Your easy-to-understand guide to
Muslim beliefs, rituals, and history

Islam

FOR

DUMMIES®

Malcolm Clark
Professor Emeritus of Religion

A Reference for the Rest of Us!™

FREE eTips at
dummies.com®

Islam For Dummies®

The Five Pillars of Worship

The Five Pillars include worship and basic ritual requirements: the basic acts that a Muslim is expected to fulfill. See Chapter 9 for details.

- ✔ **Shahada:** A person becomes a Muslim by making the basic statement of testimony or witness. "I testify that there is no God but God, and I testify that Muhammad is the Messenger of God." Variations of the *shahada* are used in many different situations.

- ✔ **Salat:** *Salat* is a formal, ritualized prayer performed at five specified times each day while facing Mecca. *Salat* consists of a sequence of recitations and bodily positions, including prostration with one's forehead touching the ground.

- ✔ **Zakat:** *Zakat* is an obligatory charitable contribution, due annually from every Muslim at the rate of 2.5 percent of liquid assets and income-producing property. *Zakat* supports charitable works and the promotion of Islam.

- ✔ **Saum:** Fast from dawn to dusk each day during the ninth month (Ramadan), Muslims aren't supposed to eat, drink, or engage in sexual intercourse. This is a time of spiritual renewal.

- ✔ **Hajj:** At least once in his or her life, if physically and financially able, each Muslim makes the pilgrimage to Mecca during the twelfth Muslim month. During the five main days of the *hajj,* those on the pilgrimage duplicate the ritual first performed by Abraham, including circling the sacred shrine *(Ka`ba)*, standing on the plain of `Arafat, and offering a sacrifice.

The Five Essential Beliefs of Islam

In contrast to the acts of worship listed in the Five Pillars of Worship, this section lists the five basic beliefs of Islam. These are sometimes called the Five Pillars of Faith, not to be confused with the Five Pillars of Worship. See Chapter 3 for the lowdown.

- ✔ Belief in God (Allah) as the only god.

- ✔ Belief in the angels of God, such as Gabriel.

- ✔ Belief in the book of God and in the messengers and prophets who revealed this book. The book is an eternal heavenly book that was partly revealed in the Jewish and Christian Bibles and is fully revealed in the Qur'an. God sent his prophets and messengers to reveal his word and to warn people what would happen if they didn't return to the path of God. Muhammad is the final prophet in a series that began with Adam, and includes Abraham, Noah, Moses, and Jesus, among others.

- ✔ Belief in the Day of Judgment and Resurrection at the end of time, when all will be raised from the dead, judged according to their faith and deeds, and sent to the gardens of paradise or to the fires of hell.

- ✔ Belief that God is responsible for everything that happens, both good and evil, because everything happens according to the will of God. The individual, however, is still responsible for his or her own moral and immoral actions.

For Dummies: Bestselling Book Series for Beginners

Islam For Dummies®

Differences Among Muslims

Muslims may belong to one or more of several institutionalized groupings in Islam:

✔ **Sunni** Muslims include from 84 to 90 percent of all Muslims. Sunni means "tradition," and Sunnis regard themselves as those who emphasize following the traditions of Muhammad and of the first two generations of the community of Muslims that followed Muhammad.

A number of movements to reform Islam have originated mainly in the 20th century. Some are limited to one country, and others have a broader influence. Most are Sunni movements, such as the Wahhabis, the Muslim Brotherhood, and Jama`at-i-Islami. See Chapter 18.

✔ **Shi`ite** Muslims form about 10 to 16 percent of all Muslims. Shi`ites are the "party of `Ali," who believe that Muhammad's son-in-law `Ali was his designated successor *(imam)* and that the Muslim community should be headed by a designated descendent of Muhammad. Three main subgroups of Shi`ites are Twelvers *(Ithna-`Asharis),* Seveners *(Isma`ilis),* and Fivers *(Zaydis).* See Chapter 12 for more information.

✔ **Sufis** are Islamic mystics. Sufis go beyond external requirements of the religion to seek a personal experience of God through forms of meditation and spiritual growth. A number of Sufi orders, comparable to monastic orders, exist (see Chapter 13). Most Sufis are also Sunni Muslims, although some are Shi`ite Muslims. Many conservative Sunni Muslims regard Sufism as a corruption of Islam, although most still regard Sufis as Muslims.

✔ **Baha'is** and **Ahmadiyyas** are 19th-century offshoots of Shi`ite and Sunni Islam, respectively. Bahai's consider themselves the newest of the major world's religions but recognize that, historically, they originated out of Shi`ite Islam in the same way that Christianity originated out of Judaism. Ahmadiyyas do regard themselves as Muslims. Most other Muslims, however, deny that either group is a legitimate form of Islam and regard members of both groups as *heretics* — people who have corrupted and abandoned Islamic belief and practice. See Chapter 14.

✔ **Druze, Alevis, and `Alawis** are small, sectarian groups with unorthodox beliefs and practices that split off from Islam. Druze and Alevis don't regard themselves as Muslims and aren't considered Muslims by other Muslims. `Alawis have various non-Islamic practices, but debate exists as to whether they should still be considered Muslims. See Chapter 14 for details.

For Dummies: Bestselling Book Series for Beginners

Islam
FOR
DUMMIES®

by Professor Malcolm Clark

WILEY

Wiley Publishing, Inc.

Islam For Dummies®

Published by
Wiley Publishing, Inc.
111 River St.
Hoboken, NJ 07030
www.wiley.com

Copyright © 2003 by Wiley Publishing, Inc., Indianapolis, Indiana

Published simultaneously in Canada

For general information on our other products and services or to obtain technical support, please contact our Customer Care Department within the U.S. at 800-762-2974, outside the U.S. at 317-572-3993, or fax 317-572-4002.

Wiley also publishes its books in a variety of electronic formats. Some content that appears in print may not be available in electronic books.

Library of Congress Cataloging-in-Publication Data:

Library of Congress Control Number: 2003101858

1B/TR/QR/QU/IN

ISBN: 0-7645-5503-0

Manufactured in the United States of America

10 9 8 7 6 5 4 3

WILEY is a trademark of Wiley Publishing, Inc.

About the Author

Warren Malcolm Clark (who goes by the name Malcolm) is Professor of Religion Emeritus at Butler University in Indianapolis, Indiana, where he taught for 30 years. A former chair of the Department of Philosophy and Religion, he taught courses in Biblical studies, Islam, the Qur'an, World Religions, American Religion, Women and Religion, Modern Religious Movements, and Egyptology. Prior to teaching at Butler University, he taught at Princeton Theological Seminary for six years.

Professor Clark's undergraduate degree is in American History from Harvard University, and he holds a Master of Divinity and Ph.D. from Yale. His doctoral studies focused on Hebrew Bible and Ancient Near Eastern studies, and he did a year of post-graduate study at Hebrew University in Jerusalem. Professor Clark is an ordained minister in the Christian Church (Disciples of Christ). He began teaching courses on Islam 12 years ago and helped develop a unit on the rise of Islam that all Butler students take as part of a required World Civilizations course. He grew up in Texas, is married to Sharon Raven Clark, and has two married daughters (Sabrina and Rebekah) and two grandchildren. Retired in 2002, he and his wife will soon move to Mammoth Lakes, California.

Dedication

I dedicate this book to colleagues and former students at Butler University, including those students who studied Islam with me, and especially Muslim students who helped broaden my knowledge and appreciation of Islam.

Author's Acknowledgments

I wish to think my acquisitions editor, Pam Mourouzis, who initially contacted me and encouraged me to consider writing this book. I soon found out that writing a *For Dummies* book is unlike anything I've written before. The more I worked on the book, the more I wished I had additional time and space to explore topics in more depth. With a limited amount of time to produce my manuscript (in comparison with more open-ended deadlines in my previous academic writing), my project editor, Tere Drenth, kept me on track. She provided much help on style, content, and organization and pushed me to include materials I may have omitted.

The technical reviewer, Professor Jamsheed Choksy of Indiana University, also provided great help in refining my thoughts and avoiding errors that I would otherwise have made.

My wife, Sharon, carefully read each chapter of the book as I produced them, proclaiming herself a good substitute for a typical *Dummies* reader. She also went beyond anything I could reasonably ask of her by carefully rereading the entire manuscript as it went through proofing and production.

Although I was retired by the time I began work on *Islam For Dummies,* I must also acknowledge my students. By teaching them, I learned much more about many religion — including Islam — than what I knew when I emerged from graduate school.

Local Islamic organizations in Indianapolis have been a great resource for the teaching of Islam at Butler. I especially acknowledge the Islamic Society of North America (ISNA), which has its headquarters in the Indianapolis area, and two local mosques, Masjid-al-Fajr (Mosque of the Dawn) and Masjid Nur Allah (Light of God Mosque), all of which have graciously hosted visits by Butler students. Finally I wish to acknowledge Laila Ayoubi, an Afghani Muslim, and her family. I've had the pleasure of having two of her sons in my Islam classes, and my wife and I have both been charmed by our contacts with her and her family over the past years.

Publisher's Acknowledgments

We're proud of this book; please send us your comments through our Dummies online registration form located at www.dummies.com/register/.

Some of the people who helped bring this book to market include the following:

Acquisitions, Editorial, and Media Development

Project Editor: Tere Drenth

Acquisitions Editor: Pam Mourouzis

Technical Reviewer:
Professor Jamsheed K. Choksy,
Indiana University

Editorial Manager: Michelle Hacker

Editorial Assistant: Elizabeth Rea

Cover Photos: © Andrea Pistolesi/Getty Images

Cartoons: Rich Tennant, www.the5thwave.com

Production

Project Coordinator: Maridee Ennis

Layout and Graphics: Jennifer Click,
Seth Conley, Michael Kruzil, Tiffany Muth,
Jackie Nicholas, Julie Trippetti,
Jeremey Unger

Proofreaders: Laura Albert, John Greenough,
Angel Perez, TECHBOOKS Production
Services

Indexer: TECHBOOKS Production Services

Publishing and Editorial for Consumer Dummies

Diane Graves Steele, Vice President and Publisher, Consumer Dummies

Joyce Pepple, Acquisitions Director, Consumer Dummies

Kristin A. Cocks, Product Development Director, Consumer Dummies

Michael Spring, Vice President and Publisher, Travel

Brice Gosnell, Publishing Director, Travel

Suzanne Jannetta, Editorial Director, Travel

Publishing for Technology Dummies

Andy Cummings, Vice President and Publisher, Dummies Technology/General User

Composition Services

Gerry Fahey, Vice President of Production Services

Debbie Stailey, Director of Composition Services

Contents at a Glance

Table of Contents

Introduction

● ●

Welcome to *Islam For Dummies,* the book that keeps you from mixing up Muhammad, Mecca, and Medina. These pages divulge what you want to know about the beliefs, practices, and origins of Islam, as well as current developments in the Islamic world.

About This Book

Shocked and grieved by the events of September 11, 2001, people around the world are coming to understand that they have questions, misconceptions, and perhaps even fear about Islam, and this book is here to help. From giving information about the 1,000-year-old wound left on Islam by the Christian Crusades to understanding the Five Pillars of Faith, this book helps you put today's conflicts into perspective.

In addition, if you live or work among Muslims or have seen a new mosque near your church or synagogue, this book can help you understand and relate to the Muslims in your midst. Muslims are poised to become the second largest religious group in the United States. With this book, you can understand the appeal of this faith without ever having to step foot in a mosque or pray toward Mecca.

I'm not Muslim, so this book isn't written to either defend or attack Islam. Without getting hung up on points of tension between Muslims and non-Muslims, I don't pretend that valid reasons for such differences don't exist. This book is also not a textbook. You find some references to other works but no footnotes detailing the support for each point that's made in the text. A number of good, short introductions to Islam exist, but their brevity means that their treatment of issues is highly selective. *Islam For Dummies* is longer than the typical 100- to 150-page introduction and, thus, more comprehensive.

Conventions Used in This Book

Keep the following conventions in mind as you read this book:

✔ *Muslim* refers to the people who practice Islam; *islam* is Arabic for submission to God; *Islam* refers to the name of the Muslim religion and to all the areas of the world that practice that religion; an *Islamist* is someone who supports Islamic political rule.

✔ Normal dating of years in the West uses B.C.(before Christ) and A.D. (after the birth of Christ—literally "in the year of our Lord") dates. A.D. and B.C.are Christian terms because the very abbreviations affirm Jesus as Christ or as Lord. Today many — certainly not all — books aimed at a general audience that includes non-Christians use the designations B.C.E. and C.E., where B.C.E. stands for *before common era* and C.E. for *common era*. In terms of actual year, a B.C.E. date is the same as a B.C. date, and a C.E. date is the same as an A.D. date. That's why many books, especially those talking about religion and aimed at a general audience, today use the equivalent, more neutral abbreviations of B.C.E. and C.E., as I do in this book. And often, if the context of a sentence makes clear that I'm talking about the common era, I list only the year and not C.E.

✔ I refer to the Qur'an in this manner: Sura 93:6–10. The Qur'an isn't a collection of books like the Bible, so Sura doesn't refer to different books of the Qur'an. Instead, sura is similar to the chapter designation of many books. Scholars have hypotheses but don't even agree on the origin and original meaning of the word sura.

The most helpful comparison I have seen is to the Biblical book of Psalms: You don't refer to Chapter 1 of the book of Psalms but to Psalm 1. Similarly, you refer not to Chapter 1 of the Qur'an but to Sura 1. The numbers after the colon are the verses in each sura. Just as Genesis 12:1–3 is a way of referring to the first three verses of Chapter 12 of the book of Genesis, Sura 12:1–3 refers to the first three verses of Sura 12 of the Qur'an. (Islam uses the term *aya* [sign] for these verses.) Versions of the Qur'an differ slightly in how they number verses (see Chapter 7), so if you look up a verse mentioned in this book and it doesn't seem relevant, read the seven preceding and following verses, and you should find the cited verse in your translation.

✔ An essential assertion of the Qur'an is that it's the word of God in the Arabic language. A translation of the Qur'an into another language is regarded as a paraphrase or interpretation of the Qur'an, distinct from the Arabic original. Islam has always required Muslim converts to acquire at least a minimal knowledge of the Qur'an in Arabic. Therefore, in discussing Islam and the Qur'an, one can't avoid Arabic terms, which I use throughout this book. The words that you encounter in this book, often in parentheses, are transliterations of the essential Arabic terms. A *transliteration* is different from a translation. A translation gives the meaning of one word in another language, while a transliteration represents the writing or pronunciation of a word in one language (in this case, Arabic) in another language (in this case, English).

- The Arabic language uses different letters and words than does English, but I try to simplify as much as possible. For example, the Arabic language has several different "t" letters, and each is a little different from the others because of markings above and below the letters. In this book, I simply write, "t."

- Similarly, Arabic, like other Semitic languages, has two essential consonants not represented in Western languages. These are referred to as `aliph` (from which eventually comes English "A") and `ayin` (a guttural sound in the back of the throat). While sounding strange and hard to pronounce to Westerners, these are distinctly different letters, which I represent in this book with ' and `. Some other books, for simplicity, may ignore these letters, and while that's acceptable, it can lead to confusion of two words identical except for whether they are spelled with ' or `.

- Because Arabic belongs to an entirely different language family than English, different possibilities exist for how to represent an Arabic term in English. If, when reading about Islam, you see two similar words spelled slightly differently, they probably both represent the same Arabic word. Don't be concerned about which spelling is correct. For example, `id` and *Eid* are two different English translations for the same Arabic word, which designates the two basic sacrifices of Islamic ritual. Where English has accepted normal usage that may not be technically correct, I use the common term with which you are familiar. For example, I refer to Islam's holy city as Mecca, even through Makka is a more accurate representation of the Arabic name of the most holy city of Islam.

- Complete Arabic names can be very long, so I commonly use a shortened version. For example, I refer to the founder of the Hanifite legal school as Abu Hanifa rather than using his complete name: Abu Hanifa al-Nu`man ibn Thabit ibn Zuta.

Foolish Assumptions

As I've written this book, I've had a picture of you in my mind — your background, your experiences, and your needs for this book. The following are the assumptions I've made about you:

✔ You don't need to know anything about Islam or any organized religion prior to reading this book. However, when studying one religion, you often want to contrast and compare key concepts and terms with those in another religion. In this book, I introduce such terms from Judaism, Christianity, Hinduism, Buddhism, Confucianism, and Taoism, but feel free to skip over these references to other religions, if you wish. In any book on Islam, you find more comparisons to Christianity and Judaism than to Far Eastern and South Asian religions. This is because Christianity, Judaism, and Islam are related religions of the same Abrahamic "family" (see Part V). Of course, in today's global society, the more you know about all religions and cultures, the better prepared you are to understand any one.

✔ You don't have to be Muslim in order to understand Islam. Believers and non-believers have complementary insights into Islam.

✔ My experiences haven't included all parts of the Muslim world. When I explain a particular belief or practice in Islam, don't assume that what I say is the only way to understand that particular belief or practice.

All Muslims won't agree with everything in this book.

✔ This book isn't proposing new interpretations of Islam. Instead, it conveys consensus thinking among scholars and theologians.

How This Book is Organized

While writing this book, I've had to be selective about which information to include about a religion that's over 1,400 years old, has over a billion members, and spans the globe. In this book, you won't find answers to every question you may have, but in each of the seven parts of the book, I've attempted to deal with topics that are related to one another. If the Table of Contents doesn't lead you to what most interests you, try consulting the Index at the back of the book.

Part 1: Understanding the Basics

This chapter helps you understand what Muslims believe, shares a bit of Muslim history, and gives general information about the number of Muslims in the world and which countries are predominantly Muslim.

Part 11: Muhammad: The Man, the Book, and Rules of Law

This part introduces you to Muhammad, the Qur'an, and legal and ethical teachings of Islam.

Part III: Becoming Familiar with Muslim Daily Life

In this part, I tell you about Muslim worship and about rituals surrounding birth, marriage, and death. I also discuss some Muslims customs.

Part IV: Recognizing That All Muslims Aren't the Same

Islam has different group of believers and here are some — Shi`ites, Sunnis, Sufis, Druze, and others. This part also discusses Muslims in America.

Part V: Considering Islam's Concept of Abrahamic Religions

In this part, I explore how the three Abrahamic religions (Judaism, Christianity, and Islam) relate to one another historically and today, and how Islam has adapted to modernization and globalization over the past 100 years including its contact with other, non-Abrahamic religions.

Part VI: The Part of Tens

Muslims have made outstanding contributions to civilization. This part provides summaries of some of these contributions and the Muslims who have made them. Also, I discuss Islam in a number of specific countries today. If, at some point, you find the details of Islamic belief or practice hard going, take a break and turn to one of the quick chapters in the Parts of Ten.

Part VII: Appendixes

This part tells how to convert dates between the Muslim and the Western calendar, provides a glossary to jog your memory, and has suggestions about resources available for finding out more about Islam.

Icons Used in This Book

To call attention to useful information, I've put the following graphic images (icons) beside some paragraphs in this book:

This icon indicates passages from the Qur'an and other Islamic texts.

This icon spotlights important or useful information about Islam.

I put this icon beside information that will come in handy in understanding other things about Islam.

This icon clues you into an area of controversy or misunderstanding.

This icon is beside information that goes into far more detail than you probably want, but is still important for understanding Islam. If you just want the basics, skip these sections.

Where to Go From Here

This book is planned so that you can go directly to whatever interests you most about Islam. It's not a novel that requires you to begin with Chapter 1 and end with the last chapter. You may want to begin with Chapter 1, which provides a quick overview of Islamic origins and beliefs. After that, check out the following common areas of interest:

- ✔ If you're interested in Islamic beliefs, go to Chapters 3, 4, 5, 7, 8, and 11.
- ✔ For Muslim rituals and worship, go to Part III.
- ✔ If you're more interested in Islamic history, turn to Chapters 2, 5, and 15.
- ✔ If you're primarily interested in the modern world, read Chapters 17, 18, and 21.
- ✔ To read about Islam in America and the relationship between Muslims and non-Muslims, skip to Chapters 15, 16, and 17.

Or plan your own itinerary!

Part I
Understanding the Basics

The 5th Wave   By Rich Tennant

In this part . . .

Although you can begin reading this book anywhere, this part begins by providing an overview of Islamic origins and beliefs. You find out about the main branches of Islam, the number of Muslims in the world, and the countries that have the largest Muslim populations. You may also want to read Chapter 2 to get an overview of Islamic history: Some of the references you come across in other chapters of this book are easier to understand if you have this historical background.

The real meat of this part deals with Islamic beliefs, including how God is understood in Islam. This part examines the key attribute of God in Islam — his oneness — as well as his other attributes, his names, and the signs that testify to God. In addition, this part considers key theological issues in early Islam, such as the relationships between faith and works and between theology and philosophy. I conclude this part by looking at Islamic beliefs concerning the resurrection of the dead, the final judgment, and the ultimate destination of heaven or hell.

Chapter 1

Approaching Islam

• •

• •

1n this chapter, you get a quick glance at Islam that the rest of this book expands on: how the faith began, what Muslims believe, how those beliefs diverge into various branches of the faith, and where and how many Muslims practice their faith around the world today.

Keep in mind that this chapter is only a teaser for more detailed treatment in subsequent chapters of individual topics.

Getting an Overview of Islamic Origins

In about 610 A.D., the angel Gabriel appeared to a man named Muhammad in the city of Mecca in present day Saudi Arabia. Gabriel told Muhammad that God had commissioned Muhammad as His last prophet. The revelations Muhammad received until his death in 632 constitute the Qur'an, Islam's holy book. Muhammad believed that he was restoring and completing the original religion of humanity, that he stood in the line of the Biblical prophets who had also been sent by God to call people to submit to God.

Muhammad's contemporaries in Mecca worshipped many gods and rejected Muhammad's call to worship only one God. In 622, Muhammad and his small band of believers emigrated from Mecca north to the town of Yathrib, which the Muslims renamed Medina. That year would eventually be set as the first year of the Muslim calendar (see Appendix A). At Medina, Muhammad established the first Muslim community.

In 630, Muhammad led the army of the growing Muslim community against Mecca, which submitted peacefully. By the time of Muhammad's death, two years later, most of Arabia had accepted Islam and become part of the Islamic community. Muhammad was succeeded by a series of rulers *(caliphs)* under whom Islam burst forth as a new power on the world scene. In less than 100 years, Muslim armies had incorporated most of the lands from the western border regions of northwest India in the East to Spain in the West into a single, great empire usually called a caliphate.

Gradually, the original unity of Islam was lost, never to be regained. The caliphate fell before the Mongol onslaught in 1258. Islam continued to spread in the following centuries, but new Muslim kingdoms rose and fell. By the end of the 17th century, the military power of Islam ebbed away and by the end of the 19th and on into the first part of the 20th century, most Muslim countries came under direct or indirect control of European nations. In the second half of the 20th century, Muslim nations gained their independence. Despite political and economic decline, the number of Muslims in the world increased rapidly in the 20th century, and Islam became for the first time a truly global religion.

Summarizing Islamic Beliefs

Muslims share many of the same basic beliefs as Christians and Jews, while differing fundamentally from Eastern religions such as Hinduism, Buddhism, and Taoism:

- ✔ God created the world and all that is in it.
- ✔ God established in His revealed word the principles by which to live, including concern for the poor.
- ✔ One shouldn't worship other gods, or money, or power, or oneself.
- ✔ At the end of time, God will judge all people.
- ✔ If a person had fulfilled the divine command, he or she will go to heaven.

God calls upon all people to submit to His will, as embodied in His revealed law. In fact, the word *islam* means submission; Islam comes from the same root as the word for peace. Islam is often thought of as the religion of submission to God. Basic Islamic beliefs are summarized in the Five Pillars of Faith (see Chapter 4).

Islam is the name of the religion. A *Muslim* is the name of a member of the Islamic religion. The word "Muslim" means "one who submits to God." A Muslim isn't a Mohammedan, and Muslims don't belong to a Mohammedan religion, because Muhammad is only a man. Muslims worship God and not Muhammad.

Basic Islamic practice is summed up in the Five Pillars of Worship (see Chapter 9). Muslims must confess that only God is God and that Muhammad is His messenger. They stop whatever they're doing five times a day to pray to God. Once a year, in the month of Ramadan, they fast from dawn to dusk. Each year, they give a defined portion of their wealth to serve God's purposes. And once in a lifetime, each Muslim who is able must make the pilgrimage to Mecca.

Dividing into Branches

Islam has two main branches: the Sunnis and the Shi`ites.

- ✔ Sunnis constitute from 84 to 90 percent of the world's Muslims. The term "Sunni" refers to the traditions followed by Muhammad and the early Muslims.

- ✔ After Muhammad's death, some Muslims believed that his cousin and son-in-law, `Ali, should have succeeded him (as opposed to the first three caliphs who came after Muhammad). The term *Shi`a* refers to the party of `Ali, those who believed that religious and political leadership of the Muslim community should always remain in the line of `Ali and his wife Fatima. Because of disputes that arose about the line of succession, Shi`ites divided into a number of different groups, such as Ithna`-Ashari (or Twelvers), Isma`ilis, and Zaydis (see Chapter 12 for details).

Sufis are another large group of Muslims. Sufism is Islamic mysticism, rather than a sect, like Sunnis or Shi`ites. So, a Sufi is normally also a Sunni (or more rarely, a Shi`ite) Muslim. Many Sufi orders (see Chapter 13) exist just like many monastic orders exist in Roman Catholicism.

Counting the Numbers

Determining the membership of any religion is tricky, but the surveys and studies are good at giving general ranges, as provided in Table 1-1. The *demographers* (those who study populations) don't judge whether people are active members or whether they almost never attend a temple, synagogue, mosque, or church. When one of these studies lists 360 million Buddhists in the world, this means that 360 million people consider themselves to be Buddhists.

Table 1-1 Size of Selected World Religions (2000)

Religion	Size	Percentage
Christianity	1.9 billion	31–33 percent
Islam	1.2 billion	19–22 percent
Hinduism	881 million	14 percent
Buddhism	360 million	6 percent
Judaism	14 million	under .5 percent

Christianity and Islam are still both growing, most rapidly in Africa over the past century. Muslim countries have some of the world's highest fertility figures, which accounts for much of the Islamic growth.

The figures for 1900 provide an interesting comparison to those for 2000. In 1900, the 555 million Christians represented 32 percent of the world's population, about the same as today. In contrast, the 200 million Muslims constituted only 12.3 percent of the world population, in contrast to Islam's 19 percent plus today. This percentage growth is why Islam is called the world's fastest growing major religion.

For more information on the demographics of world religions, go to www.adherents.com.

Locating Islam on the World Map

All Arabs aren't Muslims, and all Muslims aren't Arabs (the original inhabitants of the Middle East who became the dominant population of many Middle Eastern and North African countries, from Iraq to Morocco). In fact, Arabs are only 20 percent of the world's Muslims. In contrast, South Asia (Pakistan, Bangladesh, and India) has 300 million Muslims. The Middle East has 200 million Muslims, but the two largest Muslim countries in the Middle East — Turkey and Iran — aren't Arab countries. Of course, Arabic is the language of Islam, and Arabic culture has left an indelible impression upon Islam, although most Muslims don't speak Arabic.

Don't assume that all Arabs are Muslims. More Arab-Americans are Christian than Muslim. Arab Christians are a large minority of the population of Lebanon and a small but significant minority in Iraq. As late as the middle of the 20th century, Christian Arabs were an influential minority of the population of Palestine, although many have since emigrated to the United States and elsewhere. However, well over 90 percent of Arabs are Muslim.

Muslims are concentrated in a continuous band of countries that extends across North Africa, the Middle East, South Asia, and then to Malaysia and Indonesia in Southeast Asia. The percentage of the population that is Muslim in these countries (except India, where Muslims are a small minority) ranges from the low 80s to more than 99 percent. Note that Shi`ites are the largest Muslim group in Iran, Iraq, Yemen, Azerbaijan, Bahrain, and Lebanon. For about 1,000 years, most of South Asia (today's Pakistan, Bangladesh, and India, but not Sri Lanka) was ruled by Muslims. If you add together the Muslim population of these three countries (see Table 1-2), you see that the total constitutes by far the largest number of Muslims in any area of the world.

Table 1-2	The Nine Largest Muslim Countries by Population
Country	*Muslim Population*
Indonesia	170,310,000
Pakistan	136,000,000
Bangladesh	106,050,000
India	103,000,000
Turkey	62,410,000
Iran	60,790,000
Egypt	53,730,000
Nigeria	47,720,000
China	37,108,000?

Over time, through emigration and conversion, most of the population of today's Pakistan and Bangladesh became Muslim, while the majority of the population of India remained Hindu. At independence in 1948, the former British colony of India (including all three of the countries named) split into India and Pakistan, resulting in a massive displacement of population as most Hindus in Muslim-dominated areas moved to India, while a substantial number of Muslims in areas with Hindu majority moved to Pakistan. (Later, a civil war in Pakistan gave rise to the independent nation of Bangladesh in what had been East Pakistan). Since 1948, relations between India and Pakistan have been tense, coming close at times to all-out war. Because a substantial number of Muslims remain in India, clashes at the local level have often broken out between Muslims and Hindus. Both religious factors (for example, some Hindus are offended by Muslims' using cattle for food because the cow is a sacred animal in Hinduism) and political factors (for example, disputes over Kashmir, a Muslim majority area that remains with India) play a role in these conflicts.

Arabs and Muslims

Many non-Muslims simply equate Arabs and Muslims, and while most Arabs are Muslims, not all are. More Christian Arabs live in the United States than Muslim Arabs. Christian Arabs are one of the three major communities of Lebanon and prior to emigration from Palestine to the West in the years after 1967, were an important element of the population of Palestine. Other Muslim countries, such as Iraq, have a small but ancient Christian Arab population that goes back to a time when the majority of the population was Christian. In Arabia itself, Christians were never a significant element of the population except on the fringe in areas like Yemen. Prior to their conversion to Islam, most Arabs of Arabia were polytheists. At the time of Muhammad, the majority of the population of present-day Israel, Palestine, Jordan, Lebanon, Syria, and possibly Iraq were Christian Arabs. Depending on the country, Christian Arabs may be non-Latin Catholics, Greek Orthodox, or members of one of the other ancient branches of Eastern Christianity.

China may have many more Muslims than the figure in Table 1-2, but no one knows for certain because the Chinese government tends to understate the numbers of adherents of all religions and doesn't cooperate with demographers wishing to arrive at more accurate figures.

Go to www.guardian.co.uk/flash/0,5860,567574,00.html on the Internet where you'll find a click-on map. Click on 80–100 percent, and those countries light up; other percentage ranges follow suit.

Chapter 2

Tracing the Path of Islamic History

*I*slam isn't just a religion of individuals bound together for spiritual pursuits and guidance. Instead, Islam attempts to organize all aspects of human society. To understand Islam, one must pay attention to its political and cultural embodiment. While you can read other chapters in this book without having first read this chapter, some concepts make more sense when you have an overall sense of the Islamic history in this chapter.

Muslims today who want to establish a Muslim state often look to the first Islamic states for models to emulate and for inspiration. To Muslims, these times aren't simply irrelevant ancient history. Because it was during this period that Islam took shape as a civilization and a political and religious system, clues for the present are to be found in the developments of this early period from 632 (Muhammad's death) until the fall of Baghdad in 1258.

This early history falls conveniently into three periods. The first is that of the first four successors of Muhammad during whose rule Islam rapidly spread out of Arabia into Syria, Iraq, Egypt, and parts of Iran (632–661). Next came the first dynasty (in which rule remained within a single family). The Umayyads (661–750) ruled from their capital at Damascus over a unified Islamic community that extended from the borders of India in the East to Spain and Morocco in the West. Empires don't last forever, and Umayyad rule had created many enemies. The Abbasid family led a successful assault as a result of which the Abbasid dynasty (750–1258) replaced the Umayyads. The new capital of Baghdad wasn't only the political center of Islam but also its cultural center.

The realm of Islam *(dar al-Islam)*

Islam understands its mission as extending God's rule over the entire world. Practically speaking, this means that the entire world should be under Islamic rule. Islam divided the world into Islamic and non-Islamic realms:

- The *dar al-Islam* (realm of Islam) is that portion of the world under Islamic rule. God's intent, according to Islam, is that the *dar al-Islam* should expand until it includes the entire world so that all people live according to God's plan and law.

- The *dar al-harb* (realm of war) is that portion of the world not under Islamic rule. God commands Muslims to bring all peoples into Islam (although not by forced conversion).

- Sometimes a third category is mentioned, the *dar al-sulh* (realm of truce), the portion of the world that exists in a treaty relationship with the *dar al-Islam* but isn't presently under Islamic rule.

Islamic scholars debated which geographical areas were properly considered part of the *dar al-Islam* and under what circumstances an area ceases to be part of the *dar al-Islam*. They also argued about whether an Islamic state should be at war with any adjoining non-Muslim state

in order to bring it into the *dar al-Islam*. Another point of discussion concerned whether a person can properly live a Muslim life if he doesn't live in an Islamic state. Some said that those who, due to changes in political boundaries, found themselves living in a non-Islamic state should immigrate to an Islamic state (just as many Jews believe Jews living outside of Israel have a religious obligation to immigrate to Israel). These remain relevant issues in Islam today in the light of — for example — large-scale immigration of Muslims to Western countries.

Dar (as in *dar al-Islam*) is difficult to translate into English. The root meaning of the Arabic word is "to surround." Before Muhammad, *dar* designated the circular encampment of a nomadic group. It can also indicate the housing complex of an extended family with its surrounding wall, in contrast to the house proper. Thus, "compound" or "estate" is perhaps the closest you can come in English to this word, which designates a type of dwelling area. *Dar* is frequently translated into English as "land" or "house." Thus the concept of *dar al-Islam* is a bounded compound in which the entire Muslim community dwells secure under God's law.

Islam has existed for 1,400 years, includes one-fifth of the world's population, and has ruled geographical areas that are more extensive than any other world empire. One chapter can't cover all of Islamic history or all areas in which Islam came to predominate. Much of importance to the history of Islam I don't discuss in this chapter, or the chapter would become a confusing, long list of rulers and dynasties with strange names, dates, and geographical terms. Specifically, I don't discuss in this chapter the following important parts of the story of the spread and history of Islam. You can read more about these episodes in a number of books such as the one by Ira M. Lapidus, *A History of Islamic Societies,* 2nd Edition (Cambridge University Press, 2002).

✔ Islam spread during the 13th to 16th centuries into Indonesia, today's largest Muslim country.

✔ Islam from the earliest period established its presence along the coast of East Africa and subsequently spread not only in East but also in West Africa, until it became the dominant religion in the northern half of sub-Saharan Africa.

✔ In the time of the Umayyads, Islam extended across North Africa and into Spain. As elsewhere, this region, including modern Libya, Tunisia, Algeria, Morocco, and Spain, has its own unique history and accomplishments.

✔ Islam became the dominant religion in central Asia and the Caucasus Mountain regions — from the Black Sea to part of Eastern China. Much of this region was part of the former Soviet Union (see Chapter 21) and now includes a number of newly independent states.

✔ I omit any detailed treatment of developments in the Middle Eastern heartland of Islam between the later portion of the Abbasid dynasty and the rise of the Ottoman and Safavid Empires, a time in which many dynasties rose and fell, but few established lasting control over more than a limited area.

The Four Rightly Guided Caliphs

At his death, Muhammad left behind the basis for a new religion and for a new political system. However, in the case of both religion and state, the future would determine the form that both Islamic religion and an Islamic state would take. Although, for Muslims, religion and the state are closely connected, this chapter focuses on the development of Islam as a political and cultural system. Here are of the main political issues which the young Muslim community based in Medina had to resolve and work through over the next century or two of its development:

✔ Would the Islamic community, which united most Arabs for the first time in history, endure, or would it dissolve with the death of Muhammad?

✔ If it did endure, who should head the community? Should the ruler exercise both political and religious authority or only be the political leader of Islam?

✔ What was to be the nature of this community: broad-based, including all those who didn't explicitly exclude themselves from Islam, or a more narrow, puritanical community?

✔ Was the Islamic community to remain an Arab state, or should the state include non-Arabs on a basis of equality?

✔ How should Islam be consolidated and institutionalized?

The word *caliph* means successor or representative. Adam, for example, was the caliph of God — the representative of God on earth. Caliph, as a designation of an Islamic ruler, is an abbreviation of the phrase, "caliph (successor) of the messenger of God." A movement still exists today to reestablish the caliphate.

Choosing a successor: Abu Bakr (632–634)

If the political community that Muhammad had fashioned wasn't to fall apart at his death, quick and decisive action was necessary. But who should lead the community? Four groups could have staked a claim:

- **The natives of Medina who had supported Muhammad ("helpers"):** Although Muhammad lived in Medina until his death, the natives of Medina could have seen the possibility of the elite of Mecca reasserting their leadership among the Arabs.

- **The most influential leaders of the Quraysh tribe:** This group had converted to Islam only shortly before or after the conquest of Mecca in 630. Nevertheless, by lineage and tradition, they believed that a leader of the Quraysh should lead a state founded by one of their people.

- **`Ali, the son of Muhammad's uncle and guardian, Abu Talib:** Muhammad had taken `Ali into his own home, and `Ali had married Muhammad's only surviving child, Fatima. The children of `Ali and Fatima were Muhammad's direct heirs. Supporters of `Ali believed leadership should remain within the family of Muhammad and continue the combination of religious and political leadership that Muhammad exercised. However, tribal leadership in Arabia didn't automatically pass from father to son. Rather the leaders of the tribe or clan chose a new leader from among the best qualified. *Sheikh,* the word for the tribal leader, literally meant "old man," indicating that age and experience were a necessary prerequisite for leadership. `Ali, still a relatively young 34 years of age at Muhammad's death, wouldn't have been the obvious candidate. Supporters of `Ali had a different view. They pointed to a tradition that said Muhammad had designated `Ali as his successor on his return from the farewell pilgrimage to Mecca. But the wording of this tradition is ambiguous, and other Muslims didn't understand Muhammad's words to be a designation of `Ali as his successor. (See Chapter 12 for more on the Shi`ites, the party of `Ali.)

- **The companions:** This was the final group from whom a successor could've been chosen, the earliest Meccan converts to Islam, from before the time of the immigration to Medina in 622. Most of the companions came from lesser clans of the Quraysh tribe and thus weren't the people whom the elite of the Quraysh felt to be their natural leaders.

Given these options, Abu Bakr, both one of the companions and a member of the Quraysh, was the obvious compromise choice. An older man, Abu Bakr was the second or third convert to Islam. He had accompanied Muhammad on the flight (emigration) from Mecca to Medina. Known as "the Righteous," he had an unblemished reputation. `A'isha, Muhammad's favorite wife (after the death of Khadija), was Abu Bakr's daughter, and Muhammad had designated him to lead prayer during the period of Muhammad's final illness. The actual choice of Abu Bakr, however, was made by a small, inner group of the Quraysh in the absence of both `Ali and the native leaders of Medina.

Muhammad had brought together in a single federation more Arab tribes than ever before. Still, it wasn't obvious that the state Muhammad had created would endure beyond his death. Here's why: According to Arab custom, leaders who had taken an oath of allegiance to Muhammad would be released from that oath at his death. For a tribe to withdraw from the young state didn't automatically mean that the tribe rejected Islam. But for some tribes, acceptance of Islam had been more a matter of political expediency than of religious conviction. These groups could've seized upon the death of Muhammad as an opportunity to renounce Islam, and when Abu Bakr became caliph, a number of tribes did revolt, a time known as the Apostasy *(al-Ridda)* in Islam. Some of these revolts were led by individuals who claimed to be inspired prophets with their own revelations. Abu Bakr, with the aid of the future second caliph, `Umar, successfully put down these revolts. He also brought under Islamic rule the few tribes in Arabia that hadn't yet accepted Islam and made preparations for military expeditions outside of Arabia. Islam had survived its first period of crisis following the death of Muhammad.

Expanding out of Arabia: `Umar (634–644)

On his deathbed, Abu Bakr appointed the 43-year-old `Umar, already the second most important person in the young state, as his successor.

`Umar had originally been a vocal opponent of Islam. At one point in 616, `Umar set out to kill Muhammad but stopped at his sister's home to rebuke her and her husband for having embraced Islam. When he heard them recite from the Qur'an, he converted on the spot. Known for a quick temper, he nonetheless became one of Muhammad's strongest supporters.

Despite the tremendous wealth then flowing into Mecca and Medina from military conquests, `Umar led a simple life. Sunni Muslims often look back to `Umar as an ideal ruler. Among some of the highlights and achievements of `Umar's very successful rule as caliph were the following:

- `Umar took the title *Amir al-Mu'minim* (commander of the faithful), a title that became traditional among his successors.

- He oversaw the first major expansion of Islam outside of Arabia, conquering what is now Palestine, Syria, Iraq, Egypt, and Iran. To the west and north stood the Byzantine (Eastern Roman) Empire. To the east and northeast was the Sasanian Empire, the heir of the ancient Persians. With the aid of able military commanders, such as `Amr ibn al-As and Khalid Ibn al-Walid, `Umar and his army inflicted a major defeat on the Byzantine army at the Yarmuk River in southern Syria in 636, and two years later defeated the main Sasanian army in southern Iraq in 637 and occupied the Sasanian capital of Ctesiphon. While the Byzantium (Eastern Roman Empire) remained a significant power for centuries more, the victory of 637 marked the end of the Sasanian (Iranian) Empire as a major power in the region as Arab armies pressed northward into Northern Iraq and by the mid-650s had reached eastern Iran. By 642, Muslim armies had taken control of Egypt from the Romans.

- He established the basis for administering the greatly expanded Islamic state, utilizing some pre-Islamic bureaucratic structures already in place in areas conquered from the Romans. Many important mid-level positions in the government were occupied by non-Muslims who had the necessary expertise that the invading Arabs lacked.

- `Umar settled soldiers of the Arab armies in camps at Kufa and Basra in Iraq (and similar settlements elsewhere later) where they were separated from the local population. These camps became major centers for the subsequent development of Islam in their region. Soldiers were paid pensions from the spoils of war.

- As the Arabs settled in conquered areas, their leaders often became the new local elite. However, many of the pre-Islamic elites were allowed to retain their lands and positions. Many of these people weren't happy with either Roman or Sasanian rule, and by his policies `Umar was able to gain their support for the new Muslim state. A number of these members of the local, native elites converted to Islam — undoubtedly in part to improve their standing in the new Islamic order.

- He set the date of the emigration from Mecca to Medina (622) as the beginning date of the Muslim calendar.

- `Umar instituted a policy of tolerance toward Christians and Jews, fleshing out statements in the Qur'an regarding non-Muslim "peoples of the Book" (people who had a scripture). `Umar didn't force Christians and Jews to convert to Islam.

For the next 200 years, Muslims remained a minority in the Middle East. In about 637, the Christian patriarch of Jerusalem voluntarily surrendered the city to the advancing Muslim army. Muslim tradition says that when `Umar entered the city, he refused to pray at the church that marked the site of the crucifixion of Jesus lest his followers transform the church into a mosque. The document known as the Treaty of `Umar set forth the conditions under which Christians and Jews were permitted to live in the Islamic state. These protected peoples *(dhimmi)* could continue to practice their religion but couldn't make new converts or build new places of worship. The *dhimmi* wore distinctive clothing and paid an extra tax to compensate for not serving in the Muslim army. Contemporary scholars disagree as to whether Muslim accounts such as this one of the conquest of Jerusalem and the Treaty of `Umar represent what actually happened or whether it's the view of a century or more later when Muslims began to recount their early history. Much scholarly effort has been expended over the last 20 years to recover a more historically accurate account of early Muslim history — and much remains to be done. In either case, this story and the text of the Treaty of `Umar became crucial for later Muslims in determining how Muslims should treat Christians and Jews in newly conquered lands. It remains relevant to how Muslims view their relationship to Christians and Jews and indeed to other non-Muslims) today.

A disgruntled slave assassinated `Umar in 644. On his deathbed, `Umar appointed a *shura* (consultative body) consisting of `Ali, `Uthman and other prominent leaders to select the next caliph. They chose `Uthman. Today, advocates of a form of Islamic democracy point to the institution of the *shura* as an early Islamic precedent. Shi`ites naturally believe that once again `Ali was unjustly denied the position of caliph and very possibly `Ali himself only reluctantly went along with the appointment of `Uthman.

Gathering the Qur'an: `Uthman (644–656)

Although personally pious, `Uthman was a more controversial and less capable ruler than his predecessors. He was one of the early converts to Islam, had married a daughter of Muhammad, and belonged to the powerful Umayyad clan of the Quraysh. In his appointments to government positions, he favored members of his own clan, most of whom were late converts to Islam, and these appointments aroused resentment. The people of Medina resented the increasing prominence of Mecca in the affairs of the state, and many Muslims were repulsed by the increasing wealth and power being accumulated by the elite.

Groups opposed to `Uthman's policies also arose in the key Islamic center of Kufa in Iraq and in Egypt. In the end, `Uthman was assassinated — probably by Egyptian rebels — while reading the Qur'an. Although it's unlikely that `Ali was involved in `Uthman's assassination, some of `Ali's enemies including `Uthman's family (the Umayyad clan) and `A'isha (Muhammad's wife) and her supporters suggested that he was, or that at the least he hadn't acted as he should have to protect `Uthman.

During `Uthman's reign, the geographical expansion of the state continued, especially into Libya and Tunisia. Most significantly, according to Muslim tradition, he was responsible for establishing an authoritative version of the Qur'an. Thus, an authoritative version of the scripture was established much earlier in the history of Islam than was the case in Christianity and Judaism.

Rebelling against `Ali (656–661)

A legitimate council *(shura)* selected `Ali as the fourth caliph, but he never firmly established his power as ruler, because many believed he was involved in the murder of `Uthman. `Ali was personally upright and appealed to the less powerful members of the community. He moved his capital to Kufa in Iraq. From that time on, the political center of Islam was never again in Arabia.

`Uthman's death marked the beginning of the first *fitna* (rebellion) that threatened the unity of the Muslim community. Three subsequent *fitnas* would follow in the time of the first two Islamic dynasties, the Umayyads and the Abbasids. `Ali was also opposed by Muhammad's wife `A'isha and her supporters, whom he defeated at the Battle of the Camel in 656.

`Uthman had appointed his nephew, Mu`awiya, as governor of Syria. When `Ali, as the new caliph, sent his new appointee as governor to Syria, Mu`awiya refused to yield the post, and the armies of `Ali and Mu`awiya met in battle in 658. `Ali's forces were winning when the opposing cavalry put pages from the Qur'an on the tips of their spears and cried out "Let God decide." By accepting this proposed arbitration, `Ali compromised his position and lost the support of his more fervent supporters who took up arms against `Ali. This group became know as the Kharijites (meaning, the "seceders" because they had withdrawn from `Ali's camp). The Kharijites were an extremist, puritanical group in early Islam who believed that only the strictest believers should be considered Muslims and that the caliph should be chosen on the basis of his Muslim faith — not his family or political connections. In addition, the three-person arbitration panel was stacked against `Ali, and the decision went against him. `Ali managed to hang on to power in part of Iraq until a Kharijite zealot assassinated him in 661. The Kharijites intended to assassinate Mu`awiya also but that attempt failed. In some ways, the Kharijites can be seen as forerunners of extremist (but sincere) Islamist groups of the present day (see Chapter 18).

Expanding the state

Shortly before and during the time of Muhammad, no one in the central regions of the Middle East would have expected a serious threat to come from Arabia. But Muslim armies quickly eliminated the Sasanian (Iranian)

Empire and pushed back the borders of Byzantium Rome (the Eastern Roman Empire, with its capital in Constantinople). By the early 700s, the Muslim caliphate extended from the Atlantic coast of North Africa to portions of present-day Pakistan.

Muslims point to this success as a sign of God's favor. Yet those victories against the Byzantines weren't inevitable. Several of the key military campaigns could easily have gone against the Muslims, changing the entire outcome. So, besides God's favor, what else may account for this amazing success? Consider the following factors:

- Byzantium Rome and Sasanian Iran were exhausted by a century of warfare against each another. Within Muhammad's lifetime, the Sasanians had captured Jerusalem, and the Byzantines had recaptured it.

- Native populations were often unhappy with Byzantine and Sasanian rule. Although Christian, the populations of Syria, Iraq, and Egypt were persecuted by the Byzantines, who championed a different form of Christianity than they were practicing.

- The native populations of Syria and Iraq were Arabs and shared more in common with the invading Muslim Arab armies than they did with their Iranian or Byzantine masters.

- The caliphs followed a policy of conciliation rather than exploitation toward the local populations, thus gaining their support.

- Joining the entire Middle East into a single political and economic unit reinvigorated an economy that had been devastated by constant Sasanian-Byzantine warfare. Although this joining of several tribes may not have ever been intended, it was nonetheless effective.

- Several exceptionally capable caliphs and generals were important factors in the Muslim victories.

- Motivation is a crucial factor in any army and can often make the difference between defeat and victory, even in the face of what may seem like surprising odds. Islamic tradition reports that religious zeal was crucial in Muslim victories against Mecca during Muhammad's life. Religious zeal clearly was an important military factor at other times in Muslim history. Scholars have suggested that religious zeal was important also in motivating many of the Arab soldiers involved in the initial conquest. According to tradition, a Muslim who dies while fighting for Islam is assured entrance into heaven without undergoing the ordeal of the Day of Judgment. Of course, the importance of the religious factor is difficult to prove, because scholars today don't have access (and never will) to the psychology of early Muslim soldiers. The religious factor, however strong, doesn't mean that the lure of the vast spoils of war wasn't an equal or stronger factor motivating soldiers from Arabia where life was hard.

The Golden Age

A golden age wasn't always so golden to people who actually lived at that time. People like to look to the past, expecting or hoping to find a time when the complexities and problems of life in the present hadn't yet developed. Various cultures have a view of a succession of ages, each a decline from the preceding age. Islam itself developed a similar view in which original Islamic faith was pure and uncorrupted but subsequently declined until a "restorer" would come to renew the faith. Later generations of Muslims often look back longingly to the early days of Islam and specifically to three periods: the rule of Muhammad in Medina, the period of the first four caliphs, and the time that followed of the first two Islamic dynasties, the Umayyads and the Abbasids. One of the things that made this an ideal time is that everything seemed to be right for the Muslims, proving to them that God was on their side. It was also a time when all Muslims lived under the rule of a single caliph, thus embodying in political form the idea of the unity of the Muslim people. Indeed the time of the first two dynasties was a period of great accomplishments — militarily, in state formation, in the institutionalization of Islamic religion, and in intellectual and artistic accomplishments. Of course, the memory is probably more golden than the reality as regards the Abbasid dynasty and perhaps memory was less golden than reality as regards the accomplishments of the Umayyad dynasty. In this section, I turn to these two dynasties (see Figure 2-1).

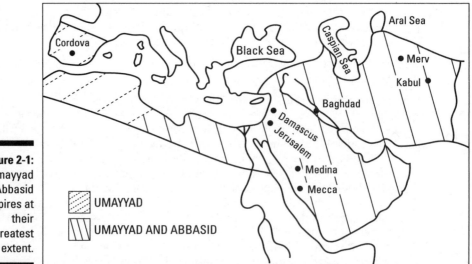

Figure 2-1:
Umayyad
and Abbasid
Empires at
their
greatest
extent.

Umayyad rule (661–750)

After the death of `Ali, Mu`awiya quickly consolidated his rule. He succeeded in passing on the rule to his son, thus establishing a dynastic principle in which the succession went to another member of the ruling family. This dynasty is called the *Umayyad dynasty* after the name of the Quraysh clan to which Mu`awiya and his uncle `Uthman belonged. However, stable transition of power at the death of the reigning caliph was a recurring problem.

Umayyad caliphs

Despite the questionable manner in which Mu`awiya came to power, he proved to be a capable ruler. He ruled in the personal style of an Arab sheikh, depending as much on his powers of persuasion as on force. As a former governor of Syria, Mu`awiya's power base was the Arabs of Syria and Palestine. He dispatched annual military campaigns against the Byzantine forces to the north to fulfill the religious mandate to expand the *dar al-Islam*. Already based in Damascus when governor of Syria, Mu`awiya made Damascus his capital. Mecca and Medina were simply too far away from the heartland of the greatly expanded Islamic state to serve as political capitals. New converts — Arabs and non-Arabs — were incorporated socially and economically into the society as clients *(mawali)* of leading families from Arabia, who had resettled in the newly conquered lands.

Some of Mu`awiya's successors lived pious lives: `Umar II (717–720) was respected as a model ruler, like his namesake; Abd al-Malik (685–705) and Walid I (705–715) followed with successful reigns. Yet, many of the 14 Umayyad caliphs followed distinctly non-Islamic lifestyles.

A key event for Shi`ite Muslims

The event of the Umayyad period that had the most far-reaching consequences for Islamic religion was the death of `Ali's son Husayn at Karbala in 680. (`Ali's older son, Hasan, had renounced his claim to the caliphate.) At Mu`awiya's death, Husayn took up the cause of his father and rebelled against Mu`awiya's son, Yazid I. Naturally, Husayn was supported by those who believed that Muhammad had appointed `Ali and his descendants as his successors. He also drew support from disgruntled elements of the population of Iraq, who felt that Umayyad rule unduly favored Syria.

On his way to Kufa, Yazid's army intercepted Husayn and his small band of supporters. Husayn was killed and beheaded. The general sent Husayn's head to the caliph in Damascus. The death of the grandson of the prophet, who had sat on the prophet's lap as a child, shocked the Muslim world. For Shi`ites, Husayn's martyrdom at Karbala became the defining event in their sacred history, and Karbala itself a holy site (see Chapter 12).

This was only the beginning of the period known as the second *fitna* (680–692). Afterward, a series of rebellions broke out in Iraq and in Arabia, including the sacred city of Mecca. Only well into the reign of Abd al-Malik was Umayyad control firmly reestablished in most areas.

Umayyad accomplishments

Accomplishments under the Umayyads included:

- The resumption of the expansion of the empire. By 715, Muslim armies had conquered the rest of North Africa and most of Spain. In the East, Islamic armies advanced into the Indus Valley (in today's Pakistan) and into areas of central Asia (today's Afghanistan, Uzbekistan, and Turkmenistan). The Umayyad caliphate had become the largest empire the world had ever known.

- Establishment of a standing army replacing and limiting the power of the original invading forces from Arabia.

- *Arabization* (use of Arabic in government records and coinage) and later *Islamization* (lesser dependence on non-Muslims to staff the expanding bureaucracy) of the government.

- Undertaking of building projects, including palaces and the development of mosque architecture. The Dome of the Rock in Jerusalem (about 691 or 692) was the first great achievement of monumental Islamic architecture.

- Developments in Islamic religious scholarship, including the gathering of traditions and study of the Qur'an.

Abbasid rule (750–1258)

The events surrounding the fall of the Umayyad dynasty and the establishment of Abbasid rule constitute the third *fitna* (rebellion).

- Mawali (non-Arab) elements of the population resented the privileges that descendants of the original invading Arab leaders enjoyed.

- Shi`ites resented a dynasty founded in denial of rule to `Ali and his descendants.

- The emerging class of religious scholars was unhappy with the worldliness of the Umayyads. However, some modern scholars believe the Umayyads have gotten a bad rap, being no less (or more) pious than the Abbasids turned out to be.

- The center of gravity of the empire was shifting east, away from the Umayyad power base in Syria.

- Internal conflicts existed between different groups of Arabs.

Thus, the enemies of the Umayyads pursued a successful public relations campaign to discredit them.

With some ups and downs, the power and unity of the caliphate was restored and maintained during the first third of the period of the Abbasid dynasty. Thereafter, the caliph became more and more of a figurehead with real power exercised by another individual, often a military figure who bore titles like sultan and "prince of princes." Centralized power declined and various regions, while still recognizing the theoretical headship of the caliph, became independent, often with governors or generals who established their own local dynasties. Nevertheless, during this time of political decline, Abbasid culture flourished artistically, religiously, and intellectually.

How the Abbasids came to power

Armed revolt had broken out against the Umayyads in northeastern Persia. The leaders behind the scenes held out the possibility of returning rule to the prophet's family, which gave the movement an apocalyptic and messianic flavor. The revolt was managed by the descendents of al-`Abbas (thus the name, Abbasid dynasty), one of Muhammad's paternal uncles. Abu Muslim led the rebel armies to victory in 750. With victory won, Abu al-`Abbas was designated caliph, to the surprise of the Shi`ites, who expected a descendent of `Ali to become caliph.

The Abbasid family set about consolidating its power and marginalizing the Shi`ite partisans who had supported the revolt. The caliph found a pretext on which to execute Abu Muslim, whose military prowess represented a potential threat to Abbasid domination. The Abbasids built the new city of Baghdad in Iraq and made it their capital. The dynasty flourished in its early years, reaching a peak in the time of Harun al-Rashid (786–809).

What the Abbasids accomplished

Politically, the Abbasids accomplished much politically, economically, and militarily during the first third of the dynasty's reign. Even after its political decline began, great accomplishes in religion, science, medicine, and literature still occurred under the Abbasids, including:

- ✔ Islamization of the population. From an estimated ten percent of the population at the end of Umayyad rule, the Muslims became the urban majority by the tenth century. Populations in the countryside were predominantly Muslim by 1300.

- ✔ Economic development, including urbanization, expansion of trade (stimulated by the disappearance of borders between previously independent states that were incorporated into the caliphate), and development of agriculture through irrigation projects and new agricultural techniques such as crop rotation.

- ✔ Reorganization of government bureaucracy with a division into various departments and with reform of the tax system.

- ✔ Development of religious scholarship including the development of theology, the systematization of Qur'anic interpretation, the gathering of the six classical collections of traditions, and the establishments of the various Schools of interpretation of law (see Chapter 8). The failed efforts of three caliphs to impose Mu`tazilite beliefs (the "ordeal") in the ninth century helped ensure the relative independence of religious institutions from government domination. Islamic law, administered by Islamic judges *(qadi)* had a central role in forming the social and moral ethos. The `ulama' (religious scholars), rather than the caliph, became the primary religious center of Islam.

- ✔ Development of the Sufi mysticism (see Chapter 13).

- ✔ Translation of the classical Greek texts in medicine, philosophy, mathematics, and science into Arabic, along with major new contributions to these areas and other disciplines, often by Iranian Muslims drawing upon Sasanian-era translations from Greek and Sanskrit (see Chapter 19).

- ✔ Development of literature in which ethnic Iranians, drawing on indigenous as well as Arab roots, played a major role.

Bridging the Gap

In this section, I take you on a whirlwind tour through a few of the dynasties and people that gained and lost political power from the latter part of the Abbasid dynasty up to the emergence of enduring new centralized empires beginning in the 15th century. By the middle of the tenth century, real political and military power was exercised not by the caliph but by leading families who established dynasties of their own, recognized and legitimated by the caliph who remained their theoretical sovereign. The first of the families was the Buyid dynasty with Shi`ite leanings (mid-tenth to mid-eleventh centuries). The further an area was from the capital in Baghdad, the more independent it became while, in fact, still recognizing the ruling caliph. The Hamdanids controlled northern Mesopotamia in the tenth century, while the Samanids controlled Eastern Iran, Afghanistan, and Transoxiania (the region north of Afghanistan and the Oxus River that flows from southeast to northwest into the Aral Sea). Power in this eastern region passed at the beginning of the 11th century to the Ghaznavids, and Mahmud (a Ghaznavid ruler) strengthened the Islamic presence in northwest India. During this period, the Arabic roots of Islam were enriched by the revival of Persian culture and the use of the Persian language in the eastern half of the empire. From there, this Arabic-Persian form of Islamic culture was transmitted to India as Islam spread into South Asia.

In the 11th and 12th centuries, Turkic peoples, many already converted to Islam, crossed from central Asia into the Abbasid Empire. In 1055, the caliph formally recognized a Seljuk Turk as the sultan, the political ruler appointed by the caliph. At the peak of their power, the Seljuks exercised power from central Turkey (with a major victory over the Byzantine Romans in 1071) to eastern Iran, although as always in these centuries the sultan's control over local rulers was sometimes minimal. Now the Persian-Arabic culture was further enriched with an added Turkish layer. In the absence of a strong caliph, Sunni Islam flourished at the local level through the activities of the scholars (*`ulama'*) and the Sufi mystics, both of whom provided the people with religious guidance. A system of Islamic schools (*madrasas*) spread under the sponsorship of the great Seljuk vizier, Nizam al-Mulk (1018–1092).

Understanding the Crusades

The Christian crusades lasted from 1098 to 1291. In 1099, the crusader armies from western Europe took Jerusalem, massacring the entire Muslim and Jewish populations. The crusaders established a number of short-lived, independent, small Christian states in Palestine and Syria. Saladin (Salah al-Din al-Ayyubi, 1138–1193) administered the decisive defeat to the crusaders at the Horns of Hattin in Palestine in 1187 and recaptured Jerusalem, sparing its Christian inhabitants. His chivalry toward defeated Christians was renowned even in Europe. A series of further subsequent crusader armies met with little success. From the Muslim standpoint, the crusaders were simply another instance of barbarian intrusion into Islamic lands, an intrusion that didn't threaten seriously any of the Islamic states of the time.

Another Christian crusade was the *Reconquista,* the reconquest of Spain from the Moors, who were Muslims from northwest Africa. Muslim forces had conquered most of Spain by 715, having crossed over from Morocco after completing the conquest of North Africa in 711. In 755, an Umayyad survivor of the Abbasid destruction of the Umayyad dynasty in Damascus escaped to Spain and established an independent Umayyad state in Spain. His successors eventually assumed the title of caliph. In the tenth century, Cordoba — the capital of Umayyad

Spain — was by far the largest and most advanced city in Europe and rivaled Baghdad as a cultural center. The Cordoba mosque (*la Mezquita)* was among its great buildings and still stands today. In the 11th century, the Christian reconquest began from northwest Spain. Gradually the Christians advanced southward, temporarily stopped by Muslim invasions from North Africa (the Almoravids, 1056–1147, and the Almohads, 1130–1269). In the 12th and 13th centuries, dialogue flourished among Muslim, Jewish, and Christian scholars in cities such as Toledo. In this way, forgotten classics of ancient Greek philosophy and science, as well as newer Muslim contributions, were transmitted to Christian Europe. The most important figure of medieval Judaism, Maimonides (Moses ben Maimon, known as Ramban, about 1135 to 1204) was born in Cordoba. Due to persecution of non-Muslims by the Almohads, the family left Spain when Maimonides was about 13 years old. He eventually settled in Cairo, where he was the physician to Saladin's vizier (second highest government official after the ruler himself), headed the local Jewish community, and produced important writings in Jewish philosophy and law. The Christian reconquest of Spain concluded with the fall of Granada in 1492 and the expulsion of Muslims (and Jews) from Spain.

Beginning about 1200, a new nomadic threat appeared from Central Asia and regions to the north, the Mongol armies of Genghis Khan (about 1162–1227). Although the empire was split among the Khan's descendants into four main parts, the Mongols continued to spread to the east (China), west (Russia and Eastern Europe), and south (Islamic lands). The Mongols were pagans and left terrible destruction in their wake. Their destruction of Baghdad in 1258 marked the end of the political system that began with Abu Bakr and `Umar. The time of a single Islamic state was at an end.

Don't confuse the Mongols of this period with the later Islamic Mughal Empire in India. The Mughal rulers were descendants of the Mongols and thus the name Mughal. Today, the mogul is synonymous with "business tycoon," and this derives from and reflects the power of the Mughal ruler. I discuss the Mughals in the "Mughal Empire: Islam in South Asia" section at the end of this chapter.

Still, eventually most of the Mongols (except those in the Far East) converted to Islam, resulting in the further spread of Islam into the area of the Crimea (north of the Black Sea) and parts of Russia (for example, present Tataristan, several hundred miles east of Moscow). In the former Abbasid lands, new regional dynasties rose to power and fell as quickly. Best known among their leaders is Tamerlane (1336–1405, "Timur the Lame"), a Turkish warrior who claimed descent from Genghis Khan. Like the earlier Mongols, Timur was a conqueror who spread fear and destruction. Yet he also established a new state with its capital at Samarqand (in Transoxiania, north of Afghanistan), and extending from central Turkey to northwest India. His son, Shah Rukh, established the Timurid dynasty with its capital at Herat (in eastern Afghanistan), which produced works of architectural and literary sophistication. With this, the stage is set for the emergence of the Ottoman, Safavid, and Mughal Empires (see the "Understanding the Crusades" sidebar for developments in Syria and Egypt during the period I've been discussing.) The preceding sketch only hints at the developments during this period, omitting many other people and dynasties that played an important role during this period of Islam's history.

Three Great Later Empires

Three post-medieval empires that arose after the fall of the Abbasids are often referred to as gunpowder empires, because their armies effectively utilized gunpowder technology. The Ottoman, Safavid, and Mughal Empires imposed highly centralized administration, based on a military model, on the areas they ruled. Each legitimated itself through Islamic ideology, military might, and patronage of the arts.

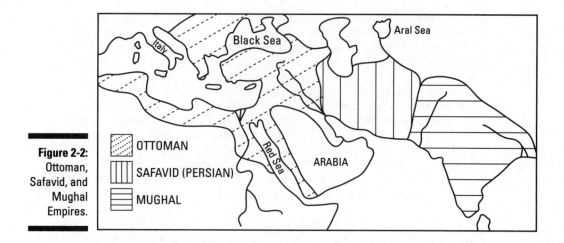

Figure 2-2:
Ottoman,
Safavid, and
Mughal
Empires.

OTTOMAN

SAFAVID (PERSIAN)

MUGHAL

Ottoman Empire: The Turks

Of the three gunpowder Islamic empires, the Ottoman Empire had the greatest influence on Islam and on the West. In the 13th century, Islamic Turkic groups were moving into Anatolia (present-day Turkey), and in the western Anatolian city of Bursa, the chief of one Turkic clan established a small state. The resulting empire grew rapidly: At the beginning of the 13th century, the majority of the population of Anatolia was Christian, but by the end of the 15th century, 90 percent of the population was Muslim, due both to Turkic immigration and conversion of the indigenous population by Sufi missionaries.

The name Ottoman derives from the name of the Turkic chief's son and successor, Osman (also known by the alternate form of his name, `Uthman I).

The Ottoman Empire was dedicated to the expansion of the *dar al-Islam* (realm of Islam) into Christian Europe, so in the 14th century, the Ottomans crossed into Europe and defeated the Serbs in 1389. From then on, the threat of the "ferocious Turks" struck fear into the hearts of many people in Europe. In the 15th century, the Ottomans conquered the rest of Anatolia and the Balkans, including Constantinople in 1453. This marked the end of the remnants of the Roman Empire. In the 16th century, the Ottomans conquered North Africa, western Arabia (with the holy cities of Mecca and Medina), Syria, Palestine, and Iraq.

The Ottoman Empire stood at the crucial crossroads of trade from Europe to the east (China, Asia, South Asia, and the Pacific) and from north to south. (Thus, the discovery of the new world and the development of new sea routes going around the tip of Africa to the east play an important role in the eventual Ottoman decline.) The Ottomans took a direct hand in promoting the production of luxury goods for the royal establishment and for export. Products included carpets, textiles (centered at Bursa) and especially ceramics, including tile manufacturing (centered at Iznik in eastern Turkey). Tulip flowers were a characteristic design motif.

Ottoman culture flourished in other ways. Scholars attached to mosque schools in the capital Istanbul (the former Constantinople) made major contributions to mathematics, astronomy, medicine, geography, and history. Miniature painting techniques derived from Persia found a new application in illustrating historical records, including portrayals of various military campaigns. In architecture, the major accomplishments were the Topkapi palace in Istanbul — more a series of pavilions and other private and public rooms than a fort — and the great mosques and mausoleums (see Chapter 19).

The Ottoman state dominated religion as thoroughly as it did other areas. The state was tolerant toward non-Muslims, who were represented by the head of their religious community. When they were forced to flee persecution in Europe, Jews frequently found a safe haven and prospered in the Ottoman Empire. Muslim religious officials were incorporated into the civil bureaucracy. The Sheikh al-Islam, appointed by the government, in turn appointed the qadis (judges) as well as the teachers in the madrasas (schools). The qadis' government duties included collecting taxes, supervising markets, and inspecting the military. Religious law was Hanifite (see Chapter 8). The state was strictly Sunni. Two Sufi (mystical) groups were particularly prominent, the Bektashis and the Mevlevis (see Chapter 13).

The caliph regarded himself as the military defender of Islam, the upholder of shari`a (Islamic law), and the heir to both Rome (by right of conquest of the Byzantine state) and to the early Islamic caliphs. To that end, Ottoman armies barely failed to take Vienna in 1529 (and again in 1683). The majority of the Balkan population remained Christian, although significant numbers of people converted to Islam in present-day Bosnia, Albania, Montenegro, and Macedonia.

Although not of Arabic (or Quraysh) descent, the Ottomans claimed that the last Abbasid caliph had ceded the office to the Ottoman ruler in 1517. A bit later, the reign of Suleyman I, The Magnificent, (1520–1566) represented the peak of Ottoman rule. The Ottomans successfully engaged the Christians on three fronts: against the expanding Russian state to the north of the Black Sea, against the Austrian-Hungarian Empire in eastern Europe, and against the Spanish on the west through control of the Mediterranean Ocean. In the east, the Ottoman state battled the Iranian Safavids for dominance. Although the Ottoman Empire came to an end only in 1922 after the end of World War I, its decline began in the 17th century. Central control weakened at the same time that the military and economic challenge from Europe became more acute. The caliphate was abolished in 1924, two years after the demise of the Ottoman state and the founding of modern Turkey.

Safavid Empire: The Iranians

The Safavid Empire provides the best example of a Shi`ite Islamic state. Twelver Shi`ism is the dominant form of Shi`ism (see Chapter 12), and it evolved in Iran. The Safavid state encompassed a larger area than just modern Iran, and its cultural and artistic contributions were comparable to those of the Abbasid, Mughal, and Ottoman Empires.

Where did it all begin? Turkic peoples poured into the northern and northeastern areas of the Abbasid Empire as central power broke down. In the absence of a strong central state after the Mongol conquest in 1258, various Sufi orders (see Chapter 13) became important means of social organization at the local level. Sheikh Safi al-Din (1252–1334) rose to such prominence in one of these orders that it became known by his name — thus the origin of the name Safavid. This order spread from its source in Azerbaijan both east (into Iran) and west (into eastern Turkey).

From 1502 until his death in 1524, Shah Isma`il, a descendant of Safi al-Din, led his followers in the conquest of Iran, thus establishing the Safavid state. Shah Isma`il claimed descent both from Muhammad and the Shi`ite *imams* (descendants of Muhammad recognized by Shi`ites as their leader) as well as from the last Sasanian king (*shah* is an ancient Sasanian word for king). He also claimed to represent the last (12th) Shi`ite *imam,* who, according to Shi`ite belief, had gone into hiding in 874 (see Chapter 12). These claims gave him both political and religious authority.

At this time, most of the population of Iran were Sunni Muslims. However, once in power, Shah Isma`il set out to establish a state based on Twelver Shi`ism (see Chapter 12). He repressed other Shi`ite groups, Sufi groups, and Sunni groups. He recruited slave soldiers from populations of the Caucasus Mountain region (between the Black and Caspian Seas), rather than depending on the groups that had brought him to power. To provide religious leadership to the population that was now forced to practice Twelver Shi`ism, he imported Twelver Shi`ite `ulama' from Lebanon, Syria, Iraq, Bahrain, and Kashmir (hence the influence to the present day of Iranian Shi`ite *mullas* — Twelver religious leaders — among Shi`ite populations in those areas). Religious institutions were under state control.

Isma`il introduced the Shi`ite practice of cursing the first three caliphs — Abu Bakr, `Umar, and `Uthman (plus `A'isha, who Shi`ites have traditionally disliked because of her opposition to `Ali's rule as caliph) — in the call to prayer. He rebuilt shrines associated with the line of Twelver *imams.* Shi`ite rituals, such as the pilgrimage to Karbala and the annual celebration of the martyrdom of Husayn, were (and are) the most important religious observances (see Chapter 12 for more on Shi`ite religious practices and theology).

Military conquest, efficient administration, and government direction of the economy allowed Safavid Iran to flourish for the first hundred years. In fact, one million people dwelt in the capital of Isfahan with its 152 mosques and 273 public baths. The reign of Shah `Abbas I (1587–1629) marked the peak of Safavid accomplishments, including a synthesis of Persian and Turkish traditions that produced the great period of Persian miniature painting. Most famous was the illustration of the Persian national epic, the *Shahnama* (story of the kings). The government greatly expanded carpet production as a major source of export revenue. Shah `Abbas brought hundreds of Chinese potters to his new capital city of Isfahan in central Iran to teach Persian potters how to make porcelain vases for export. The production of colored tiles, always a major Islamic art form, reached perhaps its highest level under the Safavids. These tiles, along with the characteristic architectural design inherited from earlier traditions of Iranian Islam, gave the great mosques their easily distinguishable appearance.

Decline set in after the time of Shah `Abbas. The `ulama' (religious scholars; the popular Iranian term for religious leaders, *mulla,* is the singular of `ulama') became increasingly independent and resistant to the religious claims of the shah. They believed that they, rather than the shah, were the guardians of the faith and the representative of the *hidden imam.* Inevitably, as centralized power declined, the regional and tribal centers of power asserted themselves and the empire began to fall apart well before the death of its last ruler in 1702. By 1779, after other minor dynasties, the Qajars emerged as a successor dynasty, to be followed in turn by the Pahlavis in 1925 and the Islamic Republic of Iran in 1979.

Mughal Empire: Islam in South Asia

Why choose the Mughal Empire as one of three examples of later Islamic states? Remember the demographics: Far more Muslims live in South Asia (India, Pakistan, and Bangladesh) than in the Arab world. Islam spread from India to Southeast Asia and Indonesia, the country with today's largest Muslim population. Also, Islam in India presents a distinctly different face from that found in Middle Eastern countries.

Islam first penetrated into western portions of South Asia as early as 711–713. Major intrusions came later, particular from Afghanistan. By 1201, the first independent Muslim states in India were established in the Delhi region. Over the next 300 years, most of South Asia was brought under the control of Muslim states. The largest and longest-lasting state was the Mughal Empire established by Barbur in 1526, which reached its peak under Akbar I (1556–1605). Barbur claimed to be a descendant of both Genghis Khan and of the great Turkish conqueror, Timur.

Mughal rulers established an elaborate administrative system of office holders who were fully under control of the central state. Government control extended to the village level, but Hindus still held many offices.

The government exercised similar control over religious affairs, appointing the chief *qadi* (religious judge), local *qadis*, market supervisors, preachers, prayer leaders, and *waqf* (charitable trust) administrators.

The Muslim population, concentrated in northwest India, the Indus Valley, and Bengal, never exceeded 20 to 25 percent of the population. This made the religious and cultural development of the Mughal Empire distinct from other great Muslim empires, where most of the population became Muslim. To the dominant mix of Iranian and Indian/Hindu cultural traditions were added elements from Arabic, Mongol, and Turkic traditions. Wealth acquired through conquest, as well as through efficient administration, made possible the flourishing of Mughal culture. Mughal India made major contributions in music, literature, painting, and architecture.

Drawing on the Persian tradition of manuscript paintings, the style and repertoire of subjects was greatly expanded under royal patronage. Some animal paintings were amazingly lifelike. The greatest accomplishment was the illustration of Hindu and Islamic epics. The *Hamzanama* is a legendary account of the adventures of Muhammad's uncle, Hamza, as he traveled throughout the world to spread Islam. The Hamzanama originally consisted of 1,400 paintings, each two feet tall. Two hundred survive today. Equally impressive were the architectural achievements in palaces, mosques, and the great garden tombs of the Mughal rulers and their wives (see Chapter 19).

In religion, Akbar I followed a policy of openness to all religions. The tax on non-Muslims was abolished and a solar calendar was used. The government financed not just mosques but also Hindu temples, and the eating of beef was discouraged in deference to Hindu sensibilities. *Syncretism* (the mixing of elements from different religions) flourished not only at the state level but also at the local level in the interaction between devotional forms of Hinduism and saint-focused forms of Sufism.

Sufi orders at this time were instrumental in converting people to Islam. These orders, such as the Chistis and the Shurawardis, emphasized *baraka* (blessing) of the Sufi saint. The writings of the Spanish philosopher/theologian Ibn `Arabi (1165–1240) were a major influence on Mughal Sufism. Urdu, a dialect based on north Indian Hindi with Persian contributions to its vocabulary, became the dominant language for religious and other literature in Muslim south Asia. Later, reformist Sufi orders, such as the Qadiriyyas and the Naqshbandis (these two Sufi orders are described in Chapter 13), rose to prominence, emphasizing *shari`a* (law) and rejecting both Hindu influences and what they regarded as undue emphasis on Sufi saints. This movement toward a stricter and more traditionalist form of Islam was supported under the emperor Auranzeb (1618–1703) with the reintroduction of the lunar calendar, the special tax on non-Muslims, and destruction of many Hindu temples.

The British, who first came to India in 1600 and subsequently became the de-facto rulers of India, deposed the last Mughal ruler in 1858, although the gradual decline of Mughal power had already begun by 1700.

Chapter 3

Submitting to God

. . . .

. . . .

Some basic beliefs about God are shared by most — and, perhaps, all — Muslims. These beliefs or affirmations are based on what the Qur'an and the traditions (called *hadiths*) say about God, so this chapter makes liberal use of quotes about God that come from Islamic scriptures. Even the most basic affirmations, however, while agreed upon by most Muslims, do lead to theological discussions about the details. And theologians come up with differing conclusions. (Chapter 4 looks at some more advanced theological debates.)

If you're familiar with Jewish or Christian understandings of God, you may find that Islamic views about God are pretty similar. Most of what Muslims say about God would be readily affirmed by traditional Christians and Jews. This contrasts with the situation in Hinduism, in which different people focus their devotion on different Hindu gods, while denying that any of these gods is the ultimate reality.

For Muslims, like members of Judaism and Christianity, God is the only ultimate reality. God depends on nothing else, but everything else depends on God. Sura 28:88 says, "Everything will perish except His [God's] face." Because God is the only necessary (rather than contingent) reality, only God is eternal. Everything else exists only to the extent and for as long as God wills its existence. Thus everything else depends on God for its existence. In recognition and acceptance of this dependence upon God, each person should submit to God. According to Muslim tradition, all humanity originally submitted to God. Humans, however, are forgetful. As a result God sends prophets to remind people to return to and submit to God. The word *muslim* means "one who submits [to God]."

Affirming the Unity of God: Tawhid

Tawhid (unity) is the Islamic term that best sums up the Muslim understanding of God. Sura 112, one of the earliest and shortest suras, is titled "unity" (an alternative name is "sincerity"), and because unity is so important, this sura is said to constitute one-third of the faith. Only the *Fatiha*, Sura 1, surpasses Sura 112 in importance. Most Muslims know this sura by heart, just as many Christians know Psalm 23 by heart. Sura 112 begins:

> *Say, he is God, One.*
> *God, eternal.*
> *He does not give birth, nor was he born.*
> *And there is none like unto Him.*

This passage was directed against the people of Mecca, who believed that Allah was one among many gods and that he had three daughters. To believe that God has a wife or children is to commit the sin of *shirk* (association), the worse sin possible in Islam. *Shirk* also occurs if one believes other gods exist and that they share power with God. Sura 4:116 says, "God does not forgive associating anything with Him; anything else He forgives according as He wills."

However, Muslims extend their understanding of God's unity and the corresponding sin of *shirk,* which denies His unity beyond simply a denial of literal polytheism. Michael Sells, in his widely praised recent book on the Qur'an, points out four understandings of God's unity to which I've added a fifth that may help you:

- ✔ **The denial of *polytheism*** (a belief in other gods) and the denial of the association of other beings with God, as I just discussed. Paganism and popular Hinduism, in accepting a multiplicity of gods, are guilty of association from a Muslim perspective.

- ✔ **The denial of absolute loyalty to anything other than to God,** including money, power, or possessions. Of course, most modern Westerners aren't inclined to cling to other gods in the literal sense, but many people put money, possessions, country, family, or reputation family ahead of God making these things into their gods.

- ✔ **The internal unity of God:** Not only do no other gods exist external to God himself, no multiplicity exists within God. Sura 112 was't originally directed against the Christian concept of the Trinity — one God in three beings. However, Muslims easily expanded Sura 112 to include a rejection of the Christian concept of the Trinity which asserts a multiplicity within the nature of God — father, son, and holy spirit.

- ✔ **The denial of the permanent reality of the self:** *Sufis* (Islamic mystics) understand Sura 112 to imply that because only God is real and eternal, the goal of spiritual development is a loss of a sense of self. Human egocentricity attests to the existence of something other than God.

⌐ **The assertion of the uniqueness of God:** Nothing else is essentially similar to God. You may say that something is like God in some way — for example, human mercy is like God's mercy — but according to the great Muslim theologian Abu Hamid al-Ghazali (1058–1111), this comparison doesn't mean that human mercy is the same as divine mercy, even though human mercy reflects divine mercy.

The Satanic Verses

In 1988, the award-winning Indian-born, British author Salman Rushdie published a novel, *The Satanic Verses,* that became a focus of worldwide controversy. Many Muslims regard Rushdie's novel as blasphemous. Ayatolla Khomeini, then the prelate of Iran, issued a decree of death *(fatwa)* against Rushdie. Muslims all over the world demanded the work be suppressed, and riots occurred in Britain and elsewhere.

The title of Rushdie's novel refers to a story found in both the authoritative biography of Muhammad and in the works of al-Tabari, the great early Muslim historian and compiler of Qur'an commentaries. While many Muslim scholars regard this story as a forgery, it would nevertheless be an early one. Western scholars of Islam, such as W. M. Watt, argue that a story like this, which is so contrary to subsequent belief, is more likely to be true than to have been invented.

Muhammad met opposition in part because in attacking polytheism, he was implicitly attacking the religious beliefs of his contemporary's ancestors. One of al-Tabari's accounts says that Muhammad was wishing for a revelation, which would make his situation with his fellow citizens of Mecca less contentious. At this point he recited Sura 53:19–20, "Have you considered al-Lat and al-`Uzza and Manat the third, the other." Al-Lat simply means "the Goddess." Al-`Uzza means "the mighty one" — equated with Venus

(the morning star), and very popular among the Quraysh tribe of Mecca. Manat means fate or destiny, which is a key concept of pre-Islamic Arabic religion.

These goddesses are referred to as the daughters of Allah, which may originally simply mean "feminine divine beings." They had shrines in the area of Mecca in pre-Islamic times. Accorded to al-Tabari's version — which I remind you is disputed — Muhammad added, "these are exalted females (or literally, great birds) whose intercession is to be desired," which seemed to allow a subordinate role for the three goddesses.

And why not, after all? Islam accepted the existence of various beings between people and God, such as angels and jinn (see Chapter 5), so why not also accept these beings as a conciliatory measure to the inhabitants of Mecca who were delighted by Muhammad's words. However, this would have been to return to polytheism. Subsequently, Gabriel informed Muhammad that he'd been led astray by Satan. Muhammad deleted the statement about the intercessory role of the goddess and substituted newly revealed verses including verse 53:23 that says that the three goddesses are mere names and don't truly exist. The deleted verses are known as the Satanic verses. Whether the story actually goes back to Muhammad himself or not, it reflects struggles with the issues of "unity" and "association."

The *shahada:* The first pillar of Islam

The basic confession *(shahada)* of Islam is the first and most important of the Five Pillars of Islam (see Chapter 9). The first half of this state-ment, called the *first testimony,* is the central Islamic expression of God's unity *(tawhid).* It says, "There is no God but God, and Muhammad is the messenger of God "While the full *shahada* doesn't occur in any one place in the Qur'an, its two parts (before the comma and after) occur a number of times separately. For example, Sura 3:18 says, "God bears witness that there is no god but himself — Angels and wise men bear witness also. He upholds justice. There is no god but Him, the all-mighty and the all-wise."

Al-Hallaj, the famous Sufi mystic who was martyred in the tenth century, said that Satan was the most consistent monotheist. The Qur'an says that when Adam was created, God commanded all the angels to bow down before Adam. Satan refused to do this. Al-Hallaj said Satan was being obedient to God's command not to worship anyone other than God himself. Satan observed this commandment even when it meant his own condemnation.

Clarifying the Terminology: Allah Equals God

The word *Allah* occurs over 2,500 times in the Qur'an. Allah is probably a contraction of two words: the *(al)* and god *(ilah).* Muslims regard Allah as the original god of the *Ka`ba,* the sacred shrine in Mecca (see Chapter 9), but in pre-Islamic times', the divinities worshipped by the Meccans were Hubal, the moon god, and al-`Uzza. Still, long before the time of Muhammad, Arabs knew Allah to be an important Arabic deity; in fact, Muhammad's father was named `Abd Allah, which means "servant of Allah."

Today, in Islam and in the Qur'an, Allah is simply the name of God. In fact, Allah in Arabic is a direct equivalent of the word God (with a capital G) in English. When early Christians translated the Bible into Arabic, they used Allah wherever God stood in the original Greek and Hebrew.

Muslims claim that Allah is the same God as the God of the Hebrew and Christian scriptures, thus affirming that Islam stands in continuity with Judaism and Christianity. Muslims believe that all three religions share the same God and the same scripture, but also believe that each, in turn, claims to reform, perfect, and complete what came before.

Yet while Muslims, Christians, and Jews usually believe they worship the same God, most would not normally say that *Vishnu* (a Hindu god) or *Amida Buddha* are the same as God or Allah. In Hinduism, at the popular level three major gods exist — Brahma, Vishnu, and Shiva. Most ordinary Hindus are devotees of Vishnu, Shiva, or a number of important goddesses. At a more sophisticated level, the level of ultimate reality is an unchanging, impersonal cosmic reality (Brahman), which is the same as the internal essence of each individual (the Atman or soul). Salvation consists of realizing — for example, through advanced meditation (yoga) — that Atman is the same as Brahman.

Christians and Jews naturally think of Islam as a religion which originates later than Judaism and Christianity. Christians and Jews will also naturally think of Muhammad as the founder of Islam in the same way they think of Abraham, Moses, and Jesus as the founders of either Judaism and Christianity. Muslims realize that the present form of Islam goes back to the prophetic mission of Muhammad in the seventh century C.E. At the same time, Muslims believe that Islam is the original religion of humanity, which Muhammad was sent to restore. In the Qur'an, Adam is the first person to worship Allah/God. Abraham is the essential founder of the Muslim religion. The Qur'an tells the story of Abraham's rejection of other gods in Sura 6:74–79.

Testifying to God's Supremacy

How is one to know that there is only one God? How did Muhammad know? How were the people of Mecca to know? The Qur'an calls a proof of God a *sign (aya)*.

- ✓ **The Qur'an itself is a sign of God.** The individual verses of the Qur'an are called *signs,* but they're generally referred to as *verses.*

- ✓ **The creation of the world is a sign of God.** Sura 13:2 says, "God is the one who raised the heavens without pillars that you can see and then seated Himself upon the Throne, ordaining the courses of the sun and moon. He regulates all affairs and sets forth his signs that you may know you're meeting your Lord."

- ✓ **The processes of nature provide additional signs testifying to God.** Sura 36:33 says, "A sign for them is the dead land, which we bring to life and bring from grain, which they eat; and we make in (the land) gardens of palms and vines, from which we cause fountains to flow forth." Rain falling on the dead land and causing it to turn green did, indeed, appear as a miracle in the desert environment of Muhammad's contemporaries.

- ✓ **God's concern for humanity is a further sign of God.** The most important expression of this divine care is God's sending of the prophets to warn people so they may escape eternal damnation, as in Sura 30:47, which says, "indeed, we sent before you [that is, before Muhammad came] messengers unto their peoples. And they brought to them the clear signs. Then, we punished those who sinned." God also provides daily care for people: the night for rest, seas for transport, food to eat, water to drink, and relief to the suffering (see Sura 27:62).

✔ **Human reason and logic provides proof of God's existence** and some basic knowledge of God's attributes according to theologians and philosophers. The logical proofs of God offered by medieval Muslim theologians are similar to those offered at the same time by Jewish philosophers, such as Maimonides, and Christian theologians, such as St. Thomas Aquinas. Al-Ghazali, the most prominent medieval Muslim theologian, said that when you look at the intricate order of the universe, you can conclude that this universe must have a creator who is different from the universe.

Defining the Attributes of God

The *Throne Verse* (Sura 2:255) is one of the most famous verses of the Qur'an. It's part of a larger group of Qur'anic passages known as *passages of refuge*. The Throne Verse is frequently inscribed on amulets (to protect one from evil) and on tombstones. It reads,

God. There is no God but Him, the living, the everlasting. Neither slumber nor sleep seizes him. To Him belongs all things in the heavens and the earth. Who may intercede with Him except with His permission? He knows what lies before them [people] and what is after them, and they do not understand anything of His knowledge except what he wills. His throne encompasses the heavens and earth; the preserving of them does not weary Him. He is the all-high, the all-glorious.

Even if one knows from revelation (the Qur'an) or human reason that God exists, people want to know more about God. As the Throne Verse shows, Islam shares with Judaism and Christianity the belief that one can assert certain things about God. Muslim theologians refer to these qualifications of God's nature as the "attributes of God." Through examination of Qur'anic passages that speak about God and especially those which list the various epithets (titles or names) of God, Muslim theologians such as al-Ghazali arrived at lists of the most essential attributes of God. Among these are:

✔ **Knowledge:** God knows everything.

✔ **Power:** God can do anything.

✔ **Will:** Everything happens according to God's will.

✔ **Life:** God lives eternally.

✔ **Speech:** The Qur'an is the eternal speech of God.

✔ **Hearing:** Nothing one says is hidden from God.

✔ **Sight:** As with "hearing" because God is everywhere nothing is hidden from His sight.

Other attributes are implied by these seven. For example, God's power includes God as creator. God's knowledge and God's will imply the idea of predestination — God both knows and wills who will be saved and who will be damned. God's hearing and seeing implies the attribute of God's justice in rendering judgment.

Loving and Knowing God

According to Abu Hamid al-Ghazali, no one other than God can ever know God. But to know that you don't know the essence of God is to come as close as possible to knowing God. That's a little tough to follow!

Humans can know something about God by knowing His attributes. This means that believers shouldn't grasp the attributes of God only intellectually, but they should also embody the attributes of God in their own lives.

But Islam balances this idea of never knowing God with statements about the nearness of God, which creates the possibility of at least a limited knowledge of God. Two verses from the Qur'an perhaps best express this immanence of God:

✔ "We created man, and we surely know what His soul whispers to Him, for we are nearer to Him than His jugular vein," says Sura 50:16.

✔ "Have you not seen that God knows everything in heaven and on earth? Three men do not consult secretly together but he is the fourth among them, neither five men but he is the sixth among them, neither fewer nor more but he is with them wherever they are," says Sura 58:7.

Although Muslims may attempt to know God in different ways, the most important is that he or she love God. Ahmad al-Ghazali (died 1126), the lesser-known brother of the famous theologian, wrote that love is what integrates the human soul, and the ultimate object of love is God. Many poets, including Rumi (1207–1273) and Farid al-Din `Attar (1119–1220), developed the theme of God's love for humanity and human love for God.

As far as scholars know, the emphasis on love is first expressed by the early female mystic Rabi`a (713–801). Although earlier sources of information about Rabi`a exist, the most important is the Farid al-Din `Attar's account in his "Memoirs of the Saints." `Attar's account includes perhaps the most-often quoted saying of Rabi`a on the importance of humans loving God:

O God, if I worship you for fear of hell, burn me in hell, and if I worship you in hope of paradise, exclude me from paradise; but if I worship you for your own sake, deny me not your eternal beauty.

In another incident, Rabi`a is hurrying down a path. She has water in one hand and fire in the other. Someone asks her why and she replies that the water is to put out the fires of hell and the fire is to burn up paradise. The reason? One should not love God out of fear of punishment in hell or reward of heaven but only out of love for God himself.

Invoking the 99 Names of God

A tradition *(hadith)* says: "Allah's Apostle said, 'Allah has 99 names, and whoever knows them will go to Paradise.'" Most of the names occur in the Qur'an or are derived from descriptions of God in the Qur'an'. Lists of the 99 names often begin with the 13 names that occur in Sura 59:22–24, which begins:

"He is God; there is no god but he. He is the knower of the invisible and the visible; he is the all-compassionate, the all-caring.

"He is God; there is no god but he. He is the king, the all-holy, the all-peaceful, the all-faithful, the all-preserver, the all-mighty, the all-compelling, the all-exalted. Glory be to God; he is above all that they associate with Him.

In actuality, God has 100 names, but the 100th name is hidden: Allah is the 100th name. In addition, if you combine various lists, you come up with more than 99 names. Some traditions speak of 1,000 names, a way of indicating that the names of God are as infinite as His qualities.

Al-Tirmidhi (824–892) is the author of one of the six authoritative collections of Sunni *hadiths*. One of his *hadiths* (number 117) contains a common listing of the 99 names among which are the King, the Holy, the Source of Peace, the Preserver of Security, the Protector, the Mighty, the Overpowering, the Great in Majesty, the Creator, the Maker, the Fashioner, the Forgiver, the Dominant, the Bestower, the Provider, the Decider, the Knower, the Withholder, the Plentiful Giver, the Abaser, and the Exalter.

Ibn `Arabi (1165–1240), regarded by some as the greatest Sufi theologian and by others as a heretic, said that the divine names are creative possibilities present in the essence of God. God causes these possibilities to become manifest in His creation of the cosmos and of humanity. Love is the force that causes God to create the universe. A favorite *hadith* of Ibn `Arabi and other Sufis says, "I was a Hidden Treasure, so I loved to be known. Hence I created the creatures that I might be known." Perhaps because light is perceived as among the most immaterial of substances, Sufis especially, but also Islam in general, emphasized God as light. The divine names are like the rays of light streaming out from the sun. "The Light," one of the 99 names, occurs in Sura 24:35, another of the key Qur'anic verses of refuge, which says:

God is the light of the heavens and the earth; the likeness of His light is as a niche wherein is a lamp, the lamp enclosed in glass, the glass as brilliant as if it were a glittering star, kindled from a blessed tree, an olive that is neither of the East nor of the West, whose oil would ignite even if no fire touched it. Light upon light! God guides to His light whom he will. For God gives parables for humans, because God knows everything.

Dividing the names into categories

The names of God are variously divided or summarized. One common grouping is the names of mercy or beauty *(jamal)* and the names of rigor or majesty *(jalal)*. Westerners often have an image of Allah as a wrathful God, because God's justice does require that he punish the wicked and admonish the living in order that they not suffer eternal torments in hell. Of course, one can point to equally or more chilling comments about the wrath of God in the Bible. Yet as is the case with the Bible, the Qur'an emphasizes God's mercy much more than His wrath.

In the 99 Names of God, the names of mercy far outnumber the names of majesty or wrath. A famous *hadith qudsi* (a *hadith* in which God speaks) says, "When God decreed the creation, he pledged Himself by writing in His book which is laid down with Him, 'My mercy prevails over my wrath.'"

Remembering the names

Sura 17:110 is another passage recommending the invoking of the names of God.

> *Say: 'Call upon God, or call upon the compassionate, using whatever name you will. To Him belong the most beautiful names. And do not be too loud in your prayer nor too soft, but seek a middle course.'*

Meditation and recitation of the names of God are central to Muslim devotional practices. The Qur'an emphasizes "remembrance of God" *(dhikr Allah)*. The practice of *dhikr* is most extensively developed in Sufism (see Chapter 13). Remembrance includes mental and inward meditation on God. But first and foremost, the Qur'an injunction refers to oral recitation of the names of God. According to tradition Muhammad said, "Let your tongue stay moist with the remembrance of God," emphasizing the vocal aspect of this remembrance. Muslims often use a string of prayer beads or rosary *(subha)* when reciting the names of God. The rosary consists of three groups of beads strung like a necklace. Three larger beads separate the groups. The beads are used to keep count as one recites the 99 names.

For a tourist in some Muslim countries, kiosks selling many different varieties of rosaries provide a colorful photo-op. Rosaries vary from the very cheap ones made of plastic to those made of ivory and other precious materials. The rosary isn't mentioned in the Qur'an and some conservative Muslims such as the Wahhabis of Saudi Arabia reject the use of the rosary regarding it as an "innovation" *(bid`a)*. Extensive use of the rosary may have become common in Islam rather late. Similar use of rosaries occurs earlier in Buddhism as an aid in reciting the name of *Amitabha Buddha* and later in Roman Catholicism as an aid in performing devotional and prayer rituals.

Chapter 4

What Muslims Believe

In This Chapter

▶ Grasping the basic Islamic beliefs

▶ Looking at key issues of Islamic theology

▶ Relating theology to philosophy

As you go through this chapter, you may find that much of this theological discussion sounds archaic and irrelevant. Some of the points may remind you of the tale of medieval Christian theologians arguing about how many angels can dance on the head of a pin. Be assured that many of these issues, however, do remain relevant to Muslims today. Accusations that one's opponents were unbelievers were readily made in early Islam, and not only by the puritanical sect. Similar accusations are made today not just against non-Muslims but also against other Muslims (as an examination of Islamic e-mail lists and Web sites readily shows). Some radicals claim that anyone who disagrees with their understanding of Islam and doesn't commit to their cause is an unbeliever *(kafir)*. Just as the legitimacy of the use of Greek philosophy was a key issue in early Islam, similar arguments concerning Western concepts and Western approaches to education exist today, for example, "Is democracy compatible with Islam?" and "Is there a universal standard of human rights that can be determined apart from revelation?" For a closer look at these issues, see Chapter 17.

Stating the Five Essential Beliefs of Islam

A well known *hadith* (tradition) says that the angel Gabriel, dressed as a man in white, once sat beside Muhammad and his companions. He asked Muhammad: "What is Islam?" Muhammad answered with a statement of the five basic ritual requirements of Islam. The man then asked, "What is faith *(iman)?*" Muhammad responded with a list of five basic beliefs. The man commended Muhammad's answer and then asked a third question: "What is virtue *(ihsan)?* Muhammad replied, "That you should worship God as if you saw Him, for if you do not see Him, nevertheless he sees you." The man in white departed.

Gabriel's three questions correspond to the traditional Islamic division of religion into three parts — worship (`ibada, literally service), belief about God (iman, or faith), and ethics (ihsan, literally virtue and including right living). In answering the first question, Muhammad names the *Five Pillars of Worship* (see Chapter 9), also called the *Five Pillars of the Religion* and the *Five Pillars of Islam* (submission). These Five Pillars are the testimony that only God is god and that Muhammad is His messenger, the five daily prayers, the observance of the daytime fast in the month of Ramadan, the giving of alms, and a pilgrimage to Mecca at least once in one's lifetime. The placing of this question first indicates the priority of these ritual obligations in the life of a Muslim. The ordinary Muslim accepts the basic beliefs of her religion but doesn't spend much time puzzling over them. Her conscious effort as a Muslim is focused on active submission to God (worship and service) more than on intellectual assent to propositions about God (beliefs).

But if you ask a Muslim about his beliefs, he'll most likely respond with the five items mentioned by Muhammad in replying to Gabriel's question about faith. The first three of these beliefs are also stated in Sura 2:285, which says that each Muslim believes "in God, His angels, His books and His messengers." The Gabriel *hadith* adds two (in some versions only one) additional beliefs to the four in Sura 2:285.

These beliefs are sometimes referred to as the *Five Pillars of Faith*, by analogy to the designation of the basic worship requirements as the *Five Pillars of Worship*. You may also see this list referred to as the *Six Pillars of Faith*. Belief in the books of God and the prophets of God is usually listed as one pillar, but some list it as two. Neither the Qur'an nor the *hadith* of Gabriel specify how to count them and the normal Arabic phrase is *arkan islam* — pillars of faith (without specification of number). Actually, different ancient variants of the *hadith* of Gabriel vary in the number of items included and in how specifically they refer to each item of belief. Whether five or six, the content is the same and the point is simply to realize that if you read about Five Pillars of Faith in one book and Six Pillars of Faith in another, both are talking about the same thing. And remember not to confuse the "Pillars of Faith" with the "Pillars of Worship."

The Pillars of Faith provide a convenient summary of basic Muslim beliefs. If you want to know more about any of them, I provide references to other chapters in which I discuss the specific belief in more detail.

Believing in God

"There is no god but God" — the first half of the basic testimony of faith (*shahada*) states unequivocally this simple, core belief of Islam. The theological term that expresses this concept is unity (*tawhid*). *Tawhid* (unity) means a numerical oneness: God is one because no other gods exist beside God. God is one in that he doesn't manifest himself in different beings. Islam rejects anything similar to the Christian concept of one God in three persons (Father, Son, and Holy Spirit), or to the Hindu concept of the manifestation of the God Vishnu in ten different incarnations. Christians who accept Jesus as a very important prophet of God but reject Him as being the same as God are called Unitarians. The Arabic word equivalent to Unitarians *(muwahhidin)* is another Islamic term for Muslims.

God is one because he has no associates — no wife, or parents, or children as gods often have in polytheistic religions. The greatest sin in Islam is "association" *(shirk),* a term that occurs frequently in the Qur'an in reference to the citizens of Mecca who continued to worship other gods. To be guilty of "association" is to be subject to the penalty of death in this world and spending eternity in hell in the next world (although ultimately God is capable of forgiving even the worst sinners should he choose to do so). To accuse somebody of *shirk* is the worst accusation one can make against a fellow Muslim and a term of derision applied to non-believers. The person who is guilty of *shirk* is a non-believer, a *kafir.*

Some radical Islamic Web sites today and some decrees *(fatwas)* issued by Islamic terrorists refer to all non-Muslims as *kafir* even though the Qur'an allows a special position for Jews and Christians and doesn't accuse them of shirk. Radical Muslims today (and even in the earliest period of Muslim history) at times refer to other Muslims who don't share their particular beliefs or join their cause as *kafir.* It's analogous to what happened during the American Cold War with Russia when some people accused political liberals of being communists. Today, *kafir* is virtually synonymous with atheist. A *kafir* as atheist is one who by his actions actively opposes the will of God more than simply one who rejects the concept of God as a philosophical proposition. Does it seem strange that the same term can designate an atheist (one who does not believe in God) and a polytheist (one who believes in many gods)? Not to a Muslim. To a Muslim, one who believes in other gods denies the one true God just as the formal atheist who believes in no gods does.

God is one because he is unique. God is "number one" and no "number two" exists alongside Him. Nothing can be compared to God because nothing is like God. Nothing can be added to or taken away from God that would make Him more perfect, wiser, more powerful, or more knowledgeable. He is perfect and the one entity (living or not) that has existed eternally and will continue to exist eternally.

While believing in God involves intellectual assent to the existence of God, more is involved in saying, "Yes, God exists." If God is what the Qur'an and Islam say he is, then to say you believe and not act on that belief is to demonstrate you don't really believe. If actions do not follow from belief, then one doesn't truly believe. Note that in the division of Islamic religion into worship, faith, and virtue or ethics, belief in God in the sense of submission to the will of God as manifested in worship of God is first in each of the three divisions (see Chapter 3 for more on believing in God).

Believing in God's angels

A number of Hollywood movies use the motif of an angel who comes to earth for one purpose or another, reflecting the fascination with angels in popular American culture. Traditional Islamic beliefs about angels are similar to the portrayal of angels in the Bible and in subsequent Christian and Jewish tradition. Eastern religions in general don't have angels, although various gods may exercise some of the same functions as angels in the Western monotheisms. The representation of an angel on a Christian card is of a human-appearing individual with wings. This is the basic portrayal also in the Qur'an where angels are mentioned more than 80 times.

While still basically humanoid, some angels as described by tradition are quite fearful looking. Angels are an order of beings between humans and God. God created angels from light. They don't (normally) sin and have many functions as agents of God. In Islam, angels have three especially important functions. First they have a heavenly function, praising God, carrying His messages, and supporting His throne. Secondly, angels may serve as an instrument of God in human affairs. Angels played an important role at key points in Muhammad's life; each person has two guardian angels. Thirdly, several specific angels play a key role in the events beginning with the death of an individual and ending with the resurrection.

Satan or Iblis is a fallen angel in Islam who was expelled from the presence of God when he refused God's command to bow down and worship Adam. Until the Day of Judgment, God allows Satan to tempt humanity and spread mischief on the earth. Although frequently mentioned in the Qur'an, Satan in Islam isn't the powerful, anti-God figure that he becomes in Christian and Jewish traditions. Believing in angels also includes by extension believing in the other major category of non-material beings, the *jinn. Jinn* are minor beings who exercise some influence, good and bad, on human affairs. (See Chapter 5 for more on the angels, Satan, and the *jinn.*)

Believing in God's books and in God's messengers

Some list this as one pillar; others list it as two. These two items of belief can be considered separately from one another in that they don't say the same thing; however, they relate logically to one another in a way that's not true of the other pillars. The messengers are the ones who bring the scripture, so to believe in one implies belief in the other. Keeping this connection in mind, I summarize them separately in the following sections.

Believing in the revealed books of God

First and foremost, one believes in the Qur'an, but the "books of God" also include the Mosaic Law, the Psalms of King David, and the Gospel of Jesus. The revealed books are specific manifestations of the heavenly book — the "mother of the Book." Although the question of the nature of the Qur'an was a hot topic in early Islamic theological debate, the consensus position for the last 1,000 years is that the Qur'an is the literal, eternal, spoken word of God. Just as God has always existed, so has His word, the Qur'an, always existed. When a Muslim recites orally the text of the Qur'an, she is actualizing God's eternal word. In a sense, this is similar to how a sacred mantra may actualize the power of a deity in Hinduism and Buddhism. Another way of putting it is to say that as in Christianity God is most fully manifest in Jesus (who is called "the word" in the gospel of John), so in Islam God is most fully manifest in His word, the Qur'an.

The revelations to Moses, David, and Jesus come from the same heavenly book as does the Qur'an. Islam says that these earlier revelations were incomplete in that they didn't contain the entire heavenly book. Muslims also believe that Jews and Christians intentionally or unintentionally corrupted the earlier books they had received. Therefore, Muhammad was sent with an uncorrupted and complete rendition. Muslims believe this Qur'an has remained unchanged since the death of Muhammad. Therefore, no need exists for future revelations from the divine book because in the Qur'an, the whole word of God is already present. Many stories and characters that appear in the Bible also appear in the Qur'an although often with significant changes. Much that is in the Bible isn't paralleled in the Qur'an and much in the Qur'an has no parallel in the Bible.

You may expect that Muslims would therefore also read the Torah (the Mosaic Law in the first five books of the Bible), the Psalms, and the Gospels — at least to supplement information in the Qur'an and perhaps provide further context for understanding some passages. After all, Christians read and study the Hebrew Bible as well as their own New Testament, so why wouldn't Muslims read and study the Law, the Psalms, and the Gospels? The answer: If you have a perfect and final edition of a book (as Muslims believe they do in the Qur'an), you've no need to read earlier, corrupted versions of that book. (See Chapter 7 for more information on the Qur'an.)

Believing in the messengers who reveal God's books

The foremost messenger is of course Muhammad himself, as the second half of the *shahada* states: "Muhammad is the messenger of God." A messenger is one who brings a revelation from the heavenly book. God has sent only a limited number of messengers to humanity to reveal His word. Muhammad is also a prophet. God has sent many prophets to warn people of their sinful ways and of the judgment that they'll face if they don't return to worshipping only God. Because Muhammad revealed the perfect and complete form of the word of God (the Qur'an), God will send no further prophets and messengers. The Qur'an itself now stands as a warning and a call to return to the service of God.

The Qur'an names about 28 prophets, most of whom occur in the Bible. A few references are uncertain so the precise number is uncertain. The Qur'an gives considerable information about some of these prophets and very little beyond their names about others. It mentions some only once and others such as Abraham, Noah, Moses, and Jesus numerous times. The Qur'an is shorter than the Bible, and it relates less about each of the Biblical prophets than what is found in the Bible. Most of these prophets bring the same message: an exhortation to justice in dealing with others and a call to return to worshipping only God, along with a threat of judgment on the Day of Resurrection if the warning isn't heeded.

Some people called prophets in the Qur'an are prominent in the Bible but not called prophets by the Bible — such as Adam, Noah, Job, Lot, and King Solomon. Along with Abraham and Muhammad, Jesus is one of the most revered Islamic prophets. The Qur'an affirms his virgin birth and his relationship to his mother Mary, who is also highly respected. Most of the story of Jesus' ministry isn't included. In two points, the Qur'anic understanding of Jesus differs radically from the Christian understanding. Like all the prophets including Muhammad, Jesus is only a man. He isn't the son of God or in any sense divine. Islam also denies that Jesus was crucified on the cross and resurrected. While Jesus is very important, he isn't the savior of humankind. (See Chapter 6 for more on Muhammad and Chapter 16 for more on the Biblical prophets and Jesus.)

Believing in the last day and the resurrection from the tomb

Muhammad's contemporaries in Mecca apparently didn't have a developed concept of an afterlife. "Fate," a power greater than the gods, determined everything. If you think this life is all there is, then the temptation is strong to enjoy it while it lasts. If you think this life is only a brief prelude to eternity, then, with hope, you'll live this life in such a way to guarantee a happy eternal life after resurrection. Muhammad warned his contemporaries that sometime after death, the Day of Resurrection would occur. An individual's deeds had been recorded in a book and on the basis of this record, placed in their left hand (a bad sign!) or their right hand, the person would go to hell or to heaven. Islamic views didn't include either a purgatory for those meriting neither heaven nor hell nor a limbo for those who couldn't get into heaven through no fault of their own. Even most Muslims who go to hell will ultimately be admitted into heaven due to the mercy of God.

The Qur'an presents many "snapshots" of hell but no detailed or comprehensive picture. Both hell and heaven have seven levels. Tradition develops the picture of the torments of hell in graphic detail. Generally, the punishment fits the sin. The picture of the tortures of hell is similar to that found in many religions. "Fire" is the basic feature of hell. Heaven is viewed as a well-watered garden in which the saved live a serene existence. The purpose of these images of heaven and hell is to motivate those still alive to live in such a way as to avoid hell and merit life in heaven at the final judgment. Although Muslims believe that all rests in the hands of God, most probably believe that as Muslims the mercy of God will eventually result in their entrance into heaven.

Islamic tradition provides a detailed picture of what happens between death and entrance into heaven or hell. Upon death, there is an examination of the person in the grave by two angels that may lead to a limited period of punishment in the grave. Various events signal the coming of the end of time at which point all are resurrected and eventually face the judgment as to their final state. (See Chapter 5 for more on the end of time, the final judgment, and heaven and hell.)

Every religion faces the problem of the relationship between free will and predestination. Most people, at the gut level feel, that their actions in this world affect to some extent their fate in this world. If you don't study, you won't get good grades. If you goof off at work, you won't get promoted. Free will says that each person makes the decision as to whether or not to study or goof off at work. Religions extend this free will concept also to one's eternal destiny. Hinduism and Buddhism share a concept of karma — as you sow, so shall you reap. They also believe in reincarnation or rebirth. What happens to us in this life is simply the working out of the inevitable effects of the actions we have chosen in past lives. If you suffer in this life, that isn't punishment but simply the result of choice made in past lives. Western monotheisms (Judaism, Christianity, and Islam) don't usually believe in reincarnation. A person has only one life and the choices one makes in this life determine one's eternal destiny. To say that I can freely make those choices is to affirm free will.

But Western monotheistic religions generally affirm that God is ultimately responsible for everything that happens. To say otherwise would be to diminish the power of God. Problem!! How can one say that people are responsible for their own actions and still affirm that God is in control of everything? But if divine predestination is overly emphasized, then I can say that my bad (or good) fortune is simply the mysterious will of God. If God determines everything (good and evil), then I may as well do whatever appeals to me because God has predetermined the end result in any case. And if my sinful actions are due to a decision of God, made even before I was born, isn't it unjust of God to condemn me to hell for doing what he had pre-determined that I would do? This is a short statement of what is one of the thorniest theological problems of monotheistic religions but hopefully you'll get a sense of its importance.

This fifth (or sixth) belief affirms that God ultimately is responsible for all that happens. Some Muslims went so far in defending this position as to effectively deny ordinary cause and effect. However, the dominant position tried to defend both free will and divine determinism. The most important ninth century Muslim theologian, al-Ash`ari, said that although God knows, wills, and determines what people will do, people acquire the responsibility of their actions by freely choosing what they were predestined to choose. I know that to many non-Muslim Westerners today, al-Ash`ari's "solution" will seem more like a semantic trick than a genuine solution. But before you criticize Islam too harshly for failure to reconcile free will with divine determinism, remember that no solution to this perennial problem is able to resolve the problem to the satisfaction of non-believers.

You've probably heard the expression "if God wills it." Muslims frequently say *inshallah* after any expression of what they'll do in the future. "I'll meet you here at 2:00 tomorrow, *insha'allah* (God willing)." This means that although the speaker makes decisions, the real decision maker even for that meeting with someone at 2:00 tomorrow is God.

The Pillars of Faith represent the starting point as to what a Muslim is to believe. A beginning Muslim accepts these statements on the authority of the Qur'an and of Muhammad. As a Muslim matures in his faith, his beliefs are deepened, and he comes to understand at a more profound level the truth of these statements.

Although you may or may not agree with each of these beliefs, they're all pretty easy to understand. Islam has an advantage over some religions in that it offers a short list of easily comprehended beliefs. New converts can grasp the basic concepts without doing mental gymnastics and becoming philosopher-theologians. It's simple! It's understandable! It's doable! Compare this with, for example, the concept of the Trinity — three Gods in One — that Christians believe, or the "no self" concept of Mahayana Buddhism, which says the belief of most people that they have a "self" or soul is precisely what prevents them from obtaining salvation. Muslims, in contrast, aren't expected to become budding theologians. Theology *(kalam)* exists among Islamic scholars, but "doing theology" isn't central to Islam. Some Muslims even reject the idea of doing theology, saying that they simply accept the words of the Qur'an and the *hadith* at face value. However, as is the case in other religions, people who claim that they're simply stating the position of the scriptural texts rather than interpreting them are basically not facing up to the reality that other interpreters come up with different views on the basis of the same texts. As soon as one begins to explain a sacred text rather than simply quote it, one is engaged in interpretation and to claim otherwise is intellectually dishonest.

Explaining the Faith to Non-Muslims

The Pillars of Faith present a consensus of basic Islamic beliefs. Two episodes from the traditional biography of Muhammad (see Chapter 6) reflect how Islam presented itself to non-Muslims. In both accounts, matters of faith or belief *(ihsan)* are intermixed with items pertaining to worship *(ibada)* and ethics (also *ihsan).* Scholars disagree as to the historic accuracy of the events, but whether historical or not, they reflect an Islamic view of how to present the faith to non-believers or new converts. These narrative accounts supplement the more systematic lists of beliefs and worship in the *hadith* of Gabriel.

The first incident occurs about 616. Muhammad sent 80 of his followers to Ethiopia to escape persecution in Mecca. When the Meccans sent two diplomats asking the king to send the band of Muslims back to Mecca, the king called the leaders of the Muslims before him and his bishops and asked them to tell him about the new religion that had caused them to abandon the gods of their fathers. The response of the spokesman, Ja`far ben Abu Talib, gives us a picture of early Muslim preaching. As a summary of early Muslim preaching, Ja`far's speech recalls sermons of the apostle Paul in the New Testament such as that to the citizens of Athens (Acts 17:22–31). Ja`far begins by referring to Arabian paganism of the fifth century. He continues with God's sending of Muhammad, the demand to abandon the worship of many gods, to be just in dealings with others, and to follow the Five Pillars of Worship (see Chapter 9). Ja`far says that when he and some others accepted this message, the non-believers in Mecca attacked them and tried to make them abandon their Islamic faith. Because of this, they came to Ethiopia seeking refuge, which they trust the king will grant them. The king asked them to read a passage from their scripture and they read a passage about Mary, the mother of Jesus, from Sura 19. The king and bishops were so moved at these words that they wept. The two emissaries from Mecca then tried to lay a trap by telling the king to ask the Muslims what they thought about Jesus. Ja`far replied that Jesus is the slave, messenger, spirit and word of God and that God put the unborn Jesus in the womb of the Blessed Virgin Mary. The king was impressed and satisfied with Ja`far's testimony and promised the Muslims protection while they were in his country.

Ja`far's speech emphasized:

✔ Oneness of God

✔ Rejection of worship of other gods

✔ Concern for the poor and weak (orphans and women)

✔ Observance of prayer, fasting, and charity (see Chapter 9)

✔ Honesty in word and in dealings with others

✔ Hospitality to others (a key virtue of Arabic culture and one which is also important to New Testament Christianity)

✔ Avoidance of bloodshed

✔ Reverence for Jesus and Mary, thus linking Islam to the Biblical tradition

The second example of Islamic missionary preaching comes from the year before Muhammad's death, a year in which most of the remaining tribes of Arabia were accepting Islam and the leadership of Muhammad. The Banu al-Harith, a Christian tribe from the Yemen (in Southwest Arabia) had submitted. As they'd already made their confession of Allah as God and Muhammad as His prophet, Muhammad sent Amr ibn Hazm to instruct them in the faith. Muhammad told ibn Hazm to tell the Banu al-Harith that they should:

✔ Avoid evil actions

✔ Teach their people the Qur'an

✔ Know the joys of paradise and the torments of hell

✔ Fulfill obligations of daily prayer, purification, pilgrimage, and payment of alms and taxes

✔ Not fight with other Muslims but rather bring disputed matters to God (namely, to Muhammad as God's messenger) for arbitration

✔ Allow Jews and Christians the freedom to practice their religions

Expounding the Faith: Dealing with Difficult Faith Issues

One of the great contributions of Islam to world civilization was in preserving, transmitting, and developing the philosophical (as well as the scientific and medical) heritage of the Greeks that had largely been forgotten in much of the West. Through their translation of ancient Greek philosophical works, Muslim scholars became familiar with both the nature of philosophical disputation and the conclusions of the Greek philosophers. Some conclusions of Greek philosophers — including whether the world was created or eternal and whether there would be a physical resurrection of the body — were in obvious conflict with the plain word of the Qur'an.

The problem of the relationship between revelation and human reason is a difficult issue in many religions, but especially in the three Western monotheisms. Most Americans are familiar with this problem through issues that arise when the conclusions of modern science contradict statements in the Bible. One example is the account of the seven-day creation of the world (Genesis 1) in contrast to the position of most scientists that formation of the earth took several million years. Another related example that everyone is familiar with is the conflict between the Genesis account of the creation of humanity and the scientific Darwinian view of the evolution of the human species over time. Those who defend the literal truth of these Biblical accounts today often call themselves "scientific creationists." Some Muslims also reject the consensus of modern science in matters of creation.

Muslim philosopher-theologians could deal with such conflicts in three different ways:

- ✔ Attempt through the use of human reason to refute the conclusions of the Greek philosophers in places where those conclusions conflicted with the Qur'an.

- ✔ Reject philosophy because it conflicted with the revelation of God, and then refuse to argue the issues. One should accept whatever the scripture says without even asking how it can be true.

- ✔ Accept the positions on these issues of Greek philosophy (as found in the writings of Aristotle, Plato, and the Neo-Platonists) and find a way to reconcile these positions with the Qur'an.

One possible way of reconciling apparent conflicts between reason and revelation — philosophy and the Qur'an — was to say that some statements in the Qur'an are metaphors or poetic language and not to be taken literally. Another way of reconciling seeming contradictions was to say that statements are meant literally, but that when applied to God they don't mean the same thing as in ordinary usage. For example, the Qur'an says God has a face and hands. Early Muslim theologians disagreed as to what this meant. Some said it was a metaphorical way of expressing the nature of God as a personal, active being. Others said the statement was meant literally and must be accepted as true but that Muslims don't know in what sense it's true when applied to God. This position of accepting "without knowing how" became the dominant Islamic position that continues to the present day.

All sides in this debate accepted the authority of the Qur'an and quoted it freely to support their positions, but they interpreted the specific Qur'anic passages differently to support their positions. All sides also accepted the basic beliefs of Islam, although they may have understood them differently. For 300 years, debates continued until finally, in the middle of the tenth century, a general consensus emerged, and it was known as Sunnism, or *Ahl al-Sunna wa-l-jama'a* (meaning, people of the tradition and the community). This consensus position is especially associated with the great Islamic theologian al-Ash`ari (873–935).

Use and limits of Islamic philosophy

Religious questions are an important part of traditional philosophy but still only one of the areas of philosophical inquiry. For those who rejected the use of philosophy to address theological problems, the question still arose as to whether the Muslim scholar could engage in these other areas of philosophical inquiry, such as mathematics, logic, the physical sciences, and ethics. Al-Ghazali (1058–1111) defended the obligation to utilize philosophy in these other realms of inquiry, while recognizing limits to the ability of philosophy to address religious topics without leading people astray in their religious beliefs. The Qur'an itself praises the scholar and commends the pursuit of knowledge. Al-Ghazali was a very important scholar of Islamic law, theologian, ethicist, and Sufi (Islamic mystic — see Chapter 13). He's possibly the most important thinker of medieval Islam, comparable in importance to Maimonides, Nagarjuna, and St. Thomas Aquinas in Judaism, Buddhism, and Christianity respectively.

Naming some theological issues

The Pillars of Faith include just the most basic Islamic theological affirmations. These affirmations are probably sufficient for most Muslims. However, other theological issues arose in Islam. I mention some of the important theological issues in this section. Some of these issues are long since settled. Others are still live issues today. Some issues may strike you as obviously important and relevant today. Other issues may make you wonder what all the discussion was about because the issue appears to you as either unimportant or even as a non-issue — but they were important issues in Islamic theology. Theology is important in Islam but not nearly as central as it is in Christianity, or as philosophy is in some forms of Hinduism. Islam is closer to Judaism than to Christianity in that it emphasizes other things (such as the law) more than it does doing theology.

Defining a true Muslim

In the past, some Protestants haven't regarded Catholics as true Christians and when Protestantism arose in the 16th century, Catholics didn't regard Protestants as true Christians. Many Orthodox Jews don't regard Reform Judaism as a true form of Judaism and do not recognize as valid conversions to Judaism performed by Reformed rabbis. Even in ordinary conversation, one person may refer to another person (usually not in his or her presence) as not being a true Christian or Jew, usually meaning he believes the person doesn't actually live his religion. Islam, from the earliest days, debated the issue of who was a true Muslim.

One group that originated in the seventh century, the Kharijites (see Chapter 2), advocated a puritanical strictness that would exclude from the Muslim community anyone who didn't totally practice their religion — for example, someone who was lax in observing daily prayers. As it turned out, through most of its history and in most places, Islam has accepted as a Muslim anyone who claimed to be a Muslim. Even today, concern for the unity of the Islamic community *(umma)* prevails over imposing uniformity of belief and action in most places. The decision as to who was a true Muslim is left for God to decide on the Day of Judgment. And even a person who is condemned to hell on that day because of his sins may ultimately gain entrance into heaven if he has, while living, sincerely affirmed the *shahada* (testimony of belief in God and in Muhammad as God's prophet).

Exceptions exist to this general attitude of tolerance and acceptance of all who say they are Muslims. Some Islamist radical groups take a position similar to that of the ancient Kharijites. Members of an extremist Islamist group assassinated President Sadat of Egypt in 1981, having declared him not to be a true believer even though Sadat was known for his personal piety and strict observance of Islamic law and ritual. The Taliban, who when they ruled Afghanistan forced their interpretation of Islam upon all people living in Afghanistan, recently issued a decree that Hamid Karzai, the current president of Afghanistan, isn't a true Muslim and thus can or should be killed by a true Muslim. To declare someone who claims to be a Muslim not to be a Muslim is to say he's an unbeliever *(kafir)*. This is very similar to excommunication, which exists in some forms of Christianity.

Relating faith to works

The relation of faith to works was another important issue. Islamic texts speak of affirmation by tongue, heart (the seat of understanding), and limbs (that is, deeds). At a practical level, all three types of affirmation are required of a Muslim. But disagreements exist as to whether tongue and heart are minimally sufficient, or whether without deeds, a person shouldn't be regarded as a Muslim.

Degrees of faith

A related issue is whether faith is an absolute. Some say you either have faith or you don't. The majority position rejects this understanding and says that the faith of a Muslim may increase and deepen or can decrease and become shallower.

Anthropomorphizing God

I've already mentioned this issue, which was very important in early Islamic theological debates, in the section "Expounding the Faith: Dealing with Difficult Faith Issues." When God is described using human terms (this is called *anthropomorphism*) are these descriptions meant literally? The majority position is "yes," but adds that such language doesn't necessarily mean the same thing when used of God as it does when used of people.

Created or eternal Qur'an

Perhaps the most bitterly debated theological issue in ninth century Islam was whether the heavenly prototype of the Qur'an had always existed or whether God had created it at some point in time. The argument is similar to the crucial argument in early Christianity (third century) as to whether Christ had always existed or whether he was the first of God's works of creation. A group called the Mu`tazilites argued in favor of a created Qur'an. Why was this issue important to Islam?

 According to the Mu`tazilites, to say that the Qur'an was eternal (has always existed) contradicts the basic Islamic concept of the unity of God which includes the belief that only God is eternal. The Islamic rulers of the time (the caliphs) tried to impose by force the Mu`tazilite belief that the Qur'an was created but weren't successful. Most Muslims since that time accept that the Qur'an has always existed although the specific explanation as to how this is so can get rather complicated. While the idea of a created Qur'an was ultimately rejected, some theologians recognized a distinction between the eternal Qur'an and the Qur'an as manifested in time and space.

Knowing what is good and evil

Does God tell people not to kill because killing is intrinsically bad or is killing bad only because God says not to do it? If God said to kill, would killing be good? The answers to this question vary. Some say that even apart from revelation and scripture, an objective standard of good and evil exists that one can at least partially know through reason and intuition. Others take the opposite view and conclude that actions are good or bad only because God says they are. This latter position tended to prevail.

Rejecting Formal Creeds

Christians, unlike Muslims and most members of most other religions, typically emphasize correct belief. From early days, Christians have written "I believe" statements. Early creeds, such as the Apostles' Creed and the Nicene Creed, are used widely in Christianity today, for example: "I believe in one God, the Father Almighty, Creator of Heaven and Earth . . . ." Traditionally, to be a Christian, you had to affirm the belief statements of these creeds, and some Christians have even gone to war with one another over differences in belief (think of Northern Ireland). Even some Protestant Christian groups that reject creeds nevertheless use "affirmations of faith" in worship or state in some other way the essential or even required beliefs of the denomination. The closest other religions come to creeds are lists like the Five Pillars of Worship and the Pillars of Faith in Islam. The Four Noble Truths and the Three Refuge Formula would be comparable examples from Buddhism.

Islam isn't a creedal religion. It doesn't make acceptance of a creed a requirement of being a Muslim. It doesn't incorporate creeds into its worship. It doesn't convene groups of Muslim theologians to write and approve official creeds.

This doesn't mean that Islam produced no creeds, however. The *hadith* of Gabriel summarized amounts to a short creed (ʿaqida). The Fiqh Akbar I is another short, early "creed" attributed to Abu Hanifa (700–767). Ultimately much longer creeds were produced — some containing 100 or more belief statements. These creeds summarize the theological position of a particular scholar or school.

To give you a feel for the content and format of these creeds, I reproduce statements from several creeds written during the first 400 years of Islam. This short list isn't an effort to summarize what Muslims believe. To find out more about Muslim creeds and to read the major creeds in their entirety, see whether your library has a copy of W. M. Watt's *Islamic Creeds: A Selection* (Edinburgh University Press, 1994).

- ✔ "We [Muslims] do not hold anyone to be an infidel on account of sin, and we do not deny their faith."

- ✔ "He [God] has always existed together with His attributes since before creation. Bringing creation into existence did not add anything to His attributes that was not already there. As he was, together with His attributes, in pre-eternity, so he will remain throughout endless time."

- ✔ "Everything happens according to His [God's] decree and will, and His will is accomplished. The only will that people have is what he wills for them. What he wills for them occurs and what he does not will, does not occur."

- ✔ "People's actions are created by God but earned by people."

- ✔ "They [Muslims] confess that faith is both word and deed."

✔ "People who innovate in religion or do as they please about it go to the fire of hell, in accord with the *hadith*."

✔ "The Qur'an is the speech of God, not something created which must therefore die out, nor the attribute of something created which must therefore come to an end."

Chapter 5

Standing Before God: Heaven and Hell

Suppose you're going on a long trip to a place you've never visited before. No Web sites post pictures of your destination. Visa requirements are uncertain, and you may not even be allowed to enter the country. Even the vaccinations you should take to protect you during your trip are uncertain. Other people have gone there, but they haven't returned, and the communications they have sent may seem mysterious.

Death is similar to such a journey. Questions concerning death and the destination of (as well as the journey to) the afterlife are prominent in most religions. In this chapter, I look at Muslim views concerning death — what happens at death and after death. In the Islamic faith, death takes you into another world, so this chapter also looks at the Muslim view of this other world. Because angels play an important role in the events concerning the end of life and beyond, I begin with a discussion of angels and other non-worldly beings.

I present an organized topography of the other world and an itinerary of the journey from life to afterlife. The Qur'an and other Islamic sources are nowhere near as organized and systematic as this chapter may suggest to you. In the Qur'an, you find many powerful images regarding the topics in this chapter, but these images aren't organized into a systematic or sequential presentation. So when I present a particular listing of the angels or of the stages from death to life, realize that other texts arrange the data in different ways. Nevertheless, I hope you get an overall impression of Islamic views in this area.

Understanding Other Beings beyond God and Humans

In addition to humans and God, the Qur'an talks about two other groups of living beings: the angels and the *jinn*. Two traditions *(hadiths)* make comparisons of humans, animals, and *jinn*. The first tradition says, "Men are created from clay, angels from light, and *jinn* from fire" (see also Sura 38:76). The second tradition says, "God created angels with intellect but without sensuality, the animals with sensuality but without intellect, and humans with both intellect and sensuality."

Gabriel and the other angels

Although details vary, the Islamic view of angels isn't much different in general from the Jewish and Christian views. Angels are mainly a feature of Western monotheistic religions where they function as intermediaries between God and humans. The English word angel derives from the Greek which in turn derives from a Hebrew word that literally means messenger. Some spirits and minor gods in Eastern religions exercise some of the functions of angels in Western religions but no clearly defined category comparable to the angels exists in these Eastern religions. Belief in angels is part of the Five Pillars of Faith *(iman)* in Islam (see Chapter 4). The Qur'an has more than 80 references to angels. These show that, as you would expect, Muhammad's contemporaries were already familiar with the concept of angels. Although angels are active in this world, angels themselves belong to a different world, which is a formless one. God created angels from light, the least material of substances. Angels are gendered but don't procreate. They don't have free will and, therefore, normally can't sin. Sura 35:1 says angels have two, three, or four wings.

Being sinless and belonging to a higher world, angels are superior to humans from one perspective. Thus when Islamic texts mention the name of an angel, they follow the name with the same formula of blessing used after the name of prophets — "and upon him be peace." However, if you look at it from another perspective, humans have greater potentiality than angels. Humans, unlike angels, are created in the image of God. Thus, after God created Adam, he commanded the angels to prostrate themselves before Adam. In the story of Muhammad's night journey and ascent to heaven, the angel Gabriel acts as Muhammad's guide. But eventually, Gabriel can go no further up through the heavens and Muhammad has to continue alone the remainder of His way to the presence of God.

Angels doing their job

So why do religions like Islam need angels? What purpose do they serve? To some extent angels — who are not gods — replace the minor gods of other religions. Here are some of the things angels do according to Islamic belief.

✔ Angels are God's messengers between Him and the earthly world.

✔ Angels praise God day and night without ceasing (Sura 21:20), as do the winged beings (who aren't actually angels) called cherubim and seraphim in the Jewish Bible.

✔ Angels support the throne on which God sits in the highest heaven.

✔ Angels guard the walls of heaven and hell and the gates of entrance to each level of heaven and hell.

✔ Each person has (one or two) guardian angels.

✔ Angels record the deeds of each person in the book that will be used in God's judgment of the person on the day of resurrection. Sura 82:1–12 says, "Yet over you are watchers, noble beings, writing down, who know whatever you do."

✔ As in both the Christian and Hebrew Bibles, angels play a prominent role at certain points in history. For example, in the crucial Battle of Badr (624, see Chapter 6), Gabriel in his yellow turban led the angels fighting alongside the Muslims and assured the Muslim victory.

✔ The angels are present whenever Muslims are engaged in prayer (*salat*) and are acknowledged by the worshipper at the end of the ceremony.

✔ In Shi`ite Islam (see Chapter 12), the succession of Shi`ite *imams* (successors of Muhammad in the Shi`ite branch of Islam) are guided by angels. At the advent of the hidden 12th *imam,* an angel will appear in the sky to herald the event.

✔ Angels play a crucial role in the process of death and resurrection.

Organizing the angels

"No one of us does not have his known station," say the angels in Sura 7:164. This verse provides the proof text for the concept of a hierarchy or ranking among the angels. One way of expressing this is to link each angel to one of the seven heavens. The most important group of angels are the four archangels — Gabriel, Michael, Israfil, and `Izra'il.

Naming the angels

In this section, you meet some of the more important angels, although this isn't a complete list. According to later tradition, God gave some angels responsibility for certain human attributes, as I note in the list.

✔ The archangel Gabriel is undoubtedly the most important of the angels — both in the Qur'an and in the Bible. In the Qur'an, Gabriel is mentioned only twice (Suras 2:97 and 66:4). However, Muslim tradition identifies Gabriel as the unnamed angel who appears to Muhammad at his call (Sura 53:4–14) and who later leads Muhammad on his night journey to heaven and ascension into Jerusalem (Sura 17:1–2). In Ibn Ishaq's traditional biography of Muhammad, Gabriel appears at a number of other crucial points in Muhammad's life. Along with the archangel Michael, he's one of the two strangers who remove the black speck (representing any potentiality for future sin) from the heart of the infant Muhammad. He leads the angels in battle on the side of the Muslims at the Battle of Badr (624) and also at the Battle of Hunayn (630 — see Chapter 6 for the preceding incidents). Gabriel later appears to Muhammad and teaches him the rituals of purification and prayer (see Chapter 9). Gabriel also appears in the Satanic Verses incident (see Chapter 3). Gabriel appears not only to Muhammad but also to the other prophets who preceded Muhammad. God gave Gabriel responsibility for human speech.

✔ The archangel Michael is mentioned much less frequently. He is named in Sura 2:97 along with Gabriel. He also appears with Gabriel in the incident of the cleansing of the heart and at the Battle of Badr (see the preceding paragraph on Gabriel). According to later tradition, God gave Michael responsibility for human memory (the ability to recall past events).

✔ `Izra'il — the angel of death (Sura 32:11) — is a third archangel. He isn't mentioned in the Bible or named in the Qur'an. He does appear in post-Biblical Jewish traditions, where his functions and appearance are similar to what Muslim traditions say about him. He's gigantic. He has 4,000 wings, 70,000 feet, and his body is covered with eyes and tongues. Clearly, he isn't a friendly figure but could fit well into a Hollywood horror movie. Later traditions report that when God determined to create humanity out of clay, the earth resisted. None of the other angels would take the risk of securing the necessary clay until `Izra'il stepped forward and did this. `Izra'il has a scroll with the names of all people on it, coded for salvation or damnation. When a leaf falls from a tree beneath the throne of God, `Izra'il knows the person's time has come. His primary function is then to separate the soul of the person from the body within 40 days of the person's death — something that the person not unsurprisingly often resists. God entrusted `Izra'il with oversight of the ability of humans to write.

✔ Israfil is the last of the four archangels and similar to `Izra'il in that he also is of gigantic dimensions. He's not named in the Qur'an but according to later tradition, his feet are beneath the earth and his head in the heavens. Like `Izra'il, his body is covered with tongues, mouths, hair, and four wings — one each facing north, south, east, and west. He reads out the divine decisions from a tablet between his eyes and transmits these decisions to the angel responsible for carrying out the decision in the world. His most important function is to sound the trumpet that will usher in the day of resurrection and judgment. God made Israfil the guardian of the human ability to think.

✔ The angels Munkar and Nakir play a particularly important role in the final events. They are black with blue eyes. They question men in the grave about their faith. They aren't mentioned in the Qur'an and don't equate with figures of post-Biblical Christian or Jewish tradition. Muslim creeds of the eighth and ninth centuries mention them along with the punishment in the grave when listing required Muslim beliefs.

Aladdin's lamp and the jinn

Back in the 1960s, a television sitcom called *I Dream of Jeannie* was very loosely based on the idea of the genie in Aladdin's lamp. A popular Disney animated movie *(Aladdin)* of 1992 gave rise to several sequels and a television series for kids. Aladdin is a character from the *1001 Nights,* a prominent staple of Muslim folklore and storytelling. Everyone knows about Aladdin's gravy-boat-shaped lamp. Rub it, and a genie will appear to grant you three wishes.

Although the English word *genie* comes from the Arabic *jinn,* these creatures aren't likely to grant you or me three wishes. Many cultures have traditions of a group of beings, normally invisible to human eyes, who may cause good or evil for humans — fairies, leprechauns, and trolls. Islam has the *jinn,* made of fire. *Jinn* are intelligent beings, imperceptible to humans. In pre-Islamic tradition, they were spirits of the deserts and springs. In the Muslim tradition, they're more important in folklore and storytelling than in theology.

Jinn are capable of salvation or damnation and, thus, can be good or bad. A group of *jinn* once overheard Muhammad preaching (Sura 72:1–5). They believed what they heard and accepted Islam at a place called the Mosque of the Jinn in Mecca. *Jinn* helped King Solomon construct the temple in Jerusalem (Sura 34:12–14).

Jinn have their own tribes and kings. They are male and female, and they marry. Occasionally, they marry humans. In pre-Islamic Arabia, *jinn* inspired prophets, soothsayers, and poets, who had enormous power and prestige at the time of Muhammad. A poet was believed to speak not his own words but the words of the *jinn* who inspired him, so they were like Greek muses. Some people thought Muhammad must be inspired by a *jinn* when he first began to recite the Qur'an and claimed revelations from God — a perception that Muhammad absolutely rejected.

Jinn isn't the only term used of such creatures. Several other terms occur for the more troublesome or evil of these creatures. The most prominent are the *shaytans* (satans with a lowercase "s"); this term occurs over 100 times in the Qur'an and refers to rebellious *jinn.* They try to disrupt the prayers of Muslims. One *shaytan* or *jinn* sits on the shoulder of each person, tempts the person, and witnesses against him on the Day of Judgment.

The Devil made me do it

Iblis is the proper name of the Devil in Islam and may have been derived from the same Greek word as the English word, "Devil." The term *al-shaytan* ("the" Satan), is also used. When God created Adam, he commanded the angels to prostrate themselves before Adam. Iblis alone refused (Sura 15:30–33) His sins were pride and disobedience (Sura 7:12); after all, he knew one should worship only God. God condemned Iblis to damnation but delayed the punishment until the Day of Judgment.

The Qur'an mentions Satan (more than 70 times) more frequently than it does Iblis (8 times). Whether or not Iblis and Satan were originally distinguished, they effectively refer to the same entity in Islam. God allows Satan and his helpers to sow discord and hatred and tempt humans to do evil, beginning with Adam in the garden. Before reciting the *basmala* formula that begins every Sura but one — "In the name of God the Compassionate, the Caring" — Muslims repeat the *ta`awwudh* formula: "I take refuge in God from Satan, the accursed one" (Sura 16:98).

Iblis/Satan doesn't assume the same importance that Satan/the Devil has in Christianity. Sometimes, in Christianity, Satan is seen as a superpower almost equal to God, although God and Jesus will ultimately defeat him at the end of time. In contrast, while Iblis/Satan is a troublesome force in the Islamic world view, nothing, including Satan, comes close to being an almost-equal counterpart to God. The concept of Satan derives from the Hebrew Bible, where he's rarely mentioned and isn't yet the major embodiment of evil that he becomes in Judaism by the time of Jesus. Christianity takes over this developed Jewish concept of Satan. Although many gods of eastern religions represent evil and misfortune, the closest parallel to the Jewish-Christian-Muslim concept of Satan is Mara ("death-causer") in Buddhism. Mara is a god who rules over the world of sensual desire and who tried to prevent the Buddha's enlightenment.

Going to Heaven or Hell: From Life to Death to Resurrection

Regarding the process of death, resurrection, and the final judgment, a detailed sequence of events emerged early on in Islamic texts. In this section, I summarize the typical sequence of events, but keep in mind that variations exist both as to sequence and details.

Islamic portrayals divide the process into two stages: the first is that of death itself and the time in the grave. The second stage includes the sounding of the trumpet, the general resurrection of all peoples in the grave, and the final judgment and dispensation.

Dying and the grave

The three Western monotheisms share the belief in an end to history and time at which point occurs the resurrection of all who have lived, the judgment of those now resurrected, and their entry into heaven or hell. However, most people die long before the Day of Judgment. What happens to them in the meantime? Are they simply dead? Do they have some form of intermediate existence in the grave? Do they have any contact with the living? Even where the scriptures have little to say, tradition will supply answers to these questions. The series of steps is a sequential one, although different traditions may slightly vary both sequence and details.

1. **Forty days before death, a leaf with the name of the person who is to die falls from the tree beneath the throne of God.**

   From this sign, `Izra'il, the angel of death, knows the appointed time has come. God determines both the length of an individual's life (Sura 6:2) and when the universe will cease to exist. When an individual dies, both death and the angel `Izra'il (see the "Naming the angels" section earlier in this chapter) appear to the dead person, who asks, "Who are you?" The person may try to turn away but death (or `Izra'il) confronts her wherever she turns. The two angels who have recorded the person's good and bad deeds show the person the record of her deeds.

2. **`Izra'il extracts the soul of the person from the body.**

   The dying person may resist, but resistance is futile.

3. **Satan tempts the dying person to abandon her faith, perhaps offering a cup of cold water to alleviate her discomfort.**

4. **The person is greeted by the grave, receiving perhaps a glimpse of the future rewards of paradise or of the evils of hell, depending on the future destiny of the person.**

   The grave is a place of darkness and isolation, containing unpleasant insects and reptiles.

5. **The person may then attempt a journey through the seven heavens to see what lies ahead.**

   The condemned person is, of course, denied entrance through the gates of heaven.

6. **The soul is reunited with the body in the grave.**

7. **In the crucial part of this stage, the angels Munkar and Nakir interrogate the dead person.**

   The person, who by now has been buried by his family, is commanded to sit up. "Who is your Lord?" ask the two angels.

   Martyrs and prophets skip the interrogation and go directly to heaven.

8. **The person is punished in the grave — distinct from the final punishment in hell.**

   All those in the grave experience at least a minimal unpleasantness — the pressure of the grave — because all will have committed at least some deeds worthy of punishment.

9. **After usually no more than 40 days, the punishment comes to an end. The person then remains unconscious in the grave until the day of resurrection.**

   This period is called the *barzakh* (Sura 23:100) — the barrier or partition and is similar to sleep. Theologians raised questions about where the person is during this time, whether spirit and body are together, and whether the dead person has contact with or awareness of the living. (No single, consistent answer is given to these questions.)

The resurrection and the final judgment

You can think of the events of the previous section as the warm-up act. Now occurs the grand finale. Life, and even the time in the grave, is but a short prologue to an eternity in heaven or hell. On the Day of Judgment, God will conduct a judicial inquiry of each person based on his conduct when alive. Again the following steps are sequential.

1. **The signs of the end of time appear.**

   Signs announce the approaching end. These signs include the reversal of the order of nature (Sura 81:1–14), such as the rising of the sun in the west rather than the east and the decline of moral order. After a time of troubles involving conflict between the forces of good and evil, God's representatives triumph over evil and the world comes to an end.

   As in the case of other religions, the human imagination and the traditions are very creative in filling the gaps of information about what happens in the "last days" or the "end times." In a typical view, a figure usually called the anti-Christ (*al-Dajjal,* mentioned in the Qur'an as "the Beast" — Sura 27:82) appears. He leads people away from Islam during the period of his rule. Jesus returns to defeat the anti-Christ. After a relatively short period of rule according to God's will (as expressed in Islam), time and history end.

2. **The resurrection (*qiyama,* which means standing) begins.**

   The angel Israfil (see the "Naming the angels" section earlier in this chapter) sounds the trumpet to announce the day of resurrection (Sura 69:13–18). The world comes to an end and with a second sounding of the trumpet, only God remains — "all that is on earth will perish, only the face of God will remain," says Sura 55:26–27. After a period of time, the world is reconstituted, and bodies are reformed in their graves. Israfil is the first of the angels to reappear and Muhammad or one of the Jewish prophets is the first person to be resurrected (spirit rejoined to body). Then comes the resurrection of all the community of Muslims, and finally the resurrection of all others. Only God knows how long a period of fearful anticipation about their fate the resurrected will endure before the actual judgment takes place.

3. **The reckoning (judgment) occurs.**

At the time of death, the book in which each persons deeds were recorded during their lives was affixed to their necks. Now those destined for heaven receive the book in their right hands; those destined for hell receive it in their left hands. The book, or the deeds themselves, are put on the balance scales of judgment and the result determines the final fate of the person. Good deeds weigh more than bad deeds and one must achieve a minimum total weight known only to God to be worthy of entrance into paradise.

4. **All move across the bridge that goes over the fire of hell and leads to the entrance to heaven.**

For the faithful, the bridge is flat and broad and the crossing is easy. For sinners, the bridge becomes as sharp as a sword and as narrow as a hair while the passage becomes dark. They fall into hell. Muhammad meets his faithful followers at a pond on the other side of the bridge. The sweetness of the pond's liquid anticipates what the saved will drink in heaven. But the possibility remains that several of those who fell into hell will ultimately be raised from there into heaven by God's mercy (and perhaps with the aid of the intercession of Muhammad).

Facing the unresolved issues

One question leads to another. The outline of the events of the Day of Judgment left many important questions unanswered. For example, what happens to children who die at a young age before clearly formulated belief is possible? These are crucial issues for ordinary, believing Muslims.

✔ **Intercession:** Intercession refers to the concept that someone of exceptional merit may petition God to reduce the punishment that a believer would otherwise receive for their sins. Strictly speaking, the justice of God demands that each individual receive what he or she deserves, in which case intercession would be pointless. Some early Muslims did deny intercession. However, intercession came to be accepted in the mainstream as a manifestation of God's mercy. Muhammad is the primary intercessor. Tradition says that after the final judgment, Muhammad will encounter his people (Muslims) at the entrance to heaven. Some will ask him to intercede to remove the effects of their sins. Other prophets may also intercede.

✔ **Children:** If you're a believer but your children die young before they can understand and practice the faith, what happens to them? Popular Islamic belief came to affirm that children of believers would enter heaven. Some said all people are born with a natural faith. In the case of young children, this natural faith that hasn't entirely disappeared will suffice to get them into heaven. Others said that the faith of the parents would enable their minor children to enter heaven.

✓ **Spending eternity in hell:** Logic and justice seem to suggest that where one was sent at the judgment is where one would remain for all eternity. But mercy triumphs over judgment in Islam. The common belief is that all sincere Muslims eventually enter heaven despite grave sins (except possibly the sin of denying God). Some say that this mercy will ultimately extend to non-Muslims.

Some Sufis and modernists of the last several centuries have emphasized a metaphorical understanding of the events concerning the final judgment and the final destiny. Other modernists argue that the Muslim view of death and resurrection is supported rather than put in doubt by modern science. Of course, even the strictest traditionalists in affirming the literal meaning of images of heaven and hell in the Qur'an and subsequent tradition would add that these are true "without our knowing how."

Envisioning Heaven and Hell

For reasons of curiosity, religions have often provided reports about heaven and hell. These reports encourage the living to conduct themselves so that they can make the ultimate trip to heaven — and avoid the no-return trip to hell.

Detailed descriptions of hell and its torments occur in the second century (Christian) *Apocalypse of Peter,* in Dante's *Inferno* and *Paradiso* (14th century), and in Swedenborg's *Heaven and Hell* (18th century), to name just a few examples. Buddhist texts provide equally graphic descriptions.

Hell and its torments

Strangely, sometimes the human mind is more fruitful in imagining the worst that can happen, such as the punishments of hell, than in creating images of the greatest possible delights, such as those enjoyed by people in heaven. While the Qur'an emphasizes the basic nature of hell as "the fire" *(al-nar),* the traditions multiply to provide graphic descriptions of the punishments experienced in the different levels of hell. Speaking of sinners destined for hell, Sura 15:44 says, "Gehenna shall be their promised dwelling for all of them. It has seven gates, and a group of them [sinners] will be assigned to each gate." This passage provides the Islamic picture of hell as having seven levels. In each level, the punishments are worse than in the preceding one because the sins committed by its inhabitants are more serious. Believing Muslims are in the upper-most level, pagan unbelievers in the next-to-lowest level, and hypocrites (those who pretended to support Muhammad but in fact secretly opposed him) are in the lowest level (see Sura 4:145). The Muslims in the upper level will ultimately be delivered by the mercy of

God, but the hypocrites will never benefit from divine mercy. Angels guard each of the gates.

The fire is the most frequent name for hell in the Qur'an and is its most characteristic feature. A number of other terms are used of which Gehenna *(jahannam)* is the most common after "the fire." Gehenna is originally a valley bordering Jerusalem whose name came to designate hell in the Jewish tradition. In the Qur'an, hell is sometimes envisioned as a large and horrible beast that comes to meet the sinner on the Day of Judgment (Sura 89:23). At the bottom of the lowest level of hell grows the zaqqum tree (Sura 37:62–68; 44:43), with devils' heads for flowers. Sinners must eat of its fruit, which burns their insides like melted brass (Sura 44:45).

The Qur'an contains a number of images of the torments of hell, such as boiling water, smoke, and searing wind. In his ascent into heaven — see Chapter 6 — Muhammad, while still in the lowest level of heaven was given a peek into hell by the angel Malik, the keeper of hell. The fire is fueled by the bodies of the condemned, who receive new skin to be burned as soon as the previous skin is consumed by the fire. The inhabitants of hell try to escape but are pulled back into the pit with iron hooks.

The general rule is that the punishment fits the sin. For example, adulterous women who gave birth to illegitimate offspring are hanging by their breasts. Men guilty of adultery are forced to eat lean, stinking meat while leaving untouched the good fat meat displayed before them. (The good meat represents the wives permitted to them while the stinking meat represents the women they illegitimately desired and pursued.)

Heaven and its delights

Enough doom and gloom. The real purpose of these descriptions isn't to gloat over those who suffer but to scare them into changing their lives so they can take the road to heaven. Remember that God's mercy goes before His wrath. In Sura 6:160, the Qur'an says that a good deed counts ten times as much as a bad deed. God wants Muslims to enter heaven but ultimately it all depends on the person himself.

The garden *(al-janna)* is the most common name for heaven in the Qur'an. This isn't surprising for a religion that arises in a harsh desert region, where rain and vegetation are rare and precious things. Elaborate gardens are one of the glories of Islamic architectural planning, with the gardens mirroring the garden that is paradise. The word garden also refers to the Garden of Eden where the first human couple lived. Another term used in the Qur'an is paradise *(firdaws)*, a Persian word which originally meant a garden or park. Long before the time of Islam, the Greek translation of the Bible used this Persian word for the Garden of Eden, and from there paradise passed into other Western languages.

On the basis of Sura 23:17, Muslims believe heaven has seven layers — the seven heavens Muhammad ascended through on his night journey and ascent. Later tradition develops specific organization of the gardens and those who dwell in them. As there was a tree at the bottom of hell, so another cosmic tree grows at the top of heaven under the throne of God. Water and fruit-bearing trees are plentiful. Sura 47:15 mentions four rivers of wine, milk, honey, and water that run through heaven.

In contrast to the torments of hell, those in heaven enjoy a serene existence with no deprivation or worries. Delightful food and drink abound — including wine that doesn't make one drunk. People wear silk garments and lounge on couches while being attended by male servants and young, virgin maidens.

The climate is peaceful and shade is plentiful. People are always healthy. But the greatest joy available to those in heaven is to behold the face of God, as described in Sura 75:22–23.

Women and the houris in heaven and hell

Something of a media sensation occurred in August, 2001 when a recruiter of suicide bombers for Hamas (a radical Palestinian group) said in a CBS interview on the 60 Minutes program that he told young recruits, that God had promised martyrs such as themselves that God would give them 70 virgins in paradise. The broadcast generated much controversy. Some claimed that the recruiter had been misquoted. Others said that this objection was irrelevant because the content of what was reported was correct except that all men in paradise would have the 70 or 72 virgins (*houris*) and not just martyrs. This incident raised in the public eye the question once again of women in Islam. Many Westerners were well aware of the image of young virgins in paradise serving the sexual desires of men and Western feminists pointed out the lack of any suggestion of a similar reward awaiting women in paradise. The following is some relevant information for you to consider regarding this topic.

✔ The Qur'an, in a number of passages, unequivocally states that men and women are equal when it comes to the final judgment, being judged on the basis of their own deeds, and as a result gaining entrance into heaven. Women of righteous men such as Lot and Noah are condemned to hell because of their unbelief. A wife of an unbeliever — Pharaoh's wife — gains entrance to heaven because of her saving of Moses.

✔ Nothing in the Qur'an or even in later traditions supports the accusation that the Qur'an says that women have no souls.

✔ The Qur'an does refer explicitly in four passages to the *houris (hur)* — Sura 52.20; 56:22; 55:72; and 44:54 (in likely chronological order). These passages and several others that likely refer to the same females are all from the Meccan period of Muhammad's mission, before the emigration to Medina in 622. The terms doesn't occur in the later Qur'anic passages revealed after 622, which instead talk of purified wives (or literally companions) of men.

✔ The term *hur,* referring to whiteness, was originally applied in Arabic to gazelles — their large, black eyes offset by white irises. So, literally, *houris* are women with large, penetrating, black eyes and, by extension, fair (white) skin. In the Qur'an, the *houris* are amorous virgins with full breasts, untouched by men or *jinn.* They live in pavilions and conduct themselves modestly. These descriptions of paradise from the Meccan period seem mainly directed to men and graphically emphasize the delights which Arabian men of the time would envision in order to make clear that paradise was an infinitely more desirable place than any vision one may have of life on earth.

✔ The Qur'an and later tradition has much less to say about what awaits women in paradise. Some Muslims say this does not mean that women do not have corresponding sexual delights in paradise but rather that modesty precludes describing these delights in the case of women. I do not find this argument convincing but maybe you do.

✔ Later traditions greatly expand on the description of the *houris.* They're perpetual virgins with translucent flesh; on one of her breasts is the name of her human husband and of God on the other breast. They wear precious stones and their face is like the crescent moon. They live in pavilions with 70 beds and are attended by 70,000 maids of honor. They don't get pregnant and have no menses. Men have as companions (depending on the text) their human wives and a houri, or even 72 *houris.* At the same time, we're told that human wives are vastly superior to the *houris* because they're believers who have observed the ritual requirements of Islam.

✔ Other traditions have a much less egalitarian view of women than that expressed by the Qur'an. Some say that women are inferior to men, created from the tip of the bent rib of Adam. Others say that women are temptresses, introducing a motif not found in the Qur'an — that Adam's fall was due to the temptation of Eve. A tradition with a number of variations says that when Muhammad looked into hell, he saw that the majority of its inhabitants were women. Other traditions seem to make a woman's salvation dependent on her submission to her husband even as the man's salvation is dependent on his submission to God. Islamic feminists point out that the authenticity of many of these traditions is dubious and regard them not as part of revelation but rather as an expression of male dominance which emerged in the history of Islam that ran counter to the egalitarianism of the Qur'an.

✔ I doubt that many Muslim theologians would endorse the idea of luring young men to engage in suicide bombings by promises of incredible sexual delights as compensation. If such martyrdom is permissible, it must be done out of submission to and service of God, not out of what one hopes to get out of it. The West in the last 100 years has made the the treatment of Muslim women one of its major criticisms of Islam. Westerners are fascinated by *houris,* belly dancing, and images of harems that contain many women to service the sexual desires of their owners. In the 19th century, Westerners criticized Islam for its treatment of women at a time when, in many ways, the rights of Western women were more severely restricted than those of Muslim women.

Islam also has no clear concept comparable to *limbo* — a place to which go those deserving of neither heaven nor hell. But many commentators find something similar to limbo implied in Sura 7:46–48. This passage refers to people on the "heights." These people see the people in hell suffering their torments and the people in heaven enjoying their pleasures. But the people on the heights belong to neither group. It seems they'll never enter hell. Interpreters differ as to whether they'll eventually gain entrance into heaven.

Purgatory, limbo, and heaven

Islam has no purgatory in the sense of a place, distinct from heaven and hell, in which the sins of those not yet ready to enter heaven are purged. Yet popular belief is that due to the mercy of God, even sinful Muslims who haven't worshiped other gods will ultimately be saved even though they find themselves in the upper level of hell at the time of the final judgment. Also discussed, with less agreement, is the extent to which divine mercy would ultimately deliver others, including non-Muslims, from hell.

Part II

Muhammad: The Man, the Book, and Rules of Law

The 5th Wave   By Rich Tennant

"I told him we were lost and needed directions. He offered a road map for the former, but suggested the Qur'an for the latter."

In this part . . .

In this part, I retell the story of Muhammad and examine the role he plays in the daily lives of Muslims. Because Muhammad's only miracle was the transmission of Islam's scripture — the Qur'an — you find out about the origins, organization, style, content, and interpretation of the Qur'an. You also discover that an oral presence of the Qur'an in Muslim faith is very important.

Like Judaism, Islam emphasizes living according to God's revealed law. The traditions of what Muhammad did and said along with the Qur'an are the primary sources for this law. The final chapter in this part considers how Muslims derive knowledge of God's will from the Qu'ran and other sources.

Chapter 6

The Prophet: Muhammad

Some religions have a single founder. Siddhartha Gautama Buddha, Confucius, Jesus, and Muhammad are the founders of Buddhism, Confucianism, Christianity, and Islam, respectively. Other religions such as Hinduism have no central person who members consider the founder or have several individuals who share the role of founders (Abraham and Moses in Judaism). Even Taoism (a Chinese religion) has a founder, Lao Tzu, although many scholars doubt whether Lao Tzu (the name means "old man") is a historical figure and whether he is truly the founder of Taoism.

Religions with a single founder typically place major emphasis on the story of the founder. The founder's story is the "sacred story" of the religion (see Chapter 3 regarding sacred stories). Believers know the traditional story of the founder and an outsider who wants to understand the religion will also need to know the founder's story and its importance in the religion. The outsider is usually concerned about the biography of the founder as an aid to understanding why members of the religion believe and do the things the religion teaches them. To the believer, the founder is usually a key source of authority in the religion, and in many religions the founder has the most direct link to God or the divine and the path to salvation. The founder is also the primary paradigm for believers. He not only tells believers what to believe and do but also exemplifies in his life what he tells them.

The traditional story may originate shortly after the founder's death or much later. It may cover most of his life or only certain portions of his life. The founder's story isn't the same as a modern biography. The founder's story that is well known by most believers may be essentially the same as the scholars' version of the founder's life or it may differ significantly from scholarly reconstructions.

Most Muslims, like members of other religions, care more for the traditional story of their founder than for scholarly reconstructions. In this chapter, I preface my summary of Muhammad's life by describing the world into which he was born. Then after having summarized the traditional story, I end with a discussion of the historical sources for the life of Muhammad and modern scholars' evaluation of those sources.

After each mention of Muhammad's name, Muslims add "peace and blessings be upon him" (PBUH).

Setting the Stage: Arabia before Muhammad

Although only 20 percent of Muslims are Arabs, Islam is closely linked to the Arabs culturally and historically. The most important feature which binds all Arabs is a common language, Arabic. Arabic is a Semitic language, which means that it belongs to the same family of languages as does Hebrew. Arabia is the original homeland of the Arabs. Long before the time of Muhammad, Arabs had spread beyond Arabia into Iraq, Palestine, and Syria. In the century after Muhammad's death, with the Muslim conquests, Arabs spread into additional areas — especially North Africa.

Arabia is the peninsula that's mainly occupied by Saudi Arabia today (see Figure 6-1). This large peninsula lies across the Red Sea to the east of Egypt, south and southeast of present Syria, Palestine, and Jordan, and southwest of modern Iran across the Arabia Gulf (also called the Persian Gulf). Arabia is part of the area called the Middle East. (Depending on context and time period, this region extending from Egypt to Iran and including Arabia may also be called the Near East or the Ancient Near East).

Life in Arabia was hard. Much of the peninsula was desert, which supported only a sparse population. Prior to the discovery of oil in the 20th century, Arabia didn't have much in the way of natural resources. Before the rise of Islam, Arabia had never been united into a single state. A centralized state with a developed, complex civilization existed only in Yemen, where the first Yemenite state was established about 1,000 years B.C.E. The great empires at the time of Muhammad in this part of the world were the Byzantine or Eastern Roman Empire with its capital at Constantinople (modern Istanbul, Turkey) and the Persian Empire (also called the Sasanian Empire), which ruled over Iran and much of Iraq. These two great empires engaged in a series of wars. Each exercised some influence, directly or indirectly in Arabia, but neither tried to conquer and rule directly the entire peninsula.

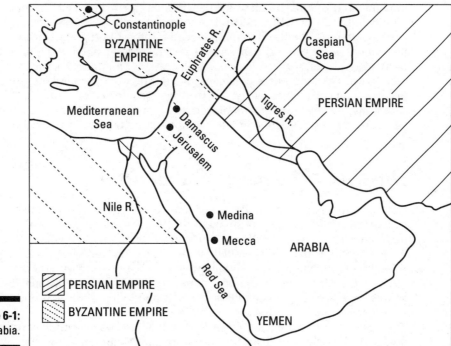

Figure 6-1:
Arabia.

Two key cities

One of the two cities that played the key role in Muhammad's life, Mecca, was located inland along the west central coast of Arabia, in an area that is still called the Hijaz. Mecca's roots go back to about 400 C.E., and it was one of the most important holy places of Arabia because it contained the sacred pilgrimage shrine called the *Ka`ba* (see Chapter 9). According to the traditional Muslim understanding, Mecca was flourishing at the time of Muhammad. Its economy was based on trade, with trade routes passing through Mecca that connected Yemen to Damascus in Syria. Two trading caravans set out each year — one to the south and another to the north. As in the case of trade across the Sahara desert in Africa, camels, which can go long periods without water and carry substantial burdens, made possible trade routes across Arabia. Treaties, a trading fair at Mecca, and a truce during the months of the fair and the pilgrimage facilitated trade. A number of scholars think this picture of a bustling commercial city playing a major role in international trade is greatly overblown. F.E. Peters (*Muhammad and the Origins of Islam,* State University of New York Press, 1994) points out that we have no archaeological evidence to support this picture of Mecca (in contrast to substantial archaeological remains from earlier Arab trading centers elsewhere) and that no non-Muslim contemporary records refer to Mecca as an important trading city. Peters thinks that Mecca was a very modest village with few if any substantial buildings and that its trade was basically local (within Arabia) rather than international.

Medina, on the other hand, was a prosperous (for Arabia) agricultural community with fertile fields and a secure water supply — things Mecca lacked. Located about 250 miles north of Mecca on the route to Palestine and Syria, its original name was Yathrib. Later it became known as Medina (meaning city), a shortened form of "city of the prophet" (Muhammad). Dates were its main crop. The settlement consisted of a number of independent farmstead-like dwelling complexes with a few fortified structures for refuge in times of war. A number of Jewish clans played an important role in the settlement, which by the time of Muhammad was dominated by two Arabic tribes.

Outside the cities: The beduin

Outside of trading towns and agricultural villages lived desert herders (the *beduin*) who had no fixed, permanent dwelling location. The word "Arab" originally applied only to the beduin, and while beduin and village dwellers were sometimes in conflict, each also depended on the other. As a general rule, the beduin valued love, honesty, generosity, hospitality, and courage in war and love; however, in the commercial city of Mecca, traditional beduin values were breaking down in the face of individual pursuit of wealth.

The *clan,* composed of a number of extended families, was the central social unit of Arab society, both settled and nomadic. Members of the clan claimed common ancestry reaching back several generations. Elders from leading families chose the clan head — the *sheikh* — who ruled by consent and consultation. Above the clan were shifting tribal federations. Desert clans engaged in raids *(razzias)* against each other or against villages and caravans in which the purpose was not to kill the opponent but to take slaves, women, camels, horses, and other booty. Of course, the defense of one's own honor and the honor of the women of one's clan was important.

Arabian religious practices

Islam says that God, through the angel Gabriel, called Muhammad to be a prophet in 610. This call marks the beginning of Islam, which refers to the time before Muhammad's call as the *al-Jahiliyya* — the time of ignorance. Most Arabs were *polytheists* (believers in many gods). The *Ka`ba* shrine in Mecca (see Chapter 9) contained images of 360 gods, including its chief god, Hubal. Allah was a distant god called upon only in times of crisis. More important for daily life were three goddesses usually regarded by pre-Islamic Arabs as Allah's daughters — al-Lat, Manat, and al-`Uzza — all discussed in Chapter 3. Vague spirits inhabited caves, stones, streams, and trees, and jinn spirits (see Chapter 5) abounded. Polytheistic Arabs had no expectation of an afterlife; instead, "fate," which was more important than the gods, eventually extinguished everything.

Islamic tradition says that before the time of Muhammad, some individuals may have sought a religious alternative to polytheism and had a vague sense of a single God. Muslims say they were reaching back to the original *monotheism* (belief in one god) of Abraham. Islamic tradition calls such a monotheist a *hanif*. Muhammad, prior to his call, is said to have been a *hanif*. As in the case of Mecca, pre-Islamic poetry, and the life of Muhammad in general, the only evidence on this is from the Qur'an and Islamic traditions, and non-Muslim historians will naturally ask, as they do about any historical evidence, how accurate it is.

Other religious practices included Judaism and Christianity. Some Jewish clans lived in Medina, in Yemen, and in other scattered locations. Christians, on the other hand, were located on the geographical periphery (across the straits in Ethiopia were Monophysite Christians, while on northern border regions, Nestorian Christians were important), and caravan traders from Mecca encountered these Christians. Neither Christian group, however, had orthodox *Trinitarian* (God as Father, Son, and Holy Spirit) views. *Zoroastrianism* was the official religion of the Sasanian (Persian) state, and, along with several offshoots, was widespread in present Iran and parts of eastern Iraq. Zoroastrianism is a form of ethical dualism, in which an uncreated god of good is locked in conflict with a god of evil. A small number of Zoroastrians known as Parsees (the name given the religion in India) survive today in a number of countries, including the United States.

Telling the Story of Muhammad

Now that you know something about the religious and historical setting at the time of Muhammad, I turn to a summary of the traditional Islamic version of the life of Muhammad. My intention isn't to try to reconstruct the "historical Muhammad" but rather to help you see Muhammad as Muslims see him and to appreciate why he's so important to Muslims.

Growing up

Muhammad belonged to the dominant tribe of Mecca, the Quraysh. The Quraysh traced its ancestry back a number of generations to Fihr, its founder. Before Fihr, the genealogy extended to Isma`il, the son of Abraham, and then to Adam, the first man. A number of generations after Fihr, the Quraysh settled in Mecca. Muhammad's clan was named after his great-grandfather Hashim. The Hashim were one of the less important clans of Mecca, but because the clan head was the guardian of the *Ka`ba,* the Hashim had considerable prestige.

Muhammad was born in about 570 C.E., the "Year of the Elephant" (see Sura 105). Tradition reports that shortly before Muhammad's birth, an army led by the Abyssinian (modern Ethiopia) governor of Yemen, was on the verge of conquering Mecca. Abyssinia at that time ruled Yemen. Upon nearing the city, the elephant leading the army supposedly refused to advance further and bowed down toward the city in reverence. Muslims believe God delivered Mecca because of Muhammad's impending birth there.

Because Muhammad's father, `Abd Allah, died on a trading journey prior to his birth, Muhammad was raised by his mother, Amina, and his grandfather `Abd al-Mutalib, the clan head. As was traditional among city-dwelling Arabs of Mecca, Amina sent the infant to be wet-nursed by a beduin woman named Halima. The people of Mecca believed that the beduin preserved pure, Arab values and that a child would benefit from early contact with people who lived according to those values.

One day two men came upon Muhammad, cut open his breast, and took out his heart, removing the black spot within. Tradition identifies the two men as the angels Gabriel and Michael and the event is regarded as a miracle. The black spot represents the human tendency to sin. By removing this spot, Muhammad was protected from sin, in accordance with the belief that later developed that, despite being only a human, Muhammad was sinless. After this, Halima brought Muhammad back to his mother. When Muhammad was six, his mother Amina died and two years later his grandfather died, leaving Muhammad in the care of his uncle Abu Talib, who had succeeded the grandfather as clan head and Muhammad's guardian.

Muhammad's own experience of being an orphan — having lost father, mother, and grandfather — is reflected in the concern of the early Qur'anic revelations for the poor and powerless, as in Sura 93:6–10:

> *Did he not find you an orphan and shelter you? Did he not find you wandering and guide you? Did he not find you in need and provide for you? So do not oppress the orphan and do not reject the beggar.*

Once, while accompanying his uncle on a trading trip, the caravan stopped at Basra in Iraq. Bahira, a local Christian monk, saw a light above the caravan and took this as a sign that the awaited prophet was among the travelers. When the young Muhammad was finally brought before him, Bahira examined Muhammad for the "sign of prophecy" on his back between his shoulders and recognized him as the prophet promised in sacred books in Bahira's possession. To Muslims, this incident presents Muhammad as a fulfillment of Christian expectations, recognized as such even by a Christian monk. The text doesn't say what precisely this sign was — perhaps a lump or special birthmark.

Because his father died before he was born, Muhammad received no inheritance. Khadija, a wealthy widow about 15 years older than Muhammad, hired Muhammad as the overseer of her trading ventures. The young man impressed her, and she proposed marriage in about 595. Until her death, Khadija was Muhammad's only wife. She bore Muhammad four daughters and one or more sons. Of their children, only Fatima survived both her mother and father.

Summoning the people of Mecca

In the Muslim view, the function of a major prophet like Muhammad is twofold. He's to convey God's word (the Qur'an, for Muslims) to His people. He's to call His people to return to serving only God and to practice justice, warning them of the punishment they'll face on the Day of Judgment if they don't respond. According to tradition, dissatisfied with the local polytheism, Muhammad went periodically on private religious retreats in a cave on Mt. Hira outside of Mecca. There, in 610, when Muhammad was about 40 years old, on one of the odd-numbered days of the last ten days of the month of Ramadan (the night of power — *laylat al-qadr*), the angel Gabriel appeared and told Muhammad that he was "the messenger of God" (that is, the one who would convey God's book to His people). Gabriel told Muhammad to recite from the book. Initially, Muhammad responded, "I cannot recite" (or "What shall I recite") as he tried to avoid the task God had entrusted to him. Sura 53:5–18 portrays Gabriel as filling the horizon in whatever direction Muhammad turned, so that Muhammad ultimately yielded.

After this experience, Muhammad was afraid. Was he mad or inspired by one of the *jinn* spirits (see Chapter 5) as were poets and soothsayers? Some people believed this of Muhammad when he later went public with his message. But Muhammad insisted he was neither poet nor soothsayer. He went to his wife Khadija, who consoled him and suggested that the two of them consult her cousin, Waraqa ibn Nawfal, who had become a Christian. Waraqa confirmed from scripture that Muhammad was the expected prophet bringing the word of God to the Arabs, who had never yet received a scripture of their own.

What verses from the Qur'an, the first verses to be revealed, did Muhammad receive on this occasion? Most Muslims believe Muhammad recited the opening verses of Sura 96, which say (verses 1–5), "Recite in the name of your Lord who created — created humanity from an embryo. Recite your Lord is all-giving who taught by the pen, taught humans what they didn't know previously."

Muhammad was worried when a couple of years passed without further revelations. In Sura 93:3–4, God assures Muhammad saying, "Your Lord has not abandoned you and doesn't hate you. What is after will be better than what came before." Throughout the remainder of his life, Muhammad continued to receive the revelations that, when collected together, constituted the Qur'an. Muslim tradition says that Muhammad was illiterate and, therefore, he couldn't himself have composed the Qur'an.

Picturing Muhammad

From Western art — both great art and popular art — Christians and Jews often have mental images of what Moses and especially Jesus looked like. The same goes for Buddhists and Confucianists. However, almost no ancient sources provide information upon which to base these images. In contrast, except for some representations of Muhammad in Persian miniature paintings (where Muhammad's face is blank), Muslim artists don't paint pictures or make statues of Muhammad. This goes back to the prohibition against making an image of any living thing (Deuteronomy 4:16–19) in the Bible, a prohibition applied most strictly in Islam to the representation of God and His prophet, Muhammad. The lack of pictorial representation is made up for by detailed textual descriptions of Muhammad's appearance. The following composite description is based on several of the *hadiths* about Muhammad collected by al-Tirmidhi (824–892) in his *Shama'il.*

Muhammad was somewhat taller than a person of average height. His shoulders were broad and his thick hair reached his ear lobes. He was large boned and had a large head. His face was oval and its complexion was neither very light nor very dark. His face shone brighter than the full moon. He had long eyelashes and between them he had a vein that swelled when he was angry. He had dark, black eyes and a heavy beard. His teeth were shinning white. The seal of prophethood [recognized by the monk Bahira] was between his shoulders. Muhammad leaned forward when walking.

In contrast to the many movies about Jesus produced for Christians, film makers have produced only one full-length movie about Muhammad, *The Message* (1977). How do you make a movie about someone without representing the person onscreen? In some scenes, Muhammad is just off-camera. In others, Muhammad is unseen behind the camera lens. Also, you can convey much about a person by focusing on key figures in his life.

Initially, Muhammad confined his mission to his immediate circle. After Khadija had accepted that God had appointed Muhammad His prophet, his slave boy Zayd, his cousin `Ali (the son of his uncle-guardian Abu-Talib), and a number of other cousins also became Muslims and recognized Muhammad as God's prophet. For a couple of years, the small group of Muslims quietly practiced their new faith, including daily morning prayers. Then God told Muhammad to proclaim the message of Islam publicly. Abu Bakr, who was to be Muhammad's successor *(caliph),* was his first important convert from outside the Hashim clan. Most remaining converts were young people, along with some adults from less influential clans. Most of the people of Mecca didn't accept the message of Muhammad. Not believing in an afterlife, they had no reason to fear the threat of eternal damnation conveyed by Muhammad. Muhammad pointed to the signs of God in creation as proof that God would settle accounts at the final judgment.

Facing opposition

As Muhammad converted more of their sons and daughters, opposition grew from Arab adults. In a society in which family and clan were everything, Muhammad's mission was causing rifts within families. Muhammad was now putting more emphasis on the worship of only one god (in Sura 112; see Chapter 3 on the Satanic Verses episode). Although Muhammad's uncle Abu-Talib protected Muhammad, many converts were without such support, and their adherence to Islam put them in danger. About 615, Muhammad sent about 80 Muslim men and their families to Ethiopia, whose Christian ruler granted them refuge (see Chapter 4). Shortly afterward, Muhammad's uncle Hamza, one of his fiercest opponents, and `Umar (the future second caliph, see Chapter 2) converted. Concerned about these conversions, the main Quraysh clans enforced a boycott of the Hashim clans from about 616–618.

In 619, Muhammad's situation took a decisive turn for the worse when both his wife, Khadija, and his uncle and protector, Abu Talib, died. Abu Lahad, another uncle and the new clan head, opposed Muhammad (see Sura 111).

Muhammad's night journey to Jerusalem *(isra`)* and ascent to heaven *(mi`raj)* occurred in about 620 (see Chapters 9 and 13). Sura 17:1 may refer to this incident. The angel Gabriel came in the night and put Muhammad on a winged donkey named Buraq that carried him to Jerusalem. Tethering Buraq on the wall of the ancient Jewish temple mountain, Muhammad then ascended up through the heavens from the place where Abraham almost sacrificed his son and the Jewish temple had once stood. After being shown the torments of hell, Gabriel led Muhammad up through the seven heavens, each of which was guarded by angels. In each heaven, different prophets, such as Adam, Moses, and Jesus, met Muhammad. Finally, beneath the throne of God, Gabriel could go no further and Muhammad proceeded by himself into the presence of God. After his return to earth, Buraq brought him back to his bed in Mecca in the same night.

In 620, Muhammad met with six men on pilgrimage to Mecca from the town of Yathrib (later called Medina). Conflict between the two Arab tribes of the town endangered the prosperity of this agricultural oasis settlement. They were seeking an arbitrator to maintain peace in the community and had heard of Muhammad's trustworthiness. In fact, Muhammad's reputation for honesty earned him the nickname al-Amin — the trustworthy one. From the Jewish clans of Yathrib, they had also heard of a prophet soon to appear and they thought that perhaps Muhammad was this prophet.

Then in 622, another group of men and women from Yathrib met secretly with Muhammad outside of Mecca and signed the "Pledge of War" to accept Muhammad as arbitrator of the city and to welcome his followers.

Muhammad urged but didn't order the Muslims to immigrate to Medina and some Muslims continued to live in Mecca. Muhammad's followers, who numbered about 70, set out for Yathrib in small groups until only `Ali, Muhammad, and Abu Bakr were left of those who had decided to emigrate. Muhammad's opponents felt it was time to get rid of Muhammad. Each clan selected one young man, the plan being they would jointly kill Muhammad. The Hashim, unable to take blood revenge on all the other tribes, would have to settle for payment of monetary compensation once Muhammad had been killed. The final night, `Ali occupied Muhammad's bed. The young men had decided to kill Muhammad when he emerged from his home the next morning and were surprised when `Ali came out instead of Muhammad. Squads of men pursued Muhammad and Abu Bakr. Tradition says the two men took refuge in a cave. God caused a tree to grow overnight, blocking the entrance to the cave, and had a spider spin a web covering the entrance. When the pursuing forces stopped at the cave, they could tell from the tree and the web that no one was hiding inside — or so they thought. On September 24, 622 Muhammad and Abu Bakr arrived at Medina (see Chapter 9 for the arrival in Medina), to be joined by `Ali three days later.

Hijra (sometimes spelled hegirah) is the term for the emigration from Mecca to Medina in 622. This date marks zero date of the Islamic calendar (see Appendix A). Don't confuse *hijra* with another equally important term, the *hajj* (the required once-in-a-lifetime pilgrimage to Mecca that's discussed in Chapter 9).

Establishing the community in Medina

Up until settling in Medina, Islam had been a small religious sect existing precariously in the midst of a larger, hostile community. In Medina, Muslims became the majority and with this change in situation, the subject matter of Qur'anic revelations changed. The revelations became longer and had less of the poetic splendor of the earlier suras. They often dealt with practical matters that had to be settled as Islam gave shape to a new community. Previously, primary loyalty had been to family and clan — and beyond that to tribe — and while these loyalties remained important, as a Muslim, primary loyalty shifted to the Islamic community *(umma)*. Reforms in areas such as marriage, inheritance, and commerce were instituted.

Initially, the more important clan chiefs still had more power than did Muhammad. The entire community had accepted Muhammad as arbitrator, but not all accepted Islam as their religion. Pagans were allowed to remain in the city, as long as they didn't conspire with the Quraysh tribe of Mecca.

Muslims in the city were divided into two main groups. The immigrants *(muhajirun)* included both those who accompanied Muhammad on the hijrah from Mecca to Medina and also those people of Mecca who emigrated later (but before the conquest of Mecca in 630 that's discussed later in this section). The helpers *(ansar),* those people of Medina who pledged to protect Muhammad and who became Muslims, were the other group. In addition, the Qur'an refers to a third group: hypocrites who outwardly pretended to support Muhammad but secretly opposed him.

Reconciling the interests of all these different groups was no easy task. Only a person of high personal and political skills could have pulled this off as Muhammad did. The relationship between the parties was regulated in a document called the Constitution of Medina (see "The terms of the Constitution of Medina" sidebar for details). This pact established reciprocal rights and obligations among the various groups, who in accepting the terms of this pact constituted the political community. Muslims regard the Constitution of Medina as the basic political document of Islam. Supporters of Islamic democracy also claim this document as a precedent. However, because the Constitution of Medina wasn't divinely revealed, it doesn't legislate the form of government of subsequent Muslim states.

A chronology from 622 to 630

Eight years elapsed between the flight from Mecca to Medina in 622 and the triumphal reentry of Muhammad into Mecca in 630 discussed in the following chronology. Another two years passed before the death of Muhammad in 632. The following outline presents the highpoints of this ten-year period.

- ✔ **623:** After the completion of Muhammad's new home in Medina, he sent for the remaining members of his family, including the woman he had married after the death of Khadija. At this time he married `A'isha, the very young daughter of Abu Bakr (one of his early converts, the person who fled with him to Medina, and his eventual successor) who had been betrothed to him in 620. `A'isha became Muhammad's favorite wife after Khadija's death. Muhammad entered into a number of additional marriages, receiving a revelation that granted him special dispensation to exceed the normal limit of four wives for a Muslim (see Chapter 11). Most of these subsequent marriages were to provide support for women whose husbands had died fighting for Islam.

- ✔ **624 (January):** The suras of the Qur'an revealed in Medina show increasing emphasis on links to the Biblical traditions. Originally, Muslims prayed facing Jerusalem. In 623, Muhammad had appointed a freed, black, Ethiopian slave — Bilal — to give the call each morning from the top of the tallest house. While leading the community in Friday prayer, Muhammad received a revelation (Sura 2:39) and told the congregation to turn toward Mecca to pray, as Muslims have done since that day. Also, originally, Muslims had fasted on the 10th of Muharram, the first month, in accord with Jewish tradition. Now the Qur'an instituted the month of Ramadan as the period of fasting (as described in Sura 2:182; see Chapter 9).

✔ **624 (March):** The Battle of Badr. The Muslims of Medina, in accord with the normal custom of Arabian society, sent raiding parties against Meccan trading caravans. A revelation from God (Sura 2:217) even authorized Muslims to engage in these raids during the sacred month of Rajab when Arab custom prohibited fighting. After a number of minor raids, Muhammad led a force of over 300 men against a Quraysh caravan returning from Syria. The caravan had escaped before a relief army arrived from Mecca and confronted the Muslims. Outnumbered three to one, the Muslims won a surprising victory. Tradition says that the angel Gabriel himself led the angels in combat alongside the forces of Muhammad against the Quraysh. Despite the relatively minor nature of this victory in which 45 to 70 Meccans were killed, this victory at Badr demonstrated to the Muslims that God was on their side (Sura 8:9).

✔ **625:** The Battle of Uhud. Mecca was still determined to put an end to Muhammad. Near Medina, 3,000 Meccan infantry and cavalry — a large army for that place and time — attacked the forces of Muhammad numbering about 1,000. Seventy Muslims were killed in the battle, but the forces of Mecca failed to follow up on their victory. About this time, Muhammad expelled from Medina two of the main Jewish clans because he suspected them of conspiring against the Muslims.

✔ **627:** The Battle of the Ditch. This time, the Quraysh clan from Mecca mustered an army of 10,000. A Persian convert named Salman al-Farisi advised Muhammad to dig a ditch around the three exposed sides of the city as a defense. Neither used to nor equipped for long sieges, the Mecca forces withdrew after a couple of weeks. This marked the final large-scale attempt of the Meccan forces to subdue Muhammad.

The terms of the Constitution of Medina

The Constitution of Medina, about two pages in length, deals with the most pressing concerns facing the new community rather than presenting a fully developed political system. Among its provisions are:

✔ Jews may retain their own religion.

✔ Each group is responsible for its own internal affairs.

✔ All are responsible for defense of the community of Medina against any threat from outside.

✔ A Muslim should not kill another Muslim nor help a non-Muslim kill a Muslim.

✔ Internal conflicts should be taken to Muhammad as the prophet of God for arbitration.

✔ Muslims have a responsibility for the poorer members of the community.

✔ Medina is a refuge to Muslims coming from outside the city, except that a woman who flees to Medina will not be accepted against the wishes of her family.

✔ **628–629:** The Treaty of Hudaybiyya. Muhammad led 1,600 unarmed men from Medina on an attempted pilgrimage to the *Ka`ba* in Mecca. Although the *Ka`ba* had become a pagan shrine, Muslims believed that the *hajj* had been established by God and first performed by Abraham and his son Ishmael. Muslims wished to purify the shrine from its later pagan elements. While they weren't allowed to enter the city this time, Mecca and Muhammad signed the Treaty of Hudaybiyya (Sura 48:27). The treaty established a 10-year truce and said that next year the Quraysh would temporarily leave the city of Mecca and allow Muslim pilgrims to enter. This *`umra* (lesser) pilgrimage did take place in 629.

The treaty provided an important precedent for Muslims to enter into treaties with non-Muslims.

✔ **628–630:** Mecca submits. In this period, the size of the Muslim community in Medina doubled, as many entire clans and tribes accepted Islam. Allies of the Quraysh clan were accused of breaking the terms of the Treaty of Hudaybiyya, so in January 630, Muhammad marched on Mecca with an army of 10,000. The city submitted without a battle. Muhammad cleansed the *Ka`ba* of the idols it contained, but showed mercy to the inhabitants of the city, executing only a few men. People weren't forced to convert to Islam, although most eventually did.

✔ **631:** The Year of Deputations. At the end of 630, the first Muslim army was sent to the area of southern Palestine, anticipating the expansion out of Arabia. Treaties were concluded with the Christian Arabs there — another precedent for Muslims entering into treaties with non-Muslims. Most of the remaining tribes of Arabia sent delegates to Muhammad, accepting Islam and the leadership of Muhammad.

✔ **632:** The Farewell Pilgrimage and the Death of Muhammad. Muhammad led pilgrims on a *hajj* pilgrimage to Mecca. (Chapter 9 describes the *hajj*.) On the plain of Arafat outside Mecca, he gave what is known as the farewell sermon in which he said, "Your Islam is completed." At this time Muhammad received Sura 5:4–5, the final portion of the Qur'an to be revealed. Not long after his return to Mecca, he fell sick. On June 8, 632, he died in the arms of `A'isha.

Naturally, Muhammad's death caused consternation. `Umar (the future second caliph) refused to accept that Muhammad was really dead. At that point, Abu Bakr (Muhammad's successor) addressed those assembled and said, "If anyone worships Muhammad, Muhammad is dead. If anyone worships God, God is alive, immortal."

Thinking about Muhammad Theologically

The traditional biography of Muhammad is about 600 pages long in English translation. Not all Muslims are familiar with every detail, but most are familiar with the events I mention in the preceding sections of this chapter. This biography talks about the contribution of Muhammad to the origins of Islam. However, to say what Muhammad did (or what Muslims believe he did) doesn't answer all questions about the Muslim understanding of Muhammad — what you may call the theological understanding of Muhammad in contrast to the understanding of his historical role. This section deals with the theological significance and understanding of Muhammad. Then in a further section, I look at the role of Muhammad in the popular devotion of Muslims.

Messenger, prophet, and seal of the prophets

Based on the Qur'an, Islam emphasizes three primary functions of Muhammad.

- ✔ **Muhammad as a prophet** *(nabi):* God has sent as many as 124,000 prophets according to one tradition, and all have come to warn people of the consequences of their sins and turn them back to worshipping only God. About 28 prophets are named in the Qur'an, most of them men from the Bible. Five prophets are singled out: Muhammad (the "beloved of God"), Abraham (the "friend of God"), Moses, Jesus, and Noah.

- ✔ **Muhammad as the messenger** *(rasul)* of God according to the second half of the basic Muslim confession, the *shahada* (see Chapter 4). Messengers come not only to warn the people, but also to bring a new or corrected revelation from God — as did Moses (the law), David (the Psalms), and Jesus (the Gospels). All messengers are prophets, but most prophets aren't messengers.

- ✔ **Muhammad as the seal of the prophets:** By *seal of the prophets,* Muslims understand Muhammad to be the final prophet. Why is he the last? Because he brings the complete revelation of God, so no further messengers are needed. In early Sunni Islam, the *caliph* (successor [of the prophet of God]) assumes Muhammad's role as political leader of the Muslim community but didn't share in Muhammad's religious authority as prophet and messenger.

Comparing Muhammad with Jesus and Moses

How does the role of Muhammad in Islam compare with the role of Jesus in Christianity and of Moses in Judaism? You can sum it up by saying that from a Muslim perspective, the role of Jesus and Muhammad differ considerably while Muhammad and Moses have a much more similar role. Of course, Islam regards all three as prophets.

Muhammad and Jesus

For Christians, Jesus is the *incarnate* (bodily) word of God. For Muslims, Muhammad is only a man. The Qur'an is the eternal word of God in Islam. Muhammad is the witness to that word, just as the Christian Bible is the witness to Jesus as the word of God for Christians. Thus, from a theological standpoint, the Qur'an occupies the same role in Islam that Jesus does in Christianity, and Muhammad occupies the role in Islam that the Bible does in Christianity (see Table 6-1). Jesus for Christians is a divine savior figure. For Muslims, Muhammad isn't a savior.

Table 6-1	Word of God in Islam and Christianity	
Item	*Islam*	*Christianity*
Word of God	Qur'an	Jesus
Witness to the Word	Muhammad	Bible

Muhammad and Moses

The Qur'an pictures Moses in such a way as to emphasize the parallel roles of Muhammad and Moses. In a sense, Muhammad is a new Moses (but greater than Moses). Muhammad and Moses each share the following:

- Ethical prophet, emphasizing proper morals
- Exemplary prophet, who is a model to be imitated
- Lawgiver
- Ritual leader
- Judge/arbitrator
- Political head of the community
- Military leader of the people of God
- Intercessor for the people before God
- Mystic (one who has a unique, personal encounter or vision of God and provides the model for subsequent mystics)

Living like the beautiful example

Sura 33:21 says, "You have in the messenger of God [Muhammad] a beautiful pattern." Some Christians say WWJD ("What would Jesus do?") and try to imitate Christ, but this imitation by Christians pales beside the imitation of Muhammad by Muslims. Muslims obey because they accept Muhammad as the chosen one (*mustafa,* one of the most common epithets of Muhammad). To obey means to imitate the actions of the prophet, heed the words of the prophet, and accept as permissible that to which he gave his approval.

All of Muhammad's actions are worthy of imitation: what he ate, how he cleaned his teeth, how he groomed his beard, and his love of children and of cats. Imitation of the prophet creates an amazing commonality to some aspects of Muslim life across cultures and explains why a Muslim from one country often feels at home in a different Muslim culture.

Reviewing the miracles of Muhammad

In contrast to figures like Elisha and Jesus in the Bible, the Qur'an doesn't attribute miracles to Muhammad. The people of Mecca asked Muhammad to perform miracles to substantiate his claims. He refused, saying that the Qur'an was his only miracle and even that was God's miracle, because Muhammad only repeated the words revealed to him.

Nevertheless, popular faith almost always seems to demand miracles. A number of miracles are included in the eighth century standard biography of Muhammad and later poets emphasize miracles in their poems praising Muhammad. For several of these miracles, support was cited in the Qur'an, although usually from passages that have other possible understandings. These miracles include the opening of the breast when Muhammad was an infant, a story about the splitting of the moon in two ("The hour appeared and the moon was split," Sura 54:1), and the night journey to Jerusalem and his trip through the heavens (Sura 17:1).

But many other miracles come to be told of Muhammad. Here is one of my favorite miracle stories. When preaching, Muhammad originally leaned against the trunk of a palm tree. When a pulpit was built from which Muhammad could preach, the palm tree was no longer needed, and it sighed full of sorrow that it no longer experienced the touch of the prophet's hand. Muhammad took pity, and had the palm tree brought before him to relieve its grief. Among others, this miracle is reported by Abu Nu`aim (948–1038), Sufi and *hadith* scholar, in his *Proofs of Prophethood.*

Exploring the sinlessness of Muhammad

Early Muslim theology outlines the attributes of a prophet: He should be truthful, intelligent, honest, and should proclaim the word of God. But this doesn't mean a prophet is without sin (`isma`). Some passages in the Qur'an can be read to suggest that Muhammad wasn't without sin: "Did He not find you erring and guide you?" says God to Muhammad in Sura 93:7. Why should Muhammad pray for forgiveness, if he's without sin?

Early Muslim theologians discussed these considerations and some allowed that while Muhammad may have committed minor misdeeds, he was free from major, intentional sins. Nevertheless, the dominant Muslim view is that Muhammad was without sin. Although only human, he was a perfect human.

Respecting Muhammad as intercessor

According to Sura 2:255, Muhammad is the primary intercessor for the sins of humans at the Day of Judgment (see Chapter 5). Living Muslims also invoke Muhammad in their prayers. Some Sufi orders use formulas of intercession as a litany in their *dhikr* (remembrance) ceremonies. Poets also use the theme of Muhammad as intercessor.

Muhammad as intercessor is closely linked to the use of the *tasliya* — the formula of blessing upon Muhammad. "May God give him blessings and peace" occurs in many variant forms including the one spoken or written after every name of Muhammad (PBUH, "peace be upon him"). "God and His angels bless the Prophet. O believers, you also should bless him," says Sura 33:56.

Relating Personally to Muhammad

Having looked at Muhammad's role as the historical founder of Islam, and how Muslim theologians understand Muhammad, an important topic remains. Most Muslims are neither historians nor theologians. For ordinary Muslims, Muhammad plays an important role in their life of religious devotion. Muhammad isn't only a figure of the past; instead, he's a living presence in the life of all Muslims. In this section, I look at how Muslims approach Muhammad in popular faith, prayer, and devotion.

Naming Muhammad

For Arabs, a name contains the essence of that which is named. Naturally, Muslims give attention to the names of Muhammad. The name Muhammad means "worthy of praise." In *calligraphy* (ornamental writing), elaborate designs are made using Muhammad's name. Other common names of Muhammad include *Ahmad* (most worthy of praise), *al-amin* (trustworthy), *al-habib* (beloved of God), and *al-mustafa* (chosen one). While lists of the 99 noble names *(asma' al-sharifa)* of Muhammad have been created analogous to lists of the 99 names of God (see Chapter 3), different lists vary slightly as to which names they include.

More poetry honoring Muhammad

The most famous *Burda* is that of Muhammad al-Busiri (1213–1298). Copies of the poem were inscribed on walls, while portions of it were used as good luck charms. Al-Busiri's *Burda* acquired a blessing power *(baraka)* of its own. Later poets wrote poems in which they reproduced the text of the *Burda*, adding their own additional lines after each line of al-Busiri's poem.

In addition, a number of different Arabic and non-Arabic (particularly South Asian) literary genres have been readily utilized for praise of the prophet, genres such as the *qasida* (traditional, three part pre-Islamic poetic form), the *ghazal* (description of the beloved), and the *mathnawi* (long poem composed in rhyming couplets). Other genres by definition focus on Muhammad: the *na`t* (poem in praise of Muhammad enumerating his qualities) and the *maulud* (poem celebrating the birthday of Muhammad, which are recited or sung on many occasions.)

Here is an excerpt from the most frequently recited portion of the *Burda*:

> Muhammad, leader of the two worlds, and of men and the jinn, and of the two groups, Arabs and non-Arabs. Our prophet, who commands good and prohibits evil, No one is better qualified to say 'No' or 'Yes'. Beloved by God is he, whose intercession is hoped for.

Exalting Muhammad in poetry

A vast poetic literature focuses on Muhammad. Hassan ibn Thabit was a sort of official poet during Muhammad's life and thus the model for subsequent poets known for poems praising Muhammad. Another poet, Ka`b ibn Zuhair, originally wrote poems satirizing Muhammad. In about 630 or 631, he composed a poem in the traditional *qasida* style that ended with an expression of hope that Muhammad would forgive him. Muhammad was so moved by the beauty of the poem that he threw his cloak over Ka`b's shoulders, indicating his acceptance of the plea. Ka`b's poem, known as the *Burda* (mantle) became famous and stimulated subsequent mantle poems.

Celebrating Muhammad's birthday

Although condemned by puritanical movements, such as the Wahhabis of Saudi Arabia, the celebration of Muhammad's birthday *(maulid)* is a major religious celebration in many Muslim countries and plays a large role in popular piety (see Chapter 10 for more information).

Preserving the relics of Muhammad

Just as the Buddhist may revere the tooth of the Buddha and Christians may revere the shroud of Jesus and pieces of the cross, relics of Muhammad are important in Islamic piety. Relics claimed by various Muslim shrines include hairs from Muhammad's beard, the cloak worn by Muhammad, Muhammad's sandals, and impressions left by the foot of Muhammad.

Viewing Muhammad as the light of the world and the pole of the universe

Tradition says that at Muhammad's birth, a light shone forth that illuminated the world. This tradition is linked to Sura 33:46, which speaks of Muhammad as a shining lamp. Sura 22:35, the "light verse" describes God as the light of the cosmos (see Chapter 3) and goes on to speak metaphorically of a lamp within a niche as the reflection of the light of God. Naturally, Muslims understand Muhammad to be this lamp.

Searching for the Historical Muhammad

Often, a major point of tension between Muslims and non-Muslims concerns attitudes toward Muhammad. The account of Muhammad's life that I recount in this chapter (in the "Telling the Story of Muhammad" section) is mainly an abridged version of the traditional account believed by most Muslims and passed on for the last 1,200 years from generation to generation. This section explains the sources for the traditional account and also alerts you to some modern Muslim narrations of the life of Muhammad. I also discuss the approach of the majority of non-Muslim Western scholars to the study of the life of Muhammad.

Traditional biographies

Ibn Ishaq's (704–768) *Sirat Rasul Muhammad* is the traditional biography of Muhammad. Ibn Ishaq's biography comes down to us in a version edited by Ibn Hisham in the first part of the ninth century. The biography is available in an English translation by Guillaume, but it's almost 700 pages! Ibn Ishaq compiled his biography from individual *hadiths* (traditions about Muhammad). The other main early source for Muhammad's life is a portion of al-Tabari's history. In addition, many *hadith* collections focus specifically on Muhammad. The Qur'an mentions Muhammad by name only four times, so if you had only the Qur'an, you would know little about Muhammad's life.

Naturally, Muhammad's story has been retold over and over in different times and places. In the 19th and 20th centuries, some less traditional biographies appeared that maintained the traditional story line but were written in such a way as to be more appealing to people with a Western-style education. Such modern biographies may downplay the miraculous elements in the story or reinterpret them or emphasize, for example, the role of Muhammad as a social reformer who provides a model for today's society. Among widely circulated modern biographies by Muslim authors are those of Syed Ameer Ali (1873, with subsequent revisions), Muhammad Husain Haykal (1935), Taha Hussan (1933–1944), and Muhammad Hamidullah (1959).

Non-Muslim biographies

Most serious Western scholarship on Muhammad in the 20th century took a fairly conservative approach. These scholars usually accepted the basic outline of the traditional biography, which they supplemented with additional perspectives of a historical, economic, sociological, and anthropological nature. Because the authors weren't Muslims, even when they believed Muhammad was inspired, they maintained a critical — although often sympathetic — stance regarding Muhammad. These historians didn't automatically accept everything the tradition reported about Muhammad nor did they always go along with the traditional reasons given for why events occurred as they did.

Quite distinct from these mainstream Western retellings of the origins of Islam are re-examinations by a handful of Western scholars who have challenged the whole biography of Muhammad, the traditional views of the origins of the Qur'an, and the early history of Islam. Patricia Crone, John Wansbrough, and Michael Cook present a radical reconstruction of Islamic origins, which essentially denies the historical validity of the traditional Muslim accounts.

Muslims are sensitive to anything that raises doubts about Muhammad. The type of questions that any college freshman would be expected to raise in a term paper on any historical person may be taken as intentional insults when raised about Muhammad. Of course, non-Muslims by definition don't believe everything Muslims do about Muhammad any more than non-Christians accept traditional Christian beliefs about Jesus.

Chapter 7

The Book: The Qur'an

• •

In This Chapter

▶ Approaching the Qur'an as scripture and as God's book

▶ Hearing the Qur'an

▶ Getting a clue about the style of the Qur'an even if you don't read Arabic

▶ Interpreting the Qur'an

▶ Examining the opening sura of the Qur'an

• •

Y ou can't understand Christianity or Judaism without dealing seriously with the Bible, or Confucianism or Taoism without reading the *Analects (Sayings of Confucius)* and the *Tao Te Ching (Book of the Way and the Power)*. Likewise, you can't understand Islam without coming to grips and spending time with the Qur'an. Yet a paradox faces non-Muslims. Muslims regard the Qur'an as a work of perfection both in its expression and in its content. Non-Muslims who know the Qur'an only in translation often agree with the British historian Thomas Carlyle who in 1841 described the Qur'an as "a confused jumble, crude, incondite; endless iterations, long-windedness, entanglement; most crude, incondite, insupportable stupidity in short." (And keep in mind that these are the words of a man who, compared to most Westerners, was sympathetic toward Muhammad and Islam.) Which view is correct? Read and decide for yourself.

One of the characteristics of the scriptures of the three major Western monotheisms (Islam, Judaism, and Christianity) is that at the core of each is a scripture contained in a single book (in present form) that claims to be a revelation of God. All three claim that each of their books is or contains the direct word of God. In Islam, that book is the Qur'an, which Muslims believe God revealed to Muhammad in a series of revelations over a period of 22 years. In contrast, the *Analects (Sayings of Confucius* and the *Tao Te Ching* don't claim to be revealed by a god or to be the word of a god.

Introducing the Qur'an

Many people can't tell you the name of the scriptures of Buddhism or Hinduism. Most people do, however, know that the Qur'an is the scripture of Islam. Some people even refer to the Qur'an as "the Bible of Islam."

Interestingly, Bible comes from a Greek word for book, and "the book" is a frequent designation in the Qur'an of Islam's scripture.

What is scripture?

The scripture of a religion may be one book or many. People who study world religions point out that a has many, if not all, of the following characteristics. (As you read this chapter, note how many of these characteristics apply to the Qur'an.)

- ✔ The text is of divine origin or a product of inspiration.
- ✔ The text is treated as sacred, powerful, and inviolable.
- ✔ The text is regarded as self-authenticating.
- ✔ The text is regarded as authoritative for a community, providing guidelines for worship, belief, and behavior.
- ✔ The text is closed — nothing may be added to it or taken away.
- ✔ The text provides an understanding of the meaning of life.
- ✔ The text is a sufficient basis for life.
- ✔ The religion has procedures as to how to study and apply the text.
- ✔ A group of people (such as `ulama' or religious scholars, rabbis, magi, or priests) have primary responsibility for transmitting and interpreting the text.

The basics of the Qur'an

You can make much better sense of any book on Islam if you have handy a copy of the Qur'an to refer to as you read. The Qur'an is about four-fifths the length of the New Testament. Perhaps you won't read it all in one night, but it's certainly not too long to read in a week. The Qur'an is divided into 114 primary units, each of which is a *sura*. (Scholars aren't certain about the origin of the word "sura.") You can think of the suras as chapters (as in the Bible), but if you do, think of them as chapters in the same way one refers to the individual psalms as chapters of the book of Psalms.

Each sura is divided into verses. Sura 2, the longest sura, has 286 verses. Several suras (103, 108, 110) have only three verses. Like most non-Muslims, I refer to a specific passage by sura and verse or *aya* number; for example, 24:35. (Note that *aya* means sign; Islam refers to the verses as signs because Muslims regard the Qur'an as God's greatest sign.) Listing the sura and verse helps anyone not well acquainted with the Qur'an find a specific passage. Muslims traditionally refer to the suras by name, such as the "opening" *(al-Fatiha)* for Sura 1 and the "cow" *(al-Baqara)* for Sura 2. Occasionally, names do relate to the dominant content of a sura, as in the case of Sura 12, the Joseph Sura. More often, the title is taken from a rare word or a word that occurs in the first couple of lines. Like musical symphonies, one can remember a sura more easily by name than by number.

For Islam, the Qur'an is the basic revelation or incarnation of God in the world. The Qur'an is God's spoken word in a literal sense *(kalam Allah)*. This goes considerably further than the view of some Christians that God dictated the words of the Bible. The entire Qur'an is the first person word of God. In contrast, most of the Bible isn't presented as direct speech of God. For Muslims, the prototype of the Qur'an, called the *mother of the book* (Sura 13:39), has existed eternally in heaven (see Chapter 4) and unlike the Bible, the Qur'an is a perfect replica of that book.

Most people today think of the Bible primarily as a book. Islam refers to Christians, Jews, and eventually, Zoroastrians (see Chapter 5) as "people of the book." Muhammad brings an Arabic book to a people who previously had no book (scripture) of their own. In Christianity and Judaism, the concept of the revelation as a book develops over a period of time, as does the book itself. For Islam, the concept of revelation as a divine book is present from the beginning.

Hearing the Qur'an

Because the Qur'an is a book, one may assume that the best approach is to read the book. On car trips, for example, I listen to "books on tape" but still I think of this as a convenient but secondary manner of "reading" the book, because most authors don't write novels to be consumed through the ears rather than through the eyes. Prior to the Protestant Reformation of the 16th century, most Christians became familiar with the content of the Bible through portions read out loud in worship, as well as through portrayal in pictures, statues, and stained-glass windows. The Hindu Vedic scriptures were primarily oral texts to recite rather than written texts to read. Even today, more people have exposure to novels through movies made from novels than through reading a novel itself.

The word *Qur'an* means "the reading" or "the recitation." The corresponding verb occurs at least 80 times in the Qur'an and means to recite, proclaim, or read out loud. In what is often regarded as the call of Muhammad, Sura 96:1–5, Gabriel tells Muhammad to "recite." He doesn't tell Muhammad to read or to write. The verb "say" occurs in over 300 passages. In the Qur'an, various forms of the word Qur'an can refer to three things:

- ✔ The entire holy book (this is the normal usage of the word)
- ✔ An individual revelation contained in the Qur'an
- ✔ A reciting of portions or the complete Qur'an

When Muhammad received a new revelation, he would need to convey it to his followers. Because according to Muslim tradition, some revelations were written down by scribes, one could think he would have a scribe make a copy of the written text and send that copy to Muslims living elsewhere. But instead, Muhammad sent "reciters" to convey the new revelation orally just as Muhammad had originally conveyed it to those who were with him. In reciting the Qur'an, a Muslim actualizes the word of God. In the spoken word God is present, just as Christ is present in the consecrated bread and wine for many Christians.

The newborn infant first hears the language of the Qur'an when the father whispers in his or her ear the *shahada* (testimony that God is the only God and Muhammad is His messenger). From that time on, the child hears the Qur'an frequently. When he or she learns to read, a primary purpose is so the child can recite the passages of the Qur'an needed for required prayer *(salat)*. In *salat,* the Muslim recites passages from the Qur'an in Arabic without the aid of a written text.

Jews and many Christians have an official prayer book for use during the worship. While Muslims can buy books with collections of prayers for devotional use, Islam has no official prayer book; instead, the Qur'an *is* Islam's prayer book. As one of the *hadiths* says, "In every *salat,* there is a recitation (of the Qur'an)."

As a child grows up, sounds of the Qur'an are everywhere. On the radio and on television, she hears readings from the Qur'an. A Muslim may gather with others before or after Friday noon prayer service to recite the Qur'an. In these groups, the Muslim has a copy of the Qur'an before her, but she still recites it out loud. When she takes a bus to work or a taxi to visit friends, the driver is as likely to be playing a tape of Qur'anic readings as playing the latest popular songs.

Phrases from the Qur'an punctuate everyday speech, such as *insha'allah* ("if God wills"). Several of these phrases are listed in Appendix B. Muslims recite specific suras or verses on particular occasions, including the following:

- ✔ The *Fatiha* (see the "Opening the Qur'an: The Fatiha" section in this chapter) is recited on many occasions, such as at the conclusion of a wedding contract.

- ✔ Suras 113 and 114, as protection against evil.

- ✔ Sura 26 on the 15th of the month of *Sha`ban,* the night when destinies are determined by God for the coming year.

- ✔ The *basmala,* which is recited before meals and as an act of consecration before many other actions. The *basmala* is the phrase "in the name of God the Compassionate, the Caring" that opens every sura except Sura 9.

- ✔ Sura 112, Sura 2:255 (the throne verse), and Sura 24:35 (the light verse) on any number of occasions.

The dominance of the spoken Arabic Qur'an is one of the chief common features shared by all Muslim cultures, regardless of their native languages. To read the Qur'an but never recite it in Arabic is like trying to appreciate a song by only reading the score.

Treating the Qur'an with Respect

Although the oral Qur'an is as important as the written Qur'an, don't get the idea that the written Qur'an is ignored. On the contrary, the Qur'an, written or oral, is treated with the greatest of respect. Muslims do the following with the Qur'an:

- ✔ Keep it in a clean and honored place. Wrap it in a cloth or keep it in a box.

- ✔ Put no other things on top of or above it.

- ✔ Purify themselves before touching or reciting the Qur'an.

- ✔ Say their intention *(niyya)* to recite the Qur'an before beginning the recitation.

- ✔ Face in the direction of Mecca when reciting.

- ✔ Before beginning to recite the Qur'an (and before reciting the *basmala* on other occasions) seek God's protection from Satan (see Sura 16:98 and 7:200–201) by reciting the *ta`awwudh* — "I take refuge in God from Satan, the accursed (or "stoned") one."

- ✔ Conclude the recitation by saying, "God the Great One spoke the truth."

- ✔ Offer a voluntary prayer *(du`a)* — a call or plea — for acceptance of the recitation.

Gathering and Organizing the Qur'an

On the one hand, Muhammad received individual revelations throughout his life. On the other hand, the present Qur'an is an organized collection of many or all of those revelations. How does one get from the individual revelations to the Qur'an as an integrated book? When did this happen? By what principle were the suras compiled? Is there basically a single tradition as to the text of the Qur'an going back to Muhammad or were there variant traditions?

Putting the Qur'an into writing

The written text that lies behind all Qur'ans today was originally a consonantal text without vowels. The Arabic alphabet at that time had only 15 characters for 28 consonants. Later special markings were added to distinguish letters which appear similar or identical in Arabic. Due to the absence of written vowels and the possible confusion of consonants, no one could pick up and read a copy of the early written Qur'an unless they already knew the oral Qur'an. When in 1924, Egyptian scholars were preparing what became the standard printed edition of the Qur'an, they first consulted the living oral tradition. When later, vowels were added to the text of the Qur'an, they were written with a different color of ink so the reader understood that the vowels weren't part of the Qur'an itself.

The early text that underlies all Qur'ans in use today was divided into lines but didn't indicate the verses *(aya)*. In most cases, stylistic considerations make clear where in the Arabic text a verse ends. However, in some cases, the division isn't entirely clear. The verse division of the 1924 Egyptian text is used in Arabic Qur'ans today. Traditional printed (or handwritten) texts indicate verse divisions with a rosette, a rose shaped icon between verses. Some Western translations follow the verse division of a 19th century scholar named Flügel that differs in some cases by as much as seven verses from the Egyptian edition. If you're looking up a citation in an English translation of the Qur'an and can't find the indicated passage, read the seven preceding and following verses.

Pronouncing the Qur'an

The early, consonant-only text lent itself to minor variant readings. Imagine writing "like" with only consonants: lk. You could read "lk" as like, lake, Luke, alike, leak, and so on. Even today, Arabic (and Hebrew) newspapers are printed without vowels. Context usually made clear the correct reading of the Qur'an. However, cases existed where different readings were equally possible. Different oral traditions developed as to how to actually read the text — in other words how to fill in the vowels and accents. Over time, a fuller version of the Arabic script developed that indicated vowels and accents with markings above and below the consonants and thus written Qur'ans came to include the vowels. Remember that only the consonants are considered by Muslims as part of the revealed text.

Michael Cook in his book, *The Koran, A Very Short Introduction* (Oxford University Press, 2000), gives this simple example. Sura 1:4 says "master of the Day of Judgment." The consonantal text for "master" is "mlk." If you pronounce this as "maliki" with a long "a," the meaning is master. If you pronounce or read it with a short a, the meaning is "king."

Organizing the Qur'an

How are the suras put together to form the Qur'an? You can see that after Sura 1, the longer suras come first. In general, the suras are arranged according to decreasing length. However, many exceptions to this rule occur. I give two examples: by length (counting the number of lines), Sura 15 would be Sura 40 and Sura 40 would be Sura 22. So clearly length isn't all that was involved.

Twenty-nine suras are prefixed with what in English are called the "mysterious (or detached) letters" — from one to four letters of the Arabic alphabet that occur after the *basmala* but before the body of the sura. Muslims accept these as part of the original revelation. In some cases, suras with the same mysterious letters are grouped together. For example, the letters A (that is, `alif), L, and R stand at the start of Suras 10–15. This grouping may be one reason why some suras appear out of place when viewed in terms of length alone. What do the letters mean? No one agrees which is why they are called the mysterious letters.

Compiling the Qur'an: The Muslim view

According to the traditional biography, Muhammad received his call to be a prophet in 610. On that occasion (discussed in Chapter 6), the angel Gabriel transmitted to Muhammad the first revelation, usually regarded to be the opening verses of Sura 96. The Qur'an says, "We sent it down during a blessed night" (Sura 44:3). "Sent down" may refer to God's having sent down the entire Qur'an from the seventh heaven to the lowest heaven on one of the odd numbered nights of the last third of the month of *Ramadan*.

Throughout the remainder of his life, Muhammad continued to receive individual revelations. Only in the case of some of the short suras did a single revelation correspond to an entire sura. Instead, individual revelations were combined together to form the suras.

Some Muslims say that whenever Muhammad received a new revelation, he indicated where it should be placed (that is, in which sura) and what was the proper sequence of the suras. Although the Qur'an didn't exist as a single, physical book during the lifetime of Muhammad, according to this view, Muhammad had already determined the structure of the Qur'an. A typical English translation of the Qur'an is about 500 pages. Divide this over the 23 years from the call to the death of Muhammad, and you come up with about two pages a month or 25 pages a year. Or take the approximately 6,200 verses and it amounts to a little less than a verse a day. Of course, revelations didn't come at such a regular pace and weren't all of the same length.

What follows is a summary of several traditions that relate the common Muslim view of how the individual revelations Muhammad received in his life were collected into a single, authoritative version of the Qur'an. Within the first two years after Muhammad's death in 632, `Umar (the future second caliph) urged Abu Bakr (the first caliph), to collect the Qur'an out of fear that the reciters who preserved the Qur'an would all die in battle. Abu Bakr sent for Zayd ibn Thabit. Zayd sought out the preserved written versions of individual revelations — some written on stone, others on palm leaves, and others on bones. He also collected and wrote down portions of the Qur'an that were preserved only "in the hearts of men." Zayd gave the results of his work, which was on separate pages, to Abu Bakr, who passed them on to `Umar at his death. `Umar, in turn, gave them to his daughter Hafsa (a widow of Muhammad's) when he died. This is the first complete, written Qur'an, according to tradition. During the reign of `Uthman, the next (third) caliph, an army general named Hudhayfa came to `Uthman. He was concerned that different groups of the army had had different versions of the Qur'an. `Uthman sent for the pages of the Qur'an that were in Hafsa's possession. He ordered the same Zayd ibn Thabit to head a committee to organize the sheets into a book, resolving any differences in readings. `Uthman sent copies of this Qur'an to four of the major Muslim cities. All other written copies of the Qur'an (whole or partial), he ordered burned.

What does the traditional account tell you?

✔ The story clearly has the purpose of legitimating the `Uthamanic version of the Qur'an, the version that is the basis for all Qur'ans used by Muslims today. Whether or not one accepts the historicity of the account of its origin, the text of the Qur'an used today is usually referred to as the `Uthman text or `Uthman version.

✔ The story indicates that even after Abu Bakr, different versions of the Qur'an were in use in the time of `Uthman.

✔ At Muhammad's death, the Qur'an didn't exist as a single manuscript.

✔ The text of the Qur'an was finalized in written form much more quickly than happened for the Biblical texts.

How complete is the present text of the Qur'an? While some Shi`ite Muslims believe the received Qur'anic text omitted some passages that speak about `Ali and his descendants, most Muslims agree that the present text of the Qur'an contains most of the revelations that Muhammad received during his lifetime. Tradition says the following principles guided the process of collection:

✔ The revelation was written down in the presence of Muhammad. In other words, no secondhand accounts were included.

✔ At least two witnesses heard Muhammad recite each specific revelation.

✔ All the revelations that Muhammad received were included. Nothing was omitted except for some passages that God explicitly nullified (see the section "The abrogated verses" in this chapter).

Compiling the Qur'an: The view of non-Muslim scholars

Some Western, non-Muslim scholars basically accept the account of the fixing of the text of the Qur'an under `Uthman. In contrast to the Muslim view, these scholars point to evidence that other versions continued to circulate for several hundred years, and they cite the following evidence:

✔ Qur'anic commentators and legal scholars occasionally quoted from non-`Uthmanic versions of the Qur'an in the several centuries after `Uthman.

✔ Muslim tradition itself refers to at least four other early versions of the Qur'an. Muslim tradition says `Uthman destroyed these versions, but texts from about 800 complain about the use of the version of Ibn Mas`ud, indicating that at least his version was still in circulation.

✔ The earliest texts of any portion of the Qur'an that have been preserved date to the end of the seventh and the early eighth century. The great shrine, the Dome of the Rock in Jerusalem, was inscribed in 691–692 with some verses from the Qur'an. In 1972, a number of ancient manuscripts containing portions of the Qur'an were discovered in Yemen. These manuscripts, dating probably to the early eighth century, if not a little earlier, in some places have slightly different texts of specific passages than in the `Uthman version. The Yemenite texts also have a different way of writing some words, and some fragments which contain the end of one sura and the beginning of another suggest that in some cases the sequence of suras may differ from the `Uthman version.

Muslim reactions to views such as these is often dismissive and many Muslims take offense at scholars even making such arguments and regard these views as another example of Western attacks on Islam. Muslims believe the Qur'an is a totally accurate copy of the heavenly book. Western scholars, such as Michael Cook, don't see it this way. What's striking isn't how many variants exist to the text of the Qur'an but how few exist, especially compared to the texts of the Jewish and Christian Bibles. What is surprising in this view isn't that the text wasn't fixed already at the time of Muhammad, but that it was fixed in written form as early as it was and transmitted as accurately as it was — again in contrast to the Bible.

Compiling the Qur'an: A radical view

In Chapter 6, I mention the radical approach to early Islamic history taken by Crone, Cook, and Wansbrough. Wansbrough focused on the Qur'an and its history using the techniques of analysis developed in modern Biblical studies. Crone and Cook offered a reconstruction of Islamic origins radically at odds with traditional views. For example, the original emigration (*hijra*) was not from Mecca to Medina but from Arabia to Jerusalem. Remember, this is just one point in a total reconstruction of Islamic origins.

Regarding the Qur'an, this radical view suggests that it emerged in the eighth century at the end of the early history of Islam, and that it was hurriedly put together to provide a "salvation history," a sacred story, of the new Muslim religion and state. In this view the Qur'an, which contains material from different periods and sources, provides evidence for the eighth century but not much evidence for the time of Muslim origins. According to Wansbrough, the reason no physical evidence exists for the Qur'an prior to the building of the Dome of the Rock (about 691) is because the Qur'an didn't yet exist.

You can certainly understand that such views would upset many ordinary Muslims who aren't scholars. Even Michael Cook in his *The Koran: A Very Short Introduction* (Oxford University Press, 2000) now takes a much more moderate view of Qur'anic origins. Toby Lester gives an excellent popular presentation of the issues in his article "What is the Koran?" published in the January 1999 edition of *The Atlantic Monthly*. You can find a more detailed consideration of some of these issues in Neal Robinson's *Discovering the Qur'an* (SCM Press, 1996).

The Style of the Qur'an

I now turn from the discussion of how the Qur'an came to exist in its present format to consideration of the style of the Qur'an. To a non-Muslim, the Qur'an often appears strange and difficult to get a handle on. A reader may wonder why Muslims praise its beauty so highly when a Western reader may find it boring and repetitive. How does it make its impact on the hearts and minds of Muslims? The effect of the Qur'an on a Muslim is due as much to how it presents its message as to the content of that message.

The Qur'an as evocative speech

The Qur'an isn't a book organized by content or chronology. Think of the suras of the Qur'an as analogous to a body of sermons by a prominent pastor or rabbi or speeches by a major political figure. Part of the impact of these sermons and speeches results from repetition. Think of a sales manager trying to fire up the sales team or a coach pepping up his team prior to a game. An editor could try to group these speeches, but this would be a secondary structure that wouldn't be intrinsic to the original speeches. Keep in mind that the Qur'an, too, is made up of oral communications intended to evoke responses.

The Qur'an makes contact with its audience through sound, visual images, and content. It appeals to the imagination, emotions, and mind. In revealing the Qur'an, Muhammad is trying to establish a connection with the audience to move them to action and to focus their attention on the ultimate speaker (God). Body gestures and intonation would have played a crucial role in Muhammad's delivery and marked changes of mode and topic. These gestures and vocal clues aren't preserved in the written text.

Most people are used to linear speech. They expect either a chronological progression or a topical organization, in which A leads to B, which leads to C. Computer technology, with its web of hyperlinks, offers people today the option of a non-linear reading of a text. The non-linear nature of the Qur'an often makes the book difficult to follow for a non-Muslim who hasn't lived with the Qur'an his entire life. The Qur'an is like a montage of different images or a kaleidoscope, in which different elements continually recur but in different arrangements. The Qur'an rarely gives the "whole story" in one place. Moses is mentioned in many passages, but the reader of any one passage must already know something of the Moses story for an individual mention of Moses to make sense.

The idiom of the Qur'an

The language of the Qur'an isn't the normal Arabic of Muhammad's day. Some suggest the Qur'anic idiom derives from a kind of high literary idiom used and understood across Arabia at the time. Just as Shakespeare and the King James Bible had a formative influence on English, the Arabic of the Qur'an exercised a decisive influence on the development of Arabic.

The language of the Qur'an isn't normal prose or normal poetry. When one considers that some of Muhammad's contemporaries said he was a poet, a soothsayer, a madman, or a magician, it appears they were having trouble fitting the idiom of Qur'an into a recognized category of speech. Qur'anic language uses a form of rhymed and rhythmic prose.

Dating the suras

Even if the suras aren't organized chronologically, can one nevertheless date them? Many Muslim traditions speak of the "occasion of revelation" of specific passages in the Qur'an. Unfortunately, these traditions sometimes disagree amongst themselves and in general, Western scholars don't think they're of much value for dating.

Still, both Muslim and non-Muslim scholars agree that on the basis of content and style one can determine which suras belong to the Meccan period (610–622) and which to the Medinan period (622–632) of Muhammad's life (see Chapter 6). Because a single sura may contain more than one revelation, some Meccan suras may contain a section that is a revelation from the later Medinan period.

And what are these content and stylistic criteria that help distinguish between Meccan and Medinan suras? The shorter, more poetic and lyrical suras mainly belong to the Meccan period. The longer, more prosaic and detailed suras belong to the Medinan period. In the first period, Muhammad was mainly a preacher addressing a largely unconvinced audience. In Medina, Muhammad was the statesman and legislator addressing a community composed primarily of Muslims and dealing with matters of practical concern to that new community. You can find several Muslim and non-Muslim listings of the suras in chronological order in a table at the end of W.M. Watt's and R. Bell's *Introduction to the Qur'an* (Edinburgh University Press, 1970).

In many translations of the Qur'an, without even reading the text, one can see that it's formatted like poetry. While lines don't have a fixed meter or set number of syllables, you can clearly see a pattern that's more like poetry than prose. Qur'anic language makes extensive use of assonance in which lines of a unit all end with the same sound.

Even though you won't understand it, if you want to sense something of the effect of the sound of the Qur'an on Muslims, listen to some suras being recited. Even better is to listen to the recitation as you follow along with a printed transliteration of the Arabic. Michael Sells' *Approaching the Qur'an: The Early Revelations* (White Cloud Press, 1989) includes transliterations of a number of short suras, along with a CD of recitations that enables you to do just that.

The inimitability of the Qur'an (i`jaz)

Tradition says that Muhammad was illiterate and uneducated. Thus the Qur'an is a miracle which Muhammad couldn't have produced on his own. In several places in the Qur'an, Muhammad challenges those who doubted his inspiration to produce ten suras (11:13) or even one sura (10:38) comparable to the Qur'an. None could do this. From this developed the concept of the i`jaz (inimitability, meaning "can't be imitated") of the Qur'an.

Subsequently, Muslim scholars, such as the 11th century theologians al-Baqillani and al-Jurjani, tried to define what constituted the *i`jaz* of the Qur'an. They emphasized the choice and arrangement of the words *(nazm)*. If one changes the words or keeps the same words and changes the arrangement, the meaning changes.

Consideration of *i`jaz* led to significant advances in understanding the rhetorical effectiveness of the Qur'an — why it has had such an effect on the minds and hearts of Muslims throughout the centuries. Modern scholars — Muslim and non-Muslim — are beginning to utilize modern techniques of literary analysis to advance the understanding of the Qur'an and to produce better translations of the Qur'an. Some Islamist writers of the 20th century, such as Sayyd Qutb, tried to articulate an Islam that spoke more convincingly to the modern world. In addition to the artistic achievements of the Qur'an, al Sayyd Qutb pointed to its prophecies about the future, its wise legislation which is as valid today as in the time of Muhammad, and its anticipation of modern scientific knowledge about man and the universe.

Recurring thematic elements in the Qur'an

In addition to analyzing the structure of words and sentences in the Qur'an, you can also look at the component elements that make up the various suras. Neil Robinson in his book, *Discovering the Qur'an, A Contemporary Approach to a Veiled Text* (Trinity Press International, 1997) speaks of six *registers* or modes of speech that make up the individual suras.

- Passages directed against pagan opponents in Mecca and subsequently against the "hypocrites" in Medina
- Signs testifying, for example, to the power of God to resurrect the dead
- Communications to Muhammad, including His call
- Signs that indicate the end of the world and the final judgment
- Material to establish the truth of the message and its messenger
- Narratives, such as accounts of earlier prophets who warned their people of impending destruction if they didn't change their ways

According to Robinson, blocks of material in these six modes of speech combine to construct entire suras. What appears on first reading as a series of unrelated units can now be understood as a coherent unity. Of course Robinson's list of six modes of speech isn't the only way to analyze the recurring elements; for example, some additional common types of material include oaths, legislative passages, and parables.

Any number of other people have tried to organize the content of the Qur'an under certain themes. A. A. Islahi, a contemporary South Asian Qur'anic scholar, divides the Qur'an into seven sections, each with a different primary theme:

- ✔ Law
- ✔ Abrahamic religion (meaning, Judaism, Christianity, and Islam — all of which claim descent from the Biblical Abraham — see Chapter 16)
- ✔ The struggle between truth and deceit
- ✔ The proof of Muhammad's status as messenger
- ✔ The unity of God (the monotheistic emphasis that God is one, without children, parents, or spouse)
- ✔ The judgment
- ✔ Warnings to unbelievers

Such arrangements of the Qur'an according to content can help the non-Muslim reader, but such arrangements don't correspond to the structure of the Qur'an.

The problem of shifting perspectives in the Qur'an

Look at a snow capped mountain from the east. Then move to the south, look at the same mountain, and you get a different perspective. Put the different perspectives together, and you have a fuller and richer view of the mountain. Shifts in person, number, and tense are called *ilitifat* in Arabic. These shifts achieve specific rhetorical effects. "We" conveys a majestic, transcendent image of God. "I" conveys a more personal image of God. Arabic, like Hebrew, has two primary tenses. One indicates completed and the other uncompleted action rather than past and future times as in English tense. Frequently the tense shifts in the middle of a passage. The grammatical subject also shifts between "I" and "We" or even "He" and various nouns such as "the Lord" within the same unit of text. Muslims regard these various shifts as one of the riches of the Qur'an.

Interpreting the Qur'an

Islam has a long tradition of commenting on its scripture. In Islam, this is called *tafsir*, from a verb meaning "to explain." Interpretations began with Muhammad answering questions from his followers. For example, `A'isha (Muhammad's young wife) heard him say, "Whoever is called to account will be punished." `A'isha challenged Muhammad by quoting Sura 84:8, "His account will easily be settled," implying a less harsh judgment upon sinners.

The process of interpreting the Qur'an

A traditional commentary starts at Sura 1:1 and then works its way through the Qur'an verse by verse. The author quotes the full verse, breaks the verse into phrases, and then comments on each phrase. This produces a sense of what individual words and phrases mean but often no overall interpretation of the full text. The author explains any unclear words and points of grammar, notes the occasion of revelation if a relevant tradition exists, includes relevant comments about the passage from Muhammad or his companions or their successors, and uses other passages from the Qur'an to help explain the verse he's discussing. He may point out the legal or ritual implications of the passage or discuss pertinent philosophical and theological issues. The scholar may also make rhetorical observations. He won't explain the passage in the light of its historical setting or try to relate it to his own time. Al-Tabari's 39-volume commentary (tenth century) is one of the most important commentaries. Al-Tabari distinguishes between verses that everyone can understand, verses that only God can understand, and verses that the reader can understand only because they were explain my Muhammad.

Exoteric and esoteric interpretation

What I describe thus far in this section is exoteric interpretation *(zahir)*, which deals with the literal, "surface" meaning of the text. In the past, many Muslims have suggested that the text has additional levels of hidden or esoteric meaning. *Ta'wil* interpretation dealt with this deeper level of meaning. Although more literalistic Sunni scholars rejected *ta'wil*, other Sunni scholars recognized the legitimacy of such interpretation and said the Qur'an itself often signaled when a deeper meaning was the key to the text. Sufi (mystic) interpreters downplayed the literal meaning in favor of an allegorical interpretation intended to illuminate the spiritual significance of the text. Shi`ite interpreters emphasized an interior meaning *(batin)* passed on from `Ali to the Shi`ite *imams* who, unlike Sunni interpreters, could provide new interpretations of the texts. To Sufis and Shi`ites, this interior meaning was often more significant than the exterior meaning of the text.

The abrogated verses

The concept of *abrogation (naskh)* says that God revealed some verses of the Qur'an that he later annulled (abrogated). Abrogation proved especially useful in dealing with two situations.

> ✔ Cases where two different verses from the Qur'an conflict with each other.
>
> ✔ Instances where Islamic law based on tradition and custom conflicts with statements in the Qur'an.

The Qur'anic basis for the concept of abrogation is three passages (Suras 2:106; 22:52; 16:106) in which *naskh* or a synonym is used to indicate a verse that was removed by God or replaced by another. Sura 22:52 is usually taken to refer to the Satanic verses episode (see Chapter 3) in which the verse about the three goddesses was revealed to Muhammad by Satan instead of by God (Sura 53:19). God later annulled that revelation. From the eighth to the eleventh centuries, scholars drew up lists of the abrogated and the abrogating verses. The earliest preserved treatise lists 42 abrogated verses, but this number expanded until a maximum of 238 abrogated passages were listed in one 11th-century book.

The most common form of abrogation is when God annulled the rule, but the verse itself remains in the Qur'an. Comparing three verses that speak of drinking wine illustrate how the concept of abrogation is applied. Sura 16:67 mentions wine along with food as a gift of God. Sura 2:219 says that both good and bad come from wine but the bad outweighs the good. Sura 4:43 warns believers not to come to prayer while drunk. Sura 5:90 says that wine along with gambling are works of Satan. Of course, this all depends on the assumption that the Qur'an is entirely self-consistent (it can't say one thing in one place and a contrary thing in another place) and on the correct dating of the passages.

Using the Qur'an in Daily Life

Many Muslim children learn to read through the study of the Qur'an. When they grow up, they hear Qur'anic recitations over radio and television. Wherever they look, they see verses from the Qur'an written out in artistic style. This section looks at this aspect of the Qur'an in the daily life of ordinary Muslims.

Educating through the Qur'an

Prior to the introduction of modern, state-run education systems that were based on a European model, formal education began with instruction in reading the Qur'an at about the age of seven. Today, this pattern of local Qur'anic schools for kids often continues alongside the state educational systems. And in Islamic countries, state schools incorporate religious education and Arabic into their curriculums. Remember that Arabic isn't the native language of most Muslim children.

In a typical example reported from a West African village, a group of young students gathers around the teacher with writing tablets, pen, ink, and copies of the Qur'an. The teacher begins with the first two verses of the Qur'an, teaching the name and pronunciation of each new letter as it occurs until all 28 letters have been learned. Then the student begins to combine the letters with the different vowels, using passages from Suras 105–111 in addition to Sura 1. Next the students combine the syllables to make words so that they can repeat the first two verses of Sura 1. So far, this is all reading and reciting of the Qur'an. Now the student learns to write. First he traces an outline of individual letters following the example given by the teacher. At each stage the teacher corrects him. By the time he has learned to read, recite, and write, he has covered about one-fourth of the Qur'an. The minority of students who persevere to the end (four years or longer) are able to recite and write the entire Qur'an. Such a major accomplishment is marked with a graduation ceremony and gifts to the student and the teacher.

Reciting the Qur'an

Recitation of the Qur'an *(taliwa)* is a highly honored performance art in Muslim countries that confers a blessing *(baraka)* on both the reciter and the listener. A person who memorizes the whole Qur'an can use the honorary title of *hafiz*, one who preserves the Qur'an in her heart.

GOING DEEPER

Tajwid: Techniques of *taliwa*

Sura 73:4 says to recite the Qur'an slowly and distinctly. Over the centuries, specific techniques of Qur'anic recitation developed. *Tajwid* ("making beautiful") refers to the rules or science of recitation. *Tajwid* can also refer to Qur'anic recitation in general or specifically to the more elaborate form of recitation.

Two basic forms of recitation are used:

✔ *Murattal* is the more conservative, less melodic form of recitation. It's the form used in worship contexts. It's slow and strives for maximum clarity *(tartil)* in articulating the text. Thus *murattal* is close to the form used in study but with more of a chanting aspect.

✔ *Mujawwad* is the more melodic, ornamental style of recitation. The performer shows off her skill and particular style. *Mujawwad* recitation isn't used in a worship context, and may even sound like singing. But one shouldn't "sing" the Qur'an to a predetermined melodic line.

Tajwid not only includes the rules of the actual recitation but also other requirements imposed on the reciter, such as how and when to clean the mouth, where to recite and not to recite, and how to approach the recitation with the proper attitude.

In theory, any Muslim willing to invest the time and effort can memorize the Qur'an. To recite it in a beautiful manner, however, is an art form. In many Muslim countries, Qur'an recitation competitions are major events. Like a sports league or a spelling bee, winners at the local level move on to competition at a district level and then the national level. Such contests are especially well organized in Indonesia.

Some people obtain a professional rank as Qur'an reciters, performing at public and private events. They make CDs, and their recitations are broadcast on radio and television. Egyptian Qur'an reciters in particular have a high reputation and provide a model for others to emulate.

Reproducing the Qur'an: Calligraphy

Reproduction of the written Qur'an is as important as oral recitation of the Qur'an. Calligraphy is one of the two greatest art forms (along with architecture) of Islamic culture. Like professional recitation, calligraphy is a highly honored professional skill that requires years of practice to master. Only in China does calligraphy achieve the same perfection as in the Muslim world.

You can find two early calligraphic styles, although over time, many other scripts evolved:

✔ *Kufic* is the more boxy, angular, heavy, and formal script.

✔ *Naskhi* is the more elongated, rounded, cursive script.

Written verses from the Qur'an are used in many contexts:

✔ They adorn the walls of mosques and other religious buildings.

✔ The cloth covering of the *Ka`ba,* the sacred shrine of Islam in Mecca, has a band of Qur'anic verses near the top.

✔ Short verses with appropriate content are posted at the entrance to schools, hospitals, and other buildings.

✔ Certain suras and verses are inscribed to be used as a sort of good-luck charm to ward off illness and evil.

✔ Although frowned upon by conservative scholars, the practice persists in some quarters of writing a passage down, and then dissolving the ink from the page in a liquid solution that is swallowed as a healing potion.

Opening the Qur'an: The Fatiha

To give you some feeling for Qur'anic commentary, I conclude this chapter with a brief discussion of the *Fatiha* (Sura 1, the "opening"). The *Fatiha* is said to be equivalent to the whole Qur'an and is by far the most frequently recited sura. In addition to its recitation 17 times a day as part of daily prayers, Muslims recite the *Fatiha* on many other occasions, such as when contracts are signed, on behalf of a dead person when visiting his tomb, and to help heal a sick person (it's also called "the sura of healing"). When the *Fatiha* was revealed, tradition says that the Devil wept. "May God open for you" is used as a shortened prayer formula.

The *Fatiha* has three parts: invocation, followed by affirmation, and ending with petition. It has a clear sound pattern in which verses end in "im" or "in" (in Arabic). Each non-indented line corresponds to one verse. Sura 15:87 refers to the "seven often repeated verses" of the Qur'an that many understand to refer to the seven verses of the *Fatiha:*

> *In the name of God, the Compassionate the Caring*
> *Praise is to God, the sustaining Lord of all worlds*
> *The Compassionate the Caring*
> *Master of the Day of Judgment*
> *You do we worship*
> > *And you we ask for help*
> *Guide us on the straight road*
> *The road of those whom you have given on them*
> > *Not those with anger on them*
> > *Nor those who have gone astray*

The *Fatiha* is the only sura in which the *basmala* (the phrase which begins with "in the name of God" is considered an integral part of the sura rather than a preface to it. As the *Fatiha* is said to be equivalent to the whole of the Qur'an, so the *basmala* is equivalent to the entire *Fatiha.* The two attributes translated here as "the Compassionate the Caring" both come from the Arabic word for womb and point to God's care of humanity being like a mother's concern for her children. The first attribute is used only of God, while the second is used of God and people, who should try to emulate God's attributes.

Verse two is the source of the common interjection, *al-hamdulillah* (praise is to God). The syntax is nominal rather than verbal, which means the verse doesn't say "praise God" or "may praise be to God" but rather states a fact ("praise is to God"). In the second part of the verse, *worlds* (plural) include all that isn't God and thus implies God as the creator of all that is.

As God alone stands at the beginning, so in verse 4, he alone exists when the world comes to an end on the Day of Judgment. The worshipper is quoted in verse 5 and God is personally addressed ("you" in contrast to the nominal references to God in verses 1–4). "Worship" is also the word for "serve." "We" places the believer in a community of believers. One submits to God (remember that "Muslim" means one who submits to God) and in return God helps the submitter in time of need.

"Straight road" (verse 6) is one metaphor used for the Islamic religion. A straight road is a paved road in contrast to a small, rough path. Paved roads are rare in the desert. "Guide us" prepares the reader for Sura 2, where in verse 2 the Qur'an is called a guidance for the believer.

Verse 7 concludes by contrasting the fate of the believer with the fate of the unbeliever. "Whom you have given on them" means those whom God has blessed because of their faith and submission. Note the verse doesn't speak of God's being angry with the unbeliever. It says anger is upon them because they have left the path (gone astray).

When one finishes reading the *Fatiha,* he should say "Amen."

Chapter 8

Islamic Tradition and Law

● ●

● ●

All religions emphasize both beliefs and actions, but they all differ in the relative emphasis placed on each. While Christianity emphasizes belief (believe in Jesus and obtain eternal life), Islam emphasizes actions (submit to God by living life according to the guidance God has given, and on the Day of Judgment you will enter paradise). The closest parallel to Islam's emphasis on *shari`a* (law) is Judaism's emphasis on law. Both develop a substantial literature to derive from their scripture (the Bible and the Qur'an) legal rulings on matters not explicitly addressed in the scripture. Indeed, many scholars believe that the means of legal argumentation in Islam were strongly influenced by the already developed tradition of Jewish legal scholarship. Hinduism also places a major emphasis on law, the Code of Manu being one of the oldest and most important Hindu books of law. The Code of Manu and other similar texts are part of what is called the Way of Works (*Karma Marga*), in contrast to the Way of Devotion and the Way of Knowledge — the other two main paths to salvation or liberation in Hinduism. In contrast to Judaism, where the content of law and the method of legal scholarship are similar to Islam, the content in Hindu law is fundamentally different from that of Islamic law. Confucianism is also concerned about how people should act, but its law (or perhaps better, advice) in this area derives not from revelation but from human reasoning and human experience.

In Islam, the first priority is to determine proper action. This chapter looks at how Islam determines what is God's law *(shari`a)*. Because Muhammad was the messenger of the Qur'an and the best testimony to the path God lays forth for humanity, the traditions concerning Muhammad are, after the Qur'an, the primary source of determining God's will. Thus before turning to an examination of Islamic law, I discuss the customary practice of imitating Muhammad *(sunna)* as determined through study of the traditions *(hadiths)*.

Imitating Muhammad

The slogan "WWJD" ("What would Jesus do?") which asks how Jesus would have reacted to a similar situation, sums up a popular movement in recent American Christianity. But in asking WWJD, no one suggests that a Christian should model every aspect of his life on Jesus. The Christian doesn't try to eat the same food that Jesus ate or sleep on the same side of the body that Jesus slept on.

Understanding the two parts of a hadith

Hadith is an Arabic word meaning speech or report. The term *hadith* designates any tradition passed on orally to others about what someone said or did. When Islam was new and spreading quickly, the companions of Muhammad shared with newly converted peoples their knowledge of what Muhammad did and said. People from such far-flung Muslim communities as orocco and Indonesia who were going on pilgrimage to Mecca (see Chapter 9) exchanged *hadiths* with one another. Sharing among scholars during the pilgrimage continues today but the age of gathering new hadiths is long past.

Hadiths consist of two parts.

- ✔ **Isnad, Part I:** The first part is the chain of people who have passed on the report (*isnad*). If somebody tells me something about someone, I want to know the source of her information, because the information is no better than its source.
- ✔ **Matn, Part II:** The second part is the actual content *(matn)* of the report. You can think of the *isnad* as the introduction and the *matn* as the body of the *hadith*.

A typical *isnad* is, "Bukhari, from Muslim ibn Ibrahim from Hisham from Yahya ibn `Ikrima from Ibn `Abbas." Then follows a story about Muhammad condemning men who act like women and vice versa (the *matn*).

Uncovering the contents of a hadith

A *hadith* contains one or more of four main types of materials:

- ✔ Something Muhammad did
- ✔ Something Muhammad said
- ✔ Something that happened in Muhammad's presence
- ✔ Words of God to Muhammad that aren't in the Qur'an *(hadith qudsi)*

Another way of viewing the content of the *hadiths* is as follows:

- ✔ Story-type material that fills in information about the life of Muhammad or earlier figures (for example, Biblical Joseph) that's not in the Qur'an.

- ✔ Legal material in which Muhammad interprets and applies the Qur'an or otherwise gives specific guidelines for questions of ritual and law.

- ✔ Preaching-like material that provides motivation to live according to Islamic values.

TIP

Understanding tradition: Sunna or hadith?

You may have difficulty grasping the distinction between the terms *sunna* and *hadith,* both of which are usually translated as "tradition." Here's the difference:

- ✔ The *sunna* of Muhammad is the totality of what Muhammad did and said. *Sunna* isn't a form of literature or writing.

- ✔ A *hadith* is an individual report of what he did or said. *Hadith* is a literary form.

But how does one know what he did and said? Well, one knows the *sunna* of Muhammad from the *hadiths* passed on about Muhammad. Collections of *hadiths* constitute the written record of the *sunna of Muhammad.* Thus the *sunna* is logically prior to the *hadiths* in the same way that the traditions of your family (or your school or social organization) are prior to any oral or written accounts of those traditions.

The word *sunna* has a basic meaning of "customary practice or model behavior." Before the time of Muhammad, each tribe or clan had its customary ways. Eventually, the *sunna* of the Muslim *umma* (community) replaced the *sunna* of the tribes. Because contemporaries of Muhammad had firsthand knowledge of Muhammad, the *sunna* also included the customs of the first and second generations. But gradually, as Muslims became further removed

from the time of Muhammad, they began to understand *sunna* as referring primarily to the tradition of Muhammad (rather than the tradition of the whole community) as attested to in the *hadiths.* Sura 33:21 reflects this view of Muhammad when it says, "Indeed you have in the messenger of God a beautiful exemplar."

The opposite of *sunna* is innovation *(bid`a).* For some, innovation in religion is equivalent to heresy. But in Islam, innovation can be good or bad. Good innovation enables the Muslim to live a more authentically Islamic life. Bad innovation involves abandonment of beliefs and patterns set forth in the tradition and the Qur'an. Thus whether an innovation is good or bad is more a matter of how the scholar views the issue than something intrinsic to the innovation itself. For example, legal scholars agree that the celebration of Muhammad's birthday (the *maulid*) was an innovation, which means it isn't mentioned in the Qur'an and isn't reported in the traditions which supposedly come from Muhammad and the first generation of Muslims. To the conservative 14th century legal scholar Ibn Taymiyya, the *maulid* celebration was a bad innovation while to the equally important 11th century theologian al-Ghazali, the *maulid* was a good innovation (see Chapter 10 for more on the *maulid*).

Collecting the hadiths

The traditional biography *(sirat)* of Muhammad (see Chapter 6) was a compilation of the first two types of *hadiths*. Muslims who wish to imitate the life of Muhammad down to the smallest detail utilize these accounts.

Early *hadith* collections were organized according to the companion from whom a *hadith* originated. Later, a topical ordering was used. These collections are second in importance only to the Qur'an as an authority in Islam. Muslims will quote specific *hadiths* to support particular Islamic beliefs and practices, much as they quote the Qur'an. For example, Bukhari 24:13 refers to a *hadith* in Book 24, Chapter 12 of al-Bukhari's collection of *hadiths*. In addition to Bukhari's collection, you're likely to encounter references to the *hadith* collections compiled by Abu Da'ud, al-Nasa'i, al-Tirmidhi, and Ibn Majah (all famous *hadith* scholars of the eighth and ninth centuries). Shi`ites have their own collections of *hadiths* (see Chapter 12 for the lowdown on this branch of Muslims and their own traditions.) The typical collection contains several thousand *hadiths*. You can buy CDs containing the main collections or consult them at a number of Muslim sites on the Internet (see Appendix C).

Reviewing the 40 traditions

Major *hadith* collections contained thousands of *hadiths*. Something simpler was needed to make *hadiths* available to ordinary Muslims, and so some scholars made small collections of what they regarded as the most important *hadiths*. Possibly the most popular, and still in wide use today to instruct young Muslims, is the *40 traditions of al-Nawawi* (1233–1277). As an example, here are five hadiths from al-Nawawi's *40*. As is usual for *hadiths,* Muhammad is understood to have spoken these words:

- ✔ "What I have declared forbidden to you, avoid; what I have bidden you do, comply with as far as you're able."
- ✔ "Don't get angry."
- ✔ "Where there is no injury there is no requital."
- ✔ "Whosoever acts with enmity toward a friend of mine, against him I indeed will declare war."
- ✔ "God has for my sake overlooked the mistakes and forgetfulness of my community."

Evaluating the hadiths

As time passed, traditions attributed to Muhammad multiplied. Muslim scholars recognized that not all *hadiths* were historically accurate. In some cases, sincere people had simply made honest mistakes in passing on words they believed went back to Muhammad but didn't. Some people invented *hadiths* that they attributed to Muhammad to support a particular position in theological or political battles of the day (eighth to ninth centuries). *Hadith* scholars developed criteria to determine how likely it was that any specific *hadith* was valid (meaning that it went back to Muhammad). These scholars ranked *hadiths* in three descending categories according to how likely they were to be true:

- ✔ **Sound** *(sahih):* Almost certainly true.
- ✔ **Good** *(hasan):* Very possibly true.
- ✔ **Weak** *(da`if):* Cannot be considered true unless confirmed by other traditions.

How did *hadith* scholars determine the validity of a tradition? They examined mainly the *isnad* (the chain of people who passed on the report), considering points such as:

- ✔ Evaluation of the character of a transmitter. Was he of good moral character? Were other traditions from this person reliable?
- ✔ Was a specific link in the chain logically possible? Did two adjacent people in the chain actually overlap in their adult lives so that one person could have passed on the information to another? Did evidence exist that they were ever in the same place at the same time?
- ✔ Were there multiple chains of transmission? If so, this was much stronger than a tradition with only a single line of transmission.
- ✔ Did the tradition occur in both the collections of Bukhari and Muslim (the two main collections).

GOING DEEPER

Understanding hadith history

By the time of caliph `Umar II (ruled 717–720), Muslims were concerned to preserve *hadiths* for future generations. `Umar commissioned the historian al-Zuhri to collect and write down the *hadiths*. Subsequently, the effort to gather all of the traditions of Muhammad gained momentum. *Hadith* scholars traveled far and wide to gather additional traditions. Elaborate rules developed to safeguard the transmission of *hadiths*.

Some Western scholars (including Goldziher, Schacht, and Coulson) regard many of the *hadiths* as fabrications without historical value. These scholars point to *anachronisms* in the text (allusions to disputes within Islam after the time of Muhammad and to places and people of periods later than Muhammad). They argue that one can't separate the valid from the invalid *hadiths*. They contend that the detailed *isnads* were added later to the older *hadiths* and, therefore, *isnad* criticism doesn't establish the historicity of the traditions.

Using hadiths in more modern times

Some Muslim reformers of the 19th and 20th centuries have utilized the *hadiths* in support of various proposals of modernization or in support of traditionalist proposals aimed at restoring Islam as it existed at the beginning. These reformers may positively utilize a *hadith* to support a practice today, arguing, for example, that traditions show Muhammad allowed women to attend mosques. This is cited against those who have discouraged the participation of women in mosque services.

Here's an example. The contemporary feminist Islamic scholar Riffat Hassan has examined six *hadiths* which have been used in Islam to support the idea that women are inferior to men. All six mention the creation of woman from the rib of man, several going further and saying she's created from the curved tip of the rib (the weakest part). Three of the *hadiths* are from the Bukhari collection and three from the Muslim collection, the two most important collections, which suggests they are "sound" hadiths. On closer examination, Hassan points out that all six *hadiths* go back in their *isnads* to a contemporary ("companion") of Muhammad named Abu Hurairah. The prominent eighth-century legal scholar Abu Hanifa didn't regard Abu Hurairah as a reliable transmitter of *hadiths*. Therefore, Hassan concludes, these six traditions are "weak" rather than "sound" and shouldn't be used to support a subordinate role for women. The implication of the argument is that the words do not really go back to Muhammad but represent a prejudice against women that came into Muslim culture after the time of Muhammad.

Understanding God's Law

Sura 5:48 says God "has sent to each people a *shari`a* and an open path." In non-religious use, *shari`a* was the path to a watering hole. Applied to religion, however, *shari`a* is the path to life and the divinely revealed laws that define that path.

GOING DEEPER

Locating the origins of Islamic law

When Islam was new and spreading rapidly, the first caliphs were faced with the necessity of organizing the state. There was as yet no class of legal scholars and no theory by which laws in accord with Islam could be derived. Naturally, the four rightly guided caliphs (see the section of this name in Chapter 2) looked to Muhammad and the Qur'an as they made their decisions. But they had to make many legal decisions on an ad hoc basis.

Soon the caliph couldn't handle all legal questions and disputes himself. So the early Umayyad caliphs delegated some of their legal responsibilities to an Islamic judge *(qadi),* who usually came from a class of Islamic scholars *(`ulama).* The cases that came before a *qadi* dealt mainly with inheritance, personal status, property, and commercial transactions.

Over time the *qadis* acquired various non-judicial functions including the administrations of trusts *(waqfs),* execution of wills, accreditation of wills, guardianship functions for minors, and enforcing public morals. In additional to the

qadi, another religious office was the *muhtasib,* sometimes translated as "market enforcer." While the *qadi* dealt with disputes that were brought to him, the *muhtasib* initiated action. These officials checked weights and coinage, reviewed the quality and pricing of goods, and kept an eye out for cases of charging interest, which is contrary to Islamic law. They also made people attend prayer services, concerned themselves with repair of mosques and city walls, and oversaw the cleaning of the streets. By the twentieth century, the office of *muhtasib* had generally disappeared.

In the mid-eighth century, the emerging scholarly class, the *`ulama,* assumed increased importance. This class was self-perpetuating and didn't depend on government appointment, and they became experts in Islamic law. These scholars engaged both in the derivation of new legal rulings and in developing legal theory. Scholars who derived new legal rulings were called *mujtahids* ("those who exert themselves," from the same Arabic word as *jihad*)

Shari`a* is God's blueprint for living one's life and organizing society, and Muslim communities are organized such that they enforce *shari`a and allow Muslims to live according to it.

From the earliest period of Islam, Muslims have attempted to live their lives according to *shari`a.* To know what God's plan is, a Muslim is expected to turn first to the Qur'an. However, only about 500 to 600 verses out of a total of 6,219 verses in the Qur'an contain legal materials, and the majority of these verses concern ritual and worship. Legal material in the Qur'an often addresses areas where Islam differed from the existing customs of the Arabs at the time the Qur'an was written: These customs include the rules of inheriting or in protecting female infants. But in many areas, the Qur'an provides relatively little explicit legal guidance.

Stages in the consolidation of Islamic law

You can trace five stages in the early development of Islamic law:

1. **At first, legal scholarship centered in the cities of Kufa (Iraq) and Medina.**

   Personal opinion and local custom dictated the law.

2. **Increasing attention in the mid-eighth century was directed to the textual basis of Islamic law.**

   Extensive reference to Muhammad's words and actions wasn't possible until collections of *hadiths* existed, and they didn't that time.

3. **At the end of the eighth and the beginning of the ninth centuries, the four legal Schools *(madhhabs)* emerged, along with a new understanding of the sources (roots) of law.**

4. **In the tenth century and beyond, legal scholars wrote books dealing in detail with theoretical aspects of each of the roots of law.**

5. **After the "closing of the door of *ijtihad*" by the end of the tenth century, *muftis* could issue legal opinions *(fatwas)* on matters not covered by previous legal rulings.**

   Muftis were highly trained legal scholars *(mujtahids)* within a particular legal School. *Fatwas* (legal opinions) could be requested by individuals for private guidance or by the judge as an aid in making a judicial decision.

Muhammad ibn Idris al-Shafi`i (767–820) is considered the founder of Islamic law and the person responsible for establishing the concept of the four roots of the law.

Rooting out the four roots of law (usul al-fiqh)

Fiqh is distinct from *shari`a. Fiqh* is the human activity that determines what God's law is. *Fiqh* is Islamic law in both its theoretical aspects and in its practical application. Different Schools of legal interpretation developed in Islam, each with their own major *fiqh* scholars, schools, and rulings on different questions. Islam refers to these Schools as *madhhabs* (*madhhab* literally means "way). (See the "Getting legal: The Schools of law (madhhab)" section in this chapter for discussion of the Schools of law.)

In order not to confuse a School of law *(madhhab)* with the ordinary use of school to designate an educational institution *(madrasa),* I use School (capital "S") for School of law. Each law School has its own *madrasas,* which is a theological (religious) school or seminary, and I spell these schools with a small "s."

The four roots of Islamic law as articulated by al-Shafi`i (also discussed in the "Stages in the consolidation of Islamic law" sidebar) are:

- ✔ **The Qur'an:** In several places the Qur'an says, "obey me and obey my prophet." To "obey me (God)" means to obey any injunctions contained in God's word, which is the Qur'an.

- ✔ **The tradition *(sunna)* of Muhammad:** Malik (see the "Malikite School" section later in this chapter) assumed that the local custom of Medina was the tradition of Muhammad because that was where Muhammad had lived. But with the emergence of *hadith* collections, al-Shafi`i argued that a valid written text (that is, in the Qur'an or the *hadiths*) must exist before any tradition of Muhammad could serve as a basis for a legal decision.

- ✔ **Consensus *(ijma`)*:** In a frequently cited tradition, God says to Muhammad that he'll never allow his community to remain unanimous in error. Al-Shafi`i understood consensus as the consensus of the entire Muslim community. But how do you determine the consensus of all Muslims? Because of the impossibility of this Islamic consensus, subsequent scholars understood *ijma`* to be the consensus of the qualified scholars of a particular generation and School. After consensus is reached on an issue, that consensus is a third written text alongside the Qur'an and the *sunna*.

- ✔ **Analogy *(qiyas)*:** Al-Shafi`i believed that because God had provided in *shari`a* a guide for all of human life, it must be possible to extend (by use of analogies) the applicability of legal material in the Qur'an and in the *sunna* so that they apply to other cases. For example, al-Shafi`i points to the Qur'anic injunctions to face the *Ka`ba,* the sacred shrine in Mecca, to pray. Most Muslims when praying can't actually see the *Ka`ba,* so they must use reason to determine the correct direction. Similarly, legal scholars may use reason to extend the cases covered by the Qur'an and the *sunna*.

Analogy doesn't apply to religious ritual. No rational principle explains why God told Muslims to pray five times rather than ten times a day. Muslims are also cautious in using analogical reasoning to determine the appropriate penalties for action contrary to Islamic law.

In addition to the four agreed on roots of law, some Schools use additional principles. While Islamic law, to an outsider, may initially appear rigid and inflexible, the application of the four roots and the supplementary principles often makes it quite flexible in application (obvious exceptions such as the Taliban in Afghanistan do exist).

- ✔ *Istihsan* (judicial preference, literally "seeking the good") is used by the Hanifites. Judicial preference means that the judge (or legal scholar) has the discretion, when two possible ways of making a ruling exist, to exercise his judgment (preference) in choosing the ruling that will promote the common good.

- ✔ *Istislah* (literally "seeking what is correct") is a principle approved by the Malikites that is similar to *istihsan* in that the ruling, so long as it doesn't contradict the Qur'an and the *hadiths,* should promote public and private welfare. Thus, this principle looks more to the spirit of the law in the Qur'an and the *hadiths* than to the letter of the law.

- ✔ *Istishab* says that a situation existing in the past is presumed to continue into the presence in the absence of contrary evidence. Most Schools use this principle when relevant. For example, suppose a person disappears and never shows up again. For inheritance law, he is presumed to be alive until what would have been his normal lifespan elapses.

- ✔ *Ibaha* ("permissibility") is associated with the Hanbalites. Acts that don't contradict the Qur'an and the *sunna* are presumed to be legitimate. For example, the Hanbalites allow a woman to include in a marriage contract a clause that her husband can't marry any other women.

- ✔ *Urf* is an exception, made on the basis of local custom, by some scholars of the Hanifite and Malikite Schools. For example, a legal contract requires oral acceptance by both parties. But the judge could recognize written acceptance of a contract if that were the custom locally.

- ✔ *Darura* ("necessity") is a special principle established by analogy from Sura 2:239 and associated with Abu Hanifa but not limited only to the Hanifite School. For example, must a soldier in battle dismount his horse in order to carry out the prayer ritual? The Qur'an says no. During a time of battle to defend the faith, necessity requires he remained mounted and ready to fight so he may pray from his horse. A modern example: While Islamic law in theory should apply in all situations, necessity requires that modern Muslim nations act on the basis of international law in relating to other sovereign states.

Getting legal: The Schools of law (madhhab)

Every Muslim takes one of the Schools of law as his guide in legal matters. *Madhhab* literally means "direction" and is sometimes translated as sect or rite.

Schools aren't religious denominations. Regardless of what branch of Islam one belongs to (see Part IV of this book), each Muslim adheres to one of the Schools. Each School has an accepted body of key texts and cultivates a strong bond between teacher and student.

Most Shi`ites follow the Ja`farite school, associated with the sixth Shi`ite *imam* (see Chapter 12 for more on the Shi`ites). In this section, I discuss the four Sunni Schools that exist today.

Hanifite School

Abu Hanifa (700–767) was the grandson of a freed slave from Afghanistan. He was born in Kufa and died in Baghdad, so he worked in Iraq. He traveled extensively and refused to take sides in the political struggles between the Umayyads and the Abbasid families for control of the Islamic state (see Chapter 2). He was one of the first to articulate general principles to guide scholars in making legal decisions. He emphasized analogy *(qiyas)* and utilized hypothetical cases to make his point. The Hanifite School is the most lenient of the four Sunni Schools, partly because of its use of "juristic preference" *(istihsan)* to moderate harsh rulings.

The Hanifite School was the official School of both the Abbasid and Ottoman Empires (see Chapter 2). The Hanifite School, by far the largest Sunni law School today, is dominant in most regions that were ruled by these two empires, with the exception of Iran and Saudi Arabia. Iran, as a Shi`ite country, follows the Ja`farite school and Saudi Arabia follows the Hanbalite School (see the "Hanbalite School" section, later in this chapter). Afghanistan, much of central Asia, and most of South Asia also follow the Hanifite School.

Recalling which legal School is dominant in which country is easiest if you remember the areas where the Hanifite school isn't dominant.

Malikite School

Malik ibn Anas (716–795) spent most of his life in Medina. His *al-Muwatta'* (book of the smoothed path), the first book of Islamic law, combined a collection of legal decisions with the traditions of Muhammad. Malik also favored the legal customs of Medina and utilized *istislah* (consideration of public good) and analogy. When Caliph Harun al-Rashid asked Malik to come to Baghdad to teach his sons, Malik replied, "Knowledge does not travel but is traveled to."

The Malikite School is dominant in West Africa and Northwest Africa, and it's prominent in southern Egypt, the Sudan, Bahrain, and Kuwait.

Shafi`ite School

I discuss al-Shafi`i's systematization of the four roots of Islamic law in the "Rooting out the four roots of law (usul al-fiqh)" section earlier in this chapter. He rejected the Hanifite use of juristic preference and the Malikite use of the customs of Medina (unless confirmed by written *hadiths*).

The Shafi`ite School is dominant in lower Egypt, southern Arabia, East Africa, Malaysia, Indonesia, and it's found in central Asia and in parts of the Caucasus mountain region, such as Dagestan.

Hanbalite School

Ibn Hanbal (780–855), the founder of the most conservative of the four Sunni Schools, is known for resisting the efforts of al-Ma'mun to impose Mu`tazilite beliefs (see Chapter 4). He survived imprisonment and torture to emerge as the hero of the traditionalists.

Hanbalite conservatism is evident in its ranking of the Qur'an above *sunna*. This School says that prophetic tradition may not be used to "abrogate" a verse in the Qur'an (see Chapter 7). Ibn Hanbal went further than al-Shafi`i in limiting both reason and analogy, but his use of *ibaha* (permissibility) made the Hanbalite position more flexible than other Schools, in some cases. Ibn Taymiyya (1263–1328) was an important Hanbalite jurist in Damascus whose work has greatly influenced the conservative Wahhabi movement in Arabia and Islamist movements of the 20th and 21st centuries (see Chapter 18).

Although the influence of the Hanbalites remains strong, Hanbalite law today is dominant only in Saudi Arabia, Qatar, and Oman.

Making a decision

Making a legal decision is more complex than simply deciding that an action is legal or illegal; instead, intermediate categories exist. Islamic law also deals with the question of penalties in the case of illegal acts and has some techniques for avoiding legal rulings that create undue hardship.

Observing the five categories of action

In Islamic law, all actions fit into one of five categories.

- ✔ **Obligatory actions (*fard* or *wajib*)** are divided into two categories: those (like prayer) required of every Muslim and those (like fighting in defense of Islam or attending a funeral) that some people fulfill on behalf of the entire community.

- ✔ **Recommended actions (*mustahabb* or *mandub*)** are meritorious but not required. Voluntary charity and monogamy are examples.

- ✔ **Neutral actions (*muba*)** have no moral or legal consequences. The Qur'an and the *sunna* don't address these actions.

- ✔ **Discouraged actions (*makruh*),** such as divorce, should be avoided. No penalty is imposed, however, and they won't keep a Muslim out of paradise.

- ✔ **Forbidden actions (*haram*)** are the opposite of obligatory actions. For example, to marry a close female relative is forbidden.

Assessing penalties

Islam receives much bad press for some of its stricter penalties *(hudud)* that come from the Qur'an, such as penalty of death for murder, cutting off of the hand for theft, and lashing for certain other acts. *Hudud* (literally, statues) is the Arabic term for these crimes and their punishments mandated by the Qur'an. A tradition says to "avoid *hadd* [singular of *hudud*] punishments by any doubt." This tradition is saying that one should impose *hudud* penalties only as a last resort.

The carrying out of these penalties has many restrictions. For example, the Qur'an imposes a penalty of 100 lashes for adultery in Sura 24:2, but the Qur'an also requires four witnesses to the act of sexual penetration in a case of adultery, and they aren't likely to be found. Sura 24:2 also adds, "unless they repent," which can negate the penalty if the person who committed the crime repents. As to cutting off of the hand for theft, Sura 5:48 also has a repentance clause. The judge must also consider the value of the item(s) stolen and whether extenuating circumstances existed. If a Muslim is starving through no fault of his own and steals, the local community that failed to respond to his hunger is as guilty as he is and the penalty isn't imposed. True, some Muslim countries have reinstituted and occasionally carry out the *hudud* penalties, but what's probably involved is a Muslim politician's version of a "get tough on crime" policy rather than genuine piety and faithfulness to Islamic law.

Closing the door of ijtihad

By the end of the tenth century, legal scholars felt that all major legal issues had been decided. They said that the "door of interpretation" *(ijtihad)* was closed and Muslims henceforth had to consult past decisions collected in the books of the various law Schools *(taqlid).*

Rulers determine which School of law applies in their countries, while individuals choose which School of law to follow in their personal lives. Most follow the School that is dominant where they live. When legal cases arise that aren't addressed in older law, a judge or ruler or individual asks the opinion of a *mufti* (legal consultant) about the case. The *mufti* issues a *fatwa*. Other qualified individuals can render contrary decisions, but the decision had to be based on the "four roots of law." Decisions made after the closing of the door aren't part of a School's consensus and can't serve as the basis for a new decision.

Ibn Taymiyya and some other Hanbalites rejected the concept of the closing of the door.

Here's an example of a *fatwa*. The Ottoman Empire had a Grand Mufti who was a high government official. Once the Grand Mufti was asked whether local authorities must force a village without a mosque to build one. His answer, the *fatwa*, was "Yes," and the *fatwa* cited both earlier government decrees and the importance of the call to prayer in Islam.

Getting a *fatwa* is easier today than in the past. Just dial 1-800-95-FATWA, or go to a number of Web sites such as www.fiqhcouncil.org and ask a question. I'm not kidding! Of course, the person responding with the *fatwa* may or may not be a qualified Muslim legal scholar, and the *fatwa* may or may not be valid.

Getting around the law

Within Sunni Islam, any of the four Schools constitutes a valid body of law, even when they disagree with one another. Because one School can be strict on an issue while another is more lenient, by picking and choosing (*takhayyur* means selection) among the different rulings of the four Schools, a person or a government gains considerable flexibility.

The concept of patching *(talfiq)* goes further than the idea of selection. On a specific issue, by combining part of a ruling from one School with part of a ruling from another School, a person or government can come up with a new legal ruling that doesn't mesh with any previous ruling. For example: Hanifite law said that a woman whose husband has disappeared must wait until the end of his expected lifespan before she can remarry. In the Malikite School, the waiting period is only four years. By adopting the portion of the Malikite ruling on the waiting period in a country governed by Hanifite law, the country avoids imposing a waiting period that was longer than she's likely to live on a woman whose husband has deserted her.

A further technique utilized by Hanifite and Shafi`ite jurists is the *hiyyal* (trick) — essentially a legal slight of hand used to avoid the plain intent of a passage in the Qur'an. For example, for merchants involved in long-range buying and selling of goods, the prohibition of usury (interest) was a problem in ancient times and is even more so today because Muslims must function in a capitalistic world economy. Whether one needs a mortgage to buy a house or a major business loan, interest is usually involved. Muslim lawyers, through complicated legal language, are able to draw up contracts that accomplish the purpose of interest without taking the form of interest.

Reforming the law

Many of the issues Islam has faced over the last two hundred years have to do with law. Along with colonial rule of most Muslim countries came Western law and the concept of systematically organized body of law (law codes) and

Fiqh and *fatwa* books

Legal scholars produced two basic types of books:

✔ The first dealt with theory. Al-Shafi'i's *Risala* is an early example, while the *Mustasfa* of al-Ghazali is the classical work. These works dealt with topics such as the five categories, the four roots of law plus any additional sources, and the rules for deriving new ruling from the sources.

✔ The second group of books is called literature of rules. Works of this type include both a practical summary of rulings in different areas and a theoretical section showing that the work is both in accord with the procedures of its School and agrees with the Qur'an and the *sunna*. The practical summary contains two basic sections: the first deal with obligations to God (basically worship and ritual), while the second deals with obligations to other people. This second section typically covers family law, commercial law, land law, criminal law and penalties, and judicial procedures. Subsequent works include summaries of the rule books for easier reference and may also include commentaries on earlier fundamental rule books of a particular School.

After the door of interpretation was closed, similar books provided collections of *fatwas* issued by *muftis* (legal scholars) of a particular School, as well as more theoretical works dealing with the qualifications to be a *mufti* and the duties and decision-making procedures of a *mufti*.

---

the concept of making laws by legislation. Western-based law codes came to prevail in most areas of the law, with Muslim law remaining valid mainly in areas like family law.

In Western thought, legal legislation derives from the will of the people. Traditional Islam has no need for legislation because the law is God's unchangeable blueprint. Human approval isn't required for God's law.

After Muslim countries achieved independence from colonial rule, they adopted the model of the Western nation state. Various solutions have been put forth as to how to reconcile Muslim law with the modern law of states:

✔ Selection (*takhayyur*) and patching (*talfiq*) are used by Muslims who believe that exclusive adherence to a single legal School is inappropriate today.

✔ Some advocate increased use of the "subsidiary principles" of the law such as *istislah* (seeking the common good) as a way of applying Muslim law to modern situations.

✔ Traditional legal scholars say that the problem was caused by the abandonment of Muslim law as it existed in the 11th to 14th centuries. If Muslims returned to the situation that existed before the intrusion of the West, the problems would be solved.

✔ Some Muslim reformers say that the problem was the scholarly class itself. Islam shouldn't return to the classical legal consensus as it existed at the time of the closing of the door of *ijtihad*. Rather, they should go back to the Islam of the first three generations and be willing to make new legal decisions, based on the Qur'an and the *hadiths*.

✔ Some modernist reformers advocate distinguishing the unchangeable basic principles of the Qur'an and the *hadiths* from the specific application of these principles in the culture of Muhammad's time. Contemporary situations require new applications of the basic principles. For example, Sura 4:3 says that a man may take up to four wives but only if he treats them all equally. Sura 4:129 says a man is unable to treat multiple wives equally. Modernists such as the founding figure of Islamic reform in Egypt, Muhammad `Abduh (1849–1905), argue that these two statements taken together means the Qur'an is against polygamy. To recap: A man may have more than one wife if he treats them equally. But no man can treat multiple wives equally. Therefore, no man may have more than one wife.

Since 1970, many Muslim countries have moved toward giving Islamic law a more central role. In some countries, this amounts only to a declaration that the law of the state is based on *shari`a*. Others propose that a council of Islamic jurists approve any laws passed by the state as not being in conflict with Islamic law. Still others want to go further and make a more systematic effort to make Islamic law the basic law of the state.

Islam today faces other legal issues that it has yet to resolve, such as:

✔ How does Islamic law relate to modern international law in which the same law applies in international relations to all countries?

✔ How are principles of universal human rights (in which all people are entitled to certain fundamental rights regardless of religion, class, race, gender, or ethnic group) to be reconciled with traditional Islamic law, which limits some of these rights? (See Chapter 17.)

Part III

Becoming Familiar with Muslim Daily Life

The 5th Wave

By Rich Tennant

@RICHTENNANT

"Excuse me, that's my pager. Okay, this is pretty important. It's a pre-set alarm reminding me of this afternoon's prayer."

In this part . . .

Rituals are crucial in shaping religious life and beliefs. Have you heard of the Five Pillars, which are the basic ritual and worship requirements for a Muslim? They're covered in depth here, from stopping five times a day to join with other Muslims in praying to God to fasting from dawn to dusk during the month of Ramadan to making the pilgrimage to Mecca — the spiritual highpoint of a Muslim's life.

Islam has other ritual observances, such as observance of Muhammad's birthday and the ceremonies accompanying birth, naming, marriage, and death. I look at these in this part, as well as some customs and requirements, such as what a Muslim may eat and what she should wear. I then conclude this part by looking at Muslim ethics, including some specific issues, such as sexual ethics, marriage and family, medicine, and social justice.

Chapter 9

The Five Pillars of Worship: Foundations of Islam

. . . .

In This Chapter

▶ Understanding the *shahada* — the Muslim testimony of faith

▶ Becoming familiar with *salat* — Islamic prayer

▶ Getting to know mosques — Islamic places of worship

▶ Appreciating *zakat* — charity in Islam

▶ Looking at *saum* during *Ramadan* — a month of fasting

▶ Grasping the *hajj* — pilgrimages

. . . .

In every religion, both adherents of that faith and outsiders instantly think of certain fundamentals, such as the Wheel of Dharma in Buddhism and the Ten Commandments in Judaism and Christianity. A similar list of basics, called the Five Pillars of Worship (*arkan al-`ibada*), exists in Islam. Like the framework of a modern building, pillars in large, ancient buildings provided the foundation and structural support. In the same way, the Five Pillars provide the foundations and basic supports of Islam. In contrast to the Pillars of Faith (see Chapter 3) that specify five basic Muslim beliefs, the Five Pillars of Worship list the five basic acts of worship. This chapter explains these Five Pillars — what each of them is called and what practices they involve. I also talk about what is sometimes called the sixth pillar, *jihad* — usually translated as striving or holy war.

The Five Pillars of Worship aren't listed together in one place in the Qur'an. Details in the observance of the pillars weren't fully fixed until after the death of Muhammad (see Chapter 5), although the pillars are regarded as implicit in the practices of Muhammad and his companions. Further, don't be surprised to find slight variations in the sequence in which the pillars are listed. You may encounter two alternative phrases to designate the Pillars of Worship. Islam also refers to them as the Pillars of Religion *(arkan al-din)* and in English the phrase *Pillars of Islam* is often used. Just realize that (five) Pillars of Worship, Pillars of Religion, and Pillars of Islam all refer to the same thing, which is different from the Pillars of Faith.

Think of the Five Pillars as the minimum of what's involved in being a believing and practicing Muslim. Imagine a person who has recently converted to Islam or is thinking about converting. She says to herself: How do I start to live my life as a Muslim? What must I believe? What must I do? Where do I begin? The Five Pillars of Worship provide a simple blueprint for a beginning and a framework for the life ahead. The pillars are like a basic checklist to help her start out on *the straight path* (*al-sirat al-mustaqim,* one of the Qur'anic terms for the Muslim way of life). Each pillar is straightforward, and each Muslim can answer for herself whether or to what degree she has fulfilled each requirement. Of course, the pillars are only a beginning. Each pillar is a gateway into deeper understanding and greater spirituality as one grows in the faith.

Purification: Getting Ready for Worship

Most religions make a distinction between the sacred and the profane (that is, the secular). The sacred is whatever pertains to God or whatever is holy or ultimate in the religion. The profane has to do with everyday life and matters. Frequently, believers think that when coming into contact with the holy (that is, with God in monotheistic religions), they should be in a state of physical and spiritual purity. Because ritual actions bring one into closer contact with God, one must be in a state of purity prior to performing acts of worship such as prayer *(salat)* and the pilgrimage to Mecca *(hajj)*. Actions that make one ritually impure aren't necessarily inferior or immoral actions. It's similar to how people used to dress up (and many still do) to go to church. Jeans and shorts weren't improper as such, but they were regarded as inappropriate when engaged in formal worship. Hinduism and Judaism also place much emphasis on ritual purity and share many but not all the same concepts as to what makes a person or thing impure and how to remove the impurity. Although not one of the Five Pillars of Worship, Muslim collections of traditions *(hadiths)* include a separate section on purification as part of the material concerning worship and ritual. One tradition says, "Purification is half the faith."

Removing impurity

If a person is in a state of ritual impurity, before touching an Arabic Qur'an, performing *salat,* or beginning the pilgrimage ritual, she either performs a minor ritual cleansing (called *wudu'*) or, for greater ritual impurities, takes a ritual bath *(ghusl)*. Before most daily prayers, only *wudu'* is necessary. *Wudu'* is a separate ritual with a prescribed sequence of actions and words. Muslims use running or poured water to wash the parts of the body, such as the forearms, mouth, and ears. Mosques include either a fountain or some other source of water (for example, spigots and basins) for *wudu'* in an outside courtyard or inside. In religions worldwide, water is the most common means of purification.

No water, no problem! The intention is what counts. Arabia has a lot of sand and little water. So at prayer time in a place with no water, Muslims may pat sand or dirt with their hands, and then carry out the sequence of hand motions and prayers for *wudu'*.

Sources of impurity

You can probably guess that Islamic scholars have devoted much attention to specifying in detail what causes minor impurity and what causes major impurity, just as they have specified in detail the ritual cleansings *(wudu'* and *ghusl)* for removing these two categories of impurity. Some examples of causes of major ritual impurity are ejaculation, menstruation, childbirth, and contact with a corpse. Examples of causes of minor ritual impurity are touching one's genitals, loss of consciousness, urination, and deep sleep. In general, chronic medical conditions, such as incontinence, don't make a person ritually impure. Most of the things that make one impure in Islam also make one impure in other religions with a major emphasis on purification. Typically, any emission from the body, anything to do with death, and anything associated with sexual intercourse are polluting in many religions. Death is polluting because God is the lord of life. Loss of blood is also polluting both because it's a bodily emission and because blood is a symbol of life in most cultures. Sleep is polluting in Islam mainly as a precaution — when asleep you may have polluted yourself so purification is recommended after deep sleep. Contact with certain animals — pigs and dogs — are polluting.

Concepts of purity and impurity also play a role in others areas of Islam. One of the names for circumcision of the newborn child is purification *(tahara).* The right hand and foot are considered pure and the left hand polluting. Thus one enters a mosque (a sacred area) right foot first and eats with one's right hand but cleans oneself with one's left hand. Anthropologists such as Mary Douglas have contributed greatly to understanding the function of purity and pollution in religions.

The Shahada (First Pillar): Testifying

Many religions condense the essence of their faith in a short statement that's simple and straightforward. At the same time, such statements or testaments have great depths of meaning that can be developed elsewhere. Such is the testimony of faith (known as the *shahada*) in Islam. This statement —

"I testify that there is no God but God, and I testify that Muhammad is the messenger of God" — sums up what it means to be a Muslim. Chapter 3 discusses this ideal of the oneness of God and Chapter 5 talks about Muhammad's designation as the messenger of God. In contrast to many other religions, Jews and Christians agree, "There is no God but God." The basic affirmation of Judaism, the *Shema* (Deuteronomy 6:44–45), and the opening of the Apostles' Creed in Christianity express the same thought. Similar in function to the *shahada* is Buddhism's three refuge affirmation ("I take refuge in the Buddha, I take refuge in the teaching, I take refuge in the community of Buddhism monks").

By speaking this statement with the intention to become a Muslim, a person does indeed become a Muslim. Muslims say that the person returns to Islam (the term "revert" is used). They believe that all people were originally Muslims, having submitted to God at the time of Adam's creation.

With slight variation, the *shahada* is spoken on many other occasions, as well. For example, the father whispers the *shahada in* the ear of his newborn child. The *shahada* is ideally the last words that a dying Muslim hears. Those carrying the body of the dead in a funeral procession also may chant it. It forms the basis of the call to prayer, and each worshipper reiterates it at the end of each of the five daily prayers — see the "Salat (Second Pillar): Praying" section.

The *shahada* affirms that being a Muslim isn't a private matter between the believer and God. Instead, a Muslim is obligated to bear witness to his submission to God and to witness to others. In other words, Islam involves an obligation to engage in what Christians call evangelism (in Islam, it's known as *da`wa*). Of course, reciting the *shahada* is only one way of witnessing to the faith. A Muslim may give up his life and die as a martyr for Islam. Such a martyr is called a *shahid,* which means witness, from the same Arabic word root as *shahada.*

Try to say the *shahada*

When the angel Gabriel called Muhammad to be a prophet and at the same time revealed to him the earliest portion of the Qur'an (see Chapters 5 and 6), Gabriel told Muhammad to recite and not simply to read. The spoken word of the Qur'an used in worship stirs the emotions and reverberates in the soul of a Muslim in the same way, a familiar old hymn may move Christians, even when they can't remember all the words.

To begin to appreciate the importance of the spoken word in Islam, try to memorize and repeat out loud the *shahada* in Arabic: *ashhadu al-la ilaha illa-Llah, wa ashhadu anna Muhammadar-rasul Allah.* Don't worry! Repeating the *shahada* won't make you a Muslim unless that is your intention. All ritual acts in Islam require one to first consciously affirm the intention *(niyya)* to perform the act in order that it be valid.

Go, team, go! What about jihad?

Jihad, typically translated as "holy war" in the West, is sometimes included as a sixth pillar in discussions of religious obligations (*ilbadat* means service or worship). Within Islam, you can find different explanations of *jihad,* often in conflict with one another. All agree that, whether it's one of the pillars or not, *jihad* is required. All agree that the word itself means "striving" or "struggle" and is used in some places in the Qur'an without military connotation. But in other texts, *jihad* does include warfare, and certainly war on behalf of God is prominent in the Islamic tradition. You can find out more about *jihad* in Chapter 17, where I look at some misconceptions about Islam.

Salat (Second Pillar): Praying

Ritual prayer in Islam, called *salat,* follows a prescribed sequence of words with accompanying bodily positions and is the most important means of worshipping God in Islam. Daily *salat* is so central to Islam that in some languages if you want to know whether a person is a Muslim, you ask, "Do you do *salat*?" rather than asking "Are you religious?" or "Do you believe in God?" Other worship rituals are important but occur at much less frequent intervals — once a year or even once in a life. But because a Muslim stops whatever she is doing to pray five times a day, she's constantly reminded to put God before all her other concerns. *Salat* as a fixed prayer ritual is different from *du`a,* which is voluntary prayer using such prayers as the person chooses. *Salat* is not simply an expression of a Muslim's faith, although it naturally is that. *Salat* is also a means by which the faith of a Muslim is molded and deepened, as indeed is prayer in most religions.

When to pray

How do Muslims know when to do the five daily prayers? The precise time varies according to geographical location and time of year. In a Muslim country, the call to prayer gives the signal. It sounds out over the rooftops and is the most characteristic sound that sticks in the mind of a non-Muslim tourist. In non-Muslim countries, printed prayer charts, computer programs, and Muslim Web sites provide the precise prayer times for any location and date. The five daily prayers are:

- Early morning prayer right before dawn (two prayer cycles).
- Noon prayer (four prayer cycles).
- Mid-afternoon prayer (four prayer cycles).

✔ Sunset prayer (three prayer cycles).

✔ Evening prayer, between an hour after sunset and midnight (four prayer cycles).

In some circumstances, two of the daily *salats* can be combined. Missed *salats* can be made up privately. Modifications may be acceptable due to situations such as illness or being on public transportation. Menstruating women don't perform *salat* because the woman is impure due to the menstrual blood just as a man is impure after seminal emission (see the section "Purification: Getting Ready for Worship" in this chapter).

In addition to the prescribed five *salats* each day, Muslims perform additional voluntary *salats* and special *salats* on the two primary festival days (at the end of the month of *Ramadan* and during the *hajj*), for funerals, and on other special occasions.

Do all Muslims observe the five daily prayers? Of course not, any more than all Christians attend church once a week. However, with the upsurge in religiousness over the last 25 years in the Muslim world, you find a greater percentage of Muslims strictly observing the five daily prayers (as well as the remainder of the Five Pillars of Worship) than would have been the case in the past. If necessity prevents a person from performing one of the prayers, God understands, accepts her intention, and allows her to make up the prayer later.

The traditional biography of Muhammad explains why Muslims pray five times a day. It says that at the time of Muhammad's night journey to Jerusalem and ascension to God's throne (see Chapter 5), God instructed Muhammad that Muslims should pray 50 times a day. On his way down, Muhammad met Moses who asked him how many prayers God had decreed. Moses said the people wouldn't be able to do 50 and told Muhammad to go back and ask God to reduce the number. This happened several times until the number was down to five, at which point Muhammad was too embarrassed to ask God for a further reduction. God told Muhammad that the Muslim who does five prayers a day will have the reward of doing 50 prayers.

Where do Muslims pray?

Muslims may perform *salat* almost anywhere. At the appropriate time, people stop whatever they're doing and face Mecca, which is the religious center of the Muslim cosmos in what is now Saudi Arabia. The direction toward Mecca is called the *qibla*.

Mosques are planned so that one wall, the *qibla wall,* faces Mecca. In the interior of the mosque, an area on the *qibla* wall — often a semi-circular arched recess — designates the direction toward Mecca and thus the direction to face when lining up for prayer. This recess is the *mihrab,* or prayer niche.

Before *salat,* people take off their shoes. If they're not in a mosque, they unroll a prayer rug upon which to perform *salat.* Usually the prayer rug portrays the Grand Mosque of Mecca, Islam's holiest mosque. If one has no prayer rug, spreading out a newspaper will do.

While a Muslim can pray alone, Muslims prefer to perform *salat* in the presence of others Muslims. Muslims line up in orderly rows, while one person stands in front and serves as *imam* (that is, prayer leader). In accord with the general emphasis on male leadership in public arenas — a tradition which some Muslim women object to and say isn't grounded in the Qur'an — a woman can act as prayer leader for other women, but not for men.

Calling to prayer (adhan)

Each time of prayer is announced with the call to prayer, known as *adhan.* If you've ever visited a Muslim country or watched a documentary about Islam on TV, you'll have heard the *adhan* whether or not you recognized it as such. In the past, about 15 minutes before the designated time of prayer, the *muezzin* (the person who issues the call to prayer) would ascend the *minaret,* a tall tower that often adorns or adjoins a mosque as a steeple may adorn a church. From there, he recited the call.

While muezzins still exist, today the call is frequently sounded by a recording broadcast from loudspeakers located on the minaret or at the top of a multi-story building. Inside the mosque, the call is repeated in a variant form (the *iqama*), ending with the words, "the prayer is established" to indicate the actual start of the *salat* ritual.

Because the *adhan* is one of the most frequently recited Islamic texts, you may be interested in both the English text and the spoken Arabic original. Table 9-1 shows four phrases, repeated a variable number of times, that make up the *adhan.*

Minarets

Like the *mihrab,* or prayer niche, the minaret wasn't part of the earliest mosques but had become a normal feature by the end of the first Muslim century. Many regions have distinctive styles of minarets, such as square style of Umayyad Syria or the thin, tall spire characteristic of the Ottoman Turks (you can read about the Umayyads and Ottomans in Chapter 2). If you become familiar with these styles and see a picture of the minaret of a traditional, unidentified mosque, you can make a good guess as to the part of the Muslim world in which the mosque was located. One famous minaret in Morocco was built to enable the *muezzin* to ride a donkey to the top — an early functional equivalent of an elevator.

Table 9-1	Four Phrases That Make Up the Adhan
English Translation	*Spoken Arabic Phrase*
God is great (recited four times — this phrase is called the *takbir*).	Allahu Akbarthis
I witness that there is no god but God.	Ashhadu al-la ilaha illa Llah
I witness that Muhammad is the messenger of God.	Ashhadu anna Muhammadar-rasulu-Llah
Rise up for prayer (twice).	Hayya `al-s-salah
Rise up for salvation (twice).	Hayya `ala-l-falah
God is great (twice).	Allahu Akbar
There is no god but God.	La ilaha illa-Llah

Before the early-morning prayer, Sunnis insert "prayer is better than sleep" toward the end prior to "*Allahu Akbar.*" Shi`tes add "rise up for the best of works," and Twelver Shi`ites add a reference to `Ali at the end of the *adhan.* You can find out more about the differences between Sunnis and Shi`ites in Chapter 12.

Doing the first rak`a (bowing)

Depending on which of the five prayer times is involved, the actual prayer ritual consists of two to four cycles of bowings *(rak`as)* — a sequence of pre-scribed movements and accompanying words. In the course of performing the five daily prayers, a worshipper completes a minimum of 17 *rak`as.* In a congregational *salat* led by an *imam* (prayer leader), much of what the individual worshippers say is spoken silently or in a very low voice. Although you may see minor variations in body position and what is said, each *rak`a* includes the following steps (preceded by each individual having explicitly avowed the intention to perform *salat*):

1. **Standing with feet slightly apart, the person raises his hands to head level, and with palms facing outward and forward says the *takbir* aloud. Moving his hands down to his sides, he pronounces the first Sura *(Fatiha)* and one other passage from the Qur'an.**

   This first position ends with another *takbir.*

2. **Bowing, with hands on the knees, the worshipper says three times: "Glory to God the Almighty."**

3. **Standing once again, he says, "God hears those who praise Him. O our lord, Praise be to you," ending with another** *takbir.*

4. **The worshipper prostrates himself, his forehead touching the ground with both hands flat on the ground, and says, "Praised be my Lord, most high; praise be to Him" (three times), ending with a** *takbir.*

   After years of doing *salat*, a person may acquire a visible mark on the forehead, which is regarded as an indication of his piety.

5. **He sits up with his left foot and leg folded under him and his right leg straight back from knee to foot with toes touching floor and heel upright (it sounds much more complicated than it is).**

   Some Muslims pronounce a short petition for forgiveness of sins, and all utter another *takbir.*

6. **To complete the** *rak`a,* **the worshipper makes a second prostration and returns to a sitting position.**

Trying to describe the *salat* ritual without making it sound dry and artificial is like trying to describe the sequence of actions involved when you greet someone with a handshake. When do I extend my hand? Do I wait for the other person to extend his or her hand first? How do I clasp the other's hand? What words accompany all this? But you shake hands without having to think of the details, and this is also true for Muslims doing *salat*. They can complete a *rak`a* in a few minutes, without thinking about the details.

While a written description must sound somewhat rigid, you find some flexibility in practice. Children may be present and moving about. Some people arrive after the beginning of the first *rak`a* and catch up silently or repeat the missed *rak`a* at the end of *salat*.

Takbir: Invoking God

You may have recognized that the *shahada* forms part of the call to prayer. The *takbir,* "*Allahu Akbar*" is another repeated part of the call. Muslims frequently use this exclamatory phrase in a variety of contexts. Although it's usually translated "God is Great," a more literal translation is "God is the Greater."

At Muslim gatherings, a speaker may call for the audience to respond with a *takbir* in the same way a cheerleader urges a crowd to respond with a school's cry. At other times, the *takbir* serves as a vocal expression of piety in the same way some Christians interject "praise the Lord" into their speech.

To appreciate the *salat*, you must observe it. Many mosques in the United States and some other countries willingly open their services to non-Muslims, embracing you (literally!) cordially before and after and making their best efforts to help you feel comfortable. Call the mosque first to ask about attending. You'll probably be seated toward the rear (or with the women, if you're female) and be free to observe but not be expected to participate. But because much is said in inaudible tones, you may need further help to catch everything that goes on. An instructional video or CD program (see Appendix C for sources) intended primarily for new converts to Islam may be the best way to comprehend the details of the *salat*.

Adding additional rak`as and voluntary prayers

Remember that each of the five daily prayers involves two to four *rak`as.* Before the second and any subsequent *rak`as,* the worshipper stands up, pronounces a *takbir*, and begins the next cycle. At the end of the second and final *rak`as,* a formulaic greeting (the *tahiyya*) asks God's blessings on Muhammad. At the end of all the cycles of a *salat*, the worshipper sits back and recites the witnessing *(tashahhud),* followed by invocation of blessing on Muhammad and Abraham. After a final prayer for peace, he turns his head to the right and then to the left, saying "peace be upon you" *(al-salamu `alaykum).* According to popular belief, he's addressing not only the people on either side but also the angels who watch over him as he prays. This concludes the formal, obligatory *salat*.

Frequently, the worshipper then says several personal, individual prayers *(du`a),* and then arises and says *al-salamu `alaykum* to the people near him. He may then perform an additional voluntary two *rak`as.*

An example of a voluntary prayer at the end of *salat* is:

"There is no God except God, the One. He has no partners. To Him belongs sovereignty and to Him belongs praise. He is all-powerful over everything. O God! None can deny that which you give and none can give that which you deny. The greatness of the great shall not prevail against you."

Of course, voluntary prayers are also used on many other occasions. Naturally, prayers attributed to Muhammad are popular, such as this one on going to bed:

> "All praise belongs to God who provided rest to my body, restored my soul to me and allowed me to remember Him."

Jum`a: Gathering for Friday congregational prayer

In Muslim cities, on Fridays, the entire community gathers in a large mosque designated for the communal Friday noon *salat (jum`a),* rather than attending the neighborhood mosques that they use the rest of the week. Of course, in very large cities, several mosques are required to accommodate those attending Friday services.

Upon entering the mosque, the believer usually performs two *rak`as.* Before the actual performance of *salat,* the *imam* or another learned individual ascends a couple of steps up the staircase of the pulpit *(minbar),* located to the right of the prayer niche. From there he delivers a sermon *(khutba).* Some pulpits are elaborately carved works of art. In more modest mosques, the *imam* stands behind a simple lectern. The sermon utilizes a specific passage from the Qur'an and explains a point of belief or conduct. In Muslim states, the sermon traditionally includes a blessing upon the ruler. All Muslims shops, offices, and workplaces close down during the Friday service, but reopen for the remainder of the day when the service concludes.

The following text from the Qur'an (Sura 62:9–10) provides the scriptural basis for the communal prayer service on Friday:

"O you who believe, when the call is proclaimed to prayer on the day of assembly, hasten to remember God, and cease your business. This is best for you if you understand. And when the prayer service is finished, scatter over the land and seek the bounty of God and remember God often that you may prosper."

If you attend a Friday service at a mosque in the United States, the sermon may strike you as fairly simple in comparison to the rhetorical elaboration often typical of sermons in Christian churches. However, the Friday service in a Muslim country provides a major opportunity to mobilize people either in support of the government or against it. For this reason, the government may maintain close control over the mosques, including appointment of the *imam.*

The mosque (masjid)

Architecture and calligraphy are the two most important art forms in Islam. Great architectural achievements include palaces (for example, the Alhambra in Spain), the Dome of the Rock in Jerusalem, and funerary shrines (for example, the Taj Mahal). But the greatest effort naturally went into the building of mosques. *Masjid,* the Arabic word for mosque, means "place of prostration," emphasizing ritual prayer as the central worship activity. Any open area that's not ritually impure may be used as a place of prayer and referred to as a *masjid.*

The plan of a classical mosque derives from Muhammad's first house in Medina. On the east side of a large courtyard were rooms for Muhammad's wives. On the south side of the courtyard, two rows of pillars supported a roof providing shade from the hot Arabian sun. The flat roof, the pillars, the courtyard, and the roofed area oriented toward Mecca became the typical early mosque plan. Only later, after the conquest of Iran, did the domed structure enter Islamic architecture and come to be used for mosques. Although not all of the following are found in every mosque, here is a list of the characteristic features of a major mosque:

- *Qibla* wall with prayer niche *(mihrab)* facing Mecca
- Pulpit *(minbar)* to the right of the *mihrab*
- Minaret
- Fountain or other facility for purification
- Prayer hall
- Elegant, hanging lighting fixture above the central prayer area
- Architecturally separated space for women

A mosque has no pews or chairs (except perhaps at the rear for the disabled). Other structures may be associated with a mosque or incorporated into the mosque itself, such as schools for young children, *madrasas* for higher training in Islamic studies, and hospices for travelers.

Mosques do vary. In some parts of Africa, the Friday service may be held in a large open area outside the mosque. In some Western countries, where Islam is relatively new, mosques may be converted church buildings or storefront structures with little on the outside to indicate they are mosques.

As with the minaret (see the "Minarets" sidebar earlier in this chapter), different regions of the Muslim world often have their own characteristic style of mosque architecture. This includes whether the typical exterior facing is of brick, stone, adobe, tile, or some other material. Figure 9-1 shows the Blue Mosque in Istanbul (top) and the Al-Aqsa Mosque in Jerusalem (bottom), which is the third most-holy mosque in Islam.

You never see human (or divine) images in mosques. You won't find stained glass windows or murals with scenes from the Qur'an or statues of the angels, Muhammad, or other key figures of Islam. Nevertheless, many mosques are decorated with elegant designs executed in tile, stucco, and brick. The most important design motif is the use of verses from the Qur'an, often so artistically and abstractly reproduced that even someone fluent in Arabic may have difficulty reading them. Strips or bands of Qur'anic calligraphy may alternate with bands of abstract geometric design or patterns of flowers, leaves, and branches (called *arabesque*).

Figure 9-1:
Two styles
of mosques.

The prohibition of images goes back to the Jewish Bible's "no images" commandment (Exodus 20:4; Deuteronomy 4:15–18). In contrast, divine images
play a major role in Buddhism and Hinduism. In Islam, the prohibition of
images is applied absolutely to mosques but not always to the decoration of
non-religious buildings. Related to this prohibition is the absence of anything
in Islamic art comparable to the tradition of pictorial art in the West. You
won't see Rembrandts or Monets in Islam. However, a tradition of illustration
of non-religious texts in Persian manuscripts is highly developed as an art
form.

The first Islamic mosque

The traditional biography of Muhammad relates the following story. When Muhammad first arrived in Medina, various prominent families wanted him to stay with them. Muhammad, however, left the matter to God. Mounted on his camel, he let the camel go where it would. Eventually, the camel came to a house belonging to two orphans with an open area used for drying dates. The camel knelt down but

Muhammad didn't dismount. The camel went a short distance away but then returned to the same spot and lay exhausted on the ground. Muhammad dismounted and went into the house. The orphans' guardian was paid for the house and grounds and Muhammad and others began to build his house, which also served as the first mosque.

Zakat (Third Pillar): Helping the Needy

Every religion urges charitable giving by its members to support religious, social service, and educational needs. In Islam, such giving is institutionalized as the *zakat,* an obligatory tax that every Muslim pays annually. Although the details can get complicated, the basic rate is 2.5 percent of all liquid assets and income-producing property. Contributions in kind are specified for livestock and crops. *Zakat* isn't levied on housing and on basic, necessary personal possessions. If one's "zakatable" property is below a certain minimum (called the *nisab*), a person does not pay *zakat.* One definition of the *nisab* is the value of three ounces of gold, which in December 2002 was worth about $1,026. Muslim Web sites and publications help the believer to figure his *zakat* obligation. For an example, go to `www.soundvision.com/Info/life/zakatcalc.asp`. Local mosque and various Islamic organizations may act as conduits to receive and distribute the proceeds of the *zakat.* The *zakat* is used to help the poor and sick, spread the Islamic faith, ransom captives, aid travelers, free Muslim slaves, help debtors, and defend Islam.

Many passages from the Qur'an and the *hadiths* extol charitable acts. Sura 2:267 says:

> *O you who believe! Give in charity of the good things you earn and of what we [God] have brought forth for you out of the earth, and do not aim at giving in charity what is bad.*

Muhammad is reported to have said that "the man who exerts himself on behalf of the widow and the poor one is like the one who struggles in the way of Allah, or the one who keeps awake in the night (for prayers) and fasts during the day." (Bukhari 69.1) Another *hadith* tells of a prostitute whose sins were forgiven by God because she took off her shoe and tied her head scarf to it in order to draw water from a well to give to a dog about to die of thirst (Bukhari 6.6).

Additional, voluntary contributions *(sadaqa)* are recommended as acts of charity and piety. These donations don't fulfill the *zakat* obligation. In addition, wealthy Muslims often establish and endow charitable foundations, either through gift or will. Like many philanthropic foundations in the United States today, these foundations are often dedicated to specific purposes, such as support of *madrasas* (Islamic schools), mosques, and hospitals; assistance to hostels for travelers; and aid to the poor.

Saum (Fourth Pillar): Reflecting and Fasting

Islam normally doesn't recommend extreme asceticism or self-denial. God created the physical world and the human body for enjoyment. Salvation doesn't come by denying one's physical needs, such as sex and food. However, the physical world is to be enjoyed in moderation.

Originally, fasting took place on the 10th of *Muharram,* the first month of the Muslim year. This is still one of a number of days of voluntary fasting. After the establishment of the community in Medina, and before the death of Muhammad, *Ramadan* was revealed as the month of fasting. *Ramadan* (whose name literally means the "great heat" or "scorcher") is the ninth month of the Muslim calendar. As with all months, *Ramadan* begins at sunset after the first sighting of the new moon *(hilal)* at the end of the previous month, *Sha`ban.*

The beginning of a new month at the time of the new moon is why the crescent of the new moon is the most common visual symbol of Islam and frequently crowns the roofs of mosques. Flags of Muslim countries also may incorporate a crescent moon.

The precise determination of the beginning of the month is crucial only for *Ramadan* and the following month, *Shawwal,* because of the fasting that begins with the start and concludes with the end of the month. Muslims, who in the medieval ages were far advanced over the West in astronomical observation, have long known that the date of the new moon can be astronomically calculated. Nevertheless, the custom of a physical sighting by a trustworthy witness is still used to determine the beginning and end of the month. In the United States, a committee composed of representatives of several Muslim organizations receives reported sightings of the new moon, checks out these reports, and then announces the beginning and end of *Ramadan.*

You may wish to greet your Muslim friends at the start of the month by wishing them *Ramadan Mubarak* (a blessed *Ramadan*), and they would respond with *Ramadan Karim* (a generous *Ramadan*).

Dawn to dust

During *Ramadan,* Muslims fast from dawn (the time when a white thread can first be distinguished from a black thread in the morning light) until sunset. Fasting includes:

- ✔ No eating
- ✔ No drinking
- ✔ No sexual intercourse
- ✔ No smoking

Islamic legal experts have gone into considerable detail as to what actions do and don't constitute a violation of the fast. For example, a person shouldn't take oral medications during the day but can receive medical injections. Pregnant and nursing women and people who are permanently debilitated or mentally ill aren't required to fast. A number of people may put off fasting for a portion of *Ramadan* but must make up the missed days over the next year. Menstruating women, the ill, and travelers on a long journey can or should postpone the fast but make up the missed days over the next year. Children begin to fast gradually, increasing the period of observance until they're able to observe the full month's fast. If a person knowingly breaks the fast, she should add a day of fasting at the end of *Ramadan.*

The faithfulness of observance varies. In some Muslim countries, the state or voluntary groups attempt to force all Muslims to observe the fast in public (it doesn't apply to tourists). However, in the privacy of one's home, some are stricter in observance than others.

A day in Ramadan

Ramadan observances vary slightly from culture to culture, but the following is typical. Muslims break the fast as soon as possible at sunset (remember that the day begins at sunset). Muslims eat the main meal later in the evening, with perhaps a final light meal in the early pre-dawn hours before the next morning's fast begins. A person shouldn't gorge in the evening to make up for not eating during the day. The evening is a time of relaxation, visiting, prayer, and Qur'anic recitation. Printed Qur'ans divide the text into 30 sections to facilitate reading the whole Qur'an during *Ramadan.* Sounds of Qur'an recitation punctuate the evening air. Pious individuals may perform a voluntary *salat* of 20 *rak`as,* sometime after the fifth prescribed prayer of the day. Some go to the mosque during the evening, especially during the last ten days of the month. On an odd-numbered day of these last ten — most commonly said to be the 27th of *Ramadan* — the *Lailat al-qadr* (Night of Power) occurred when the first Qur'anic revelation came to Muhammad. The recitation of the Qur'an during *Ramadan* recalls the giving of the Qur'an.

Sura 2:183–185 says, "O you who believe! Fasting is prescribed to you as it was prescribed to those before you, that you may learn self-restraint — (fasting) for a fixed number of days . . . . *Ramadan* is the month in which was sent down the Qur'an, as a guide to mankind."

Muslims begin the fast each day by announcing their intention (*niyya*) to observe the fast. During the day, normal activities continue. This isn't a holiday or religious retreat. But as you would expect, the pace of life is slower. Because the Muslim calendar is a lunar calendar, over a period of years, *Ramadan* occurs during every season of the year. In the coolness of winter, the daylight period of fasting is shorter and less taxing than it is in the heat of summer, when the period of fasting may exceed 18 hours.

If you're planning a business trip to a Muslim country, try to avoid the month of *Ramadan* or at least be aware that you may not accomplish your assignment as quickly during this month as you would at another time.

The meaning of saum during Ramadan

Westerners often see only the literal level of Muslim observances and may not realize that this is only a starting point. One way of looking at the significance of *saum* and the month of *Ramadan* is to highlight three levels of meaning:

- ✓ **The literal level:** No eating, drinking, smoking, or having sex.

- ✓ **The moral level:** While fasting, the believer avoids other sins, such as lying, slander, and anger, which can annul the efficacy of the day's fast and require the addition of another day of fasting. Through fasting, she experiences the deprivation that the poor suffer throughout the year, becoming more sensitive and responsive to their plight.

- ✓ **The spiritual level:** By cutting themselves off from distractions during the fast, Muslims become attuned to God as the only ultimate reality. Muslims sense a closeness to God during *Ramadan* that is more intense than at other times of the year.

The observance of *Ramadan* is a source of blessing and not a time of trial. Tradition says that during *Ramadan,* the gates of heaven are opened, the gates of hell are closed, and Satan is put into chains. Fasting during *Ramadan,* therefore, is 30 times better than at any other time. The great Muslim theologian al-Ghazali said that fasting at *Ramadan* is one-quarter of the faith.

`Id al-fitr (feast of the breaking of the fast)

As the evening of the 29th of *Ramadan* approaches, Muslims eagerly wait to see whether the new moon is sighted, signaling the end of *Ramadan* and the beginning of one of the two great festivals of Islam: `*id al-fitr* (the other great festival is the sacrifice during the celebration of the pilgrimage). This time of rejoicing lasts for three days. People attend a special *salat* with sermon in the mosque on the first day. Muslims give an additional *zakat (zakat al-fitr)* directly to the poor. Local customs include going to graveyards, visiting friends, exchanging small gifts, and preparing and sharing special foods.

During `*id al-fitr,* you may greet your Muslim friends with *Eid Mubarak* (blessed `*id*) and get a response of *Eid Karim* (generous `*id*). To send an electronic `*id* card, go to www.soundvision.com.

Hajj (Fifth Pillar): Making the Pilgrimage to Mecca

Even people who know nothing about Islam use Mecca as a synonym for an ultimate goal. The pilgrimage last from the 8th to 12th of Dhul-hijja, which is the 12th and last month of the Muslim year. Many pilgrims set out several months ahead of time in order to spend an extended time in the holy cities. Due to safe travel conditions and modern air transportation, more than two million people make *hajj* each year. Caring for the pilgrims — food, housing, guides, movement from place to place, even sanitation and toilet facilities — is a major logistical challenge for the Saudi government.

The requirement is that each Muslim make the pilgrimage once in his or her life, if able to do so. Muslims don't go into debt or sacrifice the material well being of their families in order to undertake the trip. Not surprisingly, then, to go on *hajj* gives prestige to the individual, who can then use the honorific title of *hajji* (*hajja* for a woman).

The pilgrimage was important from the earliest Islamic times as illustrated in Sura 22:27, 29, which says, "Proclaim the Pilgrimage among men: they will come to you on foot and on animals lean from the journey through distant mountain highways and deep ravines…. Then let them complete the prescribed rites, perform their vows and circle the ancient house [the *Ka`ba*]."

If you're not Muslim, you may still have the opportunity to observe Muslim practices, such as *salat* and the observance of *saum* in *Ramadan.* However, you'll never be able go to Mecca and Medina in order to see the *hajj* in person. The area around these two cities is a sacred area prohibited *(haram)*

to non-Muslims. Fortunately, nothing about the *hajj* itself is secret. Through several videos, you can vicariously experience the *hajj*. A widely distributed video is the ABC *Nightline* account of the *hajj*, narrated and photographed by Michael Wolff and an ABC team of Muslim photographers (see Appendix C).

The center of the earth

Why are Mecca and the *hajj* so important to Islam? Mecca was already an important Arabian pilgrimage sanctuary in pre-Islamic times, and important elements of the *hajj* ritual go back to before the time of Muhammad. At first, due to warfare between the young Muslim community in Medina and the city of Mecca, Muslims were unable to make the pilgrimage. When the Muslims conquered Mecca in 630, the first act was to cleanse the *Ka`ba,* the ancient sanctuary of Mecca, of its many pagan statues. Shortly before his death in 632, Muhammad made his farewell pilgrimage to Mecca. This pilgrimage provides the definitive model for subsequent performance of the pilgrimage.

The *Ka`ba* (literally "cube") is a simple cube whose walls are 35 feet on two sides, 40 feet on the other two sides, and about 50 feet high. It is covered with a black cloth decorated with a band of verses from the Qur'an embroidered in gold. This covering is renewed each year. A sacred black stone (about 11 x 15 inches) in a silver frame is set about 5 feet off the ground in the southeast corner of the *Ka`ba.* To the left of the Black Stone, in the center of the east wall is the entry door leading into the empty *Ka`ba.* The center of the *Ka`ba* is the place toward which one faces in prayer. When inside the *Ka`ba,* one may pray in any direction. The Grand Mosque *(al-masjid al-Haram)* encloses the *Ka`ba,* which stands in its open, central courtyard.

Get me to the *hajj* on time

Before World War II, 10,000 or fewer people made the pilgrimage each year. The journey not only took a long time, but often was physically and economically dangerous due to attacks of bandits and exactions of tolls on pilgrim caravans on the way to Mecca. Many people who made the trip in pre-modern times stopped along the way for extended periods. Scholars from distant lands stayed in Mecca and Medina for months or years, exchanging ideas with other scholars. Many *hajj* journeys took two years to get there and one to two years to return home.

One estimate is that ten percent of Muslims alive today will, at some point, go on pilgrimage, although that proportion may increase. Although the Saudi government exercises strict control over the pilgrimage and the number of pilgrims allowed from various countries, the *hajj* remains a major opportunity for interaction among people from various parts of the Muslim world.

According to the Qur'an, Adam built the first *Ka`ba*. Later, Abraham and his son Ishmael rebuilt it. In performing the *hajj*, Muslims not only re-enact the final pilgrimage of Muhammad, but also recall events associated with Abraham. A *hadith* (tradition) says the Black Stone came down from heaven and Adam placed it in the first *Ka`ba*. Later, the angel Gabriel took the stone out of hiding and gave it to Abraham to place in the rebuilt *Ka`ba*. Another tradition says the stone was originally white but was turned black by the sins of humanity. The *Ka`ba* is also called the house of God and is believed to be a replica of the house of God in the seventh heaven, where God's throne is located. Worshippers, in circling around the *Ka`ba,* duplicate the movements of the angels continuously circling around the throne of God.

Ibn Ishaq's eighth-century biography of Muhammad reports that when the *Ka`ba* was rebuilt in about 605 — five years before Muhammad's call to be a prophet — quarreling among the clans for the honor of putting the stone back into its place almost led to civil war. Muhammad, because of his reputation for fairness, was asked to settle the dispute. He put the stone on a cloak and told each clan chief to grasp one end of the cloak and thus all together carry the stone to the wall of the *Ka`ba*. Muhammad then replaced the stone into its place in the corner of the wall.

The days of pilgrimage

Muslims going on *hajj* sign up with a religious tourist agency in their home country and go with a group. Upon arrival in Saudi Arabia, each group is assigned a guide who helps them perform the various activities of the *hajj*, which can be confusing to a Muslim who speaks little Arabic and hasn't previously been on *hajj*.

Consecrating oneself: Ihram

The pilgrims begin their *hajj* when they leave their normal mode of life and enter into a state of consecration *(ihram)*. Most pilgrims arrive at the Jeddah airport and enter into *ihram* there if they haven't already done so on the plane or at their departure airports. First, they perform the major purification *(ghusl),* which involves a total washing of the body. Then, the pilgrims affirm the intention to perform *hajj*. Men put on two plain, white, seamless garments, one covering the body from the waist down and the other draped over the right shoulder and gathered at the waist. No specific dress is prescribed for women. They cover their hair but don't wear a veil, jewelry, or perfume. Because sewn and leather items aren't permitted, pilgrims wear plastic sandals and a plastic belt for money and documents. No longer can one tell by appearance who is rich and powerful and who is poor: all stand as equals before God. While in the state of consecration, Muslims aren't permitted to cut their hair or nails, or have sexual relations. At this time, pilgrims utter the prayer called the *talbiya,* which they repeat frequently over the following week: *labbayk allahumma labbayk* ("here I am, my God, here I am"). Tradition attributes this prayer to Abraham when he instituted the pilgrimage ritual.

Circling the Ka`ba: Tawaf and `umra

After purification and entrance into Mecca, the pilgrims proceed to circle seven times counter-clockwise around the *Ka`ba*. This circling is called the *tawaf* and it expresses the unity of God *(tawhid)*. All try to touch the Black Stone but most have to settle for making a gesture toward the stone. Lest it be thought that Muslims are worshipping the stone, a *hadith* reports that the caliph `Umar said, "I know that you're only a stone which doesn't have the power to do good or evil. If I hadn't seen the prophet kissing you, I wouldn't kiss you." Following the *tawaf*, pilgrims offer a personal prayer at a spot between the Black Stone and the door of the *Ka`ba*.

At the station of Abraham a few steps to the northeast, pilgrims perform a two-*rak`a salat*. Here, Abraham stood while building the *Ka`ba*. Next, pilgrims drink from the well of Zamzam. As his mother, Hagar, ran to and fro seeking water lest they both die of thirst, the infant Ishmael kicked his heel into the ground and water appeared, making a gurgling noise (sounding like *zam*). Pilgrims take small bottles of this water home. Today, pilgrims go down a flight of steps to a gallery where the sanitized water flows through a number of faucets. Finally, pilgrims walk and run *(sa'y)* seven times between the two small hills of Safa and Marwa, in memory of Hagar's search for water. Since the 1970s reconstruction of the mosque, this 900-plus-foot course is within the northeast wall of the mosque.

The activities mentioned so far, if performed outside of the *hajj* season, constitute the `*umra* (meaning lesser pilgrimage), which is an act of piety but not a fulfillment of the *hajj*. If not on *hajj*, at this point pilgrims terminate the state of consecration.

The Grand Mosque

Even in the Qur'an, the term *masjid* is used for any place where God is worshipped. The term is not limited to Muslim sites and need not be a building. The Grand Mosque was built by `Umar, the second caliph (successor to Muhammad) and has been expanded and rebuilt a number of times since. The essential form of the present structure goes back to the Ottoman rebuilding under the direction of the famous architect Sinan in the 16th century. The only major subsequent rebuilding and expansion took place in the 1970s under King Faysal and retained as much as possible of the Ottoman structure. Today's mosque accommodates up to a million people and is 20 times the size of St. Peter's basilica in Rome.

Statistics and logistics of the *hajj*

Here are some interesting statistics about the *hajj* from the May/June 2002 issue of *Saudi Aramco World*. From a logistical standpoint, the *hajj* has become one of the most astounding annual events. In 2002, 2,371,468 pilgrims (45 percent of whom were women) made the *hajj*, compared with 294,000 pilgrims in 1965. They arrived in 6,226 flights at the Jeddah airport, where pilgrims boarded one of 15,000 buses.

The $275 fee for the *hajj* visa included guides, tent housing, local transportation, and Zamzam water. There were 43,200 tents at Mina, housing an average of 40 pilgrims each. Tents have full facilities, including electricity, bathrooms, and evaporative cooling. 2,100 guides, 26,500 crowd-control officers, 14,000 garbage collectors, and 3,300 barbers (for the shaving at deconsecration) serviced the pilgrims. Over a million goats and sheep (each costing $131.57) were sacrificed.

Standing at `Arafat: Wuquf

Before nightfall, the pilgrims depart for the village of Mina, about five miles from Mecca, where they spend the night. Some continue on and spend the night at the plain of `Arafat, 12 miles southwest of Mecca. The next day, the ninth of the month, they spend standing for all or a portion of the time between noon and sunset on the plain of `Arafat or the low "mount of mercy" from which Muhammad delivered his sermon on his farewell pilgrimage. A misting spray of water from sprinklers mounted atop tall poles helps reduce the temperature on the plain of `Arafat. The standing at `Arafat provides a foretaste of the Day of Judgment, when some traditions say that Muslims who completed the *hajj* will appear in their *hajj* garments. This day is the peak of the pilgrimage experience.

Sacrificing: `Id al-adha

After sunset on the 9th day of the month, the overflowing or rush occurs. The masses of pilgrims hurry back toward Mina and Mecca, with the night being spent at Muzdalifah. The next day the pilgrims gather 49 or 70 pebbles (no smaller than a chickpea or larger than a hazelnut) and depart to Mina. At Mina, they cast seven pebbles at the largest of three pillars. This recalls the incident when Abraham was called upon by God to sacrifice his son Ishmael. The birth of Isaac was a reward to Abraham for being willing to obey God's command to sacrifice Ishmael. (In the Bible, Genesis 22, it's the younger son Isaac who was to be sacrificed rather than Ishmael). Tradition reports that Satan three times called out to Ishmael, tempting him to opt out of being sacrificed. The casting of stones represents the rejection of the temptation of Satan. Details of the temptation vary in the traditions, some of which include also the temptation of Abraham and of Ishmael's mother, Hagar.

At this point or any time through the 12th of the month, the sacrifice of the `id al-Adha*, the great `id*, is performed at Mina. On the 10th of the month, Muslims around the world perform this same sacrifice. The traditional greeting is the same as for *Ramadan: Eid Mubarak.* A goat, sheep, camel, or cow is sacrificed in memory of the ram provided to Abraham by God as a sacrifice in place of his son. The family head performs the sacrifice in the specified manner and shares the meat with neighbors and with the poor. How to handle and distribute all the excess meat resulting from the observance at Mina is a major logistical challenge for the Saudi government.

Just as Abraham was willing to sacrifice that which was most precious to Him, so every Muslim should be willing to sacrifice everything for God. Anyone who dies during the course of his *hajj* journey is a martyr who will go immediately to paradise.

The state of consecration comes to an end, symbolized by shaving the head (men only) or cutting a lock of hair. Pilgrims may remove their pilgrimage clothing and resume normal activities (except for sexual intercourse). They return to Mecca for the second circling of the *Ka`ba (tawaf al-ifada).* If they didn't do the *tawaf* on arrival or did the *tawaf* without the running between Safa and Marwa, they do these now.

Ending the pilgrimage

The final three days of the *hajj*, the 11th, 12th, and 13th of Dhul-hijja, are called the *Days of Drying Meat.* Each day, those remaining cast seven pebbles at each of the three pillars at Mina. A modern two-story ramp accommodates the large numbers of people involved.

Pilgrims may end the pilgrimage on the 12th day. During this period, a new covering is put on the *Ka`ba.* Before final departure from Mecca, pilgrims usually make a third circling of the *Ka`ba (tawaf al-wada).* meaning circling of farewell) and offer a farewell prayer: "O Lord, do not make this my last visit to your house, and grant me the chance to return here again and again."

Making the side trip to Medina (al-ziyarah)

After the *hajj* is over, most pilgrims desire to make the visit *(al-ziyarah)* to the tomb of the prophet in Medina, where tradition suggests places to visit and prayers to recite. More puritanical Muslims, such as the Wahhabis, who control Islamic practice in Saudi Arabia, discourage anything that may lead to worship of a human, including visits to the graves of saints or even to the grave of Muhammad. Despite the prohibition on visits to saints' tombs, the Wahhabis are unable to prohibit visits to the tomb of Muhammad. Like

Mecca, a sacred area *(haram)* open only to Muslims surrounds this second most-holy city and second most-holy mosque *(masjid an-Nabi or al-masjid al-Sharif)* of Islam. In accord with the tradition that prophets are buried where they die, Muhammad was buried in the room of his favorite wife, `A'isha, in whose arms he died. Muhammad's first three successors, Abu Bakr, `Umar, and `Uthman, are also buried here.

TIP

Where to go next year?

Many people make the *hajj* or the `*umra* (lesser pilgrimage/circumambulation) more than once. But you can find other voluntary pilgrimages in Islam:

✔ **Jerusalem:** Jerusalem is an important pilgrimage city for Christianity, Islam, and Judaism, and is a bone of contention at various times among these great monotheistic faiths. It's the third most-holy city in Islam. The Arabic name of Jerusalem is *al-Quds* (the Holy). The *al-aqsa mosque* (the farthest mosque) is the third most-holy mosque in Islam. It and the shrine of `Umar (the Dome of the Rock) are located in the sanctuary area *(haram al-sharif,* the noble sanctuary), which is the platform area constructed by King Herod in his first century B.C.E. renovation of the Jewish temple. In addition to being holy to Muslims because of its association with Jesus, David, Solomon, Abraham, and the Jewish prophets, the city is also holy because it's identified as the destination of Muhammad on his night journey *(al-isra')*. Pilgrims and tourists visiting the Dome of the Rock can view the imprint made by his footprint as he ascended *(al-mi'raj)* up through the heavens (as noted in Sura 17:1–3).

✔ **Saint's tombs:** Although regarded as unorthodox by Wahhabis and other similar groups, pilgrimage to the tombs of Muslim saints plays an important role for many Muslims. Some of these shrines are of only local importance, but others attract pilgrims from an entire country or region and involve several days of ritual celebrations. Such annual festivals typically take place on the birthday of the saint or on the date of his death, which is his rebirth into heaven (see Chapter 10).

✔ **Special for Shi`ites:** Shi`ite Muslims observe the *hajj* as one of the Five Pillars of Worship. However, for many Shi`ites, a visit to shrines associated with the death and burial of the *imams* may be equally or more important. Most important of these Shi`ite pilgrimage sites are Karbala, where the martyrdom of Husayn, the grandson of the prophet, occurred in 680, and the shrine of `Ali at Nataf. Both sites are in Iraq (see Chapter 12).

✔ **Exploring oneself:** Although Sufis observe the *hajj*, as they do all of the Five Pillars of Worship, some emphasize the spiritual significance of the *hajj* to the point of saying that the more significant *hajj* is an inner one that the Sufi makes in approach to God.

Probably the pilgrimage best known to Americans is that of Malcolm X. As a result of his 1964 *hajj*, Malcolm X abandoned the racial separatism of the Nation of Islam, having experienced the coming together of blacks, whites, and Asians as equals during the *hajj*. His experience is narrated in *The Autobiography of Malcolm X* (Ballantine Books, Inc., 1992) as well as in Spike Lee's movie, *Malcolm X* (1992).

Chapter 10

Observing Other Religious Rituals and Customs

Scholars of religion often make a distinction between what some call the Great Tradition and the Little Tradition(s). Great Tradition is what the holy books of the religion teach and what official religious bodies have determined to be proper religious belief and practice. In the past, the Great Tradition of a particular religion has usually been what the official religious leaders — whether scholars, priests, monks, or rabbis — say it is. As a result, until recently, the Great Tradition was also religion as viewed by men, because most of these leadership positions were occupied by men. In contrast, the Little Tradition is religion as lived in the lives of ordinary people. Little Tradition religion includes popular or folk religious beliefs and practices, many of which aren't authorized in the scriptures and which may be in conflict with the official Great Tradition version of the religion. The Little Tradition also often includes many religious practices of women and provides women an avenue for religious expression (and exercise of religious leadership) which Great Tradition religion may have denied them.

Keep the following in mind as you go through this chapter:

✔ The extent to which these practices are observed and how they're observed varies widely from one Muslim culture to another, from one country to another, and from one age to another.

✔ Practices also vary according to education, social class, rural or urban setting, individual piety, and age.

> ✔ Describing what people actually do is more difficult than describing what official religious teachings say they "should" do. While official religion sets forth its beliefs and practices clearly, information isn't as easily available on the popular religion of the Little Tradition.
>
> ✔ Some Muslim theologians and legal scholars object to some of the practices associated with popular Islam because they believe such practices aren't supported by the Qur'an and the practice (tradition) of the first generation of Muslims. Movements have frequently arisen in Islam to purify the religion from practices of folk religion, some of which may have come from other religions or pre-exist Islam.

Rituals Linked to the Yearly Calendar

The Five Pillars of Worship (see Chapter 9) are more central from the standpoint of official religion than are other religious rituals, such as the celebration of Muhammad's birthday and rites of passage. In this section, I look at other ritual celebrations linked to the annual calendar, focusing on the celebration of the birthday of Muhammad and of other significant figures in the history of Islam. While not required by Islam law (and even opposed by some conservative Muslims), some of these rituals are equally important for many Muslims as are the Five Pillars.

Celebrating Muhammad's birthday

For most pre-modern religion, historians don't know the founders date of birth. Nevertheless, after a couple of centuries, celebration of the founder's birthday becomes important in religions such as Confucianism, Christianity, and Islam (but not for Judaism). Christianity eventually fixed the birth of Jesus on December 25 (the birthday of the divinities Mithras and Helios worshipped by the Roman legions), and Islam fixed the birth of Muhammad on the 12th of Rabi`a al-Awwal, the third month of the Islamic year. According to tradition, Muhammad also died on the same date.

Maulid an-nabi is the name given for both Muhammad's birthday and the celebration of the birthday, which is an official holiday in most Muslim countries except for Saudi Arabia. (The spelling of *maulid,* which means "birthday," varies from country to country: *mawlid, mulud, milad,* and *mevlut.*) This ceremony has become very popular, rivaling the two `*ids* (see Chapter 9).

Finding information about folk Islam

How does one find out about popular Islam (in contrast to the well documented official teachings)? It isn't easy. An academic discipline has developed over the past several generations to study popular culture. Popular religion is part of popular culture and can be studied in the same way. These scholars turn primarily not to the scriptures of the religion but to oral traditions, incidental reports (whose actual topic may be something else), and devotional poetry and writings. Anthropology provides another major source of information about religion. Anthropologists go to towns and villages where they may live for several years doing "case studies." They observe what is really happening and undertake in-depth oral interviews. Basically, anthropologists try to collect raw data much like a physical scientist does. A further step comes when the anthropologists tries to make sense of the data by providing an interpretative framework. The anthropologist pays attention to the explanations given by the people he's studying but looks also for other explanations of what is going on. Although they weren't trained anthropologists, some people who have lived or traveled extensively in Muslims countries in past centuries have written about what they have observed, and their works are treasure troves of information. One often cited such work is E. W. Lane's book, *Manners and Customs of the Modern Egyptians* (American University in Cairo Press, reprinted in 2002), first published in 1836 and based on five years of living in the country much as a native would live.

You can turn to many places to get information about official religion. Unfortunately, getting an overview of the popular Islam as a whole is much more difficult. Remember how the anthropologist works. She does intensive field work in a single village or group of villages. Ideally, when enough such studies have been done, the anthropologist or some other scholar of religion can combine those studies to produce an overview of popular Islam. Much more work and many more studies are required to arrive at the point of an overall description of popular Islam. A useful resource is the Islamic sections of articles dealing with folk religion, popular religion, rites of passage, and the Islamic religious year in *The Encyclopedia of Religion* (MacMillan Publishing, 1987). Another useful overview on which I draw is Chapter 14 of Frederick Denny's *An Introduction to Islam* (MacMillan Publishing Company, 1994). Several times in this chapter, I use examples from Morocco simply because that's where some of the most extensive anthropological studies have been done. A useful English-language Muslim source from the standpoint of Islamic law (rather than an effort to describe what people actually do) is Yusuf al-Qaradawi's *The Lawful and the Prohibited in Islam* (American Trust Publications).

Typical elements in the celebration of the maulid

Although details vary greatly, a typical *maulid* celebration may involve the following elements:

✔ A multi-day festival, culminating on the two evenings of the 11th and 12th of the month.

✔ A carnival-like atmosphere with tents, entertainment, and special sweets.

In recent times, some governments have deemphasized the carnival atmosphere and promoted the festival as a time to take moral inspiration from Muhammad's life.

✔ Processions with lights, recitations, and songs.

✔ Qur'anic recitations, prayers, and poems about Muhammad.

✔ A link with Sufi *dhikr* ceremonies (see Chapter 13).

Many countries have their own *maulid* customs. In Morocco, a child is considered lucky to be born during the *maulid* and thus may be named Mauludiyya. The *maulid* is also a good time to circumcise boys. People in some countries celebrate with a feast and give gifts to the poor.

The maulud poems

Maulud recitations are the distinctive feature of the *maulid* celebration. *Mauluds* are prose and especially poetic compositions celebrating the birth of Muhammad. A *maulud* may be composed in a variety of literary genres, such as the *qasida* and the *mathnavi* (see Chapter 6). A typical *maulud* contains the following elements:

✔ Opening invocation and praise of God.

✔ The creation of the "light of Muhammad" (see Chapter 6).

✔ Miscellaneous information such as the ancestry of Muhammad.

✔ Announcement of the Muhammad's conception to his mother, Amina.

✔ An account of his birth and the miracles that occurred at that time.

The history of the *maulid*

Soon after Muhammad's death, Muslims began to make pilgrimages to the house in Medina where he died. Not until 170 years later, however, did the mother of caliph (the Muslim ruler) Harun al-Rashid restore his birth house as a place to visit. The Fatimid rulers of Egypt (909–1171) were the first to make his birthday a major celebration.

One of the earliest detailed descriptions of a *maulid* is one sponsored by the Abbasid government in Iraq in 1207. The writer describes torchlight processions, singing, sermons, poems, and gifts. By the end of the 13th century, the *maulid* festival had become a major event in Egypt, and it spread from there over most parts of the Muslim world.

Mauluds may include incidents from Muhammad's life, especially the ascension into heaven. Other poems in praise of Muhammad, such as al-Busiri's *Burda,* are frequently recited (see Chapter 6). *Maulud* poems are also recited as part of circumcision rituals, when commemorating the death of a loved one, and during Sufi *dhikr* ceremonies (see Chapter 13). The recitation conveys a blessing *(baraka)* upon both reciter and the hearer. *Maulud* recordings by professional singers are popular.

Two examples relating to the conception and birth of Muhammad illustrate the type of legendary embellishment of the story that occurs in this popular literature. These birth accounts recall the tone of the popular stories of the birth of the Buddha. The first example is from a very popular Turkish *maulud,* the *mevlud-i sheriff,* written by Suleyman Chelebi in Turkey (about 1400). In the poem, three heavenly ladies, including Jesus' mother, tell Muhammad's mother of the coming birth. When the time of birth is near, Amina becomes thirsty and is given a cup of heavenly sherbet to drink. A white swan comforts Amina, Muhammad's mother, in her labor pains by touching her back with its wing. A somewhat later *maulud* popular especially in Africa is that of the 18th-century Islamic judge, al-Barzanji of Medina. His original prose account has been translated into many languages and transposed into poetry. The prose version talks about how on the night Muhammad was conceived, the fruits of the trees ripened and themselves approached the person picking the fruit. Animals spoke eloquently in Arabic of the child Amina had conceived. These miracles (and many others related in the *mauluds*) emphasize the future greatness of Muhammad and contrast with the view of the early traditions and the theologians that Muhammad's only miracle was his transmission of the Qur'an. To imagine the effect of such poetry and celebration on ordinary Muslims, think of the emotional effect upon Christians of the music and lyrics of numerous Christmas carols. See also Chapter 6 on Muhammad, and Annemarie Schimmel's *And Muhammad is His Messenger* (University of North Carolina Press, 1985) for the best treatment of the veneration of Muhammad in Islam, including a chapter on the *maulid* celebrations and *maulud* poetry.

Condemning the maulid celebrations

The 14th-century legal scholar Ibn Taymiyya condemned the celebration an illegitimate innovation *(bid`a),* and the modern Wahabbi conservatives have banned it in Saudi Arabia. Others declared the *maulid* a worthy innovation. Those opposing do so for the following reasons:

✔ The Qur'an and genuine *hadiths* don't mention the celebration.

✔ The ceremony borders on worship of Muhammad, who is only a man.

✔ The ceremonies show Christian influences.

✔ The celebration encourages emotional excesses.

✔ Improper intermingling of women and men occurs at the *maulid.*

A primer on saints' tombs

Saints' tombs can be in the congested city or out in the countryside. (In fact, a visit to a shrine out of the heart of the city may be a vacation or a day retreat with no explicit religious purpose.) The typical saint's tomb (*qubba,* which means "dome") consists of a dome on top of an octagonal drum atop a square, small building, but some are far more elaborate and include mosques, sleeping quarters for visitors, and other facilities. The tomb may have a permanent caretaker or be tended by descendants of the saint (some are even supported with endowed funds, called *waqf*). In rural areas of some countries, you're in sight of a saint's tomb no matter where you are. In fact, anthropologist Dale Eickelman calculates that one saint's tomb exists for each six square kilometers in Morocco (or one for every 150 people).

Honoring the saints

An Islamic saint, who is called a "friend *(wali)* of God," may be honored in a number of ways. In fact, more than 300 saints' festivals occur in Egypt alone. One of best documented *maulids* is that of Sayyid Ahmad al-Badawi, the founder of the Ahmadiyya Sufi order in Egypt, whose autumn *maulid* draws well over a million pilgrims.

Although neither the Qur'an nor early *hadiths* mentions *walis* as saints, the concept is well established. Sura 10:63 says, "Surely God's friends — no fears comes on them nor do they grieve."

In addition to the Wahhabis, some Islamic modernists and secularists have also attacked the admiration of saints as signs of Islamic superstition. So, with urbanization and rising educational levels, some saint shrines today are deserted, and some previously prominent saint festivals draw few attendees. But saints continue to thrive in Islam. Certain festivals for saints draw from 10,000 to 50,000 devotees a day.

In some cases, sites associated with saints were holy prior to the country or group of people accepting Islam. In Indonesia, sacred snakes *(nagas)* derived from Hinduism guard the entrances to some saint shrines. In South Asia, Muslim saints competed with Hindu saints for prestige and miracle-working power.

Revering the saints' tombs

One elaborate ritual when honoring Islamic saints focuses on visiting a saint's shrine as need arises. Upon entering the shrine, Muslims approach the saint's tomb and touch it, offer a prayer, and then withdraw some distance. Petitioners of this sort, who tend to be mostly women (see the "Looking at

Women's Rituals" section later in this chapter), seek the saint's help, for example, to cure illness, heal infertility, aid a son in his exams, mediate marital problems, or solve financial difficulties. They vow to make a gift to the saint if the petition is granted, but they give no payment in advance.

The great occasion for visiting a saint's tomb is the celebration of the saint's *maulid* — or, in some cases, his death date, which is referred to as his marriage *(urs)*. In a pilgrimage *(ziyara)* to a saint's tomb, one circles around the saint's grave just as the *hajj* pilgrim circles around the *Ka`ba* in Mecca (see Chapter 9). Qur'an recitations, sermons, prayers, gifts, foods, and Sufi *dhikr* ceremonies (see Chapter 13) occur during the *maulid.*

Finding out who is a saint

The word "saint," meaning holy person, is specific to Christianity. But many religions have the equivalent and in English we use the term saint also for holy, charismatic individuals of other religions. Unlike Roman Catholicism, no official *canonization* (saint-inducting) procedure exists in Islam. A person becomes a saint when the people treat the person like a saint. This usually happens after the death of the person but the line is somewhat fuzzy between a living holy person with perceptible charisma or "power" (or *baraka,* meaning "blessing") and a dead person who had the same attributes. The saint may have visions, be illiterate, perform miracles, be a non-conformist, or engage in ecstatic behavior. Both men and women may be saints.

In Islam, Moses, Daniel, and Elijah are saints, as are some heroic figures of Islamic history. A shrine to Ayyub is one of the most important in Turkey. He was a contemporary of Muhammad and the flag bearer who died beneath the walls of Constantinople in a failed attack on the city in 669. Legend says the Ottomans were inspired to victory in their conquest of Constantinople in 1453 by a light emanating from Ayyub's tomb. Similarly, the nine Muslims who introduced Islam to Indonesia are regarded as saints.

Most Sufi founders (see Chapter 13) are regarded as saints, but certainly not all saints are Sufis. In Shi`ism (see Chapter 12), the families of the *imams* take the place of the saints in Sunni Islam (Sunni Islam being the most popular way of practicing Islam). Some suggest that the practice of pilgrimage to the tomb of Ayatolla Khomeini indicates he has acquired saint status.

Al-Tirmidhi, ninth century author of one of the six authoritative collections of Islamic traditions *(hadiths)* wrote the first definitive Muslim work on sainthood. His work came at a time when saints had become important in Islam and thus scholars began to address the issue of saints in Islam. Many Islamic believers weren't concerned about the opinions of the scholars. For such ordinary people, stories of saints became a popular literary genre and an inspiration for their faith. Manuals were composed for pilgrims to saints' tombs. Sufi (mystic) writers developed theories about the hierarchy of saints.

Islamic belief said that Muhammad was the seal (last) of the prophets sent by God. Some individuals claimed to be the "seal of the saints," implying that they were the last of the saints of God. One such person was al-Tijani (1737–1815), founder of one of the major modern Sufi orders of West and Northwest Africa, who claimed that Muhammad himself (in a vision) had commissioned him as the seal of the saints and the founder of a new Sufi order.

Reviewing other rituals

In the following list, I describe some ritual observations that are of less importance that those in Chapter 9 or than those mentioned in the preceding sections of this chapter. Note that I discuss specific Shi`ite and Sufi rituals (the *dhikr* and the *sama*) in Chapters 12 and 13, respectively.

✔ **`Ashura':** Before the institution of the *Ramadan* fast, Muslims fasted on `ashura', and Sunnis today may observe `ashura' as a voluntary fast. Tradition says that `ashura' is also the day that Adam and Eve were expelled from paradise and that Noah exited from the ark after the flood. In some countries, `ashura' is linked with visits to tombs of the dead. In Mecca, the door which opens to the interior of the empty *Ka`ba,* the most holy sacred shrine of Islam in Mecca, is opened on `ashura'.

✔ **Fifteenth of Sha`ban:** Tradition says that on the 15th of *Sha`ban* (the eighth month), the tree of paradise is shaken. Each living person's name is inscribed on one leaf. If the leaf falls off, the person will die in the coming year. Special prayers and Sura 36 are recited after sunset. In South Asia and Indonesia, ceremonies for the dead are held on this day. This is also the date of Muhammad's entry into Mecca in 630 (see Chapter 6).

✔ **Twenty-seventh of Rajab:** This date marks Muhammad's night journey to Jerusalem and ascension into heaven (discussed in Chapter 6). Many Muslims celebrate the day with processions and prayers.

✔ **Other special days:** Various Muslim countries celebrate the days of their special saints and also other events from Muhammad's life. Turkish Muslims celebrate Amina's conception of Muhammad at the beginning of *Rajab.* Shi`ites celebrate the birth of `Ali on the 13th of *Rajab.* Iranians celebrate the pre-Islamic Persian New Year's day *(nawruz)* for 12 days at the spring equinox. This same day, God created Adam, Abraham destroyed the pagan idols, and Muhammad chose `Ali as his successor.

Marking Life's Transitions

Many religions, including Islam, claim to be a total way of life. When religion pervades all of life, most major transitions in life, such as birth, marriage, and death (often called *rites of passage*), have religious significance and are marked by religious rituals.

Born yesterday

In some Islamic countries, as in other countries, pregnancy and the period between pregnancy and birth may be marked by celebrations, visits, and special foods. I start with what is the first main event in the life cycle, the birth of the child and associated rituals. Even this event, as with all the life cycle rituals, may be marked by additional rituals from the local culture that are not closely connected with Islam. For example, among the Yoruba tribe in Nigeria, many Muslim parents conduct an ancient naming ceremony designed to ensure the child a safe entry into the world, as well as a separate Islamic naming ceremony. Also in Islam, the naming and the other events are intended to welcome the new child into the Muslim community and ensure protection from any evils that may threaten the child at this first major life transition.

At birth, the father speaks the first *(adhan)* and second *(iqama)* calls to prayer (see Chapter 9) in the child's right and left ears. The father is encouraged to chew the meat of a date and put a little bit in the child's mouth because, as a number of traditions report (without explaining why), this is what Muhammad did when his children were born. Friends bring small gifts, and Sura 1, the *Fatiha* (see Chapter 7), is recited in the presence of the infant.

Celebrations mark the birth. During these early days of the infant's life, the parents may take special action (such as good-luck charms or special spoken formulas) to ensure that evil *jinns* (see Chapter 5) don't injure the child.

Receiving a name

The father chooses the child's name in consultation with the mother and other relatives. He may name the child at birth, but naming occurs normally when the infant is one week old. In the interval, the parents may call the child Muhammad or Fatima (the name of one of the daughters of Muhammad).

What will the father name the child? Compound names that indicate a close relation to God are popular — such as Abadallah (servant of God). Also highly recommended are any names linked to Muhammad and his family, including Muhammad (or any of the other names commonly used for Muhammad such as Ahmad) and `Ali (the husband of Fatima) for boys, and Fatima for girls. Shi`ite Muslims tend to favor names of the members of the 12 imams' families (see Chapter 12). Names not connected with Islam are permitted, but modern Islamist reform movements urge the use of Arabic names which have specific Islamic meaning. As a result, Islamic names have become increasingly popular in non-Arabic countries such as Indonesia and the United States. In Arabic culture, a person usually receives a number of names — some acquired during his life — which are strung together and indicate important information about the person, which puts him or her in a social context (see the "Understanding Muslim names" sidebar).

All Muslims follow the basic naming custom of speaking the call to prayer in the infant's ear and reciting the *Fatiha*. Further details depend on the country, who is present for the ceremony (in addition to father, mother, and the infant), how the participants are dressed, and whether a feast or special meal is involved. For example, in Morocco, both mother and child wear special clothes, and their faces, hands, and feet are decorated with henna (reddish-brown cosmetic dye) designs.

Offering the sacrifice

The `aqiqa sacrifice, recalling Abraham's intended sacrifice of his son, often occurs along with the naming of the one-week-old child. Only the Hanbalites say this is a required ritual, but other branches of Islamic laws recommend it, especially for boys.

The sacrifice is two male sheep or goats for a boy and one for a girl — if the parents can afford to do so. Some of the animal is donated to the poor. In addition, wealthy parents may cut the child's hair, weigh it, and donate an equivalent amount of silver or other forms of cash or valuables to the poor or to a charitable foundation.

Circumcising (khitan)

Circumcision is not mentioned in the Qur'an but is almost universal among Muslim males, although only the Shafi`ite legal School mandates the practice for both sexes. Male circumcision is the removal of the foreskin from the penis. Male circumcision is based upon the belief shared with the Jews that Abraham, the common ancestor of Jews and Muslims, circumcised his sons (see Genesis 17). Circumcision also occurs in other cultures such as ancient Egypt. In Arabic, the rite is called purification *(tahara)*, pointing to one of its functions. Muslim scholars may also associate circumcision (male and female) with control (not elimination) of the passions of the lower self (called the *nafs*).

The age of circumcision for boys differs from birth to about age 15 depending upon the country. In some countries it is done at the time of birth or in infancy, and functions in the larger context of rituals that accompany birth and infancy. Probably most common is circumcision around the age of six to seven, when the boy is about to begin to assume his religious responsibilities by participating in *salat* (Islamic prayer). In countries such as Java (part of Indonesia) and Yemen, circumcision is a coming-of-age (puberty) ritual when the child is between 10 and 12. In these cases, circumcision may be linked with the boy having completed recitation of the Qur'an in Qur'anic school. In still other countries, circumcision is done a couple of years later and functions as a preparation for marriage and full participation as an adult in the community. Sometimes, circumcision is a major celebration with special dress, foods, and processions. In some countries, several boys may share the same celebration of their circumcision. Among modernist Muslims, circumcision is more often a private, family occasion. Circumcision is recommended but not required for male converts to Islam.

For girls, circumcision has never been marked by major celebrations. Female circumcision (also called *clitoridectomy*) can vary from removal of a small portion of the prepuce of the clitoris to removal of the clitoris, the labia minora, and portions of the labia majora. Female circumcision is common in Upper Egypt, Sudan, Somalia, Ethiopia, West Africa, Southeast Asia, Southern Arabia, and parts of Indonesia. Where we have data, female circumcision in these areas (like male circumcision) seems to have predated the advent of Islam and thus doesn't originate due to Islamic influence.

Based on a tradition in which Muhammad advised against cutting a women severely (in circumcision), some Muslim authorities discourage female circumcision entirely saying that Muhammad allowed but did not recommend the practice; others say the minimal form is recommended but not obligatory; some say it is required and still others say it's not permitted because mutilation of the body is against Islamic law. Even in the same country, one group may practice female circumcision and an adjacent group may not. A worldwide campaign has emerged against "female genital mutilation."

Coming of age

One way of defining *coming of age* in Islam is to say that this is the point at which the child becomes responsible for performing the Five Pillars of Worship (see Chapter 9). Generally at about this same time, the child is expected to observe the rules regulating contact and separation among the sexes. However, Islam does not have a universally accepted coming-of-age ritual comparable to the bar/bat mitzvah ceremony in Judaism. In some countries circumcision (depending on the age at which circumcision is done) or ceremonies celebrating the completion of learning to recite the entire Qur'an function as coming-of-age ceremonies.

Understanding Muslim names

To a non-Muslim, Muslim names can be confusing because an individual may take many names. This sidebar attempts to clarify the confusion. Typically, Muslim people have five different types of names, some of which they bear from birth and others that are acquired later in life. In giving the full name of a person, the sequence below is typically followed but isn't invariable.

✔ The *ism* is the birth name that the father gives the child as just described. The *ism* is equivalent to the personal name of Westerners and, as noted, can be a non-Muslim name.

✔ When people have their first child, they acquire another name (the *kunya*), which may precede the *ism,* in the form Abu Talib (father of Talib) or Umm Fatima (mother of Fatima). Normally, you address a person by this name.

✔ The *nasab* indicates the father or mother of the person in the form Ibn `Ali (son of `Ali) or Bint `Ali (daughter of `Ali). The name may go back more than one generation (son of A, who is son of B, and so on). More recently, one may simply juxtapose the name of son and father and dispense with "Ibn" and "Bint": "Ahmed `Ali" for Ahmed, the son of `Ali.

✔ The *laqab* includes many different types of honorific names and nicknames, such as "the deaf one" or "the baker" (but these names are always in Arabic).

✔ The *nisba* usually indicates the place a person comes from. It may also indicate tribal links or connections with a legal School (such as, "the Hanbalite").

The five names listed above represent traditional Arabic custom. Imagine that you want to look up in an encyclopedia some significant person in Islamic history. Unfortunately, there is no rule which determines under which of the five names a person is listed. You may simply have to try several of the person's names to find the entry, which is typically the name by which that individual has come to be commonly known. In countries like the United States where last names are a legal requirement, Muslim people have last names, perhaps determined when they (or their parents or grandparents) filled out their immigration or citizenship papers. Once established, that remains the family name just like anyone else's name, and that's how they are listed in the phone book. Indeed, because of respect for one's parents, one should normally retain the family name even if one has converted to Islam. Many converts in Western countries will take Arabic personal names, although this is not mandatory. Some African-American Muslims have taken different family names because they regard their original family name as a slave name which perhaps goes back to the slave owners of their ancestors.

Getting hitched

As in the case of other rites of passage, much variation exists in how marriage is celebrated. The minimum requirements involving whom one can marry and the requirements for a marriage contract and a dowry (agreed upon bridal gift from the husband to the bride) are followed by all Muslims so long as no conflict exists with local law. For example, Muslim men should not marry more than one wife in countries where polygamy is illegal. Beyond this minimum, as in the case of other rites of passage, much variation exists in terms of how a spouse is selected and regarding the various ceremonies that may begin with the contract and conclude with a wedding feast after consummation of the marriage.

Muslims are expected to marry, and the Qur'an and *hadiths* (traditions) encourage early marriage. The man and woman should be sexually mature and the man should be capable of supporting his wife financially. Practically speaking, a typical male would be in his late teens and the female the same age or several years younger, although earlier marriages occurr. Marriage isn't based on romantic love but rather on considerations like ancestry, property, how religious the proposed partner is, and benefits to both families. The couple may meet in the presence of a chaperon prior to signing the marriage contract, but this meeting isn't required. Although Muslim men may marry women of other people of the book (basically, Christians and Jews), Muslim women must marry Muslim men in order to ensure the children will be raised as Muslims. Islamic law also prohibits marrying close relatives. In countries where Muslims are a small minority of the population, Islamic organizations provide matchmaking services via the Internet, and one may place matrimonial advertisements in Islamic magazines.

In the eyes of the law

Marriage in Islam is a legal contract, not a religious sacrament. Legally, the marriage depends on a contract *(nika)* that includes the following:

✔ It is signed by the bride's father or guardian in the presence of two witnesses. This normally takes place before the actual wedding night.

The bride's father or guardian acts for the woman in marriage negotiations. Differences exist among legal Schools as to whether the guardian may force his choice on the bride, but in Islamic countries today, the bride's father or guardian is required to act in the interests of the bride. Adult women have more say in choosing a husband than young women do. In the 20th century, some Muslim states set minimum ages for marriage (for example, 18 and 16 for the man and woman respectively) and required registration of the marriage with the state.

✔ The groom's payment of a gift to the bride is based on Sura 4:4. Without this *dowry,* the marriage is invalid. The gift may be specified in the contract. While normally paid prior to the consummation of the marriage, the contract can allow for installment payments. The dowry remains the property of the wife to do with as she wishes, but in some cases she may be expected to buy furnishings for the home. The dowry may consist of money or goods. Tradition says that bridal gifts shouldn't be overly extravagant, although they should be comparable to what other brides of similar social status receive. Tradition reports Muhammad approving such things as a pair of sandals or a handful of flour in the case of a poor couple.

Here comes the bride: The ceremony

Islamic traditions agree that Muhammad commended holding a wedding celebration or feast, although this is not required by Islamic law. This is one way of fulfilling the requirement that a marriage take place in public. Beyond this, customs vary widely but at some point usually involve a party with singing, dancing, feasting, and perhaps Qur'anic recitations. Wedding celebrations (one or more) may be linked to signing of the contract, fetching of the bride to the groom's home, the night of the consummation of the wedding, and a wedding feast within two days after the wedding. However it is organized, this is a joyous occasion for the couple, the families, and the community. In these events, normal separation of men and women is observed. Honeymoons are not a traditional Muslim custom and some say Muslims in Western countries should not adopt the honeymoon custom. Others, recognizing that wedding customs in Islam generally combine Islamic requirements with local custom see nothing wrong in a honeymoon.

A person invited to a marriage celebration is obligated to accept the invitation.

Taking many wives

You've probably heard that Muslim men are allowed up to four wives. However, except among some traditional royalty, few Muslim men have more than one wife today. In parts of Africa where polygamy was traditional prior to Islam, it continued naturally under Islam.

Muhammad said that divorce is the most despised of the things that God nevertheless allows. No stigma attaches to marrying a divorced person, although tradition says it's better to choose a mate who is not divorced. Cases have existed in Muslim history of men abusing their rights of divorce. In the case where some Muslim men abuse their rights by marrying young girls, courts and legal reforms in a number of Muslim countries today endeavor to prevent such abuse. Muslims would say that today American men are more likely to have multiple wives — one after another — than are Muslim men (see Chapter 11).

Marriage as a coming-of-age passage

To some extent for men, but much more so for women, marriage is the equivalent to a coming-of-age ritual in many traditional Muslim societies. Women leave their home and assume the traditional women's tasks, such as managing the home and producing children.

In some countries, birth — even more than marriage or circumcision — marks the transition to adulthood for the mother. As in many pre-modern cultures, in some Muslim countries, special restrictions and purifications mark the integration of the new mother back into society (see Chapter 10 regarding purification requirements connected with loss of blood.) Special purifications may be required of the mother. Mother (and child) in some cases may undergo a period of seclusion — first to their room with no contacts outside the immediate family, then to the house, with broader contacts allowed during this period. Again the details of seclusion and purification after birth vary and are not specified in traditional Islamic law.

Knocking on death's door

Death, the event and its meaning, is an issue that all religions must guide its believers in how to handle it. While in other rites of passage, Islam has traditionally been willing to incorporate local customs or at least ignore them without objection, when it comes to the final transition — death — Islam is less willing to compromise with the practices of the local culture. Death in Islam is the point where it all comes together and determines the eternal destiny of the person. Death is natural, but still a momentous event. Beliefs and rituals for facing this transition should be dealt with in a strictly Islamic manner (see Chapter 5 for more on Islamic beliefs about what happens at death). Therefore, greater uniformity exists in the rituals associated with death in Islam than in any other of the rites of passage.

Dying

When death is imminent, a Muslim is placed on his right side, the first testimony ("there is no God but Allah") is whispered in his ear, and Sura 36 is recited, including verse 12, which says, "We [God] give life to the dead and record that which they have forwarded and that which they have left behind," and also, "And the trumpet [announcing the Day of Judgment] will be blown, and men will slide forth out of their tombs to their Lord."

Preparing for burial

Because death is natural, no unnatural effort should be expended to make it appear as if death hasn't really occurred. Traditionally, corpses were not embalmed, although, as in other matters, here, too, Muslims follow local legal requirements. Because the body is literally to be resurrected, cremation isn't allowed. Relatives of the same sex as the deceased face the body toward Mecca and purify it three times with soap, water, and scents. These attendants completely wrap the body in white cloths (three for men; five for women). If the deceased had performed the pilgrimage to Mecca, their pilgrimage garments (see Chapter 9) may be used for the wrapping. A special ritual prayer for the dead *(salat al-janazh)* is performed at a mosque, in a home, or, in the West, at a funeral home.

Burial

Burial occurs on the day of death, if possible. In a Muslim country, a procession winds its way through the streets, with four men carrying the bier. Strangers are encouraged to join the procession for a short distance.

Sometimes women mourners who loudly cry out their sorrow are hired, although this practice is frowned on by legal scholars.

The grave is deep enough to protect from wild animals and to conceal odors. Coffins are permitted but not normally used unless legally required. A niche is carved out in one side of the grave, where the corpse is placed facing Mecca. If the first part of the *shahada* ("there is no God but God") wasn't said while the person was dying, it's spoken at this time. Someone may give a brief talk at the grave, and the mourners recite the *Fatiha*. The niche is sealed, the mourners toss three handfuls of dirt onto the grave, and the procession departs. They may stop and recite the *Fatiha* once again after 40 steps to aid the deceased who is already being cross-examined by the angels Munkar and Nakir (see Chapter 5).

After burial

Islamic tradition recommends a simple grave marker with the name of the deceased and some verses from the Qur'an. This hasn't stopped very elaborate grave markers and mausoleums from being erected, however. Visiting the grave of the dead is recommended, especially on the fortieth day after death.

Mourning continues for three days for most friends and family, although widows observe mourning for four months and ten days.

Observing Everyday Customs

Religion as a way of life includes not only the mandatory ritual practices and the life cycle observances. Instead, any act, properly done, may have religious significance, including the most trivial and mundane actions. What nonbelievers may regard as manners, customs, or even superstitions also acquire religious meaning. Eating — both how to eat and what to eat — has religious significance in many cultures. What one wears may also have religious significance. You can recognize some Hasidic (mystical) Jews by their long, black coats and their fur rim hats. If you live in states such as Pennsylvania, Ohio, and Indiana, you instantly recognize the Amish by their fashion of dress that looks like it came out of rural America of 200 years ago. People recognize a picture of an Indian Yogi by the clothes he wears, and the turban worn by all male *Sikhs* (a South Asian religion) make them instantly recognizable.

Why do religious people observe these customs? The lead character in the musical, *Fiddler on the Roof* (a portrayal of life in a Jewish village in 19th century eastern Europe) replies when asked the same question about the traditions of his village. The answer is simple and yet frustrating: tradition. They do it, because their fathers and mothers before them did it this way, as did their grandparents before them. Traditions help mark the boundary between members of the group and non-members.

For Islam, an additional answer exists: the model of the prophet Muhammad. When a Muslim tries to determine the proper way to behave, he or she looks to see whether information exists as to what Muhammad did (or said). This section introduces you to Muslim customs and manners, some of which are mandated by Islamic law (permitted and non-permitted foods, for example) and others of which are a matter of tradition.

Finding food for thought

Most foods are permitted with the following three major restrictions:

- ✔ Sura 2:173 says, "He [God] has forbidden to you flesh from animals found dead [meaning they were not ritually killed], blood, pork, and any food offered to idols." Judaism has similar prohibitions, but in contrast to Jews, Muslims may eat shellfish. Especially in China, where pork is crucial for Chinese cuisine, avoidance of all pork is a practice which sharply distinguishes Chinese Muslims from non-Muslim Chinese. Muslim, Jewish, and other scholars have tried to offer logical reasons for the avoidance of pork (for example, dangers to health from insufficiently cooked pork) but basically it comes down to matters of purity and the word of God. Many cultures have food taboos — dog, cat, and (generally) horse in America. Avoidance of certain foods is one way, according to anthropologists, of marking group (or religious) identity. Muslims are descendants of Abraham and simply took over the prohibition on pork from the Jewish tradition.

- ✔ No drinking of alcoholic beverages.

- ✔ No consumption of blood or animals that were not properly slaughtered. (The process is much like *kosher* slaughtering in Judaism.) The gullet, wind pipe, and arteries are quickly cut at the throat (while saying God's name) so that blood is drained quickly out of the animal's body.

   Muslims may eat kosher food when *halal* (permitted) food is unavailable, because kosher foods follow an ever stricter ritual standard than halal foods.

For Muslims in a non-Muslim country, like the United States, being certain that processed foods haven't been contaminated with pork byproducts or alcohol is difficult. Some Web sites for Muslims provide detailed information about the status of various foods in America, including those at fast-food eateries.

Traditionally, Muslims eat with the right hand, with or without utensils, preceding the meal with the *basmala* ("in the name of God, the compassionate, the caring.") Muslims may eat at the homes of non-Muslims, assuming, of course, that the meal isn't pork roast with red wine! Islamic legal scholars debate whether Muslims can eat or work in restaurants that serve wine.

Dressing the part

Muslims are expected to observe good hygiene, to be clean, and to dress modestly. Both sexes may wear perfumes, because pleasant smells are much appreciated in Islam. One shouldn't eat garlic before going out in public. As usual, much of this is based on traditions concerning what Muhammad wore or what he said about clothing. Sura 7:26 says, "We [God] have sent down on you clothes to cover your shame [nakedness] as well as to be an adornment to you" (see also 7:31), clearly stating the basic guideline of being attractively but modestly dressed (men and women). Traditional sayings of Muhammad warn against extravagant dress to simply impress others and specifically prohibit silk and gold for men while allowing them (in moderation) for women. Another saying of Muhammad is, "Cleanse yourself, for Islam is cleanliness." Of course, nothing in these requirements for proper dress and hygiene are unique to Islam, nor should they be because Islam would say this is proper human behavior and dress for all people.

Clothing styles are unique to each country, however, and Muslim men may wear purely Western clothing or a Western-style sport coat over a traditional tunic or gown. Below I describe what a typical, traditional Muslim man or woman would wear. Members of Islamist movements (as well as some Muslims in the West) adopt similar clothing to emphasize their identity as Muslims. Although you see men and women dressed as described in the following bullets in places like South Asia and West Africa, you see other men and women dressed in clothing that Westerners wouldn't immediately identity as Muslim dress.

Clothing for men and women differs, as follows:

- **Women:** Long skirt or loose fitting trousers; long-sleeve, loose top that's unfitted at waist; head cover over the neck or shoulders. While some Islamic cultures say that Islam requires covering the women entirely from head to toe, including veiling the face, others disagree (see Chapter 11 regarding the veil and the key Qur'anic passages relating to the veil).

- **Men:** Long-sleeve tunic over baggy pants or a long, loose fitting gown. They also wear a head cap, and keep a trimmed beard and mustache. In the Ottoman (Turkish) Empire, the head cap (called a fez) was shaped like a cylinder with a tassel. The beduin Arabic headgear *(kafia),* such as PLO President Arafat wears, and turbans are other traditional head coverings.

  The founder of modern Turkey, Ataturk, banned veils (for women), as well as the *fez* for men.

Avoiding the evil eye

Long before the advent of Islam, Arabs often attributed their misfortunes to someone having cast the *evil eye* upon them. As with witches in the West, old, unmarried women were particularly regarded as having the power of the evil eye. Spells and *amulets* (good-luck charms) helped avert the power of the evil eye, as well as mischief caused by *jinns* (evil spirits, see Chapter 5). Another means (undoubtedly also pre-Islamic in origin) to counteract the effect of the evil eye was to stretch forth one's hand, palm forward, with the five fingers spread out. While such beliefs and practices are rather peripheral to Muslim theology and not found in the Qur'an, they continue in Islam, as folk practices do in many religions.

Minding your manners

A tradition attributed to Muhammad says, "Good breeding is a part of the faith." To be a Muslim is to act in a proper human manner, in contrast to the way that other creatures (in accord with their proper nature) conduct themselves. Thus Muslims have a whole category of literary works about proper manners and conduct. I offer three examples from such a modern manual, M. I. Al-Kaysi's *Morals and Manners in Islam: A Guide to Islamic Adab* (Islamic Book Trust, 2000).

- Be prompt to thank a person saying, "May God reward you well." According to a tradition, Muhammad said, "He who does not thank people does not thank God."

- Don't try to restrain a sneeze, which is a blessing from God. When a person sneezes, she should say, *al-hamdu lilah* ("Praise be to God").

- Mercy and kindness should characterize all aspects of the treatment of animals.

- In general, the right foot, side, and hand is favored in all positive actions such as eating, drinking, holding the Qur'an, shaking hands, putting on clothes and shoes. Remember this when interacting with Muslim acquaintances. This may seem discriminatory to lefties and probably has no logical explanation beyond the fact that in many cultures "right" is associated with positive and "left" with negative actions. It could as well be the reverse. The basic point seems to be to distinguish even by your bodily gestures which things are pure and which impure (remembering that impure does not mean "evil").

Looking at Women's Rituals

Women have traditionally been excluded from or restricted in their participation in the major religious rituals of Islam, including attending the mosque (some areas of the mosque may be shut off to women). In the United States, while separation of women from men is still the norm in the mosque, women play a crucial role in activities at the mosque. In addition, in the *hajj* (see Chapter 9), women participate equally with men.

Because women don't participate to the same extent as men in "official Islam," many Muslim women have created their own substitutes. Women play a major role in various rites of passage, such as circumcision and marriage. More women than men visit saint tombs, where women are free to assert their own interests and desires. For example, a barren woman may visit a saint's shrine and pray to God to have a child. As part of that prayer, she makes a vow to return and praise God and Muhammad when her petition is granted. Here, vow refers to a formal promise made to God by the believer, but has nothing to do with more formal vows of chastity or poverty such as Roman Catholic and Buddhist monks and nuns take. In Shi`ism (see Chapter 12), a woman with a sick son can vow to sponsor a ritual dinner for her female friends if the son is cured. At the dinner, the women listen to sermons and readings, and they also visit and share religious concerns.

In parts of Egypt and the Sudan, women are prominent in *zar* ceremonies, which deal with causes and cures of mental and physical illness. *Zar* refers to both the possessed woman and the ceremony to cure her. Some Sufis (mystics — see Chapter 13) are women, such as the legendary medieval Sufi saint Rabi`a. In addition, key Sufi figures such as Ibn Arabi acknowledged their female teachers. In this section, I mention only a few examples of how women carve out their own ritual space in Islam, because the specifics vary greatly from country to country and even from town to town.

While some traditionalist movements simply want to push women back into the shadows, other Islamist movements involve women (many of whom are college-educated professionals) actively in various ways. In Iran today, while women are required to wear the *chador* that totally covers them from head to toe in public, they're also allowed to serve in parliament and government. (And I suspect that the change in the role of an Islamic woman between 1950 and 2050 will be much greater than any changes that took place between 1200 and 1950.)

Chapter 11

Muslim Ethics: Living the Good Life

*I*n most introductory books on Islam, discussion of moral and ethical issues is scattered throughout the book, and I've always found that confusing. So, in this chapter, I bring together background information, theoretical considerations, and practical issues in Islamic ethics.

The Qur'an intermixes obligations toward God and obligations toward one's fellow humans. Some Islamic introductory ethics manuals for the layperson intermix morals and manners. For example, admonitions to sleep on your right side and not to lie occur in the same book. Therefore, in this chapter, when I speak of ethics, I'm talking about duties toward other people and toward oneself — social and personal morals.

All religions place emphasis on ethics. I use the example of the teachings of Confucius, which forms the basis for subsequent ethics not just in China but in all of East Asia. The main concern of Confucius was how people should conduct themselves in their relations with one another so that society may function to the benefit of all. Confucius offered much specific moral advice and believed that certain moral absolutes existed — things which people by virtue of being human know (or should know) to do or not to do. More important for Confucius than specific do's and don'ts was building moral character, which he believed is what distinguished human nature from the nature of other beings. A person with proper character will usually act in a moral manner instinctively without having to be told what to do. A person with proper moral character will have a positive influence on the character of others without himself being corrupted by people of inferior character, according to Confucius. Confucius also emphasized modesty in actions—not going to extremes. And finally Confucian ethics was hierarchical as defined in what are called the five relationships — between spouses, between parents and children, between siblings (brothers and sisters), with other people, and between ruler and subject. Each of these relationships is reciprocal, meaning that both sides in the relationship have some shared obligations to each other, but there are also obligations specific to one side of the relationship. For example, the child has an obligation to respect and care for the parent.

Islam would agree with almost everything in the above description of Confucian ethics. Indeed, most religions largely agree on the major moral do's and don'ts. What religion, for example, says it's okay to kill, cheat others, lie, oppress the poor, commit adultery, steal, or act harshly toward one's parents? Religions also share similar views about desirable and undesirable character traits — the virtues and the vices — for example, be generous and don't be stingy; be modest and don't be boastful. The major difference between Confucianism and Islam is that ethics in Islam are based on divine revelation — the word of God.

Although some Western ethicists make a distinction between ethics (theory) and morals (practical guidelines), in this chapter, I use the two terms interchangeably.

Reviewing the Starting Points for Islamic Ethics

Humans are made in the image of God, and that image includes moral and intellectual capability. According to Sura 33:72, God offered the "trust" to the heavens, the earth, and the mountains. They were afraid and refused it. Only humans were willing to accept it. In other words, morality is a uniquely human attribute and thus morality is central to Islam. In contrast, angels can't sin and thus don't make moral choices. (Satan is a unique exception, see Chapter 5). Moral action does not always come easily, as Satan and evil spirits *(jinn)* are always tempting people to do evil. According to Islam, people do have the ability to choose good and to avoid evil.

The principles of Islamic ethics

The Qur'an has a strong ethical thrust. For example, it contains condemnation of the people of Mecca for their oppression of the poor (see Sura 107:3) and the orphans (see Sura 17:34; 93:9), and for cheating in commerce (see

Sura 17:35). In the following list, I give what I regard as six basic principles of Islamic ethics:

- ✔ Every action has moral significance. Perhaps the phrase most often cited by Muslim ethicists comes from Sura 3:104, where Muslims are told that they're a people who should call all to do what is good and right and forbid what is wrong or dishonorable. This principle of calling to "do good and forbid evil" is a guiding light. Specific "rules" are important, but insight is required to apply the rules (or the general principal of "doing good" in specific cases).

- ✔ Moral actions are those which result in justice (`adl, see Sura 4:58). In concrete circumstances, an action may involve both good and evil consequences and then one must choose that action which will maximize the good and minimize the evil, resulting in the greatest degree of justice, according to the prominent 14th century legal scholar, Ibn Taymiyya.

- ✔ Faith and works are both required. Sura 2:23 says, "To those who believe and do acts of righteousness give the good news that they will go to paradise." The moral choices one makes are serious as they play a role in determining ones ultimate fate — to heaven or to hell.

- ✔ Intentions are as important as deeds (as is true also in acts of worship) Sincerity is crucial. The trio of "heart, tongue, and deed" is frequently mentioned. Everyone agrees that it's not enough to advocate moral actions (the action of the tongue) but then act differently. An action done just for external compliance, says Islam, isn't nearly as good as one which comes from the heart. Something that comes from the heart will be accompanied by words and actions. If circumstances prevent accomplishment of the action, then commitment of the heart is still regarded as good.

- ✔ When it comes to doing what is morally right, having the proper character (consisting of virtues such as wisdom, concern for justice, modesty, and the avoidance of vices such as lust, greed, and anger) is as important as following a set of rules. In most situations people act instinctively, in accord with their basic character, rather than by consulting a set of rules. The great 12th-century theologian al-Ghazali wrote extensively on the importance of cultivating virtue and avoiding inclination to vice. Sura 5:105 says, "Believers, guard your own souls. The person who has gone astray cannot hurt you if you are rightly guided."

- ✔ Extremes should be avoided; follow the middle path, the way of balance. One shouldn't be arrogant or exalt oneself in the eyes of others. Sura 31:18–19 says, "Do not be disdainful of other people, nor walk in arrogance in the earth. God does not love any person who boasts arrogantly. Be moderate in your pace and lower your voice. The most unpleasant of voices is the ass's."

Illustrative texts

According to tradition, Muhammad said, "None among you is a believer until he wishes for his brothers and sisters what he wishes for himself." This is similar to the Golden Rule, versions of which occur in Judaism, Christianity, Confucianism, and most other faiths.

On the other hand, Islam has no Ten Commandments, although several Qur'anic texts do summarize basic moral requirements. Sura 23, 3–11 says, "Believers are those . . . who avoid vain talk; who are active in deeds of charity; who abstain from sex except with their wives, or whom their right hands possess. Thus they're free from blame, but those whose desires exceed those limits are transgressors. Believers faithfully observe their trusts and covenants and keep their prayers. They will be the heirs, who will inherit Paradise, where they will dwell." Sura 70:22–35 has a similar list of good and bad deeds.

Muhammad gave a summary of some of the moral duties of a Muslim in his farewell sermon on the pilgrimage to Mecca in 632. Along with worship and other obligations, he included the following moral instructions:

- ✔ Return any property belonging to others.
- ✔ Don't hurt anyone.
- ✔ Don't charge interest on money loaned to others.
- ✔ Husbands should treat their wives well, as they are partners together.
- ✔ Don't make friends with people of bad character.
- ✔ Don't commit adultery.

Sources for ethical guidance

As in any religion, beyond specific ethical commands in the scriptures, other resources exist for arriving at ethical guidelines in Islam:

- ✔ The Qur'an is naturally the primary source, with its explicit laws and its moral principles.
- ✔ The traditions *(hadiths)* give guidance based on Muhammad's words and actions.
- ✔ Islamic legal scholarship, by the use of analogy and other means of argument, derives additional moral directives based on the Qur'an and the *hadiths.*
- ✔ Pre-Islamic Arabic virtues, such as honor, courage, loyalty, hospitality, self-control, and endurance, continue to be important in Islam.

✔ Certain people from Islamic history, such as the four rightly guided caliphs and Fatima (see Chapter 2), provide important role models.

✔ Philosophical reflection on issues of justice and ethics by the Mu`tazilites (see Chapter 4) and others helped refine ethical issues.

✔ Works of Greek ethicists, translated into Arabic, are another source.

✔ God's attributes and names (see Chapter 3) provide a model for Muslims to imitate in their actions toward one another. Such names include the gentle, the grateful, the just, the giver, the equitable, the loving, and others with ethical implications.

✔ Sufism (see Chapter 13) cultivates a set of ethical values, including humility and poverty.

✔ *Adab* (etiquette, manners) works were written for various professions and for ordinary Muslims, and they still exist today. Two examples are manuals of advice for kings on how to rule and for physicians on how to care for patients. Works of literature (also called *adab*) provide further moral exemplars.

Dealing with sins, major and minor

Some sins are more serious than others. Like other religions, Islam recognizes gradations of seriousness in sins. Serious sins are those which are most likely to land one in hell on the Day of Judgment. To Muslims, for whom this life is only a prelude to what comes after death, the distinction between more and less serious sins is very important.

The 12th-century theologian al-Ghazali provides a good example of how Islam organized sins into different categories (although other theologians may express the distinctions somewhat differently):

✔ The first rank sins are unbelief in God *(kufr)* and idolatry *(shirk,* associating anything else with God, worshipping others in addition to God, see Sura 4:48). These two sins are often regarded as unforgivable and earn a person a stay in hell either permanently or, depending upon the grace of God, for a very long time.

✔ The second rank sins are against life and family (for example, murder and adultery).

✔ The third rank sins include wrongful appropriation of property. Perhaps sins of the second and third rank will cause a Muslim to spend some time in the top (and least painful) level of hell, but if they were sincere believers in God while living, they'll eventually make it into heaven.

✔ The fourth category is a catch-all, including consuming alcohol and lying. While not unimportant, these sins may not keep a Muslim out of heaven on the Day of Judgment.

Applying Ethics to Practical Issues

What do Muslims think about the hot moral issues of today? The remainder of this chapter addresses specific moral issues. As in any culture, expert opinions on moral issues vary widely. Someone may tell you what the Islamic position is on some issue, without a hint that other Muslim scholars may hold a completely different view on the issue. Don't expect all Muslims to agree on any complicated moral issue any more that you and your friends agree on all moral issues. In the remainder of the chapter, I try to give you a sense of where Muslims stand on these issues but don't expect that all Muslims would agree with my statement of the Muslim position on any particular issue.

Keep in mind that the comments I make on specific issues represent the position of Islamic ethicists as to what people should do. I don't attempt to describe, as an anthropologist or sociologist would, how ordinary Muslims actually conduct themselves.

Understanding Sexual Ethics

Honestly speaking, who doesn't think of sex when they think of ethics? Ethics concern how people relate to one another, and because sexual relations are the most intimate of human interactions, sexual ethics occupies an important role in most discussions of ethics. To a non-Muslim, Muslim sexual ethics would probably appear fairly puritanical. Sex is good, but is to be expressed only within carefully prescribed limits.

- ✔ **Sexual intercourse is a gift of God and is good.** Islam doesn't believe that a *celibate* life (no sexual relations or marriage) is a more holy life. Christians assume that Jesus was celibate throughout his life and are shocked if someone suggests otherwise. Buddhist monks do not marry (with some exceptions in Japanese Buddhism) and some Hindu men, in the fourth and final stage of life (that of the *sannyasin*), depart from house and wife to focus entirely on achieving liberation. Jews, Confucianists, Taoists, and Muslims don't share this attitude that marriage and sexual relations can interfere with the religious quest. For Muslims, like any other action undertaken in moderation and with the right attitude, sexual relations can be regarded as an act of worship and should be preceded by prayer.

- ✔ **Sexual relations cause ritual impurity.** One should perform the major ritual purification after intercourse or the next morning before engaging in ritual prayer (on this and the next point, see Chapter 9). Sexual relations involve bodily emissions and all bodily emissions require purification before acts of worship.

✔ **Sexual intercourse isn't permitted during menstruation, in part because contact with blood requires purification.**

✔ **Impotency is a medical problem to be dealt with by the best medical means.** So the use of Viagra is okay if it doesn't lead to unreasonable sexual demands made on the wife. Lustful tendencies should be controlled and so Viagra wouldn't be taken by an otherwise sexually healthy male to increase sexual appetite.

✔ **Masturbation (the texts contemplate only male masturbation) is regarded as undesirable (Sura 23:5–7).** However, it's not clear that verse 7 actually refers to masturbation. The Hanbalite legal School (see Chapter 8) allows masturbation in order to avoid committing fornication or adultery when the man is unable to marry. Education and delayed financial independence often lead to delayed marriage, while health and nutrition lead to earlier sexual maturity. This presents an obvious challenge to Islam with its severe legal penalties against sex outside of marriage.

✔ **Despite legal penalties for "fornication," Muslim cultures have shown tolerance toward premarital male sexual relations with females.** Premarital sexual relations by females, however, are strongly condemned and bring severe disgrace on the family. (I've never understood how the math works for a society that tolerates premarital sex on the part of young males but not young females.) Premarital sex by a Muslim woman may even lead to an *honor killing,* where in some cases even a woman who has been raped is considered to have shamed the family and a male member of the family may kill her to redeem family honor. Honor killings are contrary to Islamic law but nevertheless sometimes happen in some Muslim countries.

✔ **Prostitution is morally and legally wrong in Islam.** However, prostitutes exist in Muslim societies. Sura 24:33, along with various traditions *(hadiths),* condemn forcing female slaves to serve as prostitutes (perhaps for the financial benefit of her owner).

In Twelver Shi`ite Islam, a form of temporary marriage *(mut`a)* is legal. The marriage contract specifies how long the marriage will last (from hours up to 99 years) and what the payment will be. The wife has no rights of inheritance but the children from such a marriage are legitimate and do inherit. Sunni Muslims regard *mut`a* as equivalent to prostitution. Sura 4:26 is cited by both Sunnis and Shi`ites, the former reading the crucial word as "gift of consolation" (given to a divorced woman) and the Shi`ites as "temporary marriage." Even Sunnis recognize and traditions confirm that Muhammad did originally allow temporary marriage for Muslim men away on military campaign or commercial journeys. Sunnis argue this was a concession to human weakness, temporary marriage being better than adultery. Sunnis say that Muhammad later prohibited temporary marriage and compare the situation to drinking of alcohol that (with restrictions) was originally allowed but later prohibited in the Qur'an (according to the normal interpretation). Shi`ites attribute the prohibition of temporary marriage not to Muhammad but to `Umar, the second caliph (successor of Muhammad). Shi`ites do not recognize `Umar as a legitimate successor because he was not a descendant of Muhammad and therefore Shi`ites do not recognize his prohibition of temporary marriage as binding on Shi`ites.

✔ **Anal sex is wrong.** Islam teaches that some acts are contrary to God's intent as manifested in the created order — a concept similar to what in the West is sometimes called "natural law." To Muslim ethicists, vaginal intercourse between a man and a woman is natural, while anal intercourse isn't.

✔ **Homosexuality is wrong both because it's contrary to God's intention and because it's explicitly condemned in the Qur'an and the *hadiths*.** In Sura 26:165–175, Lot condemns the male homosexuality of the people of Sodom. Sura 4:16 apparently refers to male homosexuality and says the men involved should be punished but doesn't say what the punishment is. A few *hadiths* recommend stoning people guilty of homosexual practice on the basis that God destroyed Sodom and Gomorrah by raining down stones on the cities. However, while the Hanbalite legal School imposes severe penalties for homosexual acts, the Hanifite School doesn't. (In Malaysia, a Muslim country, the premier used a charge of homosexuality to imprison the vice-premier whom he viewed as a political threat.) Homosexuality is illegal in Muslim countries, but it's often tolerated if practiced discreetely. So you won't find many openly gay bars in Muslim countries, but you'll find a few.

The Qur'an, *hadiths*, and historical records say little about lesbianism. Most Muslims would say that lesbian sexual relationships are sinful. Transvestitism and cross-dressing are also wrong according to Muslim ethicists. Sexual roles should be clearly distinguished and anything which confuses the distinction is wrong.

✔ **Pornography is condemned because it intentionally excites rather than constrains lust, and also because it degrades women.** In a frequently cited book, *The Lawful and the Prohibited in Islam* (American Trust Publications, no date), Yusuf al-Qaradawi explains that as a general principle, Islam prohibits anything which may lead to sin. Pornography, and less explicit actions which may cause erotic arousal (such as mixed dancing — that is, of a male with a female), are therefore prohibited as a safeguard against possible adultery or illicit (from the Muslim standpoint) sexual intercourse.

✔ **Modern birth control methods (other than abortion) are generally accepted in Islam.** Having too large a family to properly care for is a legitimate reason to use birth control, so in the last 50 years, the birth rate in a number of Muslim countries has dropped dramatically. Many conservative Muslims joined with Roman Catholics, however, in opposing recommendations of a United Nations population conference held in Cairo in the 1990s. Muslims objected to government imposition of birth control and suspected a Western plot to reduce the number of Muslims.

✔ **Artificial insemination of the wife with the husband's sperm is usually permitted, although some disagree.** However, use of another male's sperm in the case of the husband's sterility is regarded as adultery. Surrogate motherhood is also illegal under Islamic law. A child born to a surrogate mother is illegitimate according to Islamic law.

✔ **Islam strongly condemns the use of sex to sell products**. You won't see scantily clad women showing off their wares at car shows or reclining men dressed only in Calvin Klein underwear on billboards in Muslim countries.

Outlining Ethics Regarding Marriage and Family

A Frank Sinatra song from 1955, written by Sammy Cahn and Jimmy Van Heusen and entitled "Love and Marriage," says they are linked like a horse and carriage. If you want one, you have to have the other. As the discussion of sex in the preceding section makes abundantly clear, sex and marriage certainly are supposed to go together in the Muslim world.

✔ **Marriage in Islam is a social contract with divine sanction (Sura 25:54).** A marriage celebration is highly recommended and almost always occurs, but the crucial religious requirement is the contract negotiated by the man and the male representative of the woman and signed in the presence of two witnesses (see Chapter 11). Elopement is contrary to Islamic practice because marriage is a public event (the celebration feast makes it public). Although prior romantic attachment isn't a basis for marriage, love is important in marriage. Sura 30:21 says that marriage is one of the signs of God's concern for humanity and that God "has put love and kindness between" husband and wife.

✔ **Marriage is encouraged at an early age — mid- to late teens.** Because the man is expected to support the woman, the realities of modern life, with extended education prior to having a full-time job, may lead to a somewhat later marriage (See Chapter 11).

✔ **Islam sanctions polygamy.** Some Islamic modernists say the Qur'an prefers monogamy but allowed polygamy because of the conditions of the early Muslim community. The husband can have up to four wives, but he must treat them equally. "Treating equally" refers to financial support of the wives, not to loving them equally. Muslims living in non-Muslim countries that prohibit polygamy are expected to obey the law of the host country. Some Muslim countries have limited or even outlawed polygamy (Tunisia is one).

Women can have only one husband, and most Muslim men today have only one wife. In some cases, a wife may include in the marriage contract a clause that prohibits the husband from taking another wife.

✔ **Adultery is one of the most severe crimes.** The Qur'an mentions a punishment of 100 lashes (Sura 24:2), but a *hadith* (tradition) supports death by stoning. The *hadith* is normally considered to have superceded (or abrogated) the Qur'anic punishment. In either case, procedural safeguards ensure that the sentence is rarely carried out. In Nigeria, several state courts in Muslim northern regions of the country have imposed the death by stoning penalty. The president, a Muslim, has actively intervened to try to prevent this travesty of Muslim law procedures. A false accusation of adultery is punished by 80 lashes (Sura 24:4) and, thus, according to the Qur'an, is almost as bad as the act of adultery itself.

✔ **Divorce *(talaq),* according to a well known *hadith,* is the most detestable of the permitted actions in Islam.** The Qur'an recommends reconciliation with the help of arbitrators (Sura 4:35). A husband may divorce his wife, basically by saying "I divorce you" during each of three successive months. After the first and second time, the couple may reconcile. During the three months, the wife continues to live in their (husband and wife's) home, and the husband continues to support her financially during this period (see Sura 65:1). After the third time, the divorce is final and the couple may not remarry unless the woman has had another marriage (and divorce) in the interval (these details are specified in Sura 2:228–232, 236–237). Later, custom came to accept saying it three times all at once. This quick divorce was legally permissible but not recommended and lent itself to abuse by the husband. Modern legislation in some Muslim countries provides protection for the wife from arbitrary divorce by the husband.

For a wife to divorce her husband is difficult. Grounds for divorce by a wife include abuse or non-support by the husband, impotency, debauchery, desertion, chronic disease, insanity, or his converting to another religion. In the case of divorce, the woman normally gets to keep her dowry.

✔ **The husband is responsible for the support of the wife (Sura 4:34).** The wife is responsible for the care of the children and the management of the home. If she fulfills these duties, she may have a job outside of the home. Any income she earns is hers to do with as she pleases; she isn't required to contribute to the basic expenses of the family. In countries where total seclusion (confinement of women to an area of the house where unrelated men won't see them) of women is practiced (as for the Taliban in Afghanistan), opportunities for employment are obviously going to be very limited. However, throughout Muslim history and in the majority of Muslim countries, many women have had various occupations.

✔ **Despite a strong egalitarian emphasis in Islam, the patriarchal family is considered the divine norm.** Everyone submits to God. Citizens submit to the ruler. The wife submits to the husband, and children submit to the parents. Mutuality is encouraged between husband and wife, and the husband normally defers to his wife in matters pertaining to the home and bringing up young children. Still, if a difference of opinion arises and a decision must be made, the husband has the final word (see Sura 4:34, speaking of the righteous women being obedient to their husbands.)

✔ **Children are a joy.** Children should honor their parents, and parents should treat each of their children equally, unless extenuating circumstances exist, such as having a handicapped child. A *hadith* says, "Fear God and treat your children with equal justice." The parents are responsible for meeting the basic needs of the child — food, clothing, shelter, religious training, and education.

Fathers should show love and affection to their children as it's reported that Muhammad did to his children. Islam assumes that mothers will show love. In one famous saying, Muhammad says, "Paradise is at the feet of the mother." In another *hadith*, Muhammad is asked, "to whom should I show kindness? He replied: Your mother, next your mother, next your mother, and then comes your father, and then your relatives in order of relationship."

✔ **Islamic law doesn't allow legal adoption (Sura 33:4–5), in which the adopted child has the same rights of inheritance as the other children.** If a child is orphaned, it's the duty of the extended family to care for that child. A childless man may take in and care for an orphan. He can will that child up to one-third of his estate, but the child doesn't inherit the way a natural child would.

✔ **Grown children care for their elderly parents and show them respect,** according to Sura 17:23, "Say not to them a contemptuous word nor repel them, but address them with respectful words." The same respect should be extended to all the elderly, as Muhammad said, "No youth will honor an old man because of his years without God appointing someone to honor him when he is old."

✔ **The extended family is morally responsible for the debts of a family member who is poor through no fault of his own and for the debts left behind by a family member who has died.** However, the extended family isn't legally responsible for those debts and can't be made to pay them.

The role of women

The status of women in Islam is one of the points which most grabs the attention of Westerners and indeed offends many Westerners, who feel that women are second-class people in Islam. I share these concerns, but I also agree with Muslim critics who point out that up until 100 to 150 years ago, women had more legal and economic rights in many Muslim countries than they did in Western countries. Also, both Muslims and many Western scholars agree that at the time of the origin of Islam, Qur'anic stipulations about women marked an advance in the legal, social, and economics rights of women compared to what existed prior to Islam. A view I share is that the position of women subsequently declined in portions of the Islamic world not because of the Qur'an but essentially contrary to the intent of the Qur'an.

- ✔ **Islam claims it has a separate-but-equal policy regarding women.** Interestingly, some Hindu writers have claimed the same about Hinduism and as in the case of Islam, argue that Western perceptions of unfair treatment of women in Hinduism (or Islam) is due to lack of appreciation of the complementary roles of women and men and the high respect in which women are held. Having grown up in part of the American South where supposedly separate but equal treatment of blacks was the rule (separate schools, separate drinking fountains, and so on), I remain suspicious of any claims of separate but equal.

- ✔ **Women have the same religious rights and duties as men.** They must, however, remain in separate parts of mosques, and they can't lead a congregation in prayer if a man is present because of the belief that men take the leadership role in the public arena as women do in the domestic area. (Sufis are the exception because mysticism helps dispense with such social boundaries.)

- ✔ **Infant girls are to be welcomed.** Because male children were preferred in pre-Islamic Arabia (see Sura 43:17), infant girls were often killed (see Sura 81:8–9). The Qur'an condemns this practice. Prophetic traditions say a Muslim should rejoice as much at the birth of a daughter as of a son. However, cases of female infanticide undoubtedly continued and, as in many societies (China, for example), traditional Muslim families have continued to rejoice at the birth of a son and regard the birth of a daughter as a burden, regardless of what their religion says they should do.

- ✔ **A daughter gets only one-half of the inheritance of a son.** Muslims say this is fair because the son has to support himself and a wife, while the daughter can do whatever she wishes with her inheritance, and she gets a dowry in addition.

- ✔ **The Qur'an (Sura 2:221; 60:10) explicitly prohibits a Muslim women from marrying a non-Muslim man but allows a Muslim man to marry a non-Muslim woman.** The concern is to prevent a Muslim from leaving Islam. The assumption is that a woman is more likely to adopt the religion of her husband than vice versa.

- ✔ **Women are to be veiled.** The specific Qur'anic text applies to Muhammad's wives (Sura 33:53). Two other texts (Sura 24:31–32; 33:60) speak of the Muslim women covering their private parts and their bosoms and wearing a cloak when outside. The extreme interpretation is the woman must completely cover herself from the top of the head to the feet including the face. Many Muslim women understand the texts only to command dressing modestly and covering their hands but not necessarily their faces.

Obviously, the dress requirements for women is an area of dispute within Islam. Over the centuries, head covering and veiling styles for Muslim women have varied considerably. You may have seen pictures of women in Iran, Saudi Arabia, and Afghanistan wearing outer garments which cover them from head to foot, perhaps with only slits for the eyes to see through. This garment may be a single garment or several. *Abaya, chaddor,* and *burqa* are not exact synonyms but all are cloak-like garments which cover the entire body. The *khimar* is a head covering that extends down to the breast and may be combined with the *jilbab,* which covers the rest of the body. *Hijab* is the general term for a veil of whatever type, whether or not it actually conceals the face from view. To affirm their Islamic identity, many women whose mothers or grandmothers rejected the veil, in cities like Cairo, have now taken to wearing the veil once more.

✔ **Opinions regarding seclusion of women vary widely.** Extreme conservatives say women should remain secluded in the house, women should go out (including travel) only with their husbands or other male family members, and work environments and schools should be sexually segregated. (Saudi Arabia has a modern shopping mall just for women.) But in most Muslim countries, you see many more women in public than this view would suggest.

Medical ethics

Medicine has always been an honored profession in Islamic countries: Jesus, regarded as an Islamic prophet, is revered for his healings. The Qur'an says, "Whoever saves the life of an individual, it is as if he saves the life of an entire people (Sura 5:32)." *Hadith* collections have sections on medicine.

In medicine, the main moral imperative is to promote health and life:

✔ **Medicine should promote life but not do anything to take away life.** Both suicide and euthanasia are condemned in Islam (Sura 4:29). Sterilization is normally prohibited. One shouldn't pray for death because God fixes the time of death. On the other hand, doctors aren't required to use extraordinary means to prolong life past its natural end.

✔ **Islam perceives no conflict between having faith in God and using the best medical science and treatment to cure disease.** In fact, people must both make their own best efforts in any endeavor including medicine and still ultimately depend on and leave the outcome to the will of God. Islamic cultures have made major contributions to medical care in areas such as hospitals, free clinics, care of the mentally ill, and the use of musical therapy. Handbooks were written to help people avoid medical quacks (see Chapter 19).

✔ **Some Islamic authorities allow organ transplants.** Some authorities, however, oppose them because they consider transplants to be mutilation of the body that has implications regarding the resurrected body on the Day of Judgment.

✔ **Abortion is prohibited (Sura 17:41) except in order to save the woman's life.** A fetus has rights of inheritance. Traditional Islam set quickening at four months, so abortion after four months is murder.

Hanbalites, however, allow abortion up to that point. During the Bosnian war, an Egyptian *mufti* (a scholar trained in Islamic law) issued a *fatwa* (legal opinion) allowing Muslim Bosnian women raped by Serb soldiers to abort a pregnancy within the four-month period.

Social and economic justice

The Qur'an emphasizes issues of social justice (Sura 4:135). Muhammad said, "He who strives on behalf of a widow and a poor person is like one who strives in God's path." What do Islamic ethics say in this area?

✔ **Don't be ostentatious in one's style of life.** A Muslim shouldn't buy the most expensive car or live in a palace-like home. Men shouldn't wear gold or silver or silk, although women may wear jewelry.

✔ **Property ultimately belongs to God.** One should work hard and try to prosper economically. If one succeeds, instead of buying the Rolls Royce, one should provide for the poor.

✔ **Be honest in commercial dealings.** Use honest weights and measures. Muhammad said that when selling a commodity in the market, you should put the poorer quality on top so as not to deceive the buyer. This is the equivalent of saying today that one shouldn't wrap the beef in the supermarket so that all the fat and trimmings are under the lean meat.

✔ **Avoid both atheistic communism and materialistic, unrestrained capitalism.** Communism, contrary to the Qur'an, doesn't recognize the rights of private property. At the same time, Western capitalism, with its excessive individualism that recognizes no limits on the rights of property, goes to the other extreme. With the fall of the Soviet Union and the creeping capitalism of Communist China, Islam seems to be the only social-economic-political system that offers an alternative to capitalism.

Muslims often say that while capitalism glorifies competition, Islamic economics promotes cooperation. All should prosper rather than some prospering at the expense of others. Since the 1930s, Muslims have been advocating and attempting to develop details of an Islamic economic system.

The Qur'an explicitly rejects usury, the charging of interest for a loan. To function in a capitalist economy without taking and paying interest is difficult. The first Islamic bank was founded in 1975, and Islamic banks (which neither charge interest on loans nor pay interest on deposits) now exist in a number of countries. Some Western banks have even set up Islamic branches. In addition, you can now invest in mutual funds that invest in companies that don't violate Islamic principles. Indexes such as the Dow Jones Islamic Market Index, established in 1999, track stocks suitable for Islamic investors.

✔ **Take care of the poor.** Modern Islamist/revivalist movements such as the Muslim Brotherhood in Egypt have social service programs, such as health services and disaster relief, which are often more effective and responsive than services provided by government agencies.

✔ **A Muslim can't enslave another Muslim and must treat slaves humanely.** It has been less than a century since legalized slavery was finally eliminated in all countries. Some people suggest that in some remote areas, de facto slavery still remains, and slavery is specifically allowed in the Qur'an with some restrictions. To free a Muslim slave is a meritorious act. Although Muslim states today prohibit slavery, in theory slavery is possible under Muslim law today.

Political issues

Strict ethical guidelines set forth the duties of the ruler of an Islamic state. Because of the fear of dissension within the Islamic community, Islamic law has had much more to say about the duties of citizens (what the state can demand from the citizen) than about the rights of citizens (what the citizen can expect from the state). Fazlur Rahman, a Pakistani scholar who taught for 20 years at the University of Chicago, lists four fundamental rights a legitimate state should ensure: life, religion, earning and property, and personal honor and dignity. As Muslim nations struggle today with what constitutes an Islamic state, much remains to be done to develop modern Islamic political ethics.

Only formal abandonment of Islam by the ruler justifies revolt against the state. Of course, this is theory and, in reality, revolts were and are common.

Other ethical issues

In addition to the issues discussed in the preceding section, this section discusses some other miscellaneous ethical issues:

✔ **Alcohol, drugs, and gambling are all prohibited in Islam.** These activities cater to the vices of greed and cloud the mental faculties.

✔ **Islam traditionally disapproves of representational art as an effort to duplicate the creative work of God.** Statuary is prohibited because of its use in pagan worship. Children's toys are an exception because Muhammad had no objections to his daughter `A'isha's playing with dolls. Thus you find Islamic dolls advertised in the United States for the parents of Muslim girls to buy as a replacement for Barbie dolls.

Mixed opinions exist regarding two-dimensional art. Illustrated epics and stories have flourished in Iran, Turkey, central Asia, and South Asia. Illustrations are also used in medical and scientific works.

Photographs, movies, and television shows are acceptable (but not to all Muslims) because they involve mechanical reproduction of a real image rather than creation of an image by an artist. Of course, Muslims often object to Western movies and television because of immoral content.

✔ **Ecological ethics is a relatively new field in Islamic ethics.** Muslim countries participate in United Nations conferences dealing with ecological issues, such as pollution. Humans can use the earth's resources for the benefit of humankind but have responsibility as God's vice-regents (*caliphs*) not to wreck ecological havoc. Muslims also point to texts concerning the sparing of trees from destruction during war.

✔ **Another recent focus in Islamic ethics is animal rights.** Animals are placed on earth for human use according to Islam, yet they shouldn't be abused or made to suffer needlessly. They shouldn't be castrated or neutered. Islam forbids the use of animals for target practice or sports, such as bullfights and cock fights. Animals should be respected and cared for. Although Islam discourages keeping pet dogs, Muhammad was a cat-lover.

Part IV

Recognizing That All Muslims Aren't the Same

The 5th Wave — By Rich Tennant

"These drives to the Mosque always remind me of what unites Muslims: submitting completely to Allah, praying five times per day, and that arriving early will assure you the best parking space."

In this part . . .

Diversity within a religion can both enrich the religion and become a source of controversy. When talking about Islam as a whole, Sunni Islam is naturally taken as the norm because from 84 to 90 percent of Muslims are Sunnis. In this part, you read about other forms of Islam, including Twelver Shi`ism and a number of Sevener (Isma`ili) Shi`ite groups, plus some other groups that began as Islamic sects and became independent religions.

While rituals and a list of do's and don'ts are important to any religion, some people want a deeper religious experience and more intimate contact with God. Sufism originated to meet this need in Islam and is covered in its own chapter in this part.

Finally, this part concludes with a look at Islam in America: how and when Islam came to America, what problems American Muslims face, and the future of Islam in America. American Muslims have their own unique experiences, many beginning with colonial slavery and continuing with the growing Islamic community today.

Chapter 12

Shi`ites

*B*ecause Sunnis constitute 84 to 90 percent of the Muslim population, most Westerners' picture of Islam is based on Sunni Islam. Shi`ites are mentioned when talking about the Iranian revolution, hostages in the American embassy in Tehran, or hostages taken in Lebanon. Ironically, while many Americans associate Shi`ism with terrorism and fundamentalism, historically, Shi`ism has been more open to change than Sunni Islam. (For example, the modern Iranian republic is something entirely new in Shi`ite history.)

In this chapter, I focus on Shi`ism in general and on Twelver Shi`ism (also called *Imami* or *Ithna-Ash`ari,* the Arabic term for Twelver Shi`ism). The other two branches of Shi`ism are the *Isma`ilis (Seveners)* and the *Zaydis (Fivers).* Most Shi`ites today are Twelver Shi`ites, who trace the line of their religious leaders *(imams)* beginning with `Ali and ending with the 12th in the line who disappeared in the ninth century. Fiver Shi`ites and Sevener Shi`ites derive their name from the acceptance of a different person as the designated *imam* at the fifth and seventh generations, respectively. Fiver Shi`ites, the smallest of the Shi`ite groups today, is also the closest to Sunni Islam in many ways. Sevener Shi`ism gave rise to many different Sevener Shi`ite groups over time, many of which have produced rather esoteric doctrines and practices when compared with either Twelver Shi`ism or Sunni Islam. See Chapters 2 and 14 for more on Isma`ili and Zaydi Shi`ism.

Locating and Counting Shi`ite Muslims

More than one hundred million Shi`ites constitute from 10 to 16 percent of the Muslim population worldwide. Sizable numbers of Shi`ites live in:

- **Iran:** 89 to 92 percent (about 60 million)
- **Iraq:** 60 to 65 percent (about 14 million, concentrated in the south)
- **Lebanon:** 30 to 35 percent (one million, in the south and in the Beqa'a valley)
- **Bahrain (in Persian Gulf):** 70 percent (about 200,000)
- **Yemen:** 30 to 40 percent (about five million Zaydi Shi`ites)
- **Azerbaijan (in Caucasus Mountain region):** 75 percent (about five million)
- **Saudi Arabia:** 5 percent (about one million)
- **Kuwait:** 30 percent (about half a million)
- **Pakistan:** about 20 percent (about 128 million centered in the Punjab region)
- **Specific regions of India, including Kashmir:** 15 percent of Indian Muslims (about 23 million)
- **Afghanistan:** 15 percent (about 5.5 million)
- **Syria and Turkey:** 10 to 20 percent (including the Druze, `Alawis, and Alevis, who usually don't want to be classified as Shi`ite)

Shi`ite Muslims also live in many Western countries to which they've immigrated in the last century

Keeping the Faith in the Family

Shi`ite means "party (of `Ali)." `Ali, the younger cousin of Muhammad, grew up in Muhammad's home and married Muhammad's daughter Fatima. `Ali occupied Muhammad's bed the night he left Mecca for Medina. `Ali carried the Muslim flag when they captured Mecca in 630. He acted as Muhammad's representative in Medina while Muhammad was away on his final military campaign in northern Arabia, also in 630.

The basic Shi`ite principle is that the head of the Muslim community must be a descendant of Muhammad. The first three caliphs (see Chapter 2) weren't legitimate rulers in the opinion of Shi`ites. For Shi`ites, `Ali was *imam* or spiritual (plus political) leader from the death of Muhammad in 632 until `Ali's death in 661, rather than just for the period 656–661 when, according to Sunni reckoning, `Ali ruled as the fourth caliph. Although `Ali and his supporters put forth `Ali's claims as caliph from the beginning, he didn't pursue these claims by force when he was passed over in the selection. According to later Shi`ite belief, God imposed the years of illegitimate rule (632–656) to separate true believers from the hypocrites.

All Muslim traditions honor `Ali and portray him favorably. In Shi`ite Islam, `Ali is a perfect Muslim. He's often referred to as the "Commander of the Faithful" rather than by his name. He's said to be the master of the Arabic language and a valiant, Apollo-like young man and warrior. In Muslim iconography, `Ali is represented by the two-tipped sword of Muhammad that he received as Muhammad's successor.

Designating `Ali as Muhammad's successor

According to tradition, when Muhammad returned from his night journey to Jerusalem (see Chapter 7), he cast his cloak over `Ali and Fatima. To Shi`ites, this was meant as a sign that `Ali be Muhammad's successor. More important is a *hadith* about the farewell pilgrimage to Mecca in 632, when Muhammad received a revelation designating `Ali as his successor. Muhammad delayed making this public until the pilgrims stopped at the oasis of Ghadir of Khumm on the way back to Medina. God then told him to make this designation public. This is how Shi`ites understand Sura 5:74 when it says, "O Messenger, make known what has been sent down to you from your Lord." Muhammad called the people together and said, "He whose master I am, `Ali is also his master." He then had all those present come forward and acknowledge `Ali. Subsequent retellings embellish the story.

Shi`ite understanding of the imam

While Sunni Islam uses the term *imam* for the prayer leader, in Shi`ism the *imam* is the leader of the community. He combines political and religious leadership, just as Muhammad did. Unlike prophets, an *imam* doesn't receive new revelation, but he receives guidance from angels and has unique knowledge of scripture. The *imam* is responsible for administration of the pillars of prayer, *saum* fast, collecting the *zakat* tax, supervising the pilgrimage, expanding and defending the dominion of Islam, enforcing Islamic law, and interpreting the meaning of the Qur'an.

Each prophet has 12 deputies *(walis)* according to the developed Twelver doctrine of the *imam*. `Ali is the *wali* to whom Muhammad taught the esoteric meaning of the Qur'an. `Ali also wrote down the Qur'an from Muhammad's dictation. `Ali's copy of the Qur'an is in the possession of the hidden *imam*, who will reveal it when he returns.

The *Mahdi* and the hidden *imam*

The *Mahdi* is the future one who will come in the final days. He will defeat evil, exact retribution, and rule over an ideal world in which all submit to God. Peace and justice will prevail, and poverty will be eliminated (see Chapter 5). Sunni scholars were often dubious about these popular expectations of a Messianic-type figure. The *Mahdi* isn't mentioned in the Qur'an, in the two major Sunni *hadith* collections, or by al-Ghazali.

In Sunni Islam, the idea of the *Mahdi* often combined with the idea of a provisional restorer of the faith *(mujaddid),* who appears at the end of each century. Various reformist political movements, especially in Africa, were led by individuals claiming to be the *Mahdi*. These include Ibn Tumart (1077–1130), the founder of the Almohad state in northwest Africa; Usman dan Fodio, the founder of the Sokoto caliphate in northern Nigeria (about 1800); and the founder of the Sanusi Sufi movement that established the state of Libya. In 1881, Muhammad Ahmad ibn `Abd Allah proclaimed himself *Mahdi* and founded the nation of Sudan based on Mahdi ideas of restoration of Islam as it first existed in Medina.

Twelver Shi`ism doesn't apply the term *Mahdi* to the first 11 *imams*. The hidden 12th *imam* is Muhammad al-Mahdi. He's alive on earth, while having connections to the prophets in heaven, and will one day return as *imam* and Mahdi. Thus in Shi`ism, the concept of the Mahdi merges with that of the hidden *imam*.

The following are some basic Shi`ite concepts relating to the imams:

✔ Like `Ali and his son Husayn, all the *imams* were martyred, except for the 12th *imam*. Thus the family of `Ali is known as the house of sorrow. Because the Shi`ites failed to come to the aid of Husayn on the day of Karbala (see the "The martyrdom of Husayn at Karbala" section of this chapter), suffering and repentance for sin play a major role in Shi`ite faith.

✔ The *imams* endure willingly their sufferings on behalf of believers. On the Day of Judgment, the *imams* and Fatima (Muhammad's daughter) will intercede before God on behalf of faithful Shi`ites. Fatima's sorrow over the death of Husayn is similar to Mary's sorrow over Jesus' death.

✔ As Muhammad designated `Ali as his successor, so each subsequent *imam* acting under divine inspiration designates *(nass)* his successor.

✔ The *imam* is without sin and infallible (`*isma).* He also knows the inner (hidden) and outer meanings of the scriptures and other secret books.

✔ There must be either a visible or a hidden *imam* or the world would cease to exist. According to the doctrine of occultation *(ghayba),* the *imam* may withdraw but he remains alive as leader of the Muslim community. The 12th *imam* is the hidden *imam* — gone into greater occultation under God's protection to return only at the end of time as the *Mahdi*, who will establish justice when he returns.

✔ Dissimulation *(taqiyya)* or concealment means that in order to avoid persecution, at times one may conceal one's Shi`ite identity, and a Shi`ite *imam* may submit to an illegitimate ruler, just as `Ali submitted to the first three caliphs.

✔ Esoteric knowledge of texts *(batin)* is accessible to the spiritual elite who are capable of going beyond the literal meanings of scripture.

✔ The suffering of the *imams* is a great injustice. Shi`ism's concern for justice *(`adl)* and its belief that the hidden *imam* will, upon his return, establish a just world order makes Shi`ism appealing to utopian, revolutionary groups.

Reviewing Two Foundational Events of Shi`ism

The martyrdoms of `Ali and of his son Husayn are the two foundational events in the unique sacred history of Shi`ism.

The betrayal and martyrdom of `Ali

`Ali was suspected of complicity in the murder of `Uthman, the third caliph. Although appointed as fourth caliph by a legitimate council, `Ali faced challenges to his rule throughout his short caliphate (556–561). `Ali sent his appointee to replace `Uthman's nephew, Mu`awiya, as governor of Syria. Mu`awiya refused to yield and the opposing armies met in the summer of 657 at Suffin on the upper Euphrates River (in present Syria). To avoid defeat, Mu`awiya's soldiers attached pages from the Qur'an to their weapons and called for arbitration. `Ali accepted. Mu`awiya interpreted the arbitration decision as validating his claim and assumed the role of caliph in Jerusalem in 660. The next January, `Ali was assassinated by a Kharijite who felt `Ali had betrayed the cause of God by accepting human arbitration. Thus `Ali was the first of the martyred *imams.* His burial site at Najaf (in Iraq) became the first Shi`ite holy site. When digging his grave, an inscription was supposedly found left by the Biblical Noah that indicated this would be the place of `Ali's burial. At this point, Shi`ism was still mainly a relatively minor political movement. Subsequent developments led to the emergence of Shi`ism as an alternate form of Islamic religion.

The martyrdom of Husayn at Karbala

After `Ali's death, his older son, Hasan, was proclaimed *imam,* and then caliph, by `Ali's supporters. After negotiations initiated by Mu`awiya, Hasan renounced his claim to the caliphate in the mosque at Kufa, the main center of Shi`ite support. Hasan received from Mu`awiya a generous pension and lands. He lived peacefully the remainder of his life in Medina and was politically uninvolved. (The current *imam* is always the legitimate ruler of Muslims but may choose to accept the illegitimate rule of another.) Hasan died between 670 and 680 and is buried at al-Baqi` cemetery in Medina, a site holy to both Shi`ites and Sunnis. Shi`ites claim he was poisoned by his wife on Mu`awiya's instigation, but many historians believe Hasan died a natural death.

Mu`awiya died in the spring of 680, having designated his son Yazid as his successor, or next caliph, thus establishing the Umayyads as a dynasty. Shi`ite envoys came from Kufa to Husayn, the younger brother of Hasan, in Medina, and asked him to assume the caliphate and overthrow Yazid. Husayn sent a cousin to investigate the situation in Kufa. Assured that the populace of Kufa would rally to his support, Husayn set out toward Kufa in September with about 50 supporters and family members. Yazid's governor in Iraq monitored the progress of the group and had Husayn's leading supporters in Kufa killed. When the group approached Kufa, an army patrol forced them away. Despite the promises of support, none of the Shi`ites from Kufa joined Husayn.

The stage was set for the encounter of Husayn's "army" of less than 100 people with the much larger Umayyad army at Karbala to the northwest of Kufa. Having been denied access to the Euphrates River, Husayn's group was suffering from severe thirst and fared poorly. Husayn died in the battle.

The death of Husayn at Karbala is the key event in the emergence of Shi`ism as a religious movement and has much to do with the sense of suffering, justice denied, and martyrdom that pervades Shi`ism. Shi`ite theology says that Husayn set out willingly toward what he knew would be his death as an act of redemption for the sins of Muslims — much like Jesus' death for the sins of Christians. Each year, Shi`ites relive the ten days of *Muharram* much as Christians relive the events of the last week of the life of Jesus. Those days were as follows:

- ✔ Days 1–3: Failed negotiations at Karbala when Husayn refused to recognize the claim of Yazid to the caliphate.

- ✔ Day 4: Martyrdom of Hurr al-Tamimi, the commander of Yazid's cavalry, who went over to the Shi`ite side.

- ✔ Day 5: Martyrdom of the two young sons of Husayn's sister, Zaynab.

- ✔ Day 6: Husayn's oldest son, `Ali al-Akbar, dies in his father's arms. `Ali's infant son, `Ali al-Ashghar, died when an arrow pierced his throat.

- ✔ Day 7: The tent had been set up for the celebration of the marriage of `Ali's nephew, when news reached the bridal party of his death in battle.

- ✔ Day 8: Both arms are cut off `Ali's half-brother, al-`Abbas, as he attempted to get water from the Euphrates.

- ✔ Days 9–10: In the final battle, Husayn and his soldiers are killed. Husayn's battlefield burial site becomes a major pilgrimage destination.

Husayn's severed head was taken to the caliph in Damascus. One tradition says it's buried in the courtyard of the Umayyad mosque there, while another has the head ultimately being buried at the Husayn shrine in Cairo, making both of these sites important for Shi`ites. The surviving women and children, including his sister Zaynab, were taken before Caliph Yazid, who treated them with respect and allowed them to return to Medina. Yazid also allowed `Ali Zayn al-Abidin, a son of `Ali who was sick in bed at the time of the battle, to retire to Medina where he died in about 713.

Postscript: The march of the penitents

The Shi`ite leader in Kufa rebuked himself and other Shi`ites for having failed to rally to Husayn's side at Karbala. To purge their sins, in November, 684, they set out on a death march with blackened faces, lamenting their guilt. The day after they stopped at the Karbala battlefield, Umayyad troops attacked and killed them. Lamentation and self-punishment are elements of the `ashura' observances that go back to this event of collective repentance.

Following the Line of the 12 Imams

The basic religious narrative of Twelver Shi`ism continues up to the occultation of the 12th *imam* in 874. Important developments in Shi`ite history take place after this date in the later Abbasid period, and then with the founding of Iran as a Twelver Shi`ite state in 1501.

Shi`ism under the Umayyads

`Ali Zayn al-Abidin was succeeded by his son, Muhammad al-Baqir (676–about 733), as the fifth *imam*. Al-Baqir lived and died in Medina without political involvement. Later, in 739–740, al-Baqir's younger half-brother, Zayd, disappointed by al-Baqir's acquiescence in Umayyad rule, led a few hundred Shi`ites from Kufa in another futile revolt. Zayd was killed in 740, but his son, Yahya, escaped to eastern Iran where his efforts to rally the Shi`ites against the Umayyads resulted in his death in 743. The Zaydis or Fivers, who recognize Zayd rather than al-Baqir as the fifth *imam,* form one of the three branches of Shi`ism (see Chapter 14).

Despite remaining politically uninvolved, the sixth *imam,* Ja`far al-Sadiq (699–765), established Shi`ism on a firm basis as a religious movement. His law School is the official Twelver Shi`ite School of law and is recognized by Sunnis as a legitimate School of law, along with that of the Zaydi Shi`ites.

Shi`ism under the Abbasids

The Abbasid revolt that overthrew the Umayyads in 750 drew on Shi`ite resentment fanned by the failed Shi`ite revolts of 740–743. Abul `Abbas al-Saffah, a descendant of Muhammad's uncle, al-`Abbas, became caliph rather than a descendant of `Ali. The Abbasid rulers kept a close watch on the Shi`ite *imam,* who was left alone so long as he stayed out of politics. Shi`ites became a significant minority of the population of the newly founded Abbasid capital city of Baghdad.

A disputed succession at Ja`far's death led to a split in the line of *imams* with the Seveners recognizing as the seventh *imam* Muhammad, the son of Ja`far's designated successor, Isma`il, who died before Ja`far (see Chapter 14).

Most Shi`ites recognized Ja`far's eldest surviving son, Musa al-Kazim (745–799) as the seventh *imam.* The Abbasid caliph brought Musa to Baghdad where he could be closely watched. Musa and the ninth *imam,* Muhammad al-Jawad (810–835), were buried at a cemetery north of Baghdad. This site, known as *al-Kazimiyya,* is another Shi`ite shrine. The Abbasid caliph al-Ma'mun designated the eighth *imam,* `Ali al-Rida, as his intended heir. Whether he ever intended to carry through with this is uncertain. Al-Rida died (818) before al-Ma'mun, and Shi`ite tradition again attributed his death, as well as the death of his father, to the caliphs. Al-Rida is the only *imam* buried in Iran (at Masshad in eastern Iran).

Ar-Rida's sister, Fatima al-Ma'suma, went to visit her brother in Iran and when she fell ill and died, she was buried in the city of Qumm, which had been settled by Shi`ite refugees in 712. Qumm became a major pilgrimage site and, much later, the major center of Shi`ite scholarship in Iran. The caliphs brought the tenth and eleventh *imams* to Samarra, the new capital, where they lived under Abbasid supervision. Their tombs at Samarra also became a Shi`ite holy site.

The 11th *imam,* al-Hasan al-Askari, died in 873 leaving no known male heir. Twelver Shi`ism claims that al-Askari had a four-year-old son whom he had hidden away. This son, Muhammad al-Mahdi, is the 12th, hidden *imam,* who will one day reappear as *imam* and Mahdi. From 874 to 941 during the lesser occultation *(ghayba),* Shi`ites believe this hidden *imam* maintained contact with the Shi`ite community through a succession of four messengers *(safirs).* In 941, the "greater occultation" began. The 12th *imam* is still alive and appears in dreams. The imam's absence created questions as to how the Shi`ite community should be led until his return. The hidden 12th *imam* is the official "head of state" in modern Iran.

By now the Abbasid caliph was a figurehead and real power was exercised by military strongmen with titles like *vizier* or *sultan*. The Buyid family filled this role from 945–1055. The Buyids were Shi`ites — at first Zaydis, then they switched to being Ithna-Asharis, because the 12th *imam* had gone into occultation and there was, therefore, no communal leader to challenge their authority. Although they didn't try to impose Shi`ism on the Sunni majority, Shi`ite religious practice and scholarship flourished under them. Shi`ite populations expanded west to Damascus and east to Iran. Although today Shi`ites are a relatively small minority of Muslims, at the end of the tenth century an outside observer could have thought Shi`ism was about to become dominant. The Buyids, the Fatimids ruling in Egypt, and several smaller Shi`ite dynasties together ruled the majority of the Muslim world, including the holy cities of Mecca and Medina. But this wasn't to last.

Iran becomes a Twelver Shi`ite state

The Abbasid Empire fell to the pagan Mongols in 1258. The Mongols who settled in Muslim areas gradually converted to Sunni Islam. Over the next several centuries the political situation was unstable. Most of the decentralized states were ruled by Sunni dynasties, although some areas fell under Shi`ite control. In the 15th century, there arose in Azerbaijan a Sufi military-missionary order linked to Isma`ili Shi`ism. Supported by some Turkic tribes, its power extended from northern areas of Iran to eastern Turkey. Its leader, Isma`il, claimed descent from Musa al-Kazim, the seventh *imam* and also claimed to be the *Mahdi*. Isma`il was the founder of the Iranian Safavid dynasty (1501–1722) that ruled over Iran and Iraq and made Twelver Shi`ism the state religion. As Shi`ites were still a minority in Iran, Arab scholars were brought from Shi`ite centers in Lebanon, Iraq, and Kashmir to implant Shi`ism among the people and serve as religious leaders and as theologians in the *madrasas* or seminaries at Meshed, Nishapur, and later Qumm. A government official supervised the religious leaders, appointing judges, prayer leaders, and regional religious authorities.

While the Safavid rulers could claim religious authority as descendants of the seventh *imam,* this wasn't true of the Qatar (1796–1925) and Pahlavi (1925–1979) rulers. The relationship of the Iranian state to the Shi`ite religious establishment was always tense. The Shi`ite clergy were financially independent and most Shi`ite holy sites and intellectual centers were in Iraq, outside of Iranian control. Prior to 1979, the religious establishment didn't aspire to actual rule. When interests coincided, they cooperated with the state but when their interests were threatened, they opposed state actions. The best example of successful opposition to the government is the tobacco boycott of 1891. The government had granted the British a long-term tobacco monopoly. This threatened the livelihood of the local merchants who were the traditional supporters of the Shi`ite scholars. They issued a *fatwa* (legal decision) against smoking tobacco. With no one smoking, the tobacco monopoly became useless and the government was forced to cancel the grant.

In the 20th century, the Iranian state secularized education and the courts abolished the veil and chador garment worn by women, and mandated Western dress for men. These actions that threatened religious interests explain why a minority of Shi`ite leaders like Khomeini became politically active in efforts to overthrow the state (see Chapter 18).

Worshipping in Twelver Shi`ite Fashion

In most areas of belief, law, and ritual, Shi`ites are the same as Sunnis. The following sections look at the ways Shi`ites differ from Sunni Muslims.

Remembering Husayn at `ashura'

To an outsider, the `*ashura'* celebrations are the most distinctive aspect of Twelver Shi`ite worship. During the first two months of the Muslim year, but especially during the first ten days of the first month *(Muharram)*, the events of Karbala are reenacted. The celebration includes:

- ✔ Lamentation and wearing of dark clothes.
- ✔ Cries of "Ya, Husayn."
- ✔ Blackening of faces and bodies.
- ✔ Erection of tents, pulpits, and special structures *(tekyeh* or *hoseyniyyeh)*. Decorative tiles in the *tekyehs* illustrate episodes from Karbala.
- ✔ Begging for water (recalling the thirst at Karbala).
- ✔ Beating with the fists on one's chest. Men's shirts, which open on the side rather than down the front, make it easy to expose the chest.
- ✔ Self-mutilation by males with knives, chains, and razor blades on the last three days. First aid stations take care of the participants' wounds.

The fully developed ceremony in Iran has three parts:

- ✔ **Public recitation of the events of Karbala (*rawzah-khvani* means "garden recitation"):** The typical sequence is a funeral elegy in honor of Muhammad, then the stories and songs about Husayn performed by the *rowza* singer, ending with the audience's singing of lamentations. The most famous recitation is the "Garden of the Martyrs" *(Rawdat al-shuhada')*. The audience is actively involved and speakers may draw parallels between Karbala and current events and governments.

✔ **Processions through the streets, which go back to at least the tenth century:** This is like a Thanksgiving Day or Rose Bowl parade with various floats prepared and carried by different guild and neighborhood groups. Coffins represent the martyrs of Karbala, standards on poles represent the *imams,* and Husayn's white horse, which is also the horse the hidden *imam* will ride when he returns, appears in the procession.

✔ **Dramatic reenactments (*ta`ziya,* from the Arabic word for mourning):** These full-scale dramatic performances emerged in developed form in the 18th and 19th centuries. This is "theatre in the round" in which actors, audience, and producer interact. Actors, scripts in hand, representing Husayn and his troop, dressed in green, sing their parts. The Umayyad villains dressed in red speak their parts. The climax comes when Husayn is wrapped in his death shroud. The Iranian state in the 1920s banned *ta`ziya* performances in its drive to modernize, and some scholars opposed certain aspects of the celebrations. Since 1979, the celebrations in Iran have revived, although they're less elaborate than those of the 19th century. More limited versions of the celebration are observed by Shi`ites in Iraq, Lebanon, and Azerbaijan. Indian and Pakistani Twelver Shi`ites' `ashura' celebrations include the recitations and processions but not the dramatic performances.

Making pilgrimage to the imams' tombs

Similar to the celebration of the birthdays of Sufi saints and pilgrimage to saints' tombs are pilgrimages to the tombs of the 11 *imams,* all but one located in Iraq. The shrines housing the tombs typically have large golden domes. The major celebration takes place on the death date of the *imam* rather than his birth date. Because the 12th *imam* is still alive, he has no tomb and his birthday is celebrated on the 15th of *Sha`ban.* Many of the shrines have enormous endowments and a large complex of buildings. As a person who has completed the *hajj* is called a *hajji,* so a person completing a pilgrimage to a major Shi`ite shrine assumes a comparable title. A person buried at one of these sacred sites doesn't undergo the examination by the angels Munkar and Nakir when placed in the grave.

Pilgrimage is also made to the tombs of descendants of the *imams* and to the tombs of some famous religious scholars. As in Sunni Islam, Muhammad's descendants (the *sheriffs,* or noble ones) are specially honored and may use the title *sayyid* (sir) and wear black turbans.

Some differences in Shi`ite rituals

GOING DEEPER

The differences between Sunnis and Shi`ites in shared rituals are minor but still distinguish Shi`ites from Sunnis. Some differences are:

✔ In the call to worship, Shi`ites add "I attest that `Ali is close" and when prostrating, may touch their heads to a clod of clay from Karbala.

✔ Shi`ites combine the second daily prayer with the third and the fourth with the fifth so that they do three ritual prayers a day.

✔ On the *hajj* to Mecca, Shi`ites make one more circle around the *Ka`ba*.

Thinking like Shi`ites

Shi`ites developed their own brands of Islamic law, theology, philosophy, textual interpretation, and religious leadership.

Shi`ite religious law (shari`a)

The Twelver Shi`ite law School is called the Ja`farite School after the sixth *imam,* who is regarded as its founder. So long as a living *imam* was in their midst, he gave divinely inspired and infallible interpretations of divine law. While the *imam* is in hiding, the first two sources of law are the same as for Sunnis: the Qur'an and the *hadiths*. Shi`ites have four major collections of traditions *(hadiths);* the oldest was collected by al-Kulayni (tenth century). These collections differ from Sunni collections in containing additional traditions relating to `Ali and in including traditions (sayings and actions) of the *imams*. A group called the *Ashkaris* were strict literalists and believed that an ordinary Shi`ite shouldn't depend on scholarly opinion but only on the Qur'an and the *hadiths*. Their rivals, the *Usulis* (from the word for "root" as in "roots of the law"), prevailed and persecuted the Ashkaris. Usulis use reason (`aql) to apply and extend the law so long as the result doesn't contradict the Qur'an and the *hadiths*. For Shi`ites, the "door of *ijtihad* (interpretation)" was never closed. In contrast to Sunni Islam, the decisions of earlier legal scholars weren't binding on the present generation of scholars or believers, although by reason they may reach the same legal decisions.

Three areas (excluding ritual and the imams) where Shi`ite law differs from Sunni law are:

✔ A dead father's brothers have no share in the inheritance.

✔ The rights of the woman are more strongly protected as regards marriage and divorce.

✔ *Mu`ta* (temporary marriage) is permitted under Shi`ite law (based on Sura 4:24). It seems the major purpose was to provide a sexual outlet for the male when away from home. In the contract, fixed formulas are spoken, a dowry is specified, and a time period is named after which the marriage ends. The woman doesn't inherit and the husband isn't obligated to provide for her. Any children go with the father.

Shi`ite clergy: The mullas

Muslims often say that Islam has no clergy. Each believer stands directly before God without the need of human intermediaries. This is true, if by clergy one understands "priests." However, the claim of standing directly before God could be made by many Protestant Christians. The more general sense of clergy is to designate a professional class of religious leaders in a particular religious tradition. In Shi`ism, the position of the religious leaders is relatively close to what most Westerners regard as a professional clergy. *Mulla* is a common term for a religious leader in Shi`ite Islam. With the occultation of the 12th *imam,* the *mullas* gradually assumed the tasks of the *imam* in his absence.

In addition to the government and religious taxes prescribed in Sunni Islam, a special Shi`ite religious tax is called the "fifth" *(khums).* All Shi`ites contribute a fifth of their earnings to the *imam.* This tax is based on Sura 8:41, which Sunnis interpret as applying only to spoils of war but Shi`ites interpret more broadly as a tax on earnings. Half of this amount is the imam's portion, and half is to support the *sayyids* (descendants of Muhammad). In the absence of the hidden *imam,* the *mullas* assumed the task of collecting and distributing these substantial sums that are used for education, welfare, and the advancement of religion. Shi`ites can pay their "fifth" to the *mulla* of their choice. A village *mulla* will keep one-third of the tax for local use and remit two-thirds to a higher ranking *mulla.* Endowments and the "fifth" tax explain the ability of Shi`ite clergy to remain independent of the state.

Shi`ism has a hierarchy of religious leaders. Candidates obtain entrance to the lowest grade as a simple *mulla* by completing the proper training in a religious institution and being certified by the *mujtahids* (literally meaning "one who strives" and recognized as one who is qualified to give interpretations on matters of religious law). Advancement to the two upper levels is by consensus and recognition. The title *hujjat al-islam* applies to clergy at the intermediate levels. A scholar at this level is a *mujtahid.* He has followers beyond those in the place he lives. At the top of the hierarchy is the "source of imitation" *(marja` al-taqlid),* who may also be called an *ayatolla* (sign of God) or a "grand ayatolla." The number of people at the top level is relatively few but isn't fixed. Sometimes one person is recognized as the top Shi`ite "source of imitation" of his time. A layperson chooses one *marja`* as the "source of imitation" whose decisions he accepts (imitates).

Shi`ite philosophers and theologians

Shi`ite scholars were more open to philosophical thinking than was true of most traditional Sunni scholars. Shi`ites tended to accept Mu`tazilite views of the created Qur'an and allowed a greater role for human free will, two Mu`tazilite positions rejected by Sunni orthodoxy. Among outstanding Shi`ite theologian-philosophers, the following are the most important:

- ✔ Al-Tusi (995–1067) compiled two of the four main Twelver *hadith* collections and wrote fundamental works in ethics, theology, and Qur'an interpretation.

- ✔ Al-Suhrawardi (1154–1191) is the founder of a philosophical perspective known as the *Ishraqi* (illuminism) *movement*. He said that at creation souls are imprisoned in flesh and forget their divine origin. God's light (illumination) may inspire one to seek reunion with God beyond death. His work was very influential in early Safavid Iran.

- ✔ Mulla Sadra (1571–1640) is Iran's most influential philosopher-mystic-theologian. He combined elements from Aristotle, Ibn Sina, Suhrawardi, and others into his own unique world view emphasizing that ultimate being is found in different degrees in all existing things. People advanced spiritually through four stages. On the Day of Judgment, the soul will reunite with an ethereal body and the two will be one.

- ✔ Muhammad Baqir Majlisi (1628–1699) was the highest ranking Shi`ite religious leader of Iran in his generation. His best-known work is the *Bihar al-anwar* (Ocean of Light), a massive collection of prophetic traditions. Majlisi set the future course of Twelver Shi`ism both in his attacks on Sunnism and Sufism and in his emphasis on mourning for Imam Husayn and visiting the *imams'* tombs. In addition to his Arabic works, he wrote many books in Persian aimed at strengthening the dedication of the people to Shi`ite Islam.

In interpreting the Qur'an, Twelver Shi`ites placed equal emphasis on the exoteric (literal meaning) and the esoteric or hidden *(batin)* meaning. The many layers of hidden meaning are fully known by the *imams* who are the "speaking Qur'an" in contrast to the written Qur'an that is the "silent Qur'an." Esoteric interpretation *(ta'wil)* reveals many references in the Qur'an to `Ali, Husayn, and the *imams*. For example, the hidden meaning of "signs" in Sura 3:1 and 41:53 refer to the *imams*. Or, in reference to Abraham's sacrifice of his son in Sura 37:107, Abraham's sorrow over the future suffering of Husayn moved God to provide a sacrificial animal in place of Abraham's son. The sufferings of Joseph, Moses, and Jesus prefigure the suffering and sacrifice of Husayn.

Isma`ili Shi`ite philosophy and theology is much more esoteric than that of Twelver Shi`ism. A typical Isma`ili view is that history is divided into seven periods. Each period begins with a prophet who gives the revelation and law for that period. The prophet is aided by a deputy *(wali)* who interprets the secret meaning of the prophet's teaching for an inner elite. This secret meaning *(batin)* remains constant through all periods. The inner, spiritual meaning is more important than the external *(zahir)* meaning. In some Isma`ili theologies, this interpreter becomes more important that the prophet himself. The interpreter is followed by six *imams,* and then the next cycle begins. Muhammad and `Ali are the prophet and interpreter of the sixth period (as Jesus and Peter were of the fifth period, and Moses and Aaron before that). The seventh *imam* after Muhammad is in hiding and will return as the Mahdi to institute the final, seventh period of history (see Chapter 14).

Interacting: Shi`ites, Sufis, and Sunnis

The final section of this chapter discusses why Sufism (Islamic mysticism) is mainly found in Sunni Islam and why conflict exists sometimes between Shi`ite and Sunni Muslims.

Shi`ites and Sufis

The founder of the Safavid dynasty belonged to a Shi`ite Sufi order, but Sufism is more associated with Sunnis than with Shi`ism. Why?

- As objects of devotion, the *imams* and their families serve the same function as do Sufi saints for Sunnis.
- Shi`ism emphasizes the hidden meaning of scripture that is analogous but not identical to the spiritual or interior meaning emphasized by Sufis.
- Sufism and Shi`ism both provide outlets to express intense religious emotions.
- Shi`ite theologians addressed many of the same issues that Sufi theologians did and were familiar with Sufi writings.

Shi`ites and Sunnis

Today, for many Muslims Shi`ite and Sunni Islam are both legitimate. But tensions and antagonisms still arise between the two groups. The reasons are complex but include:

- For Shi`ites, what they perceive as the injustices done to `Ali and Husayn aren't simply past misfortunes to be forgotten.
- In 1802, Wahhabi Sunnis (the same group dominant in Saudi Arabia today) destroyed the shrine of *imam* Husayn in Karbala, killing 2,000 people. The Wahhabis also destroyed the tombs of the four Shi`ite *imams* buried in Mecca.
- In countries where Sunnis wish to impose Islamic law, Shi`ites suspect the result will be that Shi`ites will be required to follow Sunni law.

- ✔ Some Shi`ite ritual practices, including the cursing of the first three caliphs, are highly offensive to Sunnis.

- ✔ Sunnis have at times accused Shi`ites of hypocrisy and immorality because of their practice of dissimulation and their acceptance of *mu`ta* (temporary marriage).

- ✔ Because Saudi Arabia is a bastion of Sunni orthodoxy and Iran is the leading Shi`ite country, ancient tensions between Arabs and "Persians" resurface in modern competition for leadership in the Muslim world.

Don't be deceived by a simple equation of Arab equals Sunni and Iranian equals Shi`ite. Don't assume all Shi`ites share the same political views. For example, although Iraqi Arab Shi`ites are oppressed by and hate President Saddam Hussein, they didn't support Iran during its war with Iraq.

Chapter 13

Sufis

• •

In This Chapter

▶ Taking a look at Sufi practice and institutions

▶ Meeting some interesting Sufis

▶ Encountering Sufi poets

• •

During the 1960s, exotic foreign New Age religions attracted the attention of young Americans. Although never as popular as Hindu yoga or Tai Chi, many Americans took classes in Sufi "dancing." As most people doing yoga or Tai Chi didn't convert to Hinduism or Taoism, so people participating in Sufi rituals didn't all consider themselves converts to Islam. At the same time, the poems of Jalal al-din Rumi, founder of the whirling dervish Sufi order (the Mevlevi), became enormously popular, and remain so today. This happened before developments on the world stage brought Islam onto the radar screen of most Americans.

Sufism has always been controversial within Islam. Some deny its legitimacy and say that Sufism has nothing to do with Islam. This is a theological judgment because, historically, Sufism has played an enormous role in Islam. Others counter that Sufism represents the true essence of Islam. Many famous Muslim scholars were Sufis. Sufis produced some of the greatest works of pre-modern Islamic literature, especially poetry and were more responsible for the spread of Islamic religion outside of the Arabic world than jurists, theologians, or even armies. Sufis played a major role in converting people to Islam in regions such as sub-Saharan Africa, south Asia (today's Pakistan, India, and Bangladesh), and central Asia.

Sufism as Islamic mysticism

Historians of religion describe Sufism as the Islamic form of mysticism. Mysticism is a technical term designating a particular form of religion. Taoism is the expression of mysticism in Chinese religion, and the *Tao Te Ching* ("The Book of the Way and the Power") is one of the great mystical scriptures. The *Tao* is a non-material reality that can't even be named but it's the source of all created things. Within monasticism, one finds the highest expression of Christian mysticism in people like St. Teresa of Avila and St. John of the Cross. In Hinduism, yoga is the mystical path in distinction to the paths of devotion, knowledge, and works. Mysticism emphasizes religious experience. The mystic seeks a direct, unmediated experience of the divine. Mystical knowledge is direct knowledge, in contrast to the knowledge of science, philosophy, or scriptures. The mystic incorporates the external expressions of her religion (devotion, ritual, ethics, beliefs), but she wants to go deeper. She wants not just to obey, acknowledge, and worship God, she wants to encounter and experience God. A mystical experience is more than a sudden feeling of religious intensity. Mysticism involves discipline and a technique. To set out on the mystical path is to undertake a long and hard journey without assurance that one will arrive at the destination. Usually the novice is guided by a more advanced person as she proceeds through a sequence of steps, each bringing her to a higher spiritual level.

Searching for God

Sufism, with its emphasis on religious experience, provides a counterbalance in Islam to religious legalism and to theological dogmatism.

Sufism: An overview of its history

The four stages of Sufi history that I outline here are cumulative. Each adds something new but doesn't replace or eliminate what went before it. During the first stage of Sufism, individuals sought to come closer to God. These early Sufis were spiritual athletes pushing themselves beyond the norm. Different emphases in approach include:

- ✔ The path of self-denial and purgation (the negative approach) and the path of love (the positive approach).
- ✔ Sober mysticism and ecstatic mysticism.

The early Sufis were *ascetics* (people who practiced physical self-denial) and wore coarse woolen garments. Most likely the word "Sufi" comes from the Arabic word for "wool," although other explanations have been offered. Western scholars of Islam, several centuries ago, first popularized the terms Sufi and Sufism. The Arabic term is *tasawwuf.*

Because God is totally other and transcendent, to approach God one must strip off all attributes of the self (ego). Purgation involves restricting one's possessions, sleep, and food intake. Beyond that, one purges oneself of attachment to the self. The way of love says human love, even sexual love, is the highest expression of attachment between two beings. Human love is a preparation for love of God. God created the world because he desired to be known, and to love God is the proper response.

Often, the sober mystic follows the path of self-denial and the Sufi who emphasizes love of God tends to a more ecstatic and enthusiastic expression. The sober mystic is more acceptable to the religious establishment. The ecstatic mystic, on the other hand, experiences altered states of consciousness that may find expression in unusual actions and shocking verbal expression.

The first Sufis had little consciousness of belonging to a specific approach to Islam. The second stage involves the consolidation of Sufism and dates to about 1000 C.E. Several concerns were prominent at this stage:

✔ Defending the orthodoxy of Sufism against its critics.

✔ Making Sufism accessible to a larger group of people.

✔ Taking stock by providing manuals discussing the technical vocabulary of Sufism, classifying different types of Sufism, and providing Sufi exemplars for others through collected stories of Sufis saints.

✔ Systematic and poetic exposition of Sufism, giving attention to:

- The stations of the Sufi path

- The goal of the Sufi spiritual quest

- The theological-philosophical theory presupposed by Sufism

The third stage (12th century) is the institutionalization of Sufism, resulting in organized Sufi lodges and in the emergence of the major Sufi orders (comparable to the different monastic orders of Christianity).

In the fourth stage (after 1500), Sufism loses its creative and adaptive edge, leading to numerical and spiritual decline. New opposition to Sufism develops. Even in this stage, creative exceptions emerge: additional orders, new Sufi saints, and significant achievements in Sufi thought and literature.

Textual and historical foundations

Any expression of Islam that claims legitimacy must be based in the Qur'an and the example of Muhammad, and in the case of Sunni Islam, the examples of the four rightly guided caliphs. Legitimization of Sufism included:

✔ Quoting Qur'anic passages to support the Sufi quest:

- Injunctions to "remember God." Remembering *(dhikr),* although incumbent on all Muslims, also designates the ritual most associated with Sufism.

- Expressions of God's closeness to the believer (Sura 2:186).

- Statements that God is friend and lover/beloved (Sura 5:54–56).

- References to the face of God, which is present wherever one turns (Sura 2:115). The Sufi seeks out the face of God.

✔ Finding Sufi concepts expressed in the esoteric, inner, and symbolic meaning of the Qur'an *(ta'wil).*

✔ Using Muhammad's night journey through the seven heavens to the throne of God as the model for the stations of the Sufi path.

✔ Citing *hadiths* not in the standard collections that portray Muhammad exemplifying Sufi virtues, such as poverty and humility.

✔ Quoting *hadith qudsi* (sayings of God), such as "I was a secret treasure, and I desired to be known."

✔ Referring to the examples of the voluntary poverty of the first two caliphs. `Umar, the second caliph, embraced poverty to such an extent that his patched garments became the inspiration for the patched cloak that the Sufi received at the time of his initiation into a Sufi order.

Believing in the Sufi Manner

What are some of the features which characterize a Sufi? The following list indicates some of the most important characteristics.

✔ **Asceticism, self-denial, and purgation**

✔ **Poverty:** "My poverty is my pride," says a Sufi tradition. Physical poverty is linked to asceticism. Spiritual poverty means, like Rabi`a, desiring nothing for oneself, even paradise. Two terms often used for initiated Sufis are *faqir* and *dervish.* The first is Arabic, the second Persian, and both literally mean a "poor person."

✔ *Tawakkul,* **absolute trust in God, and** *rida* **(contentment or acceptance)** with whatever good or evil happens because it all comes from God

✔ **Love for God:** Nizami's version of the folktale of *Laila and Majnun* (1188) became for Sufis an allegory of the Sufi's love of God. Cut off from contact with his beloved, Majnun became a madman (the meaning of *majnun),* wandering the desert like a Sufi dervish, giving up all his possessions, searching for and crying out *(dhikr)* the name of his beloved. She died before they consummated their love, just as the Sufi's search for God finds its final fulfillment beyond death.

✔ **Abiding in God *(baqa):* Baqa** is what remains after annihilation *(fana)* of self and world. This "goal," which only the most advanced Sufis achieve, is described as a form of experiential union with God, like the moth that is drawn to and consumed in the flame. Others say it is perfect knowledge *(ma`rifa)* of God.

✔ *Tawhid* **(unity of God):** Sufism understands *tawhid* to mean that only God exists. God is the ultimate reality or truth *(al-haqq).* If only God exists, then everything in the world mirrors the reality of God.

✔ **Focus on the interior, spiritual, esoteric aspects of religion and religious texts in contrast to the exterior:** For most Sufis, this was a step beyond, not a replacement for, the religious ritual and law.

✔ **The master-disciple relationship:** Individual wandering dervishes existed from the early days of Sufism, but for most Sufis, spiritual advancement could take place only under the tutelage of one's spiritual guide *(murshid)* and master. He's called the sheikh in the Arabic world and the *pir* in Persian-Turkish-Indian regions.

✔ **The spiritual genealogical tree *(silsila,* "chain")** that traces a Sufi's spiritual ancestry from his sheikh back through earlier sheikhs to Muhammad or `Ali: In form, the chain resembles the *isnads* that validate and introduce a *hadith* (see Chapter 8). Most *silsilas* have either al-Junayd or al-Bistami as a crucial earlier link in the chain.

✔ *Dhikr* **(recollection), the ritual invocation of a sacred phrase**

✔ **Stations *(maqams)* and states *(hals):* Stations** are the rungs of the ladder that the Sufi ascends as he matures spiritually. States are temporary emotional and psychological experiences associated with each station. As an example, al-Sarraj (10th century) lists the stations (in sequence) as: repentance, watchfulness, renunciation, poverty, patience, trust, and acceptance. Others include gratitude, fear, hope, love, and knowledge.

Making a Contribution: Outstanding Individual Sufis

In part, the rise of Sufism was a reaction against the worldliness of the `Umayyad caliphs. Sufis rejected power, wealth, and worldly success. The Sufi must pursue the "greater struggle" *(jihad)* against his own lower self. Early Sufis extended their time of fasting, prayed all night, and avoided many things that Islam permitted in order to guard against falling into sin. To avoid worldly entanglements, many early Sufis preferred celibacy, although this was not to become the norm, given the positive endorsements of marriage in the Qur'an. The Sufi totally depended on and trusted in God *(tawakkul).* Some went so far as taking no money or food with them when traveling, refusing medical help, and eating no food not given personally to them.

Hasan al-Basri (642–728) was the first outstanding Sufi saint. Like many Sufis, al-Basri was a scholar and a famous preacher. He's an example of a "sober Sufi" who followed the ascetic path and regarded the material world as a "mistake." In one of his letters to the pious Umayyad caliph, `Umar II, al-Basri described the world as a snake, smooth to the touch but with killing poison. Hasan left no surviving writings, but he's often quoted by others and he occurs as a link in most Sufi *silsilas* (a spiritual family tree of a Sufi saint or practitioner). Another of Hasan's sayings is that "the world is a bridge which you cross over (to the afterlife) but upon which you should not build."

Another early Sufi was Ibrahim ibn Adham (about 730–770). Ibrahim wandered from place to place, working rather than begging to sustain himself. He was famous for his generosity and his asceticism. He voluntarily accepted physical abuse from others as a form of self-denial. Clearly legendary is the story of how he became a monk: One day he looked at a mirror, and all he saw was the tomb. Another time, an animal that he was hunting spoke to him and told him that he was created for other than a princely life. So, like the Buddha, he abandoned his princely life. During his wanderings, Ibrahim met al-Khidr, a mysterious companion of Moses (Sura 18:61–83). To Sufis, Moses, the transmitter of the law, represents the external form of religion, while al-Khidr represents its inner essence. Al-Khidr initiated Ibrahim as a Sufi and gave him God's name as his *dhikr* formula. It took Ibrahim 14 years to complete his pilgrimage to Mecca because he stopped to pray after every step. When he finally arrived in Mecca, the *Ka`ba* was no longer there because it had gone to meet another saint, Rabi`a.

One of the most appealing figures of early Sufism is Rabi`a al-`Adawiya (713–801). Like Hasan and Ibrahim, she was a sober Sufi, the first great Sufi to focus on the love of God. She cared nothing for herself and everything for God. In one saying, she uttered, "O my God, whatever share of this world you have given me, give it to your enemies, and whatever share of the next world you have given me, give it to your friends. You are enough for me." A number of stories tell of her meetings with Hasan al-Basri. Each time, her humility triumphs over his pride. One time, he tossed his prayer rug on the water and challenged her to join him in prayer on the water. She threw her prayer rug in the air and asked him to join her in prayer up in the air, where their piety wouldn't be on display to others. She said that what Hasan had done, the fish could do and what she did, a bird could do (see Chapter 3 for more on Rabi`a).

Al-Muhasibi (751–857) wrote on the psychology of the soul in Sufism. His most famous work takes the form of short questions asked by a student followed by Muhasibi's answers. For example, he lists four types of egoism that the Sufi must overcome: conceit, pride, vanity, and self-delusion. The section on vanity is introduced by the student's question: "Tell me about vanity, what it is, where it's located, and how it can be avoided."

Dhu al-Nun al-Misri (about 796–860) was imprisoned by the caliph al-Mutawakkil when he refused to affirm the Mu`tazilite doctrine of the created Qur'an. However, Dhu al-Nun's moving testimony caused the caliph to release him. His writings include sayings, poems, and prayers. When asked by a woman what is the end of love, he replied that love has no end. Dhu al-Nun developed the Sufi vocabulary for the stations and stages of the path. He was one of the first Sufis to joyously affirm the physical world because everything in nature from the whisper of the leaves to the songs of the birds sings the praises of God.

Abu Yazid al-Bistami (Bazeid for short), a Persian who lived in the ninth century, is one of the most prominent ecstatic or intoxicated Sufis. Different ancient writers give different pictures of Bazeid that range from a very orthodox to a rather unorthodox personality. He's most famous for his ecstatic exclamations _(shatahat),_ such as _subhani_ (Glory be to me) and "How great is my majesty." He used paradox to convey truth in an almost Zen Buddhist-like fashion. When someone came to see him, he responded that he was also seeking Bazeid. He used Muhammad's night ascension _(mi`raj)_ as a model for his own vision of approaching God.

Abu al-Qasim Muhammad al-Junayd (ninth century) was a "sober" mystic who condemned the extremes of ecstatic mysticism. He emphasized that a Sufi must return from his mystical experience to live in the ordinary world. He earned his living as a merchant in Baghdad. Rather than the union with God emphasized by the intoxicated Sufis, he spoke of "consciousness" of God, in which the person returns to the state of humankind at the time of the first covenant when God called each person forth from Adam to acknowledge God as lord (Sura 7:171).

Husayn ibn Mansur al-Hallaj (executed 922) was the most famous of the intoxicated mystics. Al-Hallaj attracted many disciples and became something of a cult figure among the masses. His poetry used many images, such as the moth and the flame that became prominent in the later Sufi poetry. He is famous for exclaiming, _"Ana al-Haqq"_ (I am truth/God). Arrested on charges of heresy, after eight years in prison, he was flogged and beheaded, and his body was burned. He accepted his death, saying, "Kill me . . . for in my death is life." Like Husayn, the son of `Ali, in death al-Hallaj became one of the great martyr figures of Islam and was an important influence on later Indo-Persian Sufism.

Abu Nasr al-Sarraj (tenth century) was the author of _The Book of Flashes,_ perhaps the first systematic description of Sufi thought and life. He discussed controversial topics, such as the ecstatic exclamations, miracles, and use of music. Like al-Ghazali, he defended Sufism as the purest expression of Islam. His book became a basis on which subsequent Sufi theologians built.

Abu Hamid al-Ghazali (1058–1111) is one of the towering figures of Islamic thought. He made major contributions to Islamic philosophy and theology (see Chapter 5), as well as ethics (see Chapter 9). Al-Ghazali's _The Deliverance_ *from Error* is one of the great religious autobiographies. Coming from Iran, al-Ghazali was the foremost Islamic scholar of his day and occupied a prestigious position in the Nizamiyya university that the Seljuk vizier Nizam al-Mulk established in Baghdad. In 1095, al-Ghazali experienced a spiritual crisis, resigned his teaching post, and set out on a personal, spiritual quest. His 11 years of wandering took him to Syria, where he found in Sufism the answer to his spiritual crisis. The fourth and last section of his masterpiece, the *Ihya (The Revivification of the Religious Sciences)* is devoted to Sufism. For al-Ghazali, Sufism was the culminating expression of Islam so long as the Sufi didn't neglect Islamic ritual, law, and theology. For most Muslim scholars, his presentation legitimized the place of Sufism within Islam. The Hanbalite jurist, Ibn-Taymiyya (see Chapter 8) and his later heirs, the Wahhabis, never accepted Sufism as legitimate, but other outstanding Hanbalite jurists were themselves Sufis.

Ibn Muhyiddin Muhammad Ibn `Arabi (1165–1240) stood at the opposite extreme from al-Ghazali. Ibn `Arabi's synthesis of Sufi theology and cosmology has been constantly defended and reinterpreted by his Sufi admirers and condemned by conservative scholars. Born and raised in Spain, two of his Sufi teachers were women. He claimed to have been initiated by al-Khidr. Settling eventually in Damascus, he produced a large number of intellectually difficult and esoteric theological works. The most important are *The Meccan Revelations* and *The Bezels of Wisdom.* He presents love as the central truth upon which the universe depends. His cosmology involves 28 levels between the unknowable divine essence (the *la ilaha* or "there is no god but God," of the *shahada*) and the level of physical existence. His most influential concept is *wahdat al-wujud,* traditionally translated "unity of being." This concept isn't as pantheistic as it sounds in English. In his desire to be known, God manifested himself in the plurality of being. Another important concept of Ibn `Arabi is the Perfect (whole) Human. This person is Muhammad because he most clearly mirrors the being of God. In each generation there exists another Perfect Human, who is the link between creator and the created. He's the "pole" *(qutb)* around which the cosmos revolves. Various later Sufi masters claimed to be the *qutb* of their generation.

Rabi`a is by no means the only female Sufi or saint in Islam. Tradition names a number of other early female Sufis, such as Fatima of Nishapur. In general, Sufism has allowed greater religious possibilities for women than has been true for much of Islam and yet at the same time, the role of women in Sufism has been limited. Some female lodges were established in the great cities of medieval Islam. But with few exceptions, a female wouldn't head a Sufi order or local lodge including men and women. Heads of some Sufi lodges allowed a greater degree of female participation than did others, or they even formally initiated women into their orders, but formal initiation was relatively rare and the norm was that women had limited (if any) participation, often from a distance in communal Sufi ceremonies. Collections of biographies of the saints include a number of female figures, and Muslims visit the tombs of these female (as well as of male) saints. Yet the link of many of these women to institutionalized Sufism was limited. A number of female teachers and transmitters of *hadiths* were mentioned. For some Sufis, distinction between male and female became irrelevant for those who achieved the highest stages of the Sufi path, and Ibn `Arabi admitted that a women could even be the *qutb* (pole), the most exalted Sufi of a given age. Nor are female saints and Sufis limited to one portion of the Muslim world. For example, Fatima Jahanara, the eldest daughter of the Mughal emperor Shah Jahan (17th century) was initiated into the Qadiriyya order.

Organizing the Sufi Community

Few, if any, organized communities of Sufis existed during the first several centuries of Islam. Al-Ghazali is mentioned as one of the first to found an organized community with a central lodge (building) for the members.

Lodges

A number of terms designate the central structure of a Sufi community. The term *khanqa* (with several variant spellings in English) originated with lodges in eastern Persia (Khorasan). The equivalent Turkish term is *tekke.* In the western Arab regions, a *ribat* (originally a frontier fortress) or a *zawiya* was the Arabic equivalent. The *khanqa* had multiple functions. The sheikh taught his disciples there. It served as a hospice for travelers, a soup kitchen, and a place for the care of the sick. Most welcomed visitors without charge.

A typical *khanqa* had a courtyard for communal ceremonies with cells for individual full-time members along two sides (not all had resident members). After Sufi orders emerged, the tomb of the founder was often part of a complex that could include a *madras* (school), mosque, and other structures. A saint's cult often grew up around the tomb that in later centuries sometimes became more important than the Sufi practices themselves (see Chapter 10).

The Sufi brotherhood

Tariqa ("way" or "path") designates both an organized, self-perpetuating Sufi order (brotherhood) and the specific path followed by that order. One can distinguish four groups of people associated with a specific *khanqa.*

- The inner elite had obtained the highest spiritual stations. They undertook advanced practices and could initiate others into the *tariqa.* The sheikh could designate one of these as his successor or send him out to found a daughter lodge.

- A larger number were full members of the order who regularly attended all the functions, such as communal *dhikr,* of the lodge.

✔ Novices *(murid)* were Sufis in training who had not yet been initiated.

✔ Lay affiliates were more loosely linked to the lodge. They recognized the sheikh as their master and had some basic Sufi training. They attended the celebration of the birthday *(maulid)* or death *(urs,* literally "marriage") of the founding sheikh. The order depended on the lay affiliates for financial support. Rulers and the wealthy supported favored orders, which built up substantial endowments *(waqfs)*. Association with a *tariqa* served social purposes also. Some orders were linked to a particular class or profession. Or a Sufi order could bring together different class, ethnic, or occupational groups. In some African countries, most male Muslims belonged to an order.

Acting in the Sufi Manner

Much variation exists in the specifics of rules, ritual, and daily life of a Sufi *tariqa*. The following descriptions are typical but not universal.

Joining a Sufi brotherhood

Although a Muslim could obtain initiation from a number of different sheikhs, he recognized one as his master. Training prior to initiation could last three years, during which he practiced humility and obedience. The novice mastered the *silsila* of the order and began basic Sufi meditation rituals. A 40-day period of seclusion came at the end. In the initiation ceremony, the initiate took an oath of allegiance while clasping the sheikh's hand. The handclasp transmitted the sheikh's power *(baraka)* to the student. The sheikh gave him his patched cloak *(khirqa)*, which was the typical garment of the Sufi, and a cap whose design varied among orders. He also received a document, like a graduation diploma, that attested to his initiation and traced his *silsila*. The sheikh gave the new member a personal *dhikr*.

Following the rules of the brotherhood

Like a Christian monastic order, each Sufi brotherhood had rules to be followed by its members. Most Sufis were married but not all. R.A. Nicholson cites ten rules used by one 11th-century *khanqa,* including:

✔ Wear clean garments and be in a state of ritual purity.

✔ Pray extensively at night.

✔ In the morning, read as much of the Qur'an as possible and don't talk until sunrise.

✔ Between evening and bedtime prayers do the special *dhikr.*

✔ Welcome the poor and needy.

Remembering God: Dhikr

Besides the general use of *dhikr* for the remembering of God as commanded in the Qur'an, *dhikr* refers to the Sufi practice of the rhythmic repetition of a phrase, alone or in a group. Common *dhikr* phrases were the divine name Allah, any of the 99 names of God, the first half of the *shahada,* or an exclamatory formula, such as "praise be to God" *(subha Allah),* or "God is greatest" *(Allahu Akbar).* The Sufi repeated the phrase a designated number of times or over a specified period of time. A distinction is made between silent *dhikr* and spoken *dhikr.* In individual *dhikr,* the Sufi may start with vocal "*dhikr* of the tongue," move to "*dhikr of the heart,*" and climax with "*dhikr* of the inmost being" in which the words no longer are pronounced even mentally. The Naqshbandiyya use only silent *dhikr.* The loud *dhikr* of the Rifa`iyya order gave rise to its nickname in the West, the Howling Dervishes. Three main types of *dhikr* are:

✔ **The daily, individual repetition by members after at least two of the five daily prayer rituals**

✔ **A more elaborate form of *dhikr* resembling yoga:** The participant coordinates repetition of the phrase with breathing patterns and mental focus on a part of the body. An example is the repetition of the *shahada,* exhaling while saying "there is no God" and inhaling while saying "but God." This advanced *dhikr* takes a long time to master.

✔ **Communal *dhikr:*** This "*dhikr* of presence" usually takes place on Thursday evenings and on special occasions. "Presence" refers to the presence of God, Muhammad, and Sufi saints at the ceremony.

Hearing God: Sama`

Sama`* is the Arabic term for a Sufi session that involves music and singing. It is often combined with communal *dhikr.* Some Sufi orders have special music halls *(sama` khanahs) for the *sama`* session. Some conservative Muslim scholars have always opposed music, saying that it excites the passions and the lower self. Outside of religious contexts, music has flourished in Muslim cultures. An outsider who hears the chanting of the Qur'an in its more elaborate forms may regard this as a form of music. However, manuals on Qur'an recitation were careful to maintain a fine line between "singing" the Qur'an, which isn't allowed, and a chant-like recitation that is permitted (see Chapter 7). The Qadiriyya and Naqshbandiyya orders don't utilize musical sessions *(sama`)* but don't oppose its use by other Sufis. The Mevlevi and Chisti orders, however, are known for their use of music. Some orders train their members to control their emotions during *sama`* sessions. In other orders, restrained bodily movement accompanies the music and a few members will enter a state of ecstasy. They may shout out, cry, stand up, dance, and fall exhausted at the end. For the Mevlevi (the "whirling dervishes"), the main communal session is a combination of music and a graceful whirling dance, starting slowly and picking up speed, with all members present participating. A *sama`* session may also use the services of a professional singer *(munshid)*.

Those defending *sama`* sessions point out that the Qur'an mentions that David sang psalms to God: Young girls greeted returning Muslim warriors with songs. Muhammad listened without objection to girls singing on one of the feast days. Still, given the opposition by some to both Sufism and the religious use of music, various Sufi writers laid down guidelines to prevent excesses during *sama`* sessions. The singer should be an adult male. No musical instruments should be used, the participants should focus their attention on God, and only religiously appropriate "lyrics" should be used. Specifics vary from group to group and some do use musical instruments.

Communal dhikr with sama`

The next best thing to being there is to watch a video of a session, such as *Celebrating the Prophet in the Remembrance of God: Sufi Dhikr in Egypt,* narrated by Valarie Hoffman. *I am a Sufi, I am a Muslim* is a video that includes more ecstatic ceremonies from Pakistan and Turkey. The description that follows is a composite taken from Hoffman's script and from J. S. Trimingham's *The Sufi Orders of Islam.*

The session begins with the participants arranged in a particular order, often a circle or in two facing rows. It opens with recitation of the *Fatiha* or a prayer written by the order's founder. The *munshid* sings a single poem or combines elements from several songs. He may repeat lines that are having an obvious, strong effect on someone. Love for Muhammad or his family is the dominant theme. Each singer has a unique style from simple to elaborate. In Egypt, the singer is accompanied by his "band" using instruments, such as a tambourine, castanets, violin, and flute. While the *munshid* is performing, the participants may repeat the *dhikr* of the order. Short segments invoking the assistance of the saints, interspersed with the more intense recitation or singing, provide a momentary emotional break. As the evening progresses, the pace and intensity picks up. Some people are moved to bodily expression: foaming at the mouth, waving their hands, standing up and pulling off their headgear. Note that the public can attend some sessions, including women who typically sit apart and are more reserved in their responses.

Putting Faith into Verse: Sufi Literature

Sufism inspired great literature in Arabic, Persian, Turkish, and various South Asian dialects. Because poetry was the primary literary genre of pre-Islamic Arabia, poetry dominates Sufi literature. The following are a few great Sufi poets.

✔ Ibn al-Farid (1181–1235) is described as the greatest Arabic poet. The Arabic language provides rich possibilities for word plays that are exploited by al-Farid, who is said to have composed his poetry in a state of ecstatic trance. His *Ta'iya* contains 760 verses, all of which end in "t." In his *Wine Ode,* he takes the traditional wine song and uses it to express the mystical experience of the Sufi. Sufism made almost as much use of wine as it did of love imagery to express the state of God-intoxication.

✔ Farid al-Din `Attar (about 1119–1220) is perhaps the outstanding Persian Sufi poet. He was a masterful entertainer, as well as a teacher of Sufism. His *Mantiq al-tayr, The Conference of the Birds,* is available in English. Based on a reference to King Solomon and the speech of the birds in Sura 27:16, this long fable tells about a group of birds that set out to seek their king, the Simurgh, of whom they have only dim memories. The search is difficult, and the way is uncertain. Many of the birds abandon the search. Finally, 30 birds arrive at Simurgh's palace. There they find out that they themselves are the sought after Simurgh. Simurgh is Persian for 30 birds. The journey is a metaphor for the Sufi quest.

✔ Jalal al-Din Rumi, known as *Mawlana* (our master), is the best-known Sufi poet. His poems have become very popular in the West. His life is as interesting as his poems are inspiring. Born around 1219 in eastern Persian, his family left due to the Mongol threat and settled in the city of Konya in modern Turkey. The area was once part of the Roman Empire and known as Rum, thus the "Rumi" in his name. Rumi succeeded his father as teacher and Sufi sheikh. The crucial event of his life was meeting Shams al-Din of Tabriz in 1244. Rumi became obsessed with Shams, finding in him the means through which to experience divine love. After two years, Shams suddenly left. Rumi was so depressed that his eldest son sought out Shams and brought him back to Konya. Rumi's family and many of his disciples were scandalized and jealous of Sham's hold on Rumi. In 1248, Shams disappeared again, probably murdered. Rumi wrote inspired poetry in the name of Shams. The *Divan-i Shams-i Tabrizi* is a collection of these poems, rich in imagery and symbolism, simple in style. At the urging of Husam al-Din Chelebi, a close disciple after Shams' death, Rumi wrote his masterpiece, the *Mathnawi.* Consisting of 26,000 verses, Rumi's *Mathnawi* is frequently called "the Qur'an in Persian." Rumi died in 1273.

✔ Yunus Emre (13th and 14th centuries) is the greatest poet to write in Turkish. His poems are rich in descriptive imagery and uplifting in tone. His style is influenced by traditional Turkish folk songs. One theme of Yunus's poetry is that all creation performs *dhikr* to God.

Establishing the Sufi Brotherhoods

Enduring Sufi brotherhoods began to emerge only in the 12th century. Some of the orders are found throughout the Muslim world, while others are confined to a single region. Eventually, leadership of most Sufi orders became hereditary. Sufi orders were a major factor in spreading Islam. Branches in some cases became new orders so most Sufi orders aren't highly centralized. The following lists brief snapshots of some of the most important orders.

✔ The Qadiriyya, the earliest Sufi brotherhood, is named after `Abd al-Qadir Jilani (1077–1166). Al-Jilani is perhaps the most widely revered Islamic saint, although the Qadiryya order was founded by later disciples rather than by al-Jilani himself. Al-Jilani was a Hanbalite jurist, and his tomb in Baghdad is still visited by pilgrims. The order, which became the largest Sufi *tariqa* from the 15th century on, is prominent in South Asia, North and West Africa, Indonesia, and Malaysia.

✔ The Rifa`iyya or Howling Dervishes was founded by Ahmad ibn `Ali al-Rifa`i (1106–1182) in southern Iraq and is an offshoot of the Qadiriyya. It spread to Egypt, Syria, Turkey, Bosnia, and the region to the north of the Black Sea. In addition to its loud *dhikr,* members of the order are famous for extreme practices, such as fire and glass eating, taking out of one's eyeballs, piercing one's hands and neck with iron rings, and biting heads off live snakes. It became the largest order until surpassed by the Qadiryya in the 15th century.

✔ The Shadhiliyya was founded by Abu al-Hasan al-Shadhili. Al-Shadhili began his career as a popular preacher in Tunisia. In 1227, a vision caused him to travel to Egypt where he founded his order. The order became prominent in Arabia, Syria, and North Africa. It has no special *dhikr* and allows its members to continue their secular occupations. Ibn `Ata' Allah (13th century) is the second major figure in the history of the Shadhiliyya. His *Hikam* (206 sayings) remains one of the most popular Sufi texts among ordinary Muslims.

✔ The Suhrawardiyya was founded by Abu al-Najib al-Suhrawardi (about 1097–1168) and his nephew Abu-Hafs `Umar al-Suhrawardi (1135–1244). This isn't the same Suhrawardi as Suhrawardi al-maqtul (see Chapter 12). The order, known for its teaching and its sober form of Sufism, became important in South Asia, including Bangladesh.

✔ The Mevlevi order was founded by Rumi's son and is centered around Rumi's tomb in Konya, Turkey. The order is famous for its Sufi dance. The order appealed to the upper class of Ottoman society. In the 1920s, however, the government of Turkey banned the Mevlevi order as a barrier to modernization. Public performances continued for tourists. Sufi ritual is once again permitted in Turkey today.

- The Bektashiyya order takes its name from Hajji Bektash of Khorasan (13th and 14th centuries). It emerged in the 15th century as a highly centralized order whose head lived in the village of Hacci Betus in modern Turkey. The Bektashis are known for a form of communion that may reflect Christian influence, for their Shi`ite sympathies, and for their de-emphasis of the ritual obligations of Islam. Women are equal to men in the order. By the end of the 16th century, the order was closely linked to the Janissaries, the elite, slave military unit of the Ottomans. When the Janissaries were abolished in 1826, the order went into decline, although it survives in Albania.

- The Chistiyya order was founded by Mu`inuddin Chisti (1142–1236) as an Indian offshoot of the Suhrawardi tradition. Chisti is buried in Ajmer, near Delhi. The order avoided political involvements and practiced extreme poverty. Members give away anything they have left over at the end of each day. The order may not accumulate wealth. Its emphasis is on devotion, and music plays a significant role in its sessions.

- The Naqshbandiyya order was founded in central Asia (Bukhara) by Baha'uddin Naqshband (1317–1390). It's a sober, orthodox, and conservative order that practices silent *dhikr*. Always politically involved, after spreading to India, it combated what it regarded as lax policies of earlier Sufi orders that tended to be somewhat tolerant of other religions. The Naqshbandiyya and some other Sufi orders were important in keeping Islam alive during the period of Soviet rule of central Asia, when the `*ulama'* of "official Islam" was co-opted by the state. As a result, Sufism is a vibrant force today in this region, as well as in Turkey, the Caucuses, and Afghanistan.

- The Badawiyya was founded by Ahmad al-Badawi (1199–1278). Born in Morocco, he led a worldly life until he had a religious experience at age 30. Eventually he settled in Tanta in the Egyptian Delta. Al-Badawi was known for feats of spiritual athleticism, such as going long periods with no food and without talking. The annual birthday festival of al-Badawi, Egypt's most popular saint, draws over 1.5 million people a year.

- The Kubrawiyya order was founded by Najmuddin Kubra (1145–1220) in central Asia, south of the Aral Sea. From there it spread to Turkey and India (especially Kashmir). Kubra taught that man is a microcosm of the divine reality, and emphasized color symbolism and visions.

- The Tijaniyya is a relatively new order founded by Abu-l-`Abbas Ahmad al-Tijani (1737–1815), on command from Muhammad. Unique among Sufi orders, the Tijaniyya claims that it's the only legitimate form of Sufism. It's prominent in West Africa, as well as in Morocco and Algeria. In some parts of West Africa, the order became active in anti-colonial movements. The same was true of another Sufi order, the 19th century Sanusiyya order, which gave rise to modern Libya.

- Although, Sufism has been in numerical decline during the past couple of centuries, new orders continue to arise, such as the Hamidiya Shazilya in Egypt, founded by Salama al-Radi in the 1930s.

Rejecting Sufism

Despite some notable exceptions, the importance of Sufism in Islam has declined over the past couple of centuries for a number of reasons.

- Some orders became too focused on the cult of the sheikh.

- Techniques to produce ecstatic experiences led to a loss of focus on the spiritual goal of Sufism.

- Some Sufi orders and sheikhs became mainly sources of magical amulets and charms for superstitious clientele.

- Other groups de-emphasized adherence to the external requirements of Islam to such an extent that they became an excuse for religiously sanctioned immoral practices.

- Well-off elites, often the families of hereditary sheikhs of the order, sometimes exploited the incredulity of its poor clientele to sustain their wealth and prestige.

Modernizing states either prohibited the practice of Sufism entirely (Turkey) or sought to restrict it and bring it under government control (Egypt).

After the success of the puritanical, Wahhabi movement in Saudi Arabia, its scholars saw their mission as the purification of worldwide Islam from what they regarded as unorthodox practices, such as saint reverence and Sufism. Wahhabis and those who shared their views regarded any ritual practice not explicitly set forth in the Qur'an as illegitimate. They rejected any idea of union with God, regardless of how Sufis interpreted such union.

Some people say that Sufism has no future in Islam, but such predictions may be premature. The religious needs to which Sufism supplies an answer are always present. A generation or two ago, many Western scholars viewed all religion as a form of superstition that faced decline in the modern world. The end of the 20th century saw such predictions confounded as religions around the world showed new growth and vitality. One can only wait and see what the future holds for Sufi forms of Islam.

Chapter 14

Exploring Lesser-Known Sects Linked to Islam

n exploring of Islam, one must start somewhere. Because Sunnis make up 84 to 90 percent of Muslims, that's an obvious place to start, and the majority of coverage of Islam in this book is about Sunnis. An introductory book often adds a chapter that focuses on Twelver Shi`ism, by far the largest of Shi`ite groups (see Chapter 12 in this book). However, Islam has given rise to a number of other fascinating religious sects, and in this chapter, I look at some of these.

You can get a pretty good grasp of Christianity if you study Roman Catholicism, Eastern Orthodoxy, and several Protestant denominations. Yet you would miss a lot of fascinating side trips if you stuck only to the interstate highways of these major religious groups. Amish, Jehovah's Witnesses, the Coptic Church, Mormons, Shakers, and Unitarian-Universalists all have a fascinating story to tell. Similarly, you can understand Buddhism by focusing on the main groups of Theravada and Mahayana Buddhism, but you miss much if you don't also look at Tibetan Buddhism (Vayrayana) and some new Buddhist groups that have arisen in Japan.

Many of lesser-known Islamic sects belong to the second largest branch of Shi`ites, called the *Isma`ilis* (see the introduction of Chapter 12 for the three main branches of Shi`ism). The origins of some groups are unclear and may combine elements from several forms of Islam and even incorporate elements from other religions (see Figure 14-1 for a family tree showing the relation of various Islamic groups to one another). Some of these sects are no longer regarded by other Muslims (or even by their own members) as Islamic. Others, while regarded as Islamic, have practices and teachings that are rejected by most Muslims.

I frequently use the term *sect* to designate the groups in this chapter, a term used by scholars of religion to designate certain smaller groups within a religion, but without implying that the sect is a less-valid form of that religion.

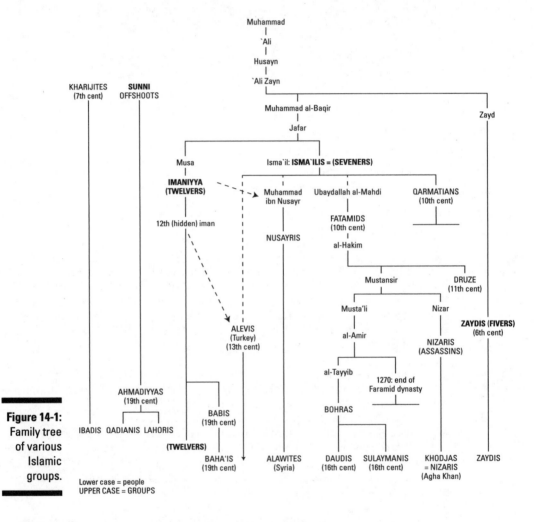

Figure 14-1:
Family tree of various Islamic groups.

`Ibadis (the early Kharijites)

`Ibadis, numbering today between one and two million, are the surviving remnant of the early Kharijites, a puritanical political and religious movement I discuss in Chapters 2 and 4. The `Ibadis, who take their name from an early leader called `Abd Allah Ibn `Ibad, broke away from more radical Kharijite groups in about 685. `Ibadis elect their own *imam* in secret and regard the absence of an *imam* as a state of disorder. Like the early Mu`tazilites and contrary to most Muslims, `Ibadis believe that the Qur'an was created rather than existing eternally. The `Ibadi School of law is similar to the Sunni Malikite School (see Chapter 8). Originally centered in Basra, Iraq, `Ibadi imamates at times controlled central North Africa and Oman (southeast tip of Arabia). Some of the earliest Muslim missionaries in sub-Saharan West Africa were `Ibadis. The largest `Ibadi community today is in Oman, where about 75 percent of the population are `Ibadis. Small, isolated `Ibadi communities survive in Saharan parts of Algeria, Tunisia, Libya, and in Zanzibar, and East Africa. Little distinguishes `Ibadis today from Sunni Muslims. Time has eliminated the original puritanical zeal of their Kharijite ancestors. `Ibadis are regarded as members of the Muslim community by other Muslims.

Zaydis (or Fiver Shi`ites)

While other Shi`ites believe the *imam* must be a descendant of `Ali and Fatima, Zaydis say any descendant of `Ali is eligible for election by the community as the person most worthy to be their spiritual leader at the time. After the death of the fourth *imam* in 713, the succession went to his oldest son, Muhammad al-Baqir. Some Shi`ites regarded al-Baqir and his father as too willing to compromise with the Umayyad caliphs. This group accepted Zayd, a younger, half-brother of al-Baqir, as the fifth *imam.* Zayd led a failed revolt against the Umayyads after which the Zaydis retreated to the mountains of Yemen and to an area on the south coast of the Caspian Sea. Zaydis ruled Yemen from the tenth century until 1962. In addition, a Zaydi state controlled, on and off, the region to the south and southwest of the Caspian Sea from 864 to 1126. Most of today's estimated 18 million Zaydis live in Yemen, where they constitute about 40 percent of the population.

Except for believing that the *imam* must be a descendent of `Ali, Zaydis differ little from Sunni Muslims. Zaydis accept the Abu Bakr and `Umar as legitimate caliphs but disagree among themselves regarding `Uthman (see Chapter 2). Zaydis recognize no fixed line of legitimate *imams.* They don't believe there must always be a living *imam,* nor do they accept the concept of a hidden *imam.* Zaydis have their own School of law and, like the `Ibadis, were influenced by the early Mu`tazilite theologians. Other Muslims recognize the Zaydis as a legitimate form of Islam.

Isma`ili (or Sevener Shi`ite) Groups

Ja`far al-Sadiq, the sixth Shi`ite *imam* (699–765), was predeceased by his son Isma`il. The larger group accepted his living son Musa as the seventh *imam.* However, some believed that Ja`far had designated Isma`il as his successor. For them, Isma`il was the seventh *imam* and his son Muhammad the eighth *imam.* These Isma`ilis or Seveners believed that Muhammad (the eighth *imam,* not the prophet) hadn't died but had gone into hiding from Sunni enemies who sought to kill him. In the ninth century, Isma`ili Shi`ism was a revolutionary movement that sent missionaries all over the Muslim world to spread its message. Where necessary, Isma`ilis practiced dissimulation *(taqiyya),* hiding their beliefs and identity. Like some Sufis, Isma`ilis also emphasized an esoteric rather than literal interpretation of the Qur'an.

Qarmatians

The Qarmatians were an important early group of Isma`ilis, named after Hamdan Qarmati, an Isma`ili missionary who was active in Iraq in the later ninth century. Qarmatians attacked the Abbasids and other groups in the Abbasid heartland. Poor peasants and beduin supported this revolutionary, messianic movement against entrenched power and wealth. In 930, they captured Mecca and carried away the Black Stone (of the *Ka`ba)* to their stronghold in Bahrain but returned it in 951. A Qarmatian state in eastern Arabia and Bahrain continued until 1076 where it formed a unique, Islamic-socialist, egalitarian community. Qarmatians were extinct by the 14th century but remain important for understanding Isma`ili Shi`ism.

Nizaris

The Nizaris are one of two main branches of Isma`ili Shi`ism — each with several subgroups — that still exist today. (The other group is the Bohras.)

From the Fatimids to the Assassins

When the Fatimid caliph of Egypt, al-Mustansir, died in 1094, the vizier put al-Mustansir's elder son Nizar in prison, where he died, and installed a younger son (al-Musta`li) as ruler. Many Isma`ilis outside Egypt didn't accept this interference and regarded Nizar as the legitimate caliph and *imam.*

Hasan-i Sabbah was the real founder of the Nizaris. Rebelling against the Abbasids, he established military strongholds from northern Syria across to northeastern Iran. His headquarters was Alamut in the Elburz Mountains of northern Iran. His successors claimed to be descendants of Nizar and, thus, in the line of Isma`ili succession. The Mongols conquered Alamut in 1256, leaving scattered groups of Nizaris in Iran, central Asia, Syria, and Yemen.

Christian crusaders knew the Nizaris as *hashishiyin* (hashish addicts). From *hashishiyin* comes the English word *assassins,* due to their practice of assassinating their political supporters.

From the Assassins to the Aga Khan

In 1817, the Nizari *imam* Abu `l-Hasan Ali married the daughter of the Iranian Shah, who awarded him the honorary title of Aga Khan ("Lord and Master"). After a falling out with the shah, the Aga Khan went first to Afghanistan in 1841 and settled in Bombay, India, in 1848. Nizari missionaries had reached India in the 12th century, and in the 15th century converted the majority of a Hindu caste to Islam, giving them the name Khojas. Khoja Islam was a mutated form of Islam, in which `Ali was regarded as the tenth avatar (incarnation) of the Hindu god Vishnu. Colonial British courts validated the claim of the Aga Khan to leadership of the Khoja community in 1886. Although the majority of the Khoja community accepted the leadership of the Aga Khan, some had become associated with Twelver Shi`ism, and a minority of the Isma`ili Khojas didn't recognize the Aga Kahn. Immigration to East Africa from India by Khoja merchants in the 19th and 20th century established an important Isma`ili community there. The third Aga Khan (1885–1957) began a program of modernization of the Nizari community, investing in education, hospitals and clinics, housing, and the improvement of the status of women. His grandson, Karim, the fourth Aga Khan (educated at Harvard University) continued this program. He is the 49th *imam* in a line of succession beginning with `Ali. More recently, Karim Aga Khan and his father brought the Khoja/Nizari sect into closer conformity with Shi`ite Islamic belief and practice.

Khoja Nizaris are found today in India, Pakistan, Sri Lanka, Burma, and East Africa. Other pre-Indian Nizari communities exist in Arabia, Afghanistan, Iran, Syria, and central Asia and recognize the authority of the Aga Khan. Nizaris number several million (some sources say as high as 20 million).

Musta`li, Tayyibis, and Bohras are all the same — almost!

After the split off of the Nizaris, the main Fatimid line (the Musta`lis) continued until a second major split occurred at the death of caliph al-Amir in 1130. The line of Fatimid rule continued irregularly through a cousin of al-Amir. This Musta`li line came to an end with the conquest of Fatimid Egypt by Saladin in 1271. A number of Isma`ili Fatimids outside Egypt objected to the decision regarding the succession to caliph al-Amir. They regarded his infant son, al Tayyib, as the legitimate ruler. Al Tayyib was said to be in hiding on earth or in heaven. Until he returns, a person called the *da`i Mutlaq* (the unrestricted summoner) represents him on earth. These Musta`li Isma`ili (sometimes called Tayyibi) were centered in Yemen. In the 12th century, Musta`li missionaries began to make conversions in India from the Hindu population. In 1556, the headquarters of the movement was moved to India: These Indian Musta`lis are known as Bohras after the merchant caste from which most came. Many Bohras are, indeed, merchants.

Isma`ili theology

Isma`ilis believe that history went through seven cycles. Each cycle started with a period in which good prevailed without the need for law. The world became corrupt in the second period. In the third period, revelation was sent to reestablish order. In this third period, law represented the external meaning of scripture.

Scripture's inner meaning was revealed to the *imams*. With the coming of Isma`il (also regarded as the Mahdi), the first period of the next cycle begins when hidden meaning is now public and law isn't needed. The cycles continue until all souls are freed from entrapment in matter and return to the Universal Soul.

A split occurred in 1591 over succession to the *da`i* office. Both resulting groups are called after their founders. Today, about 70,000 Sulaymania live in Yemen, with another 4,000 in west India. Daudis, headquartered in India, number about one million and are found in Pakistan, India, Sri Lanka, Burma, East Africa, and Yemen. Tayyibi/Bohra/Musta`li theology and practice remained close to that of the Fatimid Isma`ilis. Daudis observe seven pillars, including prayer, *zakat* (alms), fasting during *saum, hajj* pilgrimage, jihad, and purity. The first pillar is an expansion of the traditional first pillar and includes love of God, the prophets, the *imams,* and the *da`is*. Daudi Bohras renew their oath of loyalty to the current *da`i* annually. Bohras are considered Muslims, and some in the 15th century became Sunni Muslims.

On the Fringes of Islam and Beyond

The Isma`ili groups discussed in the preceding sections are generally regarded as within the boundaries of Islam, even if they have some unique beliefs and practices. Other groups, originating from a Shi`ite context are often not regarded by most Muslims as legitimate forms of Islam, and some of these groups no longer regard themselves as Muslims.

Druze

`Ubaydallah al-Mahdi, an Isma`ili missionary in tenth century Tunisia, claimed descent from Isma`il and also claimed to be the Mahdi. He established the Fatimid dynasty, which for a while rivaled the Abbasid Empire (see Chapter 2).

An enigmatic figure, al-Hakim, was the sixth Fatimid *imam*. Influenced by a Turk named al-Darazi (after whom the religion is named) and an Iranian named al-Hamza, al-Hakim became convinced he was God incarnate. Al-Darazi sent missionaries to present Lebanon to spread his teaching about al-Hakim. Al-Hakim disappeared in 1020, having gone into hiding *(occultation)* according to Druze belief. Druze communities became established in southwest Syria, south central Lebanon, and the Galilee region of present Israel. Around the year 1040, the Druze became a closed group, accepting no converts. They practiced *taqiyya* in the midst of the larger Sunni community. An elite group (`uqqal,* or the knowers) representing the hidden al-Hakim leads the community and transmits the esoteric teachings. The elite wear special clothing and follow a stricter code of living. The majority of the community are the ignorant *(juhhal)* who can strive for rebirth as one of the elite.

Fatimid *imam* al-Hakim is the Egyptian caliph who burned Cairo and destroyed the Church of the Holy Sepulcher (traditional location of Jesus' crucifixion and burial) in Jerusalem.

Druze deemphasize Islamic ritual. They don't perform the five daily prayers, observe *saum* during *Ramadan,* or make pilgrimage to Mecca. They do celebrate the `id al-adha* sacrificial festival that marks the end of the pilgrimage. Druze meet for scripture reading, prayer, and community discussion in simple places of worship on Thursday evenings; Druze deemphasize Islamic law and worship on Thursday rather than Friday. Tombs of past Druze saints are holy sites, and a five-pointed star is the main Druze symbol. Druze call themselves Banu al-Ma`ruf (Sons of Generosity), and they call their religion Muwahhid (absolute "Unity" of God).

The Druze are one of the important ethnic/political/religious groups in Lebanon. In the effort to maintain their separateness and independence, Druze have frequently been involved in bloody conflicts with external authorities in the region (the Ottoman Turks), as well as other local groups (the Marionite Christians). Druze have even served in the Israeli army. According to recent estimates, Druze number between 750,000 and 1,000,000, including emigrant communities in the United States. Because Druze recognize al-Hakim as a more complete revelation of God than the revelation by Muhammad, Druze aren't typically regarded as Muslims by other Muslims.

Druze theology

Al-Hamza taught a neo-Platonic-influenced theology. Al-Hakim was thought to be the manifestation at the cosmic level of the Universal Intelligence as al-Hamza was one of his earthly representatives. Each point of the Druze Star represents one of the key figures of early Druze history and a manifestation of the Universal Intelligence. The Druze scripture, the "Epistle of Wisdom," contains the writings of al-Hamza and al-Muqtana, a subsequent leader. Seven commandments replaced the traditional Five Pillars of Islam. An example: Submit to God's will as represented in al-Hakim. Souls are instantly reborn, and the number of Druze alive remains constant. At the end of time, al-Hakim and al-Hamza will return to establish peace and justice.

Some scholars trace the origins of Western Freemasonry to contacts of Christian Crusaders with the Druze. The symbol of the Eastern Star Masonic order, say these scholars, may derive from the Druze star. This is an interesting suggestion but hardly a proven fact.

`Alawis (Nusayris)

`Alawi is the contemporary name of this group of about one million people centered in Northern Syria. `Alawis constitute about 10 percent of Syria's population. The name `Alawi reflects the attribution to `Ali of near divine status. Mainstream Twelvers regard such extreme exaltation of `Ali as *ghulat* (extremism). `Alawis are Twelver in origin and were probably influenced at some points in their history by contacts with Isma`ili and non-Muslim religious groups.

The traditional name, Nusayriyya, goes back to the founder, Abu Shu`ayb Muhammad Ibn Nusayr (ninth century). Nusayr was a companion of the tenth *imam,* whom he proclaimed to be divine.

Nizari Isma`ilis and `Alawis often came into conflict in Syria. `Alawis were repressed or tolerated, depending on which Muslim state dominated the region. Many `Alawis served in military forces organized under the French after World War I, and they gained control of the army of modern, independent Syria. Hafiz al-Asad, who emerged as the leader of the Syrian government and the Ba`th Arab-socialist party in 1970, was an `Alawi, as were most high government and army officials. In 2000, Bashir Asad succeeded his father as head of state. Beginning in the 1970s, the `Alawis have publicly moved closer to mainstream Twelver Islam. Traditionally, `Alawis, like the Druze, were regarded as heretics who had departed from Islam. But in 1973, the leading Twelver Shi`ite cleric of Lebanon, Musa Sadr, issued a decree *(fatwa)* declaring that `Alawis were Muslims.

In the past, `Alawis downplayed Islamic rituals, such as fasting, prayer, and ablutions (purifications) and observed Christian festivals, such as Christmas, Epiphany, and Pentecost. The Christian influence may have resulted from contacts during the Christian Crusades. Traditional `Alawi theology emphasized the triad of `Ali (the *ma`na* means the "true meaning of God"), Muhammad (the *ism* is the name; *hijab* means "veil of the true name"), and Salman al-Farisi (the *bab* or gate that served as the mediator between believers and the manifestation of God). Salman al-Farisi was the Iranian companion of Muhammad.

Alevis

Some people think that Alevis and `Alawis are the same. Despite the similarity of names and proximity of location of the two groups (and despite what you may occasionally read), Alevis aren't the same as `Alawis.

Alevis are a Turkish ethnic/religious community, concentrated in central Anatolia and southeast Turkey. Alevis constitute between 15 to 30 percent of the population of Turkey (between 6 and 20 million). Alevi organizations are active among Turkish emigrants, especially the "guest workers" of Germany. About 25 percent of Turkish Kurds are Alevis. A complicating factor is the overlap between Alevis and the Bektashi Sufi order (see Chapters 2 and 13). The Bektashi order is, however, not limited to the Alevis or to Turkey. A person joins the Bektashi Sufi order, but one is born into the Alevi community, which frowns on marriage outside the community.

Alevis de-emphasize traditional Muslim rituals, such as prayer, the *hajj, saum* (or fasting) during *Ramadan,* and attending the mosque. They say the true *hajj* is the *hajj* of the heart rather than legalistic adherence to external rituals. They do fast but do so during the first 12 days of *Muharram* (the first month) in memory of the 12 *imams*. Like the `Alawis, Alevi rituals seem to have been influenced by contact with other religions. Alevis observe the August festival in honor of Haci Bektash Veli, the founder of the Bektash Sufi order. This festival seems to have been appropriated by the government as a tourist attraction, which plays down its religious aspect.

The *Cem* is the Alevis' major annual religious festival. Until recently, it was celebrated at night and in secret. The Cem celebrates the heavenly journey of Muhammad *(mi`raj),* contemplates the suffering of Husayn and the 12 *imams,* and includes a sacramental meal and sacramental alcoholic drink, singing of hymns, dancing, and lighting of candles.

Alevis have had a varying relationship with the modern Turkish state. Having been oppressed by the Ottomans, they were big supporters of Ataturk, the father of modern Turkey. Ataturk's secular state offered Alevis greater religious and cultural freedom. Also, because of their fear of Sunni influence, many Alevi youth identified with leftist political parties, because they saw a link between the leftist political and economic agenda and Alevi emphasis on equality of women, justice for the poor, and tolerance. Sunnis have generally regarded the Alevis with distain, and on a few occasions, Sunni mobs have taken violent action against local Alevis.

Modern Turkey's efforts to create a unified Turkish identity clashed with the desires of Alevis and Kurds to maintain their own culture. In the 1980s, the government began to support Sunni religion and in reaction, Alevis began to promote their own religious and cultural identity openly. They claimed to be the true Muslims, the true Turks, and the true Anatolians, in contrast to Sunnism, which Alevis said was a legalistic, Arab distortion of Islam.

Ahmadiyya

In the late 1800s, an Indian Muslim named Mirza Ghulam Ahmad (1835–1908) announced that he was a renewer of Islam *(mujaddid),* the second coming of Jesus in spirit, the Islamic *Mahdi,* and the last avatar of the Hindu god Vishnu. Jesus, he said, had not died on the cross nor had he been taken up into heaven as Muslims say. Rather, he had moved to India, lived to the age of 120, and was buried in Srinagar. The movement that Ahmad started is called the Ahmadiyya.

There is an Ahmadiyya Sufi order in Africa, which is unrelated to this Indian movement.

After Ahmad's death, a council elected a successor called the "viceroy of the Messiah" *(khalifat al-Masih).* There have been four viceroys, three of them descendants of Ahmad. The death of the first successor caused a split in the group. The Lahorites (so called because their headquarters is in Lahore) believed that the movement should be governed collectively. The Lahorites also believed that Ahmad was only a renewer. By not calling him a prophet, they remained closer to orthodox Islam.

The other group, the Qadianis (named after the birthplace of Ahmad), believes that Ahmad was a prophet but not of the same type as Muhammad. Because of these claims, most Muslims don't regard the Ahmadiyyas as Muslims. A 1984 law in Pakistan prohibits the group from representing themselves as Muslims in any way, including calling their places of worship "mosques." Qadiani Ahmadiyyas, however, regard themselves as the only true Muslims.

Both Ahmadiyya groups undertook a successful missionary program in West Africa, Europe, the Americas, and South and Southeast Asia. Current membership is estimated to be over ten million. Organizational efficiency accounts for part of its success. Ahmadiyyas established hospitals and schools and have an active publication program in various languages including English. They produced the first translation of the Qur'an into Swahili, the most widespread language of East Africa. Although unorthodox or even non-Muslim in its beliefs, the Ahmadiyyas are one example of successful and intentional modernization by a Muslim group.

Baha'is

Baha'i is often said to be the newest of the major universal religions. The religion originated in Iran with Sayyid Mirza `Ali Muhammad, a person who, in 1848, claimed to be the *bab* ("Gate"), and the forerunner of a new manifestation of God. His followers were known as the Babis. One of his followers, Baha' Ullah, in 1863 publicly claimed to be the new manifestation. Imprisoned for most of his career but active in spreading the movement, Baha' Ullah was succeeded by his son and great-grandson. The movement grew rapidly and today has about seven million members. The largest group is in India (two million). Baha'is are found in over 220 countries, including 1.7 million in Africa and 600,000 in the United States (dating back to 1894).

Baha'i teachings

The writings of the Bab, Baha' Ullah, and his son and grandson constitute the Baha'i scriptures. Baha'is believe in progressive revelation. God sends a new messenger for each new age. The message of Jesus aimed at the perfection of the individual, that of Muhammad at the perfection of the community, and that of Baha' Ullah at the perfection of humanity. Other messengers may come after Baha' Ullah, but not for 1,000 years. Baha'is actively pursues equality of men and women, equality of races, economic justice for all, universal education, and world peace. Baha'is believe in an immortal soul is immortal that will progress toward salvation in a spiritual realm after death.

Baha'i rituals

Baha'ism presents itself as a rational, modern, progressive, socially involved, and non-ritualistic religion. Baha'is pray three times a day but not as a group. Baha'ism divided the year into 19 months of 19 days each (plus 4 or 5 extra days at the end). Once a month, Baha'is gather to read scriptures and hold discussions. The last month of the year, Baha'is fast from sunrise to sunset. The calendar is a solar one with the new year occurring on the vernal (spring) equinox and includes a number of special days throughout the year.

Baha'i organization

Baha'ism is organized in a multilevel form of representative democracy. A local spiritual assembly exists wherever nine Baha'is live. Local Baha'is elect a nine-member local governing council. Local councils elect representatives to a national assembly. Every five years, elected representatives attend the meeting of the Baha'i worldwide governing body, the International House of Justice in Haifa, Israel (formed in 1962).

The already beautiful headquarters site on a Haifa hill overlooking the Mediterranean was further enhanced in 2001 with an imposing series of garden terraces going down the hill toward the sea. Baha'i temples, all with nine sides, are located in seven other locations around the world including Willamette, Illinois.

Of the various groups discussed in this chapter, Baha'ism is the one that most clearly is a new, non-Muslim religion. As an offshoot of Islam, Baha'is have suffered discrimination and persecution, especially in Iran since the establishment of the Islamic republic in 1979.

Chapter 15

Islam in America

• •

• •

The United States exhibits the world's greatest religious diversity. Because of religious liberty and immigration from around the world, American Islam is more diverse than Islam anywhere else. Thirty or 40 years ago, few Americans knew anything about Islam. Today, according to a 2002 poll, 28 percent of Americans are personally acquainted with a Muslim. The United States has moved from being a Protestant nation to a Protestant-Catholic to a Protestant-Catholic-Jewish one and now a Christian-Jewish-Muslim nation, along with many other faiths.

Getting an Overview

This section gives you a snapshot of today's American Muslim population and an overview of its origins.

Looking at Muslim origins in the United States

American Muslims come from four main groups:

✔ According to the two most recent studies, African-American Muslims account for 20 to 30 percent of all American Muslims. At least 68 percent of Muslim converts are African-American. Although Islam had largely died out among African-Americans by the middle of the 19th century, many African-Americans look with pride at the substantial percentage of their ancestors (perhaps as much as 30 percent in South Carolina) who were practicing Muslims when they were brought as slaves to America.

✔ Immigrants (first, second, and third generation) as a group make up the largest percentage of American Muslims, with an estimated 10 to 20 percent being Shi`ite Muslims. The 2002 *Mosque Study* lists 33 percent South Asian (including Afghani), 25 percent Arab, 2.1 percent Balkan and Tartars (mainly areas of the former U.S.S.R), 1.3 percent Southeast Asian (mainly Malaysia and Indonesia), 1.1 percent Turkish, and 0.7 percent Iranian. The Iranian figures appear low and may reflect an under-representation of Shi`ite mosques in the study. In addition, many Muslim students from abroad settle in America.

✔ An estimated 20,000 to 50,000 non-immigrant, white Americans have converted to Islam. White Americans, according to the *Mosque Study,* make up only 1.6 percent of all American Muslims. The most prominent early white American convert was Mohammed Alexander Webb, who was serving as the U.S. counsel (1887–1892) to the Philippians when he converted. He represented Islam at the 1893 World Parliament of Religions in Chicago. In addition to marrying a Muslim, reasons for con-version by whites include the simplicity of Islam, its emphasis on racial equality, and its sense of community. Converts often become articulate spokespersons for Islam.

✔ Sectarian groups include the Ahmadiyyas and the Druze (see Chapter 14). A number of Druze have immigrated to the United States, but the Druze don't seek converts.

Snapshot of American Muslims today

The first in-depth poll of American Muslims was conducted in November 2001, by the MAPS (Muslims in the American Public Square) project of the Center for Muslim-Christian Understanding of Georgetown University, in association with the Zogby International polling organization. According to poll results:

✔ Thirty-six percent of all American Muslims were born in the United States, and 19 percent are converts.

✔ Fifty-eight percent of American Muslims are male, and 58 percent are college graduates.

✔ The largest age group is 30- to 49-year olds (51 percent), while 23 percent of adult American Muslims are 18 to 21.

✔ Fifty percent have an income over $50,000.

✔ Twenty-two percent are professionals (such as engineers), and 10 percent are in the medical profession.

✔ Twenty-four percent attend mosque weekly for Friday prayer, and 49 percent said they have attended a *salat* at a mosque in the past week.

✔ Sixty-six percent perform at least one of the five daily *salat,* while 47 percent regularly observe all five (see Chapter 9).

✔ On social and political issues, over 55 percent favor school prayer, would like to see the Ten Commandments posted, approve of school vouchers, approve of the death penalty, would like to ban pornography, oppose legalizing gay marriage, and oppose unrestricted abortion. More than 90 percent support government-provided universal health care, anti-poverty programs, and environmental protections.

Calculating the numbers

Over the past decade, estimates of the number of American Muslims escalated rapidly until, by 2001, figures of six to ten million were frequently mentioned. If true, the U.S. Muslim population is larger than the U.S. Jewish population. Some recent studies express doubts about these figures, especially given that polls consistently indicate that no more than 4 percent of the population belongs to non-Christian religions. If the 4 percent figure is correct, the total number of Muslims, Jews, Hindus, Buddhists, and other non-Christian religions would amount to no more than 8.5 million. The most recently released figures are contained in *The North American Muslim Resource Guide* (2002). Using a variety of sources, Mohmamed Nimer estimates a total of 3.5 million Muslims, with a low-end figure of 2.5 million and a high-end figure of 4.4 million. When you read specific estimates, keep the following in mind:

✔ Accurate figures of religious affiliation are difficult to determine.

✔ The American Muslim population has expanded rapidly since 1970.

✔ Given high birth rates and continuing immigration, within the next 15 years, Islam will become the second-largest religion in the country — if it isn't already.

✔ Claims of eight to ten million Muslims today are probably too high. Between two and five million is a more likely figure.

✔ The United States population is and will remain overwhelmingly Christian in the foreseeable future. The second largest category after Christianity today is "no organized religion."

Organizing the Muslim Community

For Muslims who came in the first wave of immigration, establishing Muslim organizations wasn't a priority.

Building mosques (masjids)

In 1900, Muslims in Ross, South Dakota, held the earliest recorded prayer services. At first, local communities met in homes and rented facilities. As more immigrants arrived, the first institutional concern was to establish a local mosque. Sometimes, local Muslims converted a church or school building for use as a mosque. Not looking much like a typical mosque, therefore, a casual passerby wouldn't recognize these structures as mosques.

Early mosques were located in Michigan City, Indiana (1914), Maine (1915), Connecticut (1919), and Ross, South Dakota (1920). The oldest structure built as a mosque and still standing is in Cedar Rapids, Iowa (1934). It is referred to as the "Mother Mosque" of America. Canada's first recorded mosque was built in 1938, and the West Coast's first mosque was located in Sacramento in 1947. The first Shi`ite mosque was built in Dearborn, Michigan (1963).

By 2002, the *Mosque Report* listed 1,118 mosques, a 25 percent increase over 1994. Thirty percent were started in the 1990s, and 87 percent were founded after 1970. Even today, only about 25 percent of mosques were built as mosques, although these include a number of impressive structures in styles ranging from the traditional Middle Eastern mosque to modernistic structures. The largest number of mosques are in New York, California, and Illinois.

In addition to mosques, Muslims have built cultural centers and schools. Often, the same complex serves all three functions (prayer, community functions, and full- or part-time education). Twenty-one percent of mosques include full-time schools, and some of the larger Muslim schools are independent institutions not linked to a specific mosque. Two-thirds of the full-time schools support only the elementary grades. Many more mosques (71 percent) have some kind of weekend educational program, with half of them offering programs for children only. Some have more extensive offerings, including Arabic classes at 57 percent of mosques.

Although many early mosques had no professionally trained religious leadership, as the community expanded, trained *imams* became important to the community. Although some steps have been taken toward training Muslim clergy in the United States, most classically trained *imams* have been recruited from abroad. (Most American Muslims who want a classical scholarly training go to a school like al-Azhar in Cairo.) Still, 55 percent of mosques don't have any full-time, paid professional staff. While an *imam* from abroad may have an excellent grounding in the traditional scholarly curriculum, he often has limited familiarity with American culture and an inadequate grasp of English. He may be an excellent resource for answers to questions about Islamic law, but he may be ill-equipped for other, non-traditional roles that the American *imam* is increasingly expected to fill. The *imam* may be expected to be a counselor, a fundraiser, an administrator, an educator, and an ambassador for Islam in the non-Muslim community. Training of the leadership is one of the challenges facing American Muslims.

Establishing national Islamic organizations

As the number of Muslim communities grew, the need arose for cooperative bodies to provide a broader range of services. The Federation of Islamic Associations (FIA), started in 1952, was the first national body. Today, the largest national organization is the Islamic Society of North America, established in 1982 (located in Plainfield, Indiana). ISNA is an umbrella organization that includes many specialized associations and evolved from the Muslim Student Association, founded in 1963. MSA chapters are active on many college campuses. Member organizations of ISNA include the Association of Muslim Social Scientists (AMSS, 1972), the Islamic Medical Association (IMA, 1967), the Muslim Youth of America (MYA), the North American Islamic Trust (publications and other services), and many others. ISNA holds an annual convention over the Labor Day holiday, with over 30,000 attending in 2002. ISNA also provides for the collection of *zakat* funds (see Chapter 9), publishes a bimonthly magazine *(The Horizon),* organizes special conferences (on Islam in America, Islam and the Internet, and other topics), brings students to the Plainfield center for summer activities, and much more.

Other national bodies include the Islamic Circle of North America (ICNA, 1971); the Islamic Assembly of North America (IANA), with its emphasis on *da`wa* (Islamic evangelism); and the International Institute of Islamic Thought (IIIT), an Islamic think tank founded in 1981. Other national (and international) groups serve Twelver Shi`ites, Isma`ili Shi`ites, Ahmadiyyas, and Baha'is (see Chapter 14). The Muslim American Society (MAS), which includes most predominately black Sunni Muslim mosques, and the much smaller Nation of Islam also hold large annual conventions. A National Shura Council includes representatives of ISNA, ICNA, MAS, and the Imam Jalil al-Amin community to coordinate matters like determining when *Ramadan* begins.

Other Muslim organizations have a political function.

- ✔ CAIR (Council on American-Islamic Religions, 1994) is dedicated to combating discrimination against Muslims. CAIR has a hotline for reporting incidents of discrimination and unfair news coverage. CAIR also provides mediation services for cases of job-related religious discrimination and distributes information kits for local media, public schools and libraries, and public relation advice for local mosques.

- ✔ The American Muslim Council (AMC, 1990), in addition to combating discrimination, is active in voter registration and in political lobbying to make the voice of American Muslims heard in the government arena.

- ✔ MPAC (Muslim Political Action Committee, 1988) and the AMA (American Muslim Alliance, 1992) have interests similar to AMC.

- ✔ These four organizations (and three others) formed the AMPCC (American Muslim Political Coordination Council) in 1998.

Reestablishing a Black Muslim Community

By 1900, Islam had pretty well disappeared among the descendants of former slaves in the United States. Of course, racism hadn't disappeared in the United States, and religion was one of the ways that African Americans attempted to assert their identity and claim their place in America. Most African Americans were and remain Christians. But some African Americans rejected Christianity and turned to the religion that many of their ancestors had practiced — Islam. This section traces the development of African American Islam by focusing on the six key leaders.

Noble Drew Ali

The Moorish Science Temple of America is the first explicitly Islamic movement in the United States. Timothy Drew, its founder, was born in 1886 in North Carolina. Little is known of his first 25 years, but the various legends about him added to the sense of mystery that was part of his appeal. Was he a descendant of Bilali Mahomet or a slave descendant raised by Cherokee Indians? Did he travel to Egypt as a teenager and learn the secrets of ancient Egyptian religion? Had he been to Saudi Arabia and did the King of Morocco commission him to teach Islam in the United States? What's certain is that by 1913 he was in the north, had changed his name to Noble Drew Ali, and founded the first Moorish Temple in Newark, New Jersey. Noble Drew Ali combined elements from a number of different sources: the pan-Africanism of Marcus Garvey, Christianity, Islam, Theosophy, and Freemasonry.

Islamic elements included Noble Drew Ali's claim to be the last of the prophets of Allah and his *Holy Koran* (the *Circle Seven Koran*), composed in 1927. Ali's 64-page *Holy Koran* bore little resemblance to the Islamic Qur'an. It contained significant elements from the Bible, apocryphal "Jesus" gospels, and Rosicrucian (a form of Freemasonry) texts in addition to material from the Qur'an. Ali taught that African Americans were *Asiatics* who could trace their ancestry back to Morocco, and beyond that to Jesus. African Americans should abandon their slave identity and religion and reclaim their heritage. Converts generally dropped their slave (last) names, substituting for it El or Bey and carried a national identity card. Men often wore a fez and women a white turban. They avoided pork (regarded as a slave food) and alcohol.

The movement appealed to poor blacks who made up the first "Great Migration" from the south to the urban north from 1915–1930. By the late 1920s, there were 30,000 Moorish Americans in most major cities of the Midwest and northeast. In 1929, Ali was arrested in connection with the killing of a rival. Released from jail, he died the same year under mysterious circumstances, but the movement continued to grow. Only in the 1950s did the Nation of Islam surpass it in membership. Although small, the Moorish Temple is still active today.

Wallace D. Fard

As in the case of Noble Drew Ali, various legends surround the origins of Wallace D. Fard. He was an Arab from Mecca, or perhaps a Turk, or maybe from Jamaica if not New Zealand or Los Angeles. He used a variety of names during his life. He first appeared in Detroit in 1930 as a peddler of silks and Islamic items and established his unorthodox version of Islam among converts who initially met in homes. Problems with the police and accusations of human sacrifice on the part of members of his "Lost-Found Nation of Islam in the Wilderness of North America" led to his arrest in 1932. Given refuge in Chicago by Elijah Muhammad, who had risen to be his chief lieutenant, he disappeared after 1934. What happened and who was responsible was never discovered.

According to Fard, African Americans were Asiatics, members of the "lost and now found tribe of Shabazz." White traders enslaved the ancestors of African Americans from Mecca almost 400 years ago. Fard's mission was to redeem and restore this tribe. According to a sacred story created by Fard, an evil scientist of the tribe of Shabazz was expelled from Mecca. By genetic engineering, he bred the white race that then enslaved the blacks. The day of the final apocalyptic battle foretold in the book of Revelation is near. In this battle that will take place in America, blacks will triumph over whites and reclaim their freedom and independence.

Fard presented himself as semi-divine. To his previously Christian followers, he was a Christ-like figure or in Islamic terms, a *Mahdi*. He preached a message of racial separatism, independent nationhood (members didn't regard themselves as American citizens), and economic independence. Members led an austere life style: hard work, one meal a day, no pork, alcohol, or gambling. Schools and businesses were established to pursue the goals of Fard. Fard also founded the Fruit of Islam, a paramilitary group that was the Nation's army, police force, and security force.

Elijah Muhammad

Fortunately for the future of the Nation of Islam, it had in Elijah Muhammad a potential new leader with charisma equal to that of W. D. Fard. Born Elijah Poole in Georgia, he moved to Detroit in 1922 and worked at the Chevrolet plant as a skilled worker. His wife, Clara, who was to play an important role in the movement in the 1940s when Elijah Muhammad was in jail, may first have induced him to attend a meeting of the Nation of Islam. Quickly, Elijah Muhammad rose to become Fard's chief minister. If Fard was in some sense God, then Elijah Muhammad was his final prophet.

After Fard's disappearance, Elijah Muhammad moved the headquarters of the group to Chicago. For the next seven years, he traveled as an itinerant preacher spreading the message of the movement and surviving a series of challenges to his leadership. In 1942, Elijah Muhammad was imprisoned for urging his followers not to register for the draft. His wife kept the movement going until his release in 1946. At that time, the Nation was still quite small, having temples only in Chicago, Milwaukee, Detroit, and Washington D.C. With the second great wave of migration of blacks to the north after World War II, the Nation began to expand rapidly in the 1950s. Businesses, temples, and educational activities of the Nation expanded. Elijah Muhammad made his *hajj* in 1959, gaining a degree of legitimacy for the movement, although most orthodox Islamic organizations officially rejected the Nation as a legitimate form of Islam. Elijah Muhammad died in 1975.

Malcolm X

Malcolm Little was born in Omaha in 1925. His parents were both active in Garvey's United Negro Improvement Association, which led to the family's being run out of town. After settling in Detroit in 1929, the family house was torched and his father was killed in 1931. In the 1930s, Malcolm was placed in foster homes and in a juvenile detention center. He moved in 1940 to live with his older half-sister in Boston, where he became involved in street crime and drugs. After moving to Harlem in New York City, he ended up in prison from 1946 to 1952. While in prison, he converted to the Nation of Islam. Malcolm became a changed man who took full advantage of the educational opportunities in prison. Upon his parole in 1952, he became known as Malcolm X (the X replacing his slave name). Three of his brothers were already active in the Nation.

Malcolm devoted all his energies to the Nation. After leading temples in several major cities, he became chief minister — the number-two position — and head of the Detroit Temple # 1 in 1957. Membership of the nation had risen to an estimated 40,000. Prison ministry, already important, became even more so because of Malcolm's own experience as a young black man in prison. Malcolm appealed to young African Americans and became something of a media star. Elijah Muhammad sent Malcolm on a tour of mid-east and West Africa in 1959. From his studies, as well as the contacts made on this tour, Malcolm began to have doubts about some of the Nation's doctrines and practices that diverged from orthodox Islam. Malcolm began to see the destiny of African Americans as linked to third world liberation movements and to worldwide Islam. A CBS documentary in 1959 on the Nation of Islam, although unfavorable to the Nation, gave favorable national exposure to Malcolm X.

As Malcolm's star rose, cracks appeared in the almost father-son relationship between Malcolm X and Elijah Muhammad. The roots of the split between the two men were multiple. Jealousy may have played a role. Malcolm was disappointed when it appeared Elijah Muhammad had been involved in illicit affairs with his secretaries. Elijah Muhammad prohibited Malcolm from organizing protests after the Los Angeles police killed Ronald Stokes, a friend of his, in 1962. Elijah Muhammad silenced Malcolm for three months due to comments Malcolm made about the "chickens coming home to roost" upon the death of President Kennedy. Policy differences about the future direction of the Nation and the relationship to orthodox Islam heightened tensions. The FBI was active, as it had been since the 1930s, in promoting internal discord within what it regarded as radical, un-American black groups. The recognized climax of Malcolm's spiritual pilgrimage was his *hajj* in 1964, together with visits to Nigeria and Ghana on his return from Mecca. Coming under severe attack upon his return, he withdrew from the Nation in March, 1964, and founded an orthodox Sunni mosque in New York City. He changed his name to El Hajj Malik El-Shabazz. Rumors of plans to assassinate Malcolm X turned into fact when he was killed on February 21, 1965. The case was never solved, although theories abound.

Warith Deen Mohammed

W.D. Muhammad was born in 1933, being named Wallace D. after W. D. Fard. He later changed his name to Warith Deen Mohammed ("inheritor of the faith"). His father, Elijah Muhammad, sent him and a brother to study at al-Azhar in Cairo. A serious student of Islam, W.D. Mohammed began to see that many of the beliefs and practices of the Nation were contrary to Islam. He would later say that his father was aware of this, but felt that his version of Islam was necessary for African Americans at that time. Warith D. Mohammed was a friend to Malcolm X, even as Malcolm X fell into disfavor. Ill in his final years, Elijah Muhammad desired leadership of the Nation to remain in the family and reappointed Warith as chief minister in 1974.

Despite limited opposition from some quarters, Warith assumed control of the movement in 1975 and by 1978 had undertaken a number of actions to bring the movement into accord with orthodox Sunni Islam, such as the following:

- Rejecting racism and allowing whites to join the movement.
- Eliminating the demand for a separate black nation in America.
- Rejecting any claims to divinity and prophethood on the part of Fard and Elijah Muhammad while still honoring their role in the movement.
- Recognizing the contributions of Malcolm X.

> ✔ Disbanding the Fruit of Islam security force and selling off most of the economic enterprises of the Nation.
>
> ✔ Instituting a number of ritual changes: five times a day *salat,* celebration of *Ramadan* at the normal time for Muslims, replacing "temple" with *masjid* (mosque), and using prayer rugs rather than seats in the mosque hall.

Under W. D. Mohammed, the movement and its newspaper (now the weekly *Muslim Journal*) underwent a number of name changes; until today it's known as the Muslim American Society. Government was decentralized so that while W. D. Mohammed is the recognized head and spiritual leader, he doesn't have absolute administrative authority. The MAS is now recognized by other Muslims as an orthodox Sunni Muslim movement and the status of W. D. Mohammed was signaled by making him responsible for certifying American Muslims who wish to make the *hajj.* While many African-American Muslims worship in mosques that aren't predominantly black, the majority (perhaps 90 percent) belong to mosques of the MAS.

Reviving the Nation of Islam

Not everybody was happy about the changes brought about by W. D. Mohammed. Louis Farrakhan was born as Louis Eugene Wolcott in 1933 and converted to the Nation after meeting Elijah Muhammad in 1955. Like Malcolm X (who was a great influence), Farrakhan is a powerful speaker. In 1978, he broke with W.D. Mohammed to organize a "new" Nation of Islam based on the original teachings of Elijah Muhammad. The Fruit of Islam security force was reestablished.

When non-Muslim Americans hear about black Muslims, most probably think of Farrakhan's group and not the much larger MAS. Media attention focuses more on Farrakhan because his controversial statements are better attention getters than those by W. D. Muhammad.

> ✔ Farrakhan probably gained most attention for organizing the 1995 Million Man March on Washington, D.C. His appeal extends far beyond those who belong to the Nation of Islam as shown by the diverse group of leaders and followers who participated in this event.
>
> ✔ Farrakhan is infamous for his anti-Semitic remarks, including the accusations that the Jews are chiefly responsible for the slave trade. He's also reported to have said in the 1980s that Hitler was a great man.
>
> ✔ Some local Nation of Islam chapters have been praised for their efforts to halt the drug trade and gang warfare in inner city neighborhoods.

> ✔ At the 2000 annual Savior's Day (the annual Nation of Islam convention), Farrakhan announced closer ties to orthodox Islam and he and Warith Deen Mohammed embraced on stage. The Nation now observes Friday prayers and celebrates *Ramadan* according to the Muslim lunar calendar.

Shi`ites in America

Shi`ites constitute 10 to 20 percent of American Muslims, according to some estimates. In smaller cities, Shi`ites are likely to participate in the local Sunni mosque. In larger cities, Shi`ites will have their own mosques or even different Shi`ite mosques for Shi`ites of different ethnic origins. Partly, this is because Shi`ites from various countries differ in how they observe `ashura', the martyrdom of *Imam* Husayn (see Chapter 12). Political differences also separate Shi`ite groups. In general, Shi`ites seem to be less well organized in the United States than Sunni Muslims.

Various national and international Shi`ite groups are active in the United States, including the Kho`i Foundation (1976) in New York City, the Alawi Foundation, financed by Iran, and the World Federation of Khoja Twelver Shi`ites, based in England. The Isma`ili group headed by the Aga Khan (a graduate of Harvard University) founded its first American center in 1968 and, while small, is active in the United States (see Chapter 14).

Sufis in America

Gisela Webb distinguishes three periods of Sufism in the United States. In the first period, from 1910 to 1927, Hazrat Inayat Khan spread the Sufi message in The United States and founded the *Sufi Order in the West*. He was a Chistiyya Sufi who believed that Sufism had a universal message that transcended any one religion. Khan's Sufism emphasized harmony, peace, and the unity of all beings in its teachings and utilized music and dance in its ceremonies. Traditional Muslims don't regard this movement as a valid form of Islam.

Webb's second period of American Sufism occurred during the 1960s and 1970s when many new religious movements appealed to American youth. Hazrat Khan's son revived the *Sufi Order in the West*. He established a center in upstate New York, and its Sufi Dances at the Cathedral of St. John the Divine in New York City attracted attention and converts. During this period, the movement became even less clearly Islamic. A Sufi order that evolved from New Age Spirituality toward traditional Sufism is the Bawa Muhayiddin Fellowship founded in Philadelphia in 1971 by a Qadiriyya sheikh from Sri Lanka. Bawa Muhayiddin died in 1986, and his shrine near Philadelphia is a pilgrimage destination even for non-American Sufis. Subud is an unorthodox Sufi movement founded in Indonesia in the 1920s and brought to the United States in the late 1950s by John Bennett. One can belong to the Subud movement and be a member of any or no religion. Subud retains some outward forms of Islam such a modest dress, ritual separation of men and women, and fasting during *Ramadan*.

Webb's third period of American Sufism, from the 1980s to the present, is marked by the influence of orthodox Muslim immigrants on American Sufism. Many traditional Sufi orders have established various centers in the United States, including the Naqshbandiyya and the Tijaniyya.

Many people participate in Sufi "dancing" groups, modeled on the Mevlevi order of Rumi, without having any intention of converting to Islam. Other Americans know about Sufism through Coleman Bark's translations of the writings of Rumi and writings on Sufism by scholars like S. H. Nasr.

Facing the Future as Muslim Americans

The Muslim community is relatively young and faces the same issues of adaptation encountered by earlier immigrants. African-American Muslims face their own unique set of issues. Beyond the fact that Islam is here to stay in the United States, only a fool would predict the shape of Islam in The United States 50 years hence. This section outlines some of the issues facing Muslims.

Internal issues

An underlying issue is whether Muslims are to remain apart from the mainstream of American society, as some Christian groups like the Amish have done, or whether they're to integrate themselves fully into American society, following the path of earlier immigrants while still maintaining a clear Muslim identity. Some say a Muslim shouldn't even live in a non-Muslim society. Some say if they do, they shouldn't participate in that society. Others say the Qur'an obligates all Muslims to participate actively in order to create a more just society.

✔ **Muslim women face problems of their own.** Muslim men on the streets may appear foreign but not identifiably Muslim because they usually wear Western clothes. Muslim women who wear Islamic dress are immediately identifiable as Muslims. Muslim women face problems of how to find a spouse in a culture where "dating" is the normal way to find a mate. They face problems in relating to men in public in a culture where a handshake is expected as a simple courtesy, and yet tradition may say she shouldn't touch an unrelated male. Domestic violence is an issue that the Muslim community is just beginning to address.

✔ **A major concern is how to raise children as Muslims in a non-Muslim culture.** Parochial schools are expanding, as is home schooling, but most Muslim children continue to be educated in public schools, where they face problems of gender relations, food restrictions, occasions for prayer, and celebration of major Muslim holidays. Even textbooks may present Muslim children with negative images of Islam.

✔ **Avoiding prohibited food is difficult** because of the use of alcohol and pork byproducts in processing of foods, pharmaceuticals, and cosmetics.

✔ **Muslims have to decide how to live in one of the most capitalistic societies in the world** and still not break the prohibition against paying or charging interest.

✔ **In the military, workplace, prisons, and hospitals, reasonable accommodation of the religious needs of employees, inmates, and clientele must be balanced against the need of the organization.** While issues remain, significant progress has been made.

✔ **Immigrant Muslims come from many countries.** Sometimes ethnic identity is stronger than religious identity. An Indian Muslim parent may, for example, rather see her child marry a Hindu than a non-Indian Muslim. Many mosques are ethnically mixed, but tension between ethnic groups is sometimes a problem.

✔ **A similar issue is the relationship between black and non-black Muslims.** Despite the egalitarian teaching of the Qur'an, anti-black prejudice has existed in many Muslim cultures.

✔ **Because new immigrants are still replenishing the Muslim community, tensions exist** between new immigrants and earlier immigrants. New immigrants sometimes regard themselves as having a purer Islam and may presume to instruct other Muslims as to true Islam.

✔ **Another issue concerns foreign Muslim movements.** When these movements try to impose their view of Islam on American Muslims, they meet with both positive and negative reactions.

External issues

In addition, consider the following issues coming from those outside Islam:

✔ **Muslims face incidents of physical violence because of their faith.** In a country where synagogues still face incidents of vandalism, despite the long Jewish presence in America, you may not be surprised at the many incidents of mosque vandalism each year. Events in 2002 involved a mosque in Boise, Idaho, a plot to bomb a number of mosques in Florida, and hate materials deposited at a mosque in Honolulu. Fortunately, when such incidents happen, local political and religious leaders often publicly condemn such actions.

✔ **Some Muslims face discrimination on the job.** A Muslim policeman may feel his religion requires that he grow a beard, while department policy may say all officers must be clean-shaven. A supervisor may tell a Muslim employee that she can't wear her *hijab* (veil and head-covering) at work, perhaps because of a perceived health or safety hazard or because it doesn't project the public image the company desires. Often, these cases result from decisions made by local supervisors ill-informed as to both anti-discrimination laws and the requirements of Islamic faith and must be resolved through intervention of higher company officials, outside mediators, or the courts.

Other incidents involve not so much overt discrimination as insensitivity. In 1997, the Nike shoe company put a symbol on one of their shoes that looked much like Allah in Arabic characters. They subsequently ceased the use of this design. Insensitivity may also involve how Muslims are portrayed in the media.

✔ **Some Muslims say Muslims shouldn't participate in American politics.** But most Muslims want input into political decisions that affect their future. In 2000, the AMPCC recommended bloc voting by Muslims in the presidential election. It endorsed President Bush, having received a more favorable response on issues of concern to Muslims than it did from vice-president Gore. Forty-two percent voted for Bush and 31 percent for Gore. Traditionally, Muslims have favored Democrats (40 percent to 28 percent Republican) and would have in this election, except for the action of the AMPCC. The switch in the Muslim vote provided the margin of victory in the determinative Florida results.

✔ **Muslims must decide to what extent they may engage in interfaith activities.** May a Muslim *imam* participate in an interfaith religious service for world peace or in an interfaith community service on Thanksgiving Day? Is it proper for mosques to hold open houses for visits by non-Muslims or allow non-Muslims to attend Friday prayers?

Part V

Considering Islam's Concept of Abrahamic Religions

The 5th Wave   By Rich Tennant

"I'm glad you're able to join us. But maybe I should have explained what the Festival of Fast Breaking is all about."

In this part . . .

This part considers the lively dialogue that has occurred among Muslims, Christians, and Jews over the past half-century. *People of the Book* and *Abrahamic Religions* are two ways in which Muslims express their belief that Judaism, Christianity, and Islam belong to the same family, worship the same God, and possess related scriptures. This part begins by looking at why Muslims believe they're related religiously to Christians and Jews, giving particular attention to Biblical characters, including Jesus, who play an important role in Islam.

Also in this part, I consider views Christians have held about Muslims and views of Muslims about Christians, as well as the status of Christians living in Muslim countries. Despite dialogue, many Muslims harbor resentments against America and the West. Muslims have responded in various ways to Western political and economic power and to global forces of modernization. At the end of this part, I discuss the 1979 revolution in Iran, as well as Osama bin Laden and the Taliban in Afghanistan.

Chapter 16

Seeking Common Roots: Abrahamic Religion and Beyond

· ·

In This Chapter

▶ Tracing the Abrahamic religions' family tree

▶ Looking at the Qur'anic version of the Bible

▶ Finding Muhammad in the Bible

▶ Encountering members of other religions

· ·

A dherents of Islam, Judaism, and Christianity together constitute over 50 percent of the world's population. This chapter looks at what binds the three religions together into a single "family" in the same way that Hinduism, Buddhism, and Jainism constitute a family of related religions. As part of the picture of what Islam, Judaism, and Christianity share, this chapter examines the Biblical stories that have counterparts in the Qur'an. Finally, the chapter summarizes the Muslim belief that the Bible prophesizes the coming of Muhammad.

Belonging to the Same Family

Three points bind together Judaism, Islam, and Christianity: a common God, ancestor, and related scriptures.

Recognizing the same ancestor

Abraham is the common ancestor of Jews, Christians, and Muslims. Hagar is the mother of Abraham's first son, Ishmael, to whom all Arabs trace their lineages. Abraham and Sarah have a son, Isaac. Isaac's son Jacob/Israel is the father of 12 sons from whom the 12 Jewish tribes are descended. The New Testament traces the genealogy of Jesus back to King David and beyond him to Abraham (and Adam). See Figure 16-1.

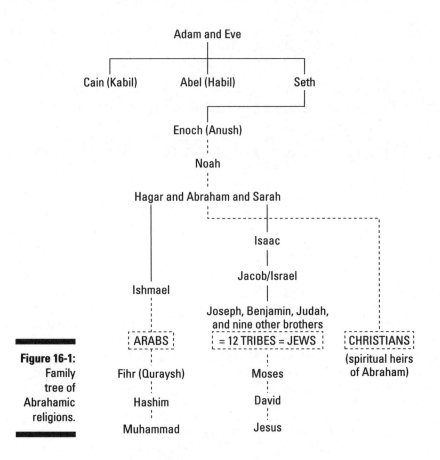

Figure 16-1:
Family
tree of
Abrahamic
religions.

Worshipping the same God

All three religions claim to worship the same God, even though some
Christians today don't accept that the Muslim God is the same as the
Christian God. When Paul, the Jew, converted to Christianity, he didn't think
he had changed the God he worshipped. Rather, he had come to a different
understanding of the God he had always worshipped. Today, when a member
of one of the three Abrahamic religions converts and becomes a member of a
different one of the three religions, she views herself as having changed her
religion but not her God. In contrast, when a pagan converted to Islam,
Christianity, or Judaism, the convert had changed both religion and god.

For Muslims, Abraham is neither Christian nor Jew (Sura 3:67). He is rather
the first monotheist and thus the first muslim (small "m") in the sense of one
who submits to the only true God. For Muslims, faithful Christians and Jews
are muslims because they submit to God.

God made a covenant with Abraham, Isaac, and Jacob that was given definitive form in the covenant mediated by Moses at Mount Sinai. God also made promises to Ishmael (Genesis 17:20), although the covenant terminology is not used for Ismael. Christians understand themselves as the spiritual children of Abraham and the inheritors of the covenant God made with Abraham (Genesis 15; Galatians 3:6). The Qur'an says that God made covenants with the Children of Israel (Sura 5:12), with Christians (Sura 5:14), and with Muslims (Sura 5:7). For Islam, underlying all of these covenants is an implicit covenant made in the time of Adam between God and all Adam's descendants (Sura 7:172). The most essential element of these covenants is the acknowledgement of the one God. This God is the only ultimate reality, the creator of the world, the Lord of history who imposes commandments on believers, and the one who will bring the Day of Judgment and the resurrection.

Sharing the same book

Muslims believe that anterior to the scriptures of Christianity, Islam, and Judaism is the eternal, heavenly prototype, the Mother of Book. The scriptural revelations (Torah, Psalms, Gospels, Qur'an) brought by prophetic messengers are exemplars of this heavenly book, although from the Islamic point of view, only the Qur'an is a complete and uncorrupted version. Because their scriptures go back to the same heavenly prototype, Muslims, Jews, Christians (and some others) are all People of the Book.

Reviewing family relations

The three Abrahamic religions obviously don't agree theologically on how to express the relationship of each to the other two. In the same manner that Christianity views itself as fulfilling, completing, and superceding Judaism (without abolishing the validity of the Jewish covenant), so Islam regards itself as fulfilling, completing, and superceding Christianity (without abolishing the Jewish or Christian covenants). Although each of these religions looks forward to the coming or second coming of a Messiah and/or *Mahdi,* each regards itself as the final revelation. Islam regards itself not only as the fulfillment of Judaism and Christianity but also as their predecessor in claiming that Islam is the natural religion of humankind at birth, as well as the faith of Abraham. Both Christianity and Islam have faced within their own ranks further revelations or prophets who challenge claims of finality. Examples are Mormonism, Christian Science, and the Unification Church for Christianity and the Baha'i religion and Ahmadiyya sect for Islam.

Each religion deals with the other two in its own way. At various times, Christianity has regarded Islam as a regression to legalism, a Christian heresy, a religion for Arabs to prepare them for true Christianity, or as a sign of the end times. Some scholars within both Christianity and Islam have used the concept that their religion is a God-given religion and thus the true one while other religions are human creations. Some modern Islamic scholars have used a thesis-antithesis-synthesis model in which Judaism is the thesis (law, materialism, particularism, worldliness) and Christianity is antithesis (love, idealism, universalism, otherworldly), with Islam representing a balanced synthesis and reconciliation of thesis and antithesis.

Reading the Bible in the Qur'an

About one-fourth of the Qur'an is devoted to stories of the prophets, most of whom are Biblical prophets (although not all of them are actually called prophets in the Bible). Because these stories and references are most often scattered throughout the Qur'an, a new reader has difficulty getting the full picture of the Bible in the Qur'an. In this section, I summarize the Qur'anic versions of these Biblical stories and also mention additions to the stories in subsequent Muslim traditions.

Biblical characters and stories circulated in pre-Islamic Arabia. When the Qur'an makes a brief mention of a Biblical character, Muhammad's audience understood the reference without the whole story being retold. According to Muhammad's biographer, Ibn Ishaq, those reconstructing the Ka`ba when Muhammad was still a youth found a stone inscribed with a Syriac translation of Matthew 7:16. According to the ninth century historian of Mecca, the Ka`ba contained pictures of Abraham, Jesus, and perhaps Mary on a column near the entrance. Some reports say Muhammad left these untouched when he cleansed the Ka`ba of its pagan idols after the Muslims conquered Mecca in 630. Muhammad and his listeners thus had some familiarity with Biblical stories circulating in Arabia. He would have heard more about the Bible from Christians and Jews with whom he came in contact. From the form of the Biblical names that occur in the Bible, scholars conclude that these stories were based on the Syriac and Aramaic (two dialects of the same language, which is related to Hebrew) translations of the Bible rather than on the Hebrew and Greek original texts. Most scholars conclude that Muhammad himself never read the Bible. The Qu'ran refers not to the "Bible" but to the torah *(taurat)*, the psalms *(zabur)*, and the gospel *(injil)*, recalling the way the New Testament refers to the Hebrew Bible (Old Testament) as "the law, the prophets, and the psalms."

Why the stories in the Qur'an differ from those in the Bible

Even a casual reader who has some familiarity with the Biblical stories easily recognizes that the Biblical stories differ from their Qur'anic counterparts. Non-Muslim scholars generally say this is because Muhammad had only an indirect and incomplete knowledge of the Bible. Also, the Biblical stories current in popular culture in the time of Muhammad included elements from post-Biblical Jewish and Christian traditions.

This explanation of the differences isn't convincing to most Muslims. After all, from the Muslim point of view, Muhammad didn't "compose" the Biblical stories in the Qur'an. Rather Gabriel transmitted them to Muhammad from the eternal, heavenly prototype, which is the word of God. Gabriel and God were unlikely to be influenced by the versions of Biblical stories circulating in seventh century Arabia. Because the Qur'an contained the original version of the story taken directly from the heavenly book, Muslims had no reason to study the Bible except for purposes of better defending their positions against Christians and Jews. Muslims believed that where the Qur'anic version of a story differed from the Biblical account, Christians and Jews had intentionally or unintentionally corrupted and altered the text. _Tahrif_ is the Arabic term for this theory of alteration. Was this alteration intentional? Many writings aimed at the general Muslim public, as well as many Muslim scholars, assert that the alteration was intentional. In contrast, Muslim scholars, such as al-Tabari, al-Ghazali, Ibn Kathir, and Ibn Khaldun, have upheld the integrity of the Biblical text as passed on by Christians and Jews.

In order of frequency, the most commonly mentioned Biblical characters are Moses, Abraham, Noah, and Adam. Multiple references are made also to Jacob, David, and Solomon. Other people, such as Lot, Isaac, Ishmael, and Aaron, are mentioned sometimes by themselves and at other times in the context of the story of one of the more common characters. The most developed single story is that of Joseph (Sura 12). Fairly complete versions of the stories of Noah, Abraham, and Moses also occur, although one must read portions of several suras to get the complete story. Brief mention is made of Elijah, Elisha, and Job. Only Jonah is mentioned from the 12 prophetic books of the Hebrew Bible (and perhaps Elijah in 21:85 and 38:49).

In my summaries of the Qur'anic stories of the Bible, I give the major accounts at the beginning of each section and only cite references from other texts in the summary. Also, I indicate incidents that are in the Qur'anic version but not in the Bible with an asterisk (*).

The Adam story

The fullest version of the creation story occurs in Sura 2:30–39; 7:11–31; and 38:71–85. God tells the angels of his intention to create a _khalifa_* (representative) on earth. The angels object*, contrasting the likely sins of humans with angelic glorification of God. God creates Adam from dust and breathes His spirit in Him. He teaches Adam the names of all things. At God's command, the angels prostrate themselves* before Adam, except for Iblis who refuses because he is created of a higher substance, fire. God expels Iblis from the garden but allows him to tempt humans.* Sura 20:115 mentions a covenant of God with Adam,* which Adam forgot. Placed in the garden, God tells Adam and his wife (unnamed) not to come near "this tree" (only one tree is mentioned). Satan (Iblis) tempts them, saying they'll live forever if they eat. So they eat and sew leaves to cover their newly realized nakedness. After God sends them from the garden to the earth, Adam asks forgiveness and God promises him guidance.*

In post-Qur'anic Muslim tradition, God sends the angels Gabriel and Michael to take clay from earth to create Adam. When the earth refuses, God sends the angel of death who takes red, white, and black clay representing the three races of men to make Adam. God creates Eve from the tip of Adam's rib. Eve makes wine, and Adam gets drunk. Satan sneaks back into the garden in the mouth of a snake to tempt Adam. Later, on earth, Adam builds the *Ka`ba,* placing on it the black stone sent from heaven. He and Eve perform the *hajj.*

The Cain and Abel story is briefly told in Sura 5:27–34. God accepts the sacrifice of only one of the two unnamed brothers. When Cain threatens to kill Abel, Abel refuses to retaliate.* God sends a raven that scratches the ground showing Cain where to bury his brother,* at which point Cain repents. The text comments that to kill a person is equivalent to killing all humankind, and to save a person is like saving all humankind*.

Abraham, Lot, Ishmael, and Isaac

Abraham is mentioned in 25 suras with longer accounts in Sura 2:124–141, 6:69–83, 19:41–50, 21:51–72, and 37:83–113. Abraham is a prophet with a book* (53:37), an *imam* for the nations*, the first Muslim (3:67), and a follower of the straight path* (16:121). Abraham is initially inclined to worship the heavenly bodies,* but realizing his folly, he determines instead to worship their creator and becomes a monotheist. He rebukes his father for his worship of idols* and smashes the idols* (21:58–65). When the people try to burn him,* God saves him. He departs for Canaan (37:99), where he receives the promise of descendants and a covenant (2:125). The Biblical promise of land isn't mentioned. Angels visit Abraham and promise the birth of Isaac (11:69–76). They tell of the destruction of Sodom and Abraham pleads for Lot.

Sura 37:83–113 tells the story of the sacrifice of Abraham's unnamed son. Rather than being asked about the sacrifice by his son as in the Bible, Abraham tells his son what's about to happen and both father and son submit to God. Although some early Muslim interpreters, including al-Tabari, agree with the Bible in identifying the son as Isaac, most Muslim commentators say the son is Ishmael and the birth of Isaac is a reward for Abraham's obedience. Both sons are named as prophets. Pride and identity play a part in the discussion as to which son is involved, because Jews trace their ancestry to Isaac and his mother Sarah, while Muslims (and more specifically, Arabs) trace their lineage (or in the case of Arabs, tribal ancestry) to Ishmael and his mother, Hagar.

The Qur'an mentions the rebuilding of the *Ka`ba* by Abraham and Ishmael, the observance of the *hajj* rituals, the settlement of Ishmael and other believers in Mecca, an infertile valley made habitable due to Abraham's prayer (14:37).

Joseph: The "most beautiful of stories"

The Joseph Sura (12) is the most developed narrative of any of the Bible stories in the Qur'an. The Qur'an calls this the "most beautiful of stories." In contrast to the narrative style of the Biblical version, the shorter Qur'anic version is structured around a series of dramatic dialogue scenes with a minimum of connecting narrative. Only Joseph and Jacob are explicitly named in Sura 12. The story tells how Joseph, envied by his brothers, is sold into slavery in Egypt, where he ultimately rises to chief minister of Pharaoh. In a time of famine, his brothers come to Egypt to buy grain, and after a series of encounters with Joseph, the family is reunited.

I highlight only a few of the most important variations of the Qur'anic story from the Biblical story. Once in Egypt, when the wife of Joseph's owner tries to seduce Joseph, he is tempted but God prevents him from yielding. As he runs to the door, the woman tears the shirt from his back. The shirt torn in the back proves Joseph was fleeing rather than attacking the woman. The wife invites the women to a banquet where, stunned by Joseph's beauty, they cut their fingers with their knives. Later in prison, Joseph preaches the message of Islam to his two cellmates. When the brothers later come to Egypt, Joseph reveals himself to the younger brother (Benjamin in Genesis) but not to the other ten brothers. When Jacob goes blind with grief over the loss of his son, Joseph sends his shirt with his brothers back to Canaan to cast over his father, Jacob, restoring Jacob's eyesight. Father and brothers come to Egypt and the family is reunited.

Later Muslim tradition emphasizes Joseph's beauty. All beauty was given originally to Adam. When Adam sinned, much of his beauty was given to Joseph.

The Moses story

REMEMBER

Moses is mentioned in more than one-third of the Qur'an's suras, making him the most frequently mentioned Biblical personality. Sura 28:1–42, 7:103–71, 20:9–98, and 26:10–58 tell a substantial portion of the story.

The story begins with God telling Moses's mother to put him into a box and cast it into the river, because Pharaoh has ordered all Jewish infants be killed. The Egyptians pick him out of the river, and he is raised by Pharaoh's wife. She later believes in God* (Sura 66:11) and Muslim tradition supplies her name, Asiya, as one of four perfect women, the other three being Mary, the mother of Jesus, Khadija, the wife of Muhammad, and Fatima, Muhammad's daughter. When Moses refuses to nurse, Moses's sister brings their mother to nurse him. After he was grown, Moses sees an Egyptian and a Jew fighting, and he kills the Egyptian. Realizing that the murder is due to the influence of Satan, Moses repents.*

After fleeing to Midian and marrying the two daughters of Jethro, Moses was traveling with his family and saw a fire on Mt. Sinai. God speaks to him, telling him to take off his shoes. God gives to Moses the two signs: the rod that turns into a snake and his hand that becomes white. God commands him to go and warn Pharaoh of his sins. Because he has a speech impediment, Moses asks that his brother Aaron be his helper. Moses and Aaron confront the Pharaoh. Moses rod devours the rods of the Egyptian magicians.* Pharaoh ridicules Moses, and orders his henchman, Haman,* to build a tower* so that he may mount up to the god of Moses (see Genesis 12). The Egyptians kill the male Israelite children (similar to the killing of the children at the time of the birth of Moses in the Bible), and the Hebrews complain to Moses about the troubles he has brought on them. Moses performs nine miracles, culminating with the separation of the waters of the Red Sea, the Israelites crossing over on the dry sea bed, and the drowning of the Egyptians when the waters flowed again.

Coming to Mt. Sinai, Moses spends 40 nights on the mountain. He asks to see God, but when God revealed himself, the mountain dissolved into dust* and Moses repented for trying to apprehend the nature of God. God gives Moses the tablets with the law. The Ten Commandments as such don't occur in the Qur'an. While on the mountain, the people, under the instigation of al-Samiri* and against the objections of Aaron, cast the molten calf from their jewelry. In punishment, al-Samiri wanders the world, crying out "Do not touch me." Later tradition identifies him as a Samaritan, a member of a Jewish sect from the time of Jesus.

The remainder of the story isn't told in detail, although various incidents are mentioned that also occur in the Bible.

Unique is the story of Moses's journey with the mysterious al-Khadir* (Sura 18:60–82), the "Green Man." Moses and his servant set out to find the junction of the two seas, taking a fish with them. They put down the fish and it swims away in the water. They then meet al-Khadir and Moses asks if they can go with al-Khadir to learn from him. Al-Khadir says yes, but they shouldn't question any of his actions. Al-Khadir sinks a boat, kills a young man, and restores a wall in a town of inhospitable people. Each time Moses questions the action. Therefore, al-Khadir leaves Moses, after first giving reasonable explanations for his strange actions. Tradition says that al-Khadir is immortal and each Friday he performs *salat* in Jerusalem, Mecca, and Medina.

According to post-Qur'anic Muslim traditions, when the infant Moses touches Pharaoh's chin, Pharaoh wants to kill him. Asiya puts gold on one side and burning coals on other side of Moses. When he reaches for the gold, Gabriel guides his hand to coals. Moses touches his lips, which is why he later has a speech impediment. When Pharaoh tries to kill the infants, Moses is hidden in a burning oven and protected by God. Moses's rod came from the first tree planted in paradise by Adam and was used by other prophets before Moses.

The death of Jesus

While all Christians, most non-Muslim historians, and the relatively few ancient non-Christian sources all accept the Gospel account that Jesus was crucified by the Romans, this is explicitly denied by the Qur'an. God always intervenes to save his prophets and to punish those who try to harm them. In Sura 4:157–58, the Jews say, "We Killed the Messiah, Jesus the Son of Mary, the Messenger of God — but they did not kill him nor crucify him, only a likeness that appeared to them. . . . They certainly did not kill him but God raised him up to himself." Sura 3:55 supplements this when God says, "Jesus, I will take you and raise you to me." Sura 4:159 says that before the death of Jesus, all the People of the Book will believe in him, and he will be a witness against them at the Day of Judgment. In Sura 19:33, Jesus speaks of "the day I was born, the day that I die, and the day that I shall be raised up alive." On the basis of these verses, Muslims say that someone else was substituted for Jesus on the cross, and Jesus himself was taken up into heaven where he is still living today. In the final days, Jesus will return, perhaps as the *Mahdi* (messianic figure of Islam), defeat the anti-Messiah, and live for 40 years on earth. He will then die (for the first time), be buried in a place reserved for him beside Muhammad in Medina, and be resurrected on the Day of Judgment when he, like all prophets, will be a witness for (or against) his community.

The disagreement between Christians and Muslims regarding the crucifixion is related to the larger issues about the nature of Jesus and the process of salvation. Christianity teaches that humanity is essentially sinful, and people can't overcome sin by themselves. Redemption is triumph over the power of sin, but this requires an act of God. Jesus "must" be God in order to overcome sin through his death. Thus, for Christianity, the divinity of Jesus is crucial.

Islam has a concept of "sin" more as individual acts of disobedience against God rather than as the basic state of human nature. Adam sinned in eating of the tree, but this was due to ignorance and forgetfulness of God. The solution is to remember God and follow the path he has revealed through His prophets. Those who do this receive blessing in this world and the next. The Qur'an's denial of the crucifixion is logically linked to its denial of the Trinity (4:171). The Qur'an emphasizes that Jesus denied saying that humans should worship him as a God (5:116). Those that say that Jesus is God are unbelievers (5:17). Like Muhammad, the Jesus of the Qur'an is an exalted being, but only a human being.

Muhammad in the Bible

In addition to the Qur'anic passage where Jesus predicts the coming of Muhammad (Sura 61:6), Muslims find in the Bible predictions of Muhammad. In doing this, Muslims are following in the footsteps of Christians who found in the Hebrew Bible predictions of Jesus. Of course, few if any Christians accept that the cited passages are speaking of Muhammad. But then Jews don't accept that passages like Isaiah 7 and Isaiah 52–53 refer to Jesus.

✔ Most important for Muslims are references to the Paraclete (Greek *parakletos*) whom Jesus, or God, at the request of Jesus, will send after Jesus and in his name (John 14:16, 26; 15:26; 16:7; I John 2:1. Christian commentators agree the texts envision someone who would be present with the young Christian community in the generation after the departure of Jesus. Subsequent Christianity naturally understood this as a reference to the third person of the Trinity, the Holy Spirit. Islam identifies this Paraclete as Muhammad. This is probably as valid or invalid as Christian identification of Jesus as the "suffering servant" of Isaiah 52–53.

✔ In Deuteronomy 18:15–18, Moses says to the Hebrews that God will raise up for them a prophet from among them. The original audience would understand this to be a Hebrew prophet. Some Christians reinterpreted this as a reference to Jesus, and Muslims in turn saw a reference to Muhammad in the passage.

✔ Other Biblical texts are cited but are less important than these two. For example, the promises to Ishmael in Genesis are said to be fulfilled in the coming of Muhammad (Genesis 21:13). Isaiah 21:13–17 is said to refer to the Battle of Badr in 624, while Habakkuk 3:3 is said to refer to the *hijra* of Muhammad from Mecca to Medina in 622. The cited texts may be convincing to many Muslims but are unpersuasive to non-Muslim interpreters of the Bible.

In summary, Muslims sincerely and quite naturally read the Bible in the light of their beliefs of a subsequent and final revelation, reinterpreting Biblical passages and giving them meaning that was never contemplated by anyone prior to the coming of Islam, just as Christians sincerely did the same to the Hebrew Bible. Obviously, one of the points of tension between religions of the same Abrahamic family is the use or perceived misuse of the scripture of another member of that family.

Muslims Facing Other Religions

Sura 5:48 says, "To each (community) among you, we have prescribed a law and a open way. If God had willed, he could've made of you one people. But he wished to test you in that which he gave to you. So strive with each other in good deeds."

This passage expresses a positive Islamic view toward other religions. Although it attacks Arabian paganism, the Qur'an is rather ambiguous regarding Christians and Jews. Some passages are favorable and other less so. Due to the early historical situation in which the treatment of Christians and Jews was the first problem faced regarding contact with people of other religions, the Qur'an says nothing about Hinduism and Buddhism. As time passes, the special status of Christians and Jews as people of the Book (that is, the scriptures all derive from the same ultimate heavenly book or word of God) was extended to other religions, such as Zoroastrians (modern Parsees), and by some Muslim theologians to Hindus (who, of course, have their own extensive written scriptures, such as the Upanishads, the Vedantas, the Puranas, and others).

Two early treaties

Although modern historians may question some of the details of early traditions, two early traditions come to be important in terms of how Muslims treated members of other religions. The Treaty of Hudaybiyyah that Muhammad concluded with Mecca in 628 provides a positive model for peace with a non-Muslim state that many Muslims today find important for addressing the question of the relation of Muslim states to non-Muslim states. The document, known as the Treaty of `Umar, supposedly originated when `Umar conquered Jerusalem in 637 set guidelines for allowing Christians and Jews to live in an Islamic state, guidelines which could easily be applied to members of other religions (see Chapter 2). During the time of the initial expansion of Islam, many people in the conquered lands welcomed Muslim rule as preferable to Byzantine or Sasanian (Persian) rule. Usually, local inhabitants weren't forced to convert to Islam and, indeed, it was to the financial benefit of the new Muslim rulers that they not convert all at once. Still, the obligation of the Muslim state to wage war on non-Muslim states in order to bring them under the rule of God's law led to negative views in many non-Muslim lands toward Islam.

Dhimmi (protected peoples)

Islamic law evolved a special status call *dhimmi* for Jews and Christians, and subsequently other "peoples of the book." Often, such people, as in the Ottoman empire, had a considerable degree of internal self-rule and were represented to the Muslim government by the head of their religious community. While the treatment of religious minorities in Islamic countries was better than the treatment of Jews and Muslims in Christian nations, the status of these religious minorities (called *dhimmi* peoples) involved religious and civil persecution that no people would willingly accept today.

In addition to special taxes levied on non-Muslims (in part, to compensate for the fact that they didn't serve in the army), non-Muslims (*dhimmis*):

- ✔ Couldn't publicly display their religious symbols, such as the cross
- ✔ Couldn't build new houses of worship
- ✔ Couldn't publicly announce their worship services
- ✔ Had to wear identifying clothing
- ✔ Couldn't carry weapons, wear armor, or serve in the army
- ✔ Had to offer seats to Muslims when in public
- ✔ Couldn't convert any Muslims to their religions

The actual status of religious minorities in Muslim countries and their relations with the Muslim majority has varied from ruler to ruler and age to age. Egypt, throughout its history, has had a sizable Christian minority, as has the area of present-day Lebanon. Muslim rulers of India had to find ways to accommodate the majority of their subjects who remained Hindus. The 16th-century ruler Akbar removed most restrictions on Hindus, but his great-grandson, Aurangzeb, revoked Akbar's policy of equal treatment. In South Asia and in Indonesia, some Sufis interacted positively with Buddhists and Hindus, while other Muslims attacked such interaction. Laws restricting the religious freedom of non-Muslims are in effect today in some Muslim countries, such as Saudi Arabia.

Moving Toward Religious Dialogue

The history of religious dialogue involving Muslims began when some early caliphs sponsored theological debates at court between Muslims and non-Muslims. Later, for limited periods of time, much fruitful interaction occurred among Muslims, Jews, and Christians in Spain. Still later (16th century), the Mughal emperor of India, Akbar, sponsored religious dialogue in his court and encouraged seeking religious truth wherever it could be found.

In modern times, an organized movement for religious dialogue first arose in the 1960s. A key event was the "Declaration on the Relationship of the Church to non-Christian Religions" produced by the Second Vatican (Roman Catholic) Council in 1965. According to the document, salvation was possible not only for Christians but also for Jews and Muslims. Beginning in the 1960s, a number of high-level international inter-religious dialogue conferences were held, some sponsored by Muslims and others by Christians. Occasionally, Jews and members of other religion participated.

Modern institutes promoting religious dialogue include the Center for Muslim-Christian Understanding (at Georgetown University in Washington, DC), the Duncan Black McDonald Center for the Study of Islam and Christian-Muslim Relations (at Hartford Seminary, Connecticut), the Centre for the Study of Islam and Christian-Muslim Religions (at the University of Birmingham in England), the Islamic Foundation (in Leicester, England), and the Henry Martyn Institute (Hyderabad, India).

In the United States, active interfaith movements exists at both the local and national level. National organizations, such as the Interfaith Alliance, mainly involved Christians, Jews, and Muslims but welcome members of other religions, too. Such organizations try to promote religious tolerance both domestically and internationally. At the local level, most large cities have a local organization to promote dialogue among members of all religions. Local organizations nearly always involve some Jewish, Christian, and Muslim organizations. When the town has a Baha'i community, it will nearly always play a leading role in such organizations. Buddhist and Hindu participation depends in part upon the nature of specific Buddhist and Hindu groups in the communities but is welcomed and sought after by the local interfaith organization. Such organizations sponsor small group dialogues in members' homes, offer educational programs, hold open houses on major religious holidays at the places of worship of the constituent organizations, and in other ways promote constructive religious dialogue.

Principles of dialogue

Participation in a local interfaith organization is one of the best ways to get to know people of other religions, because you not only find out more about other religions, you also get to know people of differing faiths at the personal level. In this time of dialogue, keep in mind the following guidelines:

- ✔ **Practicing fairness:** Each side must represent the beliefs of the other side in a way that members of the other religion can affirm as accurate.

- ✔ **Expressing empathy:** Each side must make an honest effort to appreciate the appeal of the other religion to those who are attracted to it and to understand how the religion functions for its believers and makes sense to them.

- ✔ **Avoiding misuse of scripture:** In dialogue, you can't apply your own scripture to determine what's valid or invalid about beliefs of other side. If you does this, no dialogue takes place and each side quotes its own proof texts.

- ✔ **Staying open to change and challenge:** Participants don't want to simply repeat the party line of their religions without grappling with what the other side says. Otherwise, no dialogue occurs and two monologues that pass each other in the night.

✔ **Steering clear of denunciations or debates:** No dialogue takes place when one side wants only to denounce the positions of the other side. Dialogue isn't a debate in which one side tries to get the upper hand.

✔ **Showing reciprocity:** Apply the same standards to yourself, your own religion, and the scriptures that you apply to the religion of others.

✔ **Avoiding preconditions:** Preconditions declare the most crucial issues as settled or out of bounds before the discussion begins.

✔ **Being cautious of sweeping generalizations (positive or negative):** These obscure ambiguities and differences within either religion.

✔ **Facing frankly areas of disagreement:** Have a thick skin and don't get insulted too easily.

✔ **Avoiding selective use of scripture, tradition, and history when discussing issues:** An example is citing only those passages in the Qur'an that talk about violence and comparing them to only those passages in the Bible that talk about love and peace — or vice versa.

The future of inter-religious relations

To some extent, future dialogue is always affected by political events at the regional and international level. Prospects differ in each country; for example, current conflict between Palestinians and Israelis doesn't create a healthy climate for dialogue.

Small groups of people on both sides strive for peace, justice, and tolerance, but such actions are often opposed by the mass of citizens on both sides. In India today, the continuing tensions due to the dispute over Kashmir and growing Hindu nationalism in India contrast with the early 20th century, when many Muslims and Hindus participated together in the movement for independence from the British. Fortunately, at present, contacts between members of various faiths continue to grow in the United States, and national political leaders publicly advocate religious tolerance.

Events such as 9/11, while making dialogue in the United States more necessary than ever, also make that dialogue more difficult. The same is true of open war with an Islamic state, such as Iraq.

Chapter 17

Seeking Common Ground

● ●

In This Chapter

▶ Comprehending Muslim concerns about the West

▶ Understanding Western concerns about Islam

▶ Facing key issues separating Islam and the West

▶ Deciding what can be done to reduce tensions

● ●

Clearly, problems exist between the Western world and much of the Muslim world. Each side feels aggrieved. However, in a global world, all people have to find a way to live together. Americans ask why some Muslims hate Americans. After all, Hindus and Buddhist aren't proclaiming holy war against America. Of course, Muslims also find themselves in conflict with Hindus in South Asia (India, Kashmir), and local riots break out in other countries where Muslims live side by side with other religious communities. Indeed, for this reason, some non-Muslims see the problem not as a problem of Islam versus the West. The problem, say some, is an inclination within the Islamic world view toward intolerance and violence directed against any non-Muslim community. However, Muslims abroad are attracted to American rhetoric of freedom and equality, but some of them feel that America doesn't live up to these values in relations with the Muslim world. Many in the growing Muslim-American community share this view. In this chapter, I look at these issues and concerns.

Ascertaining Muslims' Concerns

In this section, I consider problems faced by the Muslim world and Muslim attitudes toward the West.

Uncovering internal problems in the Muslim world

The Muslim world in general, and the Arab world in particular, have economic, social, and political problems that breed discontent and resentment. This anger is directed against their own governments and other countries. The Arab Human Development Report (2001) is a United Nations-sponsored study by Arab scholars of the 22 Arab countries. The report begins by highlighting gains over the past three decades:

- Fifteen-year increase in life expectancy
- Two-hundred-percent increase in adult literacy (300 percent increase for women)
- Mortality rate for children under five reduced by two-thirds
- Dire poverty levels less than in some other parts of the developing world, probably due to the obligation in Islam to care for the poor

Unfortunately, the good news is overshadowed by the bad news that the Arab world is falling behind other parts of the developing world in the areas of education, health, information and communication technology, unemployment, political participation, personal freedoms, economic productivity and trade, science and technology, and the participation and contribution of women.

- Fifty percent of women are still illiterate.
- Unemployment is higher than in any other portion of the Third World.
- Economies have remained stagnant and regional cooperation and trade is limited. State controls limit efficient economic productivity.
- Except at the lowest level, the region has fallen behind in lessening the extent of poverty while the gap between rich and poor has increased.
- Individual freedoms, human rights, and political participation are at the lowest level of any of the regions of the Third World. Corruption is a major problem.
- While the quantity of education has improved, the quality is lacking in teaching analytical skills and innovative approaches to problem solving.
- Global communications infrastructure is limited and less media freedom exists than anywhere else in the Third World.
- Foreign investment in the Arab world is minimal.
- The region suffers a severe brain drain among younger adults.
- Eighty percent of the world's refugees are Muslims.

The report isn't interested in Muslim or Arab bashing and points out resources within the Arabic cultural and religious heritage for addressing the problems, but it goes on to say that unless changes are made and problems addressed, the Arab world is likely to continue to fall further behind other Third World regions. Some Muslim countries, such as Malaysia and Indonesia, have done much better than the Arab countries in modernizing, to be better able to compete in a global economy.

Bernard Lewis pointed out that the Ottoman elite began to ask the question of "what went wrong" several hundred years ago. For its first thousand years, Islam prospered and Islamic rule expanded. Worldly success was one of the signs of God's favor. Islam was far ahead of Europe in education, medicine, science, commerce, and political and military power. However, by about 1600, the Muslim states of the time (Ottoman, Mughal, and Iranian) began to fall behind the West, and in the 20th century, behind the Far East.

The Ottoman Empire responded by adapting new Western technology (especially military), but these were superficial changes. In contrast, Far Eastern traditions were also strongly patriarchal, sexist, hierarchical, and statist, but the Confucian ethic provided resources for modernizing without becoming less Japanese or Chinese in the process.

The transformation of the Muslim world from a position of dominance to a position of weakness and dependence created disappointment and resentment. Most people find it easier to seek the cause of their problems in what others have done to them rather than looking first to what they have done or not done. Today, the United States, as the only remaining superpower, inherits much of this resentment. In societies with a minimum of opportunity for political dissent, religion often offers the only means for mobilizing and expressing opposition to the existing situation. Islamist movements offered a simple solution: If Muslims returned to the original path of Islam, God would restore Islam to its position of preeminence in the world. "Islam is the solution" became a rallying cry.

Taking the pulse of the Muslim world

Opinion polls provide a useful indicator of Muslim attitudes toward the West and America. The Gallup organization, in early 2002, polled residents of nine Muslim countries (representing 40 percent of the total Muslim population). In no country did a majority of the population have a favorable opinion of the United States. In Jordan, Saudi Arabia, Iran, and Pakistan, between 60 and 70 percent of those polled had negative opinions of the United States. They opposed American military intervention in Afghanistan.

Zogby International conducted a similar poll in the spring of 2002 in five Arab Muslim (Egypt, Jordan, Kuwait, Lebanon, and Saudi Arabia) and three non-Arab Muslim countries (Indonesia, Iran, and Pakistan), plus France and Venezuela. In this poll:

- Fifty to 84 percent had favorable opinions of American products.

- Fifty percent or more of each country had favorable opinions of American freedoms and democracy (except Iran and Indonesia).

- Eighty-five percent or more (99 percent in Iran) had an unfavorable opinion of American foreign policy toward the Muslim world, especially because of American policy regarding Palestine and Israel.

Listing Muslim complaints against the West and possible Western responses

While the fact of Western colonial domination is indisputable, Western colonialism wasn't targeted specifically to Muslim countries, and the United States wasn't a major colonial power. The borders of modern Muslim countries were often determined by colonial powers. But Islam has an imperialist and colonial past of its own. Western colonial control of Arabic countries replaced Ottoman colonial control (Muslim but non-Arab) and British control of India replaced an Islamic state that ruled over a population that had a substantial Hindu majority.

While America preaches democracy, it has consistently supported non-democratic regimes in Muslim countries, especially when these countries have been willing to support American foreign policy. The United States aided the suppression of democratic regimes in Iran (1953) and Iraq (1956). The American government remained silent when the local military annulled election victories of Islamic parties in Algeria and Turkey.

The West has been unsympathetic toward efforts of Muslim minorities in non-Muslim countries to achieve autonomy or independence, including Kashmir, Chechnya, Dagestan, western China, and the Philippians. The Muslim case would be stronger if Muslim states responded positively to movements for autonomy or independence within Muslim countries. Kurds of Iraq and Turkey have been seeking an independent state for decades. Non-Muslim rebels in the Southern Sudan have unsuccessfully sought autonomy or independence. Indonesia granted independence to East Timor (2002) only under extreme international pressure. A civil war was required by Bangladeshi Muslims to achieve independence from Pakistan.

Many Muslims believe that Western responses to situations involving Muslims involve a lack of proportionality, betraying an attitude that Muslim lives aren't important. The top grievance is the economic boycott of Iraq, which many — including Europeans — believe has caused the death through malnutrition of vast numbers of Iraqi children. They say that America advocates international law when it suits American interests, but ignores international law in other cases, such as failing to apply Geneva Treaty requirements to prisoners captured in the Afghanistan war.

The number-one complaint Muslims have against the United States is that it consistently sides with Israel against the Palestinians and the effort to establish a Palestinian state. In the United Nations Security Council, America almost always vetoes any resolution critical of Israel. Similar resolutions often pass in the General Assembly with only the United States and a few other countries voting against. Specific complaints involve American failure to intervene against Israeli seizure of Palestinian lands, destruction of Palestinian houses and of the infrastructure of Palestinian society, and human rights abuses committed against Palestinians.

The presence of American troops on Saudi Arabian soil is felt by many Muslims to be sacrilegious because of the location of the holy sites of Mecca and Medina in the same country.

Other complaints express distaste for certain aspects of American culture.

- ✔ **Moral decline, sexual promiscuity, and excessive individualism**

- ✔ **Privatization of religion leading to a lack of religious intensity**

- ✔ **Materialism:** Muslims resent the omnipresent symbols of American economic dominance in their countries. At times, boycotts are organized against American products, such as a recent Palestinian boycott of Marlboro cigarettes. Of course, global capitalism isn't especially targeted against Islam.

Listing concerns of American Muslims

While Muslim Americans share most of the above concerns, they also have concerns unique to them as Muslims living in America.

- ✔ **Profiling to detect possible terrorists:** This practice is felt to be applied indiscriminately so that all people who look like they're of Middle Eastern or South Asian origin are automatically regarded as suspicious.

- ✔ **Detention without time limits and using secret evidence (not revealed to the accused) under the 1996 Anti-Terrorism act has affected mainly Muslim immigrants:** In December 2000, the government was forced by an immigration court judge to release one such person who had been imprisoned for over three years but never expelled or charged.

- ✔ **Actions taken by the government against Islamic charities that may be channels for terrorist funds:** The Treasury Department has recently developed guidelines for American Muslim charities.

- ✔ **Negative stereotyping of Arabs and Muslims:** Characters with Arabic names and appearance have become the favorite villain in movies. Muslims also complain that broadcast media manifest anti-Muslim bias, as exhibited most famously in the immediate attribution of the Federal Building bombing in Oklahoma City to Muslim terrorists. Muslims note that when the real culprits were apprehended the media didn't refer to them as Christian terrorists.

- ✔ **Hate crimes:** Crimes directed against Muslims have increased according to the annual FBI report by 1700 percent from 2000 to 2001 (from 28 to 481). While one hate crime is one too many, some Muslim commentators remarked that given the events of September 11, the surprise is that the number isn't significantly higher.

✔ **International Religious Freedom Act of 1998:** Muslims are suspicious that this act will mainly single out cases where evangelical Christians are denied freedom to evangelize in Muslim countries while ignoring countries that restrict Muslim religious practice.

✔ **Muslim bashing:** Some prominent Christian Fundamentalist leaders have made public comments that Islam is an evil, violent religion; that Muhammad was a fanatic, a robber, and a pedophile; that Allah isn't God; and that Muslims are worse than the Nazis. President Bush and Secretary of State Colin Powell have repudiated such remarks.

✔ **The Jewish lobby:** Muslims believe that Jews exert an inordinate influence over American foreign policy to the detriment of Palestine and Muslims.

Hearing American Concerns Regarding Muslims

Poll data about American attitudes toward Muslims isn't consistent. A Gallup poll in the spring of 2002 reported that 49 percent of Americans expressed a negative opinion of Muslim countries. Only 24 percent expressed favorable views. A Newsweek poll of January 7, 2002 reported that 59 percent of Americans had a favorable view of Islam, up from 45 percent in a poll taken before September 11. After September 11, many American Muslims heard more positive than negative responses from American colleagues and friends.

The following bullet list shares some (but certainly not all) concerns about Islam voiced by many Americans and some other Westerners.

✔ **Muslim extremists have carried out a series of attacks on American targets,** beginning with the seizure of the American embassy in Iran in 1979 and culminating in the September 11, 2001 destruction of the Twin Towers of the World Trade Center in New York City. Such attacks have continued, including the murder of medical missionaries in Yemen and the bombing of a nightclub in Bali, Indonesia in October 2002.

✔ **A perception exists among the American public that Muslims have been hesitant to condemn terrorist activities carried out by Islamist groups.** The fact is, within hours of the 9/11 attack, every major American Muslim organization issued statements condemning such actions as contrary to Islam and calling on Muslims to participate in relief efforts. That most of the attackers came from Saudi Arabia, supposedly a staunch American ally, and that Saudi funds often financed Islamic schools in Pakistan and elsewhere that were the breeding grounds of Islamic radicals, made some people further dubious about the real feelings of Muslims.

✔ **Some Americans wonder whether some American mosques have willingly or unwillingly aided Islamic terrorists** and question where the loyalty of American Muslims lie. Yet the continued immigration of Muslims to America is strong evidence that given the opportunity, many Muslims prefer to live in America rather than in other countries.

✔ **It seems to some Americans as if many Muslims are totally irrational**, especially Muslims in other countries. In a Gallup poll, the majority of the population believed that Muslims weren't behind the 9/11 attacks — despite the explicit claiming of credit for the attack by bin Laden and al-Qaeda. (Jordan, Morocco, and Saudi Arabia didn't allow inclusion of this question in the poll in their countries). Remember that in the absence of a free press, public opinion of Muslims in the Third World can easily be manipulated by governments trying to deflect criticism of their own shortcomings.

One of the most fascinating examples of current popular Muslim inclination toward conspiracy theory is the story of the 4,000 Jews who didn't show up to work in the World Trade Center on 9/11, thus proving that 9/11 was really an act of Jewish/Israeli terrorism designed to cast blame on Muslims. Apparently, the story began on September 13, when a Jordanian paper published rumors of Israeli involvement. The next day, an Israeli ambassador told reporters his government had received 4,000 calls from Israelis unable to contact their relatives in New York. Finally on September 17, Hezbollah reported that 4,000 Israeli employers at the WTC hadn't showed up for work on September 11 — a "fact" for which absolutely no evidence exists. From there, the story was repeated from station to station, and Web site to Web site, until today, many Muslims outside of the West believe that Muslims had nothing to do with the event, which was actually the work of the CIA or the Israeli intelligence agency.

Facing the Major Issues

Issues arise when discussing the relationship between Islam and the West, as discussed in the following sections.

Clash of civilizations

In 1993, Samuel Huntington wrote an article about a coming clash of civilizations, in which the major antagonists would be the Western and the Islamic world. While some said that the problem the West had with Islam only concerned an extremist fringe of Islam, Huntington saw a basic conflict between the West and Islam. Leaving Huntington's explicit argument aside, many in the Islamic and the Western worlds affirm that Islam and Western civilization (or Christianity) are engaged in a mortal conflict.

In response to this apocalyptic scenario, critics respond that Islamic civilization isn't a monolith. The more essential clash is between different visions of Islam rather than between Islam and the West. Others say that the coming clash isn't between Islam and Western Christianity but between a materialistic-secular worldview and a spiritual one that encompasses Islam, Christianity and other religions.

Human rights

Since the mid-19th century, a body of principles of basic human rights and international law has developed. Under United Nations auspices, most Muslim countries have signed declarations recognizing international law and human rights, sometimes stating specific reservations. Conflicts exist between what these documents say and what Islamic law says. The 1990 Charter of Islamic Rights, while claiming to recognize international standards, says that in case of a conflict with traditional *shari`a* (Islamic law), *shari`a* takes precedence. This amounts to a denial of universal human rights. Muslim scholars, such as Abdullahi an-Na'im, distinguish between unchangeable principles of Islamic ethics and the specific embodiment of these principles that will differ from age to age. More traditional Muslim scholars don't allow this distinction. Some key conflicts include:

✔ Provisions of Islamic law sometimes conflict with human rights and international law in the area of due process.

✔ While international law requires countries to relate to one another on a basis of peace and reciprocity, *shari`a*, according to some interpretations, imposes an obligation on Islamic states to conduct war against non-Islamic states to bring them under the control of Islamic law.

✔ International law and human rights conventions recognize the rights of all people to freedom of religion. Yet many Islamic countries deny such freedom of religious exercise to non-Muslims.

✔ International law recognizes the full equality of women, yet legally enshrined discrimination against women exists in many Muslim countries. The position of Muslim women varies radically from country to country. The head of Amnesty International is a Muslim woman. Indonesia, Bangladesh, Pakistan, and Turkey have had women heads of states — something that hasn't happened in the United States.

✔ Censorship is another area of conflict between traditional Islamic law and international law.

✔ Many Muslim countries deny basic human rights not only to women and non-Muslims, but also to their own Muslim citizens. Human rights organizations are often harassed in Muslim countries, even when asserting the rights of Muslims, including Islamist groups.

Democracy and Islam

International law and human rights declarations recognize the right of people to participate in governance. The Islamic world and especially the Arabic world have lagged behind other regions in moving toward some form of democratic rule. Some Muslim countries have a democratic system on paper, but in operation this democracy turns out to be a one party state, often dominated by a strongman or military elite. Other Muslim states are ruled by hereditary monarchies. One estimate is that over half of the world's Muslims at present live in functioning democracies, including Turkey, Bangladesh, India, Indonesia, Iran, and Malaysia.

Is democracy compatible with Islam? Muslims rejecting democracy point out that in a democracy, power and governing authority are derived from the people, and government represents the will of the people. In contrast, Islamic government represents the will of God as expressed in the *shari`a.* Many Muslims perceive democracy as a Western import. Others look at paper democracies that emerged in the post-colonial period and see democracy as an experiment that has failed in the Muslim world. Some Westerners agree that democracy is incompatible with Islam because it's based on values they see as contrary to Islamic *shari`a.* People in the West are suspicious of the announced commitment of Islamist movements to democracy. They say Islamists are only interested to using democratic elections to gain power, after which democracy would disappear: "One person, one vote, one time."

Others say that democracy is as compatible with Islam as it is with Christianity. After all, Christian countries were once all ruled by kings. The Roman Catholic papacy at one time denounced democracy as incompatible with Roman Catholic Christianity. Muslims point out that the Qur'an has little to say about the specific form of a Muslim government. Monarchy, by concentrating power in the hands of a single individual, is a greater threat to the sovereignty of God than is democracy. The Constitution of Medina (see Chapter 6), the *shura* (consultation to choose the first caliphs, and consultation of the ruler with the people), the *majlis* (consultative body of tribal elders), and *ijma`* (consensus, one of the four roots of Islamic law) provide a basis on which to build Islamic democracy.

Western democracy originally excluded women, slaves, and non-property owners from political participation. Gradually, democracy was extended to include all citizens. The process of achieving stable democracy in Muslim countries will undoubtedly also take a long time. In October 2002, the first national legislative elections in 30 years took place in Bahrain, and women were allowed to vote (entering polling stations through separate doors) and to run for office. Many Westerners are surprised to discover that Iran has a working, if restricted, democracy, with contested elections whose results aren't predetermined. Otherwise, Khatami wouldn't be the current popularly elected president, contrary to the wishes of hard-line clergy. The experience of the growing number of Muslims living in Western democracies will provide a resource to Muslim countries as they move toward democratic rule.

Jihad

As I discuss in Chapter 9, the basic meaning of *jihad* is striving, and it's sometimes considered a sixth pillar of Islam. A tradition reports that when some Muslims returned from a military raid, Muhammad told them that they had returned from the lesser *jihad* but now faced the greater *jihad*. The greatest *jihad* is that of the heart against the *nafs,* one's own lower nature. The *jihad* of the tongue (words) spreads the teachings of Islam and the *jihad* of the hand engages in actions to achieve justice. Last comes *jihad* of the sword – the military struggle on behalf of God. In classical Islam, the caliph was obligated to wage war to bring non-Muslim areas under the rule of God's law. With the fragmentation of Islam into a number of states, Islamic tradition held that *jihad* of the sword in defense of Islam was required of every Muslim male.

While some limit defensive *jihad* to cases of invasion of a Muslim state, others understand defensive *jihad* much more broadly. Radical Islamists deny the validity of the distinction between internal and external (greater and lesser) *jihad* and call upon all Muslims to take military or violent action against those they consider unfaithful Muslims, as well as against non-Muslims (a "*jihad* from below" in contrast to a *jihad* declared by state authority).

Terrorism

What's an act of terrorism? Common definitions say:

- ✔ Terrorism is a political act.
- ✔ Terrorism involves physical violence.
- ✔ Terrorism intends to create fear and insecurity.
- ✔ Terrorism targets innocents.

Terrorism has been around for a long time. Years ago, news reports about terrorism in the American press usually were about IRA attacks against British control of Northern Ireland. Terrorist acts were also associated with leftist political groups. In the mid-1990s, most terrorist acts that targeted Americans occurred in Latin America. Terrorism isn't a uniquely Muslim phenomenon. What's new is the global reach of some modern terrorist groups. Individual acts of terrorism become part of an ongoing *jihad.*

Terrorists don't regard themselves as terrorists. One person's terrorist is another person's freedom fighter. The United States government has accused Iran, Syria, and Libya of engaging in state-sponsored terrorism. Muslims believe that the actions of the Russians in Chechnya and of the Israelis in Palestine qualify as state terrorism.

Some Muslims justify Muslim terrorism as the weapon of the weak against the strong. Suicide bombers have become the symbol of Islamic terrorists. Suicide is prohibited in Islam and most Islamic scholars say that death in a suicide bombing, however noble the cause, is a grave sin, as are military actions targeted at children, women, and non-combatants. How do terrorists respond? They say that Israeli and American civilians are complicit in the repression of Muslims and are legitimate targets. They say that the death of a suicide bomber is comparable to a soldier going into a battle in which he knows he'll probably be killed.

The analogy of violence committed by a few anti-abortionists is often used. Most anti-abortionists believe abortion is murder and that they should take action to stop abortions. However, only a few anti-abortionists bomb abortion clinics and shoot doctors who perform abortions. Similarly, most Muslims aren't terrorists even when they sympathize with the motives of terrorists.

Knowing What's Needed from the Muslim Side

Islam traditionally has avoided extremism; however, it needs to condemn bigots within its own ranks as forthrightly as it complains about anti-Muslim bigotry in the non-Muslim world. Moderate Muslims must speak up and not acquiesce by silence to extremist claims. Muslims need to address positively internal problems and not blame everything on Jews, secularists, and Westerners. Muslims need to undertake structural changes in their societies and not limit themselves to simplistic "Islam is the answer" solutions. The Muslim world must face up to its problems: lack of civil liberty, racism, sexism, corruption, oppression, and religious intolerance.

Knowing What's Needed from the Western Side

Non-Muslim Americans need to pursue constructive responses:

- ✔ The United States needs to wage a public relations campaign directed at the Muslim world comparable to the campaign directed to people in the Communist world during the Cold War.

- America and the West need to actively "wage peace" and not just war against terrorists. In 2000, nearly 1,000 religious leaders gathered at the Millennium World Peace Summit and pledged their support to end religious-based violence and to respect each other's religious traditions. In early 2002, Pope John Paul II sponsored an International Day of Peace meeting in Assisi, Italy.

- America must exercise patience because she holds the political, economic, and military trump cards.

- America must recognize the diversity within Islam and work with the constructive forces in the Islamic world, but not in a cynical divide-and-conquer approach. The issue isn't America versus Islam. Rather, the question is what version of Islam will prevail.

- Finally, Americans must recognize that if women's rights, democracy, and freedom are to be realized in the Islamic world, these values will have to be articulated in an Islamic dialect and with an Islamic rationale. The ultimate aim is the participation of Muslims the determination of their future.

Chapter 18

Meeting the Challenge of Modernity

....

....

This chapter gives you a brief introduction to Islam's emergence into the global, Western-dominated world of today and discusses how Islam has tried to cope with the challenges.

Considering Islamic Democracy

Democracy has become the norm to which most of the modern world gives lip service. The Arab Human Development Report pointed out that while 20 years ago democratic regimes were a rarity in much of the developing world, today, the Arab world lags substantially behind other parts of the developing world in the move toward democracy.

At the end of the 19th and the beginning of the 20th centuries, Islamic modernists, such as Muhammad Abduh in Egypt and Muhammad Iqbal and Muhammad Jinna in South Asia, envisioned a modernized Islam that would incorporate some reforms based on Western experience, while retaining an Islamic identity. This modernization usually assumed some form of democratic government in post-colonial Muslim countries, while saying that Islamic democracy wouldn't simply duplicate Western democracy.

In fact, Islamic countries in the post-colonial world tended to be either monarchies or paper democracies — *paper,* because, like communist countries, they had the form but not the reality of democratic rule. Some Muslim states came under the control of socialist parties that established one-party rule (as in Iraq, Syria, Libya, Algeria, and Tunisia), although they may allow token opposition parties. Some states experienced military rule (at times, Egypt, Pakistan, Algeria, Pakistan, Turkey, and others), although such rule was always stated to be temporary until conditions improved. The West, including the United States, has aided in the repression of democratic movements (which may lead to Islamist control, instability, or anti-Western policies) in Iraq, Iran (before the 1979 revolution), Algeria, and elsewhere. Of course, many of these countries have faced enormous problems — internal unrest; large, young, unemployed populations; lack of natural resources and economic infrastructure — that often hinder development of democracy.

Despite its periods of military rule, Pakistan has functioned as a limited democracy. Indonesia, after the long periods of strong-man rule by Sukarno and Suharto, is a functioning democracy, as is Bangladesh. In Malaysia, despite rule by one man over an extended period of time, multiple parties actively participate in the political system. Monarchies, such as those in Jordan, Morocco, and some of the smaller states of the Arabian peninsula (Bahrain, Kuwait), have begun fledging steps toward popular participation in the political process. Turkey, despite periods of military intervention, is a functioning democracy in which Islamic parties have twice won control of the government (including the most recent election).

Even some Islamist reformers such as Ghannoushi (in exile from Tunisia), and the Muslim Brotherhood in Egypt and Jordan, Jama`at-i-Islami (South Asia), and others profess commitment to democracy. In some cases, such commitment seems sincere. In other cases, Islamist statements of commitment to democracy may be merely tactical political maneuvers.

Reason for guarded optimism exists for the further progress of democratic rule in Islamic countries. Islamic radicals are a small but dedicated portion of the Muslim populations. Prognosis of the future is foolhardy, however. War between the United States and a Muslim country could either lead to increased influences by radical Islamists or could strengthen democratic forces.

Reclaiming Identity as an Islamic State

Disillusioned with the West, many Muslims felt the attraction of a call to reject Western models and return to a true Islamic society.

Naming the Islamists

Islamic modernists continue to exist in Muslim societies, although some feel compelled to maintain a low profile. Traditionalists, who want to continue the familiar Islam that has existed since the emergence of the medieval synthesis, continue to exist. Islamic radicalism threatens and challenges their claims to preeminence. Personal piety expressed in Sufi movements, despite attacks from secularists and Islamists, hasn't disappeared.

Writers use different terms to refer to Islamist movements, such as *salafis* (back to the ancestors), Islamists, political Islam, Islamic revivalism, Islamic reformism, neo-traditionalism, radical Islam, and extremist Islam. Many Westerners use a term they're already familiar with: fundamentalism. Muslims object to this term, saying that most Muslims are fundamentalists and the term properly applies to certain Christian movements in the United States. However, in the English-speaking world, fundamentalism has established itself as the term to designate back-to-the-sources movements that have become prominent in many religions during the past 30 years.

Leading the way: Three Islamist movements

Three movements and their founders greatly influenced the rise of Islamist movements in the 20th century — the Wahhabis of Saudi Arabia, the Muslim Brotherhood of Egypt, and the Jama`at-i-Islami of Pakistan. The Muslim Brotherhood and the Jama`at are active in a number of countries and have inspired and have links to other, newer Islamist organizations. The Wahhabis and their Saudi financial supporters actively support the spread of Wahhabi-style Islam in many countries, including the West.

Purifying Islam: Wahhabism and the Saudi state

The Wahhabi movement arose from an alliance of a Muslim scholar, Muhammad ibn Abd al-Wahhab (died 1791) with a local tribal chief, Muhammad ibn Saud. The Arabic term for Wahhabi is *muwahiddun,* which translates as Unitarianism. Influenced by the medieval Hanbalite legal scholar, ibn Taymiyya, al-Wahhab advocated imposing an intolerant and puritanical form of Islam on the population. He called for a return to the Qur'an and the *hadiths,* the rejection of Sufism, and pursuit of *jihad* against other Muslims who didn't accept this point of view. He rejected innovation *(bid`a),* because all behavior had be based on the example of the first Muslim community in Mecca. Ibn Saud conquered most of Arabia, destroyed the shrines at the graves of Muhammad and other early leaders buried in Medina, and also destroyed the Shi`ite shrines of *Imam* Husayn and other members of the prophet's family at Karbala.

The early Saudi state was destroyed by an Ottoman army from Egypt in 1818, but reemerged in the 20th century. Supported by the Wahhabis, Abdulaziz ibn Saud reestablished the Saudi state in 1932 and established Wahhabi-style Sunnism as the state religion. Beginning in the 1950s, oil riches allowed the Saudi state to successfully propagate the Wahhabi version of Islam abroad. Many subsequent Islamist radicals spent time in Saudi Arabia, where they adopted the viewpoint of the Wahhabis. Saudi Wahhabism provides an interesting combination of Islamic radicalism combined with support of a conservative, traditionalist government.

Seeking a theo-democracy: Maududi and the Jama`at-i-Islami

Mawlana Mawdudi (died 1979), a journalist in colonial India, founded the Jama`at-i-Islami in 1941 as a revolutionary, elitist vanguard. Mawdudi was the first to apply the concept of *jahiliyya*, the pagan society of Muhammad's day in Arabia, to non-Muslim societies of the 20th century. Mawdudi rejected both nationalist leaders who refused to institute Islamic law and the traditional `ulama'. He used the term *theo-democracy* to describe his vision of an Islamic state modeled on a romanticized vision of the state of the first three caliphs. Mawdudi and the Jama`at were moderate in their stance toward the Pakistani state, sometimes critiquing it from outside, sometimes supporting particular leaders. Despite Mawdudi's influence and popularity among Muslims worldwide (his books are still widely read), the Jama`at has never been very successful in Pakistani elections.

Making the Qur'an the state constitution: The Muslim Brotherhood, Hasan al-Banna, and Sayyid Qutb

Hasan al-Banna (died 1949) established the Muslim Brotherhood in Egypt in 1928. This movement spread beyond Egypt to Syria, Palestine (as *Hamas*), Jordan, Sudan, and other countries. "The Qur'an is our constitution" summed up his vision of an Islamic state. He said Muslims must abandon the medieval synthesis and go back to the sources. Unlike the Jama`at (see the preceding section), the Brotherhood was a grass-roots organization that, in addition to its political agenda of instituting an Islamic state, engaged in educational and social service projects at the local level, gaining popular support. The membership grew rapidly to about one million by 1949. When the Egyptian prime minister was assassinated in 1949 by a Muslim Brother, the state took action against the Brotherhood, and Hasan al-Banna was killed by the Egyptian security police. A failed effort by a Brotherhood member to assassinate President Nasser in 1954 led to a successful crackdown on the organization, and most of the leaders were jailed.

Sayyid Qutb (died 1966) is the second main figure of the Muslim Brotherhood and a more radical figure than either Maududi or al-Banna. When he visited the United States during the late 1940s, he was repelled by its materialism, racism, overt display of sexuality, and the influence of the Jewish lobby on American politics. Imprisoned from 1954 1964, he became further radicalized. His books circulate widely in the Islamic world: Democracy, capitalism, communism, Christianity, and Judaism are all manifestations of an eternal conspiracy against Islam by *jahaliyya* forces. Qutb rejected the possibility of gradual reform from within, in favor of violent, revolutionary action, which can target rulers, non-committed ordinary Muslims, and non-Muslims who are declared *takfir* (heretics or idolaters). Qutb was executed in 1966, but his death only increased his influence upon Islamic radicals.

Identifying what separates Islamist reformers from Islamist radicals

Radicals and reformers share the goal of an Islamic state but differ as to the nature of such a state. Radicals often say that only their version of Islam represents true Islam. An Islamic state representing that viewpoint will, presumably, be more authoritarian and less tolerant of differing points of view than will a state representing Islamist reformers.

Islamist reformers are willing to engage in democratic politics to win power at the ballot box. Because successful politics always involves compromise in order to build a winning coalition, reformers are often more willing to compromise than are radicals who in effect say "my way or no way." Many more Muslims support Islamist reformers than Islamic radicals.

Both reformers and radicals regard military *jihad* as a kind of weapon of last resort, although they disagree on suicide bombings and targeting of non-combatants. Islamist reform groups don't usually engage in terrorist acts directed against third parties, such as the United States, while Islamist radicals say that the United States is the true enemy and a legitimate target.

Among extremist groups active in Egypt that rejected the more moderate approach of the Muslim Brotherhood were al-Jihad and Gamaa Islamiyya. Beginning with the assassination of President Sadat in 1981, these groups engaged in attacks on foreigners, banks, bookstores, Coptic Christians, and other targets during the 1980s and 1990s. The response of the Egyptian government and military, while hardly meeting international human rights standards, was effective in virtually eliminating by 2000 terrorist attacks within Egypt. In Algeria, the FIS (Islamic Salvation Front) religious party that had been allowed to participate in the first free national election in late 1991 won a majority of the seats. The military intervened and cancelled the final round of elections in early 1992, which the FIS would surely have won. From 1992 to 1997 fierce fighting broke out, with atrocities being committed both by the government and an extremist terrorist group, the GIS (Armed Islamic Group). However, the extremism of the GIS actions, including killing of teachers and whole villages that were felt to be insufficiently committed to the GIS cause, led to a loss of support from middle-class groups that formed part of the FIS's core constituency. By 1997 the government had eliminated most terrorist incidents.

Forming a Shi`ite Islamic Republic

The two events of the last 50 years that have had the greatest impact in the Islamic world are the creation of the state of Israel and the Iranian revolution (see Chapter 12 for information on earlier Iranian Islam).

Coming of the revolution: Khomeini

In 1963 the Iranian shah began his White Revolution — a program of modernization, land reform, and industrialization that alienated important groups in Iran. Increasingly, the government ruled by decree, depending on the security forces to repress dissent. Although the clerical establishment generally didn't involve themselves in politics, they remained the one institution still relatively free of government control. The clerics' substantial sources of income, and their school and mosque network, provided a location from which to broadcast criticism of the government in sermons and mobilize the people in demonstrations. A younger cleric, Ruhollah Khomeini, became in 1963 one of the regime's most outspoken critics. In his sermons, Khomeini criticized the regime for its aping of the West, its support of Israel, its dictatorial nature, its failure to achieve social justice, and its land reform policies. His sermons during the annual celebration of the martyrdom of *Imam* Husayn in 1963 caused his arrest. He was exiled the next year to Turkey, and then went to Iraq. From his position in exile, Khomeini was free to continue his public criticism of the shah, without the shah being able to shut him up as he could domestic critics.

Khomeini, whose sermons were widely circulated on cassette tapes within Iran, became the charismatic figure around whom the opposition crystallized. By the time he moved to Paris in 1978, Khomeini was demanding the overthrow of the monarchy. He compared the shah with Yazid, the Umayyad ruler whose army killed Husayn, and those who suffered under the shah's secret police were like the martyrs of Karbala. Religious ideology was the one idiom by means of which all forces opposing the regime could be brought together in common action. The opposition included students, especially the radical *mujahiddin,* whose socialistic leanings resonated with the traditional Shi`ite attack on injustice, the communists, the liberal reformers, the clerics, the urban poor, and the traditional merchants of the bazaar. A drop in oil prices in the mid-1970s hurt the government. The end came in a dramatic series of protests in late 1977 and 1978. Mass protests and countrywide strikes paralyzed the country, forcing the flight of the Shah and allowing the return of Khomeini in early 1979.

Taking Iran in a new direction

Khomeini's supporters had conflicting ideas of what direction Iran should go. Khomeini's own ideas on government were relatively unknown. Khomeini's central — and theologically new — idea was that in the absence of the hidden *imam,* the state would be guided by *vilayat-e-faqih,* in which the council of clerical jurists or the single, best qualified jurist representing the hidden *imam* would guide the revolution. Khomeini assumed the position of Guardian or Spiritual Guide, which was institutionalized in the new constitution.

The new system of government was overwhelmingly approved by a national referendum. Essentially, there were two parallel government organizations: the religious supervisors and the constitutional government with parliament, president, and prime minister (later abolished). The Spiritual Guide retained ultimate authority although Khomeini didn't rule by dictatorial decree. Clerical bodies appointed local *mullas,* approved candidates for parliament and other offices, controlled the courts (because Islamic law was state law), and the ministry of culture (that enforced alcohol prohibition, the veil, and the elimination of Western influence, such as movies and television). Local revolutionary councils, essentially vigilante groups, helped enforce the revolution on the streets.

Over the first several years, purges and trials eliminated many potential opposition groups. Different groups jockeyed for power within the ruling establishment: a more conservative group of traditional clerics; a younger, radical group that wanted something closer to a continuing or permanent revolution that would bring about social justice internally and export revolution abroad; and a middle group of pragmatists that, while fully committed to the revolution and an Islamic republic, wanted to return to normalcy and move toward democratic rule and a more open society. While tension between different groups could've doomed the revolution, Khomeini utilized three events to rally the forces of the revolution.

- ✔ The seizure of the American embassy and the holding of hostages from late 1979 to January 1981 focused attention on the American Satan.

- ✔ The war with Iraq from 1980 to 1988 sent poor, urban youth, imbued with the martyr ideology of Karbala, off to fight against a secularist enemy. Although the Iranian revolution inspired Muslims all over the Islamic world, Iranian appeals to other Muslims to overthrow their governments had no success.

- ✔ The condemnation in 1989 of *The Satanic Verses* (Penguin USA, 1989) and the death *fatwa* against its author, Salman Rushdie, again rallied the populace, who were exhausted emotionally, militarily, and financially by the Iraqi war, and provided an opportunity for Khomeini to reassert himself as a world Islamic leader.

Facing the future

The new order easily survived the potential crisis of the death of Khomeini in 1989. Ayatolla Khamenei became the Spiritual Guide and Rafsanjani the president. As Iran moved into the 1990s, much of the population had little direct memory of the shah. The clerically dominated government was now the new entrenched power elite and the obstacle to freedom and justice. People debated in the universities, and in a more open press their concerns and visions of the future. The election of the current president, Ayatolla Muhammad Khatami, was a major surprise. Khatami won 67 percent of the vote, being strongly supported by young people (a majority of the population), women (who have the vote), and professionals. He was reelected in 2001 with 77 percent of the vote. Khatami had himself been forced out of office as minister of culture in 1992 for his relatively liberal policies.

Opponents of liberalization and true democracy remain strong, especially through their control of the courts, various military and paramilitary forces, and their veto power over legislation (through the Guardian Council). In June 2002, Hashem Aghajari, a university professor, said in a speech that laity had as much right as a cleric to interpret religious law. Aghajari was arrested and sentenced to death. Students, who played such a crucial role in other crises over the last 100 years, took to the streets. Aghajari said nothing that the premier ideologue of the revolution, Ali Shariati (see Chapter 20) or Abdolkarim Soroush, Iran's preeminent current intellectual, haven't said. The future direction of Iran, although not the permanency of the Iranian revolution and its republic, is an open question.

Reviewing the Globalization of Islamic Radicalism: bin Laden and Afghanistan

I'll first outline the events leading up to the Taliban regime in Afghanistan before going on to discuss Bin Laden and al-Qaeda.

Afghanistan

Two years ago most Americans had only a vague idea of where Afghanistan is. Prior to 1973, Afghanistan was a monarchy in which tribal conflicts between Pashtuns, Uzbeks, Tajiks, Hazaras, and Turkmen (all ethics groups), worked against national unity. Tensions also existed between the Sunni majority and a significant Shi`ite minority, and between Sufi groups and Islamists. In 1973, Prince Muhammad Daud, a cousin of King Zahir Shad, overthrew the monarchy and proclaimed himself president. Because Afghanistan bordered the Soviet Union, the Russians regarded it as within the Russian sphere of influence. In 1978, a coup installed a communist government. When Islamic groups rebelled against the new communist government, Soviet armies invaded in 1979. For the next ten years a civil war raged between the communist government supported by the Soviet army and the *mujahiddin,* Islamic freedom fighters (from the word *jihad*). Sympathizers from other Muslim countries came to Pakistan to join the Afghani rebels. The United States, Pakistan, the Saudis, and various Islamist groups supported the *mujahiddin.* By 1989, the Soviets were unwilling to continue the fight and withdrew. Without Soviet support, the communist government of Afghanistan fell in 1992. Various groups who had joined together to fight the Soviets now fought one another for dominance. The foreign volunteers, called Arab Afghans, returned home where many became involved in local radical groups.

The rise of the Taliban (the word means "student") movement began in late 1994, mainly among the Pashtuns. These "students" were refugees of the civil war who were often from *madrasas* located on the Pakistani side of the border. The *madrasas,* often supported by Saudi money, were under the control of the radical neo-Deobandi Islamic movement in Pakistan and its JUI *(Jamiyyat-i-Ulama-I-Islam)* party. This movement was militantly Islamic and anti-American and preached *jihad* against non-Muslims and other Muslims. In 1999, the JUI issued death threats against all Americans in Pakistan, stirred up mob violence against Pakistani Shi`ites, and had perhaps been involved in failed efforts to assassinate President Sharif. The schools were the indoctrination and recruiting centers out of which came the Taliban soldiers. In addition to Afghanis and 80,000 or more Pakistanis, Muslims came to the schools from all over the world to participate in the holy war of the Taliban. The Afghan people, exhausted by more than 15 years of warfare and the lack of any effective government or security, welcomed the Taliban, who offered stability and order. In 1996, the Taliban conquered the capital, Kabul, and by 1998 controlled 90 percent of the country. The tribes that constituted the northern alliance managed to hang on in only a few sections of the country. Only after the Taliban had gained power did their extremist intentions become clear. They banned music, television, and movies. They forced women out of the schools and the workplace and imposed on them the *chador* (a head to toe garment). The Taliban also persecuted the Shi`ite minority, whom they regarded as heretics. The Taliban proclaimed their version of Islam as true Islam, although Taliban leaders weren't Islamic scholars. Many Muslim leaders elsewhere condemned the actions of the Taliban as a non-Islamic aberration. Among Muslim countries, only Pakistan, Saudi Arabia, and the UAE recognized the Taliban government. The United States, ironically, supported the Taliban during the civil war. After September 11, the United States, which had previously remained largely silent regarding Taliban abuses, changed its policy, invaded Afghanistan, and overthrew the Taliban.

Bin Laden and al-Qaeda

Osama bin Laden was born in Saudi Arabia in 1957, the 17th of 52 children. His father had come from South Yemen around 1930. Starting out as a laborer, he established what became one of the largest construction companies in the country and became wealthy. Bin Laden grew up in a pious family, and during his youth had an opportunity to meet many Muslim scholars and radical Islamists. His father was strongly committed to the Palestinian cause, and the 1967 defeat at the hands of Israel made a big impression on father and son. Another influence on the young bin Laden was a radical Jordanian Muslim

Brother, Dr. Abdullah Azzam, who may have been the first to articulate a doctrine of global *jihad*. Bin Laden was one of the first Arabs to offer support to the anti-communist rebels of Afghanistan. From 1979 to 1982 he collected funds and materials to support the rebel cause and entered the country himself with construction machinery to support the rebels in 1982. By 1984, bin Laden had established a center on the Pakistan side of the border for Arabs on their way to join the *mujahiddin* in Afghanistan. In 1986 he set up his own camps of Arab Afghans under his command. He established al-Qaeda ("the base") to manage recruitment of fighters and funds.

After the Soviet withdrawal, bin Laden returned home. He offered to raise troops to defend Saudi Arabia when Iraq invaded Kuwait in 1991 and felt betrayed when the Saudis depended on infidel Americans to defend the holy sites of Islam. Bin Laden moved to Sudan in 1992. His final break with the Saudi royal family occurred in 1994. When the Sudanese government forced bin Laden to leave, he returned to Afghanistan. There he developed a close relationship with the Taliban leader, Mulla Omar. In this period, he was influenced by the leader of Islamic Jihad in Egypt, Dr. Ayman al-Zawahiri. In 1996, bin Laden issued his "Declaration of Jihad" against the West and America, attempting to show that his *jihad* met the criteria of a just *jihad* in Islamic law. To bin Laden, any action against America and the West was a defensive *jihad*, because the West had long been engaged in a crusade against Islam. In 2000, he formed an umbrella group, the World Islamic Front for the *jihad* against Jews and Crusaders, and issued a *fatwa* that all Muslims had the duty to kill Americans and their allies. The September 11 attack was part of his continuing *jihad*. Bin Laden is neither a head of state nor a person schooled in Islamic law and according to traditional Islamic law has no authority to proclaim *jihad* or issue a *fatwa*. However, as an individual who is willing to stand up to America, he's popular among many ordinary Muslims who wouldn't themselves participate in terrorist actions.

Part VI
The Part of Tens

In this part . . .

*I*slam is both a religion and a civilization. In this part, I look at ten contributions of Islam to human culture and at ten people who have made outstanding contributions to our world. While some of these people and contributions are closely linked to Islam as a religion, others have more to do with the culture to which Islamic religion gave rise.

The last chapter turns to a different topic. Here, you find information about Islamic countries in different parts of the world today, including the conflict between Palestinians and Israel that is one of the key issues creating tension today between the United States and the Islamic world.

Chapter 19

Ten Muslim Contributions to World Civilization

- -

In This Chapter

▶ Refining mathematics and astronomy

▶ Improving the health sciences

▶ Advancing engineering and technology

▶ Enriching architecture

- -

Any limited list of the great contributions of a culture, people, or religion will be arbitrary and reflect the prejudices and knowledge of the person who wrote the list. And any list of five, or ten, or even one hundred contributions will, of necessity, exclude even more significant contributions that have equal claim to attention.

This chapter isn't meant to be a list of the ten most important contributions Muslims have made to the world. Instead, it's a list of ten important contributions that I hope you find interesting and that expand your knowledge of Islam. My list of contributions doesn't attempt to represent all parts of the Muslim world nor all periods of 1,400-year Muslim history.

Islam is both a religion and a culture, and in this chapter, I mention some aspects of culture that the rest of the book — with its focus on religion — doesn't discuss. Note that I don't repeat information here that I describe in detail in other chapters.

Transmission of Greek Writings

Islamic interest in science gave rise to the collection and translation into Arabic of ancient works in medicine, astronomy, mathematics, and philosophy, mainly from Greece but also from Persia and India. Harun al-Rashid and al-Ma'mun (in the eighth and ninth centuries) sent emissaries to the Byzantine

Empire to collect ancient Greek manuscripts for the government library, *Bayt al-Hikma* (House of Wisdom), in Baghdad. Hunayn ibn Ishaq (803–873), a Christian Arab, was the most important early translator. Much of the Greek material, which had been forgotten in Western Europe, was later reintroduced by translations made from Arabic to Latin, especially in Spain and Sicily, where the Muslim, Christian, and Jewish scholars interacted with one another.

Algebra and Mathematics

The term *algebra* derives from the title of al-Khwarazmi's (about 780–850) *Kitab al-Jabr wal-Muqabala (The Book of Compulsion and Comparison),* the first systematic work on algebra. *Al-jabr* became algebra in English, and from al-Khwarizmi's name comes the term algorithm.

Al-Khwarazmiwas aware of the novelty of his work and invented new terms to express his concepts:

- ✔ *Al-jabr* designated the process of transposition of terms, by which, for example, $x + 10 = 60 - 3x$ becomes $4x = 50$.

- ✔ *Al-muqabala* refers to the cancellation and reduction in which the equation $50 + x^2 = x^2 + 10x$ becomes $50 = 10x$ and is reduced to $5 = x$.

A number of scholars developed this field of study that reached its early culmination in the work of `Umar al-Khayyam (1048–1123). The study of one field of mathematics led to advances and applications in other fields, such as trigonometry and geography, to which early and medieval Muslim scholars made major contributions. From Arabic, for example, comes the term *sine* used in trigonometry.

`Umar al-Khayyam is better known in the west through Edward Fitzgerald's very free 19th-century translation of al-Khayyam's (Persian) poem, the *Ruba`iyat*. Fitzgerald's translation was a great success in Britain and in the United States. It's interesting in its own right, but, while inspired by al-Khayyam, the translation isn't accurate translation, nor does it faithfully represent the thoughts of al-Khayyam. You can find a number of translations and books about the poem if you search under "Omar Khayyam" on any bookseller's Web site.

Arabic Numbers

Arabs didn't invent Arabic numbers but they did refine the system that they inherited from the Sasanians of Iran (who had found it in Hindu India) and passed it on to the West, where it's first recorded in 976 C.E. The key improvement was the tweaking of the indication of the placeholder — zero (meaning that no number goes in the position with 0). With this system, any number can be written using a combination of ten symbols (numbers). The Hindus used a dot or circle to indicate that a column was empty *(sunya);* the Arabs translated *sunya* as *sifr.* From *sifr* came the words zero and cipher.

For example, in Roman numerals, 321 is CCCXXI. With Arabic numbers, 321 indicates 3 times 100, 2 times 10, and 1 times 1. If the number were 320, then the zero indicates zero times 1.

Astronomy

Drawing upon the wisdom of ancient Babylon, India, and especially Greece, Arabic-speaking scientists made major contributions to astronomy, in recorded observations and in theory. They clearly distinguished astronomy from astrology. Arabic astronomy was driven by religious and practical concerns: better nautical navigation, determining the five daily prayer times, the date of the new moon (important for the religious calendar), and the direction to Mecca (for prayer and Mosque alignment). They defined this direction as the shortest arc of a great circle joining Mecca and any given place. In making these calculations, Muslim astronomers determined the latitude and longitude of many Muslim cities with great accuracy.

The second-century Ptolemaic system of the circular movement of the planets (and the sun) around the earth was accepted, but significant modifications were made as Arabic scientists noted discrepancies between Ptolemy's theory and the results of their observations.

The same al-Khwarazmi who gave the world algebra also wrote the first preserved Arabic book on astronomy. The early synthesis in the field was al-Biruni's (973–1048) *al-Qanun al-Masudi.* Many of the names of the stars come from Abd al Rahman al-Sufi's *Book on the Constellations* (1009), from which they passed into Latin and then English. Arabic gives English technical terms such a *nadir, azimuth,* and *zenith.* Ibn al-Haytham (known in the West as Alhazan, 965–1040) determined that the Milky Way was composed of many faint stars, far from the earth.

Perhaps the world's first true astronomical observatory was at Maragha (13th century) in northwest Iran under the direction of Nasir al-Din al-Tusi. While the telescope hadn't yet been invented, Arab scientists made major improvements to other instruments, such as the *astrolabe,* the basic portable instrument for observing the location of heavenly bodies. Many astrolabes are exquisite works of artistic beauty.

Engineering and Technology

Islamic advances in engineering and technology are evident in archaeological remains, historical records, and still-standing structures. Engineers didn't normally write about their work, but two books record devices that were primarily for amusement. However, the same technology was used for real world applications: switches, conical valves (including float valves), siphons, gears, crankshafts, and more. The *Book of Ingenious Devices* by the three Banu Musa brothers in ninth century Baghdad describes 100 clever mechanical devices, including a gas mask for use in polluted mines. Al-Jazari's *The Book of Knowledge of Ingenious Mechanical Devices* (1206) gives diagrams explaining materials, construction, and operation of 50 devices, including clocks, vessels, measuring vessels, fountains, and water-raising machines.

The most important real-world use was to increase agricultural production. A variety of water-raising devices made large-scale irrigation possible. One giant 44-foot-diameter water wheel still stands at Hama, Syria. Water wheels also powered mills used for grinding grain and other manufacturing functions. Crop rotation, grafting, crossbreeding of plants, and the introduction of new crops increased food production. Manuals gave advice to farmers on soil types, what to plant, when to plant, and when to harvest.

Engineering skills were also used in shipbuilding, mining, paper and textile production, and metalworking. Preserved manuals provide explicit information on fortification, siege machinery, and weapon construction. Ships on the Tigris and Euphrates rivers in the tenth century were floating water-wheel-driven mills for large-scale grinding of grain. Engineering skill was applied to dam construction and irrigation channels, including long-distance underground channels.

Medicine

At a time when healing in Europe was mainly left to God, medical care in the Islamic world was advancing rapidly. Galen's and Hippocrates' were among the first Greek texts translated into Arabic. Arabic medicine had dual purposes of preserving health and curing illness and emphasized trust between doctor and patient.

The world's first true hospital was established in Baghdad at the beginning of the ninth century. Larger hospitals had schools that granted diplomas. Arabic medicine emphasized clinical observation, diagnosis, and experiment to increase knowledge and improve treatment. Al-Razi (850–925) and Ibn Sina (known as Avicenna in the West, 980–1037) are two of many famous physicians and researchers. Al-Razi's major work was *The Comprehensive Book on Medicine*, a 23-volume medical encyclopedia. He wrote the first treatise on smallpox and measles, identified the existence and cause of hay fever, and did work on kidney stones. Ibn Sina's *The Canon of Medicine* was a compendium of all existing medical and pharmaceutical knowledge. It was still used as a standard reference work in Europe in the 17th century. Ibn Sina emphasized the importance of such factors as diet, environment, and climate.

Abu al-Qasim al-Zahrawi (936–1013) was a famous surgeon whose 30-volume manual described surgical operations and instruments. Despite religious qualms, anatomy was practiced, leading to the discovery of the pulmonary circulation of blood. Arab medical scientists also developed the fields of ophthalmology and anesthesiology.

Pharmacology

Pharmacology was recognized by the ninth century as a discipline separate from botany and a profession distinct from being a physician. Dispensaries were attached to major hospitals, and the first apothecary was opened in Baghdad in the ninth century. Pharmacists were examined and licensed by the government. *De Materia Medica (On Medical Matters)* of Dioscorides, the standard Greek text, was translated into Arabic and remained a standard textbook. Jabir ibn Hayyan (722–815) is credited with one of the first Arabic pharmaceutical treatises. Sabur Ibn Sahl (ninth century) wrote a practical handbook that gave formulas, dosage, and instructions on administering the medicines. Al-Razi and Ibn Sina (see the "Medicine" section in this chapter) also made major contributions to pharmacology. Ibn al-Baytar (about 1190–1248) compiled much of the pharmaceutical knowledge known at that time in his *Dictionary of Simple Medicines and Foods*.

Physics, Specifically Optics

Optical research began with the translation of the major Greek works into Arabic. Ibn al-Haytham (see the "Astronomy" section in this chapter) combined controlled experimentation with geometrical analysis, along with improved knowledge of the physiology of the eye, to produce a greatly improved theory of vision. Al-Haytham proved that what is sensed by the eye isn't the object. Rather the eye senses light reflected from the object and transmits this information to the brain that constructs an image of the object.

Kamal al-Din al-Farsi (about 1260–1320) is famous for providing an explanation of the rainbow, in which he combined geometrical theory, experiment, and knowledge developed about the transmission of light. He set up an experiment in which light was reflected through a sphere of water to produce a "rainbow." When the sun's rays passed through a drop of water, two refractions (bending) and one reflection of the rays inside the drop produced a primary rainbow. A second interior reflection produced a secondary rainbow with its colors reversed.

Architecture

Technology, engineering, and artistic skill come together in certain types of architecture. The two contributions I mention in this section are two of the best-known architectural monuments of Islam.

Taj Mahal

In 1631, Mumtaz Mahal, the beloved wife of the Muoghal Shah Jahan, died while giving birth to her 15th child. The next year, he began to build her tomb that is to non-Muslims the most famous achievement of Muslim architecture. In the English-speaking world, the Taj Mahal became well known from the volume of paintings of it by the English landscape painter, Thomas Daniell, in 1789.

The Taj Mahal is located on a platform, derived from Hindu architectural styles, on the left bank of the Yamuna River in Agra. It's one of the four outstanding examples of Muoghal tomb architecture from a time when the empire was at its peak (see Chapter 2 for more on the Mughals). Craftsmen were brought from the Ottoman Empire, Samarqand, Shiraz, Bukhara, and Qandahar, in addition to Hindus from India and Kashmir and Muslim masons from India. Ahmad Lahawri was probably the chief architect.

The tomb is set in the midst of a large, formal garden divided into four quadrants by intersecting pools that may represent the lake and four rivers of paradise. Over the massive entrance gate, at the south end of the garden, is a passage from Sura 89 (the "dawn") that ends with an invitation to enter paradise. The large bulbous dome of the tomb seems to float above the reflecting pools. While red sandstone had been used previously in such structures, the Taj Mahal is constructed of glistening, polished, white marble, whose color shifts as the day progresses. Many people believe the Taj Mahal is even more beautiful when illuminated by moonlight. Close to the dome on the top of the corners are four small domed cupolas. Four tall and slender minarets frame the entire complex. A large arch in the south side marks the entrance, with identical arches on the other three sides. On these is inscribed Sura 36, which is traditionally recited for the dead. A mosque and a guesthouse, basically identical on the outside, flank the tomb structure on either side and are incorporated into the walls that surround the complex of garden and tomb. Inside are cenotaphs (coffins) for Shah Jahan and his wife. Decoration, inside and out, consists of Qur'anic calligraphy and a patterns of delicate flowers in bloom. You don't need to be Muslim to be awed by the Taj Mahal or to think you've had a glimpse of heaven.

Use the image search in Goggle on the Internet to find images of the Taj Mahal.

The Alhambra

While the Taj Mahal is best appreciated from outside, the Alhambra is best seen from within, viewing its individual parts. The Alhambra is the architectural glory of the final flourish of Muslim presence in Spain. Despite being one of the best-preserved Muslim palaces, substantial parts of the Alhambra are in ruins or were overbuilt by later structures.

While the original citadel goes back to the eighth century, the most famous portions are parts of 14th-century palaces of the Nisirid dynasty of Grenada. Scholars say that, originally, there were seven palace complexes and 23 towers. The palaces consist of courtyards with pools and fountains surrounded by colonnades, connected to interior rooms. The Court of Lions is named after its famous fountain with 12 lions spouting water out of their mouths. The Court of Myrtles is famous for its long, central pool that reflects the image of the beautiful north and south porticos and north tower.

Like the Taj Mahal, the Alhambra creates an image of paradise. Ceilings of some interior rooms invoke the seven heavens and the dome of heaven. Particularly impressive are the *muqarnas* (honeycomb vault) decoration, in which staggered rows of half niches created in stucco rise up toward the ceiling, each with an individual protrusion thrusting downward from each of the niches (similar to the way stalactites grow down like icicles from the roof of a cave).

Use the image search in Goggle on the Internet to find images of the different parts of the Alhambra, including the Court of Myrtles and the Court of Lions.

Chapter 20

Ten Noteworthy Muslims, Past and Present

The vignettes of significant Muslims in this chapter are too brief to do more than excite your interest, but they give you a sense of Muslims as real people, now and in the past.

I've tried to choose a balance of significant Muslims from the past and interesting Muslims from the last 75 years. I've grouped them in pairs (or in one case, a trio) of people whose contributions were similar. If you find one of my choices uninteresting, skip it and go on to another.

I've saved one of the best for last, 20th-century Egyptian singer Umm Kulthum. If you do nothing else in this chapter, flip to the end and read about this fascinating woman, or better still, follow the clues I give for listening to some of her music.

Taking a Long Trip: Ibn Battuta

In 1325, Ibn Battuta set out from his native town of Tangiers, Morocco to make the *hajj*, a trip that normally would've taken one to three years. He returned home 25 years later. By the time he made two additional shorter trips to Spain and West Africa, Ibn Battuta had traveled 75,000 miles and visited more than 40 countries. And he didn't even earn frequent traveler miles! The Moroccan sultan commissioned the court poet Ibn Juzayy to write the memoirs that Ibn Battuta dictated to him from memory. The resulting

1,000-page account (in English translation) — called "A Gift to Those Who Contemplate the Wonders of Cities and the Marvels of Traveling" — is amazingly accurate and detailed.

Here's the abbreviated version of the itinerary.

1. **Leaving in June 1325, he traveled by land along the North African coast to Cairo, and on to Damascus to join a *hajj* caravan to Mecca, where he arrived in 1326.**

2. **Over the next five years, Ibn Battuta made two more pilgrimages while traveling around Arabia and the East African coast.**

3. **He then set off for India on a roundabout route that took him to Turkey, Constantinople, Bukhara, Samarqand, and Kabul, arriving in India in 1333.**

4. **In 1342, the Delhi sultan sent him on a diplomatic trip to China.**

   Due to various mishaps, including shipwreck, he spent some time in the Maldives.

5. **Then he was off to Sri Lanka and experienced another shipwreck before going on to Bengal, Sumatra, and China.**

6. **By 1347, Ibn Battuta had returned to India, and then went on to Syria and Cairo, which had been struck by the Black Death (plague) causing 21,000 deaths a day.**

   He went by sea back to Morocco.

7. **His final two trips took him to Grenada, Spain and then across the Sahara desert to West Africa and back.**

   Ibn Battuta served as a religious judge in Morocco until his death in 1369.

Gathering it All Together: al-Tabari

Ibn Jarir al-Tabari was born in 839 in the region south of the Caspian Sea. By the age of seven, he had memorized the Qur'an. He went to Baghdad to study with the scholar of Islamic law, Ibn Hanbal (780–855, see Chapter 8), who had died before he arrived. So al-Tabari spent a number of years studying and collecting materials in Persia, Iraq, Syria, Palestine, and Egypt. Finally, he returned to Baghdad, where he became a famous teacher of *hadith* and law. (Sources credit him with writing 40 pages a day.)

Al-Tabari followed a middle path between the positions of the Mu`tazilites and Shi`ites and the extreme traditionalists represented by Ibn Hanbal. His two most famous works are his Qur'an commentary *(tafsir)* and his *History (ta`rikh) of Prophets and Kings.* Both works are massive compilations of all previous Muslim scholarship in the field. Supposedly, al-Tabari set out to write much longer works, but his friends convinced him to cut it down, with the result that his two major books are "only" 30 volumes each. In English translation, his *ta`rikh* fills 39 volumes (SUNY Press).

His *tafsir* is a verse-by-verse rendition of the Qur'an along with all significant prior opinions on each verse. His Qur'an commentary is the primary source for understanding the early history of Qur'an interpretation and became the authoritative reference work for future scholars. Both the commentary and the history are compiled like *hadith* collection: he gives the *isnad* (chain of transmitters) for each interpretation or incident (see Chapter 8). In the way he selects material and joins the reports together, Tabari subtly indicates the weaknesses of some reports in contrast to the veracity of others. The history begins with creation, continues through the Biblical period, moves on to the time of Muhammad, and ends in 915 C.E. The history, along with Ibn Ishaq's biography of Muhammad, is one of two single most important sources for early Islamic history. Al-Tabari died at Baghdad in 933 C.E.

Wielding the Sword of Saladin

Salah al-Din (known as Saladin in the West) was a great warrior during the time of the Crusades (see Chapter 2), respected by chroniclers on both sides for his chivalry, generosity toward defeated enemies, and trustworthiness. A little more than a hundred years after his death, in his *Divine Comedy,* Dante included Saladin as the sole contemporary in *limbo* (the intermediate location for those who went neither to heaven or hell), along with ancients, such as Homer and Plato. In the 19th century, the encounter of Richard the Lion Hearted of England and Saladin became part of the plot of Walter Scott's *The Talisman.*

Saladin was a Kurd, born in about 1137. The family moved to Aleppo, serving the local Zangi dynasty who ruled northern Syria at that time. Saladin accompanied his uncle, Shirkuk, on three expeditions to Egypt, and when his uncle died in 1169, Saladin took over command of the Syrian troops and soon became ruler of Egypt and founder of Ayyubid dynasty (1169–1252) that replaced the Fatimid dynasty (see Chapter 2). Control of Egypt was part of the plan of the Zangi ruler, Nur al-Din, to retake Jerusalem and drive the European crusaders out of the region. In reaction to the crusader presence, Muslim attachment to Jerusalem became strong, and a whole literature arose to encourage *jihad* to retake the city. After Nur al-Din's death in 1174, Saladin eventually became ruler of the Zangi lands in Syria and northern Mesopotamia. Saladin decisively defeated the local crusader armies at the Horns of Hattin, in Galilee, in July 1187. In October, he retook Jerusalem, sparing its inhabitants (contrary to what the Christians had done when they conquered the city 88 years earlier). Over the next two years, most remaining Christian strongholds fell, leaving only Tyre on the coast. The French,

German, and English kings set out on a new crusade to retake Jerusalem but managed to take only Acre and a few other coastal cities in 1191. Sick, King Richard concluded a truce in 1192 and withdrew. Saladin returned to Damascus, dying the next year.

Glorifying the King: Akbar

Akbar (1542–1605) was the third Mughal ruler (see Chapter 2) but the founder of the greatest Muslim dynasty of India. On his father's side, he was a descendant of the Mongol conqueror, Genghis Khan, and of Timur, a great Turkic conqueror and founder of the Timurid dynasty (discussed in Chapter 2). On his mother's side, he was a descendant of Iranian Muslim rulers. The mother of Akbar's son and successor, Jahangir, was a Hindu princess. In his genealogy, you can see how various strands of cultural and religious tradition come together in the person of Akbar — Turkic, Persian (Iranian), Mongol, and Indian-Hindu.

Akbar's accomplishments are in four main areas: military conquest, administrative centralization of government, promoting religious tolerance, and combining of Muslim and Hindu artistic traditions. Akbar, only 13 years old when proclaimed emperor in 1556, assumed direct rule in 1560. By his death, he had expanded the small state he inherited so that it reached from the Bay of Bengal in east India to the Punjab in north India, and south to central India.

To rule his greatly expanded state, Akbar reformed the tax system so that the majority of tax revenues reached the central government while still allowing incentive for farmers to increase production, thus ensuring economic prosperity. He devised a system in which all government appointments, civil and military, derived from the ruler, and payment was from the royal treasury. High- and middle-level appointees, who included a significant minority of Hindu nobles, were frequently moved from area to area so that local centers of power wouldn't develop to challenge the ruler's power. At the local level was another layer of administrators, answerable directly to the king. Law court officials were also under royal control, and a system of reporters kept the king informed about the actions of local officials.

In a masterful way, Akbar balanced the myriad of religious currents in India at the time: various forms of Hinduism, the Islam of the legal scholars (`ulama'), different varieties of Sufism, and Shi`ism. A decree of 1579 made the king the final arbitrator on points of Islamic law. Akbar is known — and sometimes hated by conservative Muslims — for his tolerance of other religions. He abolished the special tax on non-Muslims and the tax imposed on Hindu pilgrims. He supported building both mosques and temples. He sponsored conversations between not only Muslims and Hindus, but also Roman Catholics Jesuit fathers, who resided in Goa on the southwestern coast, and members of other religions. Akbar even founded his own religion in 1582 (*Din-i-ilahi,* meaning "the Divine Faith"), although it was limited to a few people in his inner circle of friends.

The final area of his contributions was to the arts. He was a great builder renowned for several mosques, tombs, and palaces. He built a new capital city (later abandoned) called Fatehpur Sikri, much of which still stands today. He established royal art studios that merged Hindu and Persian painting traditions and produced magnificently illustrated manuscripts. All in all, Akbar, while hardly a model ruler for traditional Muslims, is a fascinating figure who accomplished a great deal.

Thinking Deep Thoughts: Ibn Rushd

Ibn Rushd, better known as Averroes to Westerners, was born in Cordoba, Spain in 1126. He had a demanding education in Qur'an interpretation, law, theology, and medicine. About 1166, he met the caliph of the Almohad dynasty that ruled northwest Africa and Spain at that time, Abu Ya`qub Yusuf, who asked him whether the sky (universe) was eternal or had it come into being at a point in time. Ibn Rushd was reluctant to respond, so the caliph answered his own question, at which point the two had a long philosophical discussion. At the caliph's request, Ibn Rushd began to prepare summaries of most of Aristotle's writings, in addition to Plato's *Republic.* He also wrote a number of commentaries on these works. Aided by royal patronage, Ibn Rushd became a judge in Seville in 1169, chief judge of Cordoba in 1171, and royal physician to the caliph at the court in Marrakesh in 1182. When he briefly fell out of favor around 1195, he was exiled and his books were burned. He was reinstated and died in 1198.

Ibn Rushd wrote three books engaging the central problems of the relationship between reason and revelation. In one, he refuted point-by-point al-Ghazali's rejection of the "incoherence of the philosophers." Instead, he felt that philosophy and religion taught the same truth: Philosophers could obtain full understanding of this truth through philosophical proof while most people accepted the truth on the authority of revelation. The Qur'an itself commanded Muslims to pursue knowledge and thus required philosophical inquiry.

To Ibn Rushd, theologians, such as al-Ghazali, were more dangerous than philosophers because theologians engaged in unproven speculations in contrast to the proof of the philosophers and the simple words of truth in scripture. Ibn Rushd examined many of the issues that concerned early Islamic philosophers, such as that of the creation of the world, the attributes of God, causation, free will and predestination, and what happens to the soul after death. As the mediator of Aristotle, Ibn Rushd became better known in Western Europe than in the Islamic world, where the age of significant Islamic philosophy was coming to an end. In Europe, his books were burned at the

Sorbonne University in Paris in 1277. His preserved works, some of which come down only in Latin translations, received renewed attention beginning in the 19th century, both in the West and among some Islamic intellectuals.

Creating the First Philosophy of History: Ibn Khaldun

Ibn Khaldun has been called the first philosopher of history and the father of sociology. He was born in Tunis, North Africa, in 1332 and died in Cairo in 1406. His autobiography, finished the year before his death, provides abundant information about the man and his times. His parents died in the Black Death in 1349, an event that made a deep impression on him. By the age of 20, he had completed a traditional scholarly education and embarked on a career that alternated periods of scholarship with periods of political activity. From 1375 to 1379, he withdrew from court life to produce the first draft of his great work, *The Muqaddima.* This long work served as the introduction to his planned history *(kitab al-`Ibar),* focusing on Arabs from pre-Islamic times to the present. After an illness, ibn Khaldun moved to Cairo, which, under the Mamluk sultans, was the greatest city in the Arabic world. There he served at times as judge and chief judge, as teacher, and as head of a large Sufi order, all the time refining his history and his *Muqaddima.*

Ibn Khaldun's primary goal was to create a science of history that would explain the rise and fall of civilizations. His *Muqaddima* is divided into six parts dealing with environmental influences on history, primitive and rural society, forms of government, urban civilization, and economic factors that influence the course of history, along with the origins, role, nature, and types of human knowledge and culture. His key concept was `asabiya, a kinship term he applied to any grouping based on a sense of common identity. This group spirit (as with the Quraysh tribe that was dominant in Mecca at the time of the rise of Islam) enabled the group to prevail over its rivals. As a result, the group accumulated the economic resources necessary for the rise of an urban society, which in turn gave rise to the cultural arts and luxuries. The original sense of shared interest dissipated due to rivalries within the group. The state weakened, opening the way for another group to rise to prominence, beginning the cycle all over again.

Becoming a Hero of the Revolution: Ali Shariati

You're likely to remain a hero if you die before a revolution. (If Voltaire and Rousseau had lived on during the French Revolution, they could've become victims of the French guillotine rather than French heroes.) Ali Shariati, who was born in 1933 and became an ideological hero of those opposed to the shah, died in 1977, two years before the Iranian Revolution. Criticized during his life by conservative clergy, Ayatolla Khomeini (who came to power during the revolution) never condemned him. As a dead hero, he inspired various groups whose revolutionary goals differed from one another.

Shariati was born in a village in eastern Iran, where he received his education from his father, who was interested in how the Islamic message could connect with modern, alienated youth. In the early 1960s, he went to Paris, where he earned a doctorate in sociology and Islamic studies. He was influenced in Paris by the writings and actions of leftist-Marxists, such as Che Guevara, Sartre, and Fanon. In Paris, he became the most prominent voice of intellectuals opposed to the shah's government. Returning to Iran in 1965, he spent six months in jail. His popularity as a teacher led to his suspension and in 1967, he moved to Tehran, where he became the star lecturer at the Husseiniya-i-Ershad, attracting thousands to his talks. His aim was to combine the radical social message of Marxism with the revolutionary, egalitarian implications of original Shi`ism.

Shariati's aim was an Islamic sociology in which the people with God on their side would initiate action to secure a just state. The unity of God *(tawhid)* implied a concern for the social order as well as the spiritual realm. Traditional Shi`ism had become too passive: God would act only when the people took the initiative (Sura 13:11). Shariati proved too popular and in 1973, the shah denounced him as an Islamic Marxist. The secret police arrested him and banned his works. He spent three years in prison and two years under house arrest. In 1977, he died in exile in England, officially from a massive heart attack, although many feel that the shah's agents murdered him.

In the subsequent revolution, he was the ideological hero to many groups, each of which emphasized that part of his message that accorded with their goals. While stressing the role of the people, Shariati felt that the people needed guidance just as in the time of the prophet. Whether he would've seen Khomeini's role as guardian or spiritual guide in the new Islamic Republic of Iran (see Chapter 18) as an embodiment or a betrayal of Shariati's revolutionary ideas, one will never know.

Building Great Mosques: Sinan

Recruitment advertisements for the American military urge young people to join the army and learn a trade or profession. Sinan would've been a wonderful poster person for such commercials because the military trained him to be an architect. Sinan became Islam's greatest architect. He's credited with 34 palaces and 79 mosques in addition to many public baths, schools, hospices for travelers, tombs, hospitals, fountains, and aqueducts — 477 buildings in all. Historians don't know for certain how many of these projects he designed and executed personally or on how many of them he was more of an architectural consultant, with much of the work being done by others. In any case, the most significant projects were designed and executed by Sinan.

Born in Anatolia in 1489, he was drafted in 1512 into the Janissary elite military corps composed of Christian youth raised by the government as Muslims. Sinan built bridges and other military structures for the army. About 1539, he turned to non-military structures and became the chief architect of the empire. Although some of his smaller structures are artistic triumphs, he's known for his three great mosque complexes:

- ✔ The Sehzade Mosque (Istanbul, 1548)
- ✔ The Suleyman Mosque (Istanbul, 1557)
- ✔ The Selim Mosque (Edirne, 1575), his own favorite

Much of the present appearance of the Dome of the Rock in Jerusalem is due to Sinan's reconstruction, including the distinctive tile work. As a model for his great mosques, he used the Byzantine church with its large central dome, but he modified the interior to provide the large, central prayer hall under the dome. Innovations in design allowed him to incorporate many more windows in the upper part, bathing the interior in light. On the exterior, he added smaller domes and half domes around the central dome, framing the whole structure with tall, slender, minarets.

The Ottoman Empire was at its peak under Suleyman I, providing the great architect the means to execute his vision. When he died in 1588, he was buried in a tomb he had designed near his masterpiece, the Suleyman Mosque.

Winning the Nobel Prize: Naguib Mahfouz

Naguib Mahfouz, the world's most popular Arabic novelist, was awarded the Nobel Prize for Literature in 1988. The Nobel citation described Mahfouz as a writer who "through works rich in nuance — now clear-sightedly realistic, now evocatively ambiguous — has formed an Arabic narrative art that applies to all mankind."

Born in 1911, Mahfouz worked in a variety of government agencies until his "retirement" in 1971, which left him free to do even more writing. He has written almost 40 novels, a number of which have been made into movies.

His first novels were based on ancient Egypt and contain allusions to contemporary Egyptian society and politics. His trilogy (1956–1957) depicts the lives of three generations of families in Cairo against the backdrop of events from World War I until the overthrow of the monarchy in 1952. They're regarded as an unparalleled record of Egyptian society at that time.

Mahfouz's most controversial novel is *Children of Gebelaawi* (*Children of the Alley*, Bantam Doubleday Dell Publishing Group, 1959; reprinted in 1996). The story traces the history of the Gebelaawi family through several generations. At the same time, the characters and incidents recall the stories of Moses, Jesus, and Muhammad. The book was banned in most of the Arab world when it first came out. Twenty years later, Mahfouz condemned the death *fatwa* issued by Khomeini against Salman Rushdie (see Chapter 3). In response, the extremist Egyptian Islamic Jihad group said that all Muslims were obligated to kill both Rushdie and Mahfouz. In 1994, radicals stabbed Mahfouz in the neck, but he recovered, and the attack was strongly condemned by the general public and by Sheikh Tantawi, Egypt's top Muslim official. Among the other translated novels of Mahfouz you may enjoy reading are *Midaq Alley* and *Arabian Nights and Days*.

Listening to Umm Kulthum

For over 45 years, Umm Kulthum Ibrahim dominated the vocal music scene of Egypt and the entire Arab world. Villagers eagerly gathered around the radio to listen to her weekly broadcasts. Later, people flew into Cairo to attend her Thursday evening concerts, where she performed in modest, long, elegant evening gowns. Her vocal and emotional range deeply moved her audiences. After the 1967 war, she became, along with President Nasser, the voice of Egypt abroad.

Umm Kulthum was born in a small village in the Egyptian delta in about 1904. Her father was the worship leader *(imam)* at the local mosque, and she attended the local Qur'an school. Hearing her older brother sing, she began to imitate him and was soon performing at festivals and weddings in the area. At first her father dressed her as a boy when performing to avoid embarrassment. The family moved to Cairo in 1923 to promote her career, but she never forgot her home village, using her influence to enable it to be one of the first to get electricity.

Her repertoire included religious, love, and patriotic songs. When she died in 1975, over four million people were said to have turned out for her funeral, with the ordinary people taking the wrapped body from the pallbearers and passing it from one person to another during the three-hour-long funeral procession. Her songs still sell in the hundreds of thousands today on CDs and cassettes.

Find out more about "the Star of the East" in Virginia Danielson's book, *The Voice of Egypt: Umm Kulthum, Arabic Song, and Egyptian Society in the Twentieth Century* (University of Chicago Press, 1997), online at `http://almashriq.hiof.no/egypt/700/780/umKoulthoum/index.html`, or hear a QuickTime video clip from a live performance at `http://almashriq.hiof.no/egypt/700/780/umKoulthoum/Films/um.kalthoum.at.olympia.MOVs`.

Chapter 21

Ten Islamic Regions in the News Today

*B*efore the September 11 terrorist attacks, before the American fight against the Taliban and al-Qaeda, and before tensions mounted between the United States and Iraq in 2002 and 2003, Islam was frequently in the news. Conflicts erupted in various regions over the last three decades, and because news coverage of foreign events in American newspapers is often rather limited, some of these conflicts have had their occasional day in the headlines only to be ignored subsequently. Others, however, such as the Israeli-Palestinian conflict are persistently in the news.

This chapter is intended to provide a basic orientation to some of the conflicts that you're likely to read or hear about in the news. Each of these conflicts requires a chapter in itself to present fully the nature of the conflict, its history, the people involved, and the present status. So my brief descriptions in this chapter are only to provide you basic information about some of the conflicts not discussed elsewhere in this book.

For more on the use of the term *Islamist* in this chapter to designate radical Muslim political movements of the 20th century, see Chapter 18.

Africa

This book has provided only limited discussion of Africa, particularly of sub-Saharan Africa. Chapter 18 has some treatment of Egypt and a brief mention of the civil war in the last quarter of the 20th century in Algeria, and I mention Africa only briefly in several other contexts. In this section, I comment on the background of the problems that recently led to Nigeria's being in the news and mention only briefly the situation in two other countries, Sudan and Tunisia.

Nigeria

Islam has been present in portions of northern Nigeria for almost 1,000 years (and longer in other parts of West Africa). Most estimates suggest that Muslims are now a majority within Nigeria as a whole, although some figures you see give Christians a slight edge.

Since independence in 1960, Nigeria, the most populous country in Africa, has experienced democratic rule, military dictatorship, and civil war. Because Nigeria has many tribes and languages, tribal divisions are more important in the conflicts than religion, but religion has often been a significant factor. Politicians, not surprising, often exploit religious tensions for their own gain.

As part of the Sokoto caliphate in the 19th century, northern Nigeria was naturally under Islamic law — one of the purposes of the war that established the caliphate was to impose a stricter form of Islamic law. Nigeria's constitution after independence didn't establish any religion or impose Islamic law upon any portion of Nigeria. But many Muslims in the north desire to see Islamic law instituted in the predominantly Muslim northern states of Nigeria. Small Christian minorities exist in the north, who object to the imposition of Islamic law. As a result, from time to time, bloody clashes have occurred between Muslims and Christians in cities such as Kano and Jos, resulting in burning of homes, businesses, and places of worship (on both sides) and in mob killings. Sometimes, these conflicts have spread for short periods to the national capital and other cities. Such conflicts will undoubtedly occur again in the future. However, Nigeria hasn't experienced full-scale civil war based primarily on religious difference.

Nigeria was in the news in November 2002, when Muslims objected to the holding of the Miss Universe contest there. When a newspaper reporter wrote that Muhammad could've chosen a wife from among the contestants, more than 200 people were killed in riots. Nigeria also made the news in 2002 when a state court condemned a woman convicted of adultery to death by stoning. Actually, more than one such case has occurred, but so far, the federal (national) government and president appear to have avoided the actual execution of any women for adultery.

Sudan

Sudan has a largely Arab and Muslim population in the north and a pagan and Christian non-Arab population in the south. The north has dominated the country politically and militarily since independence. Various forms of Islam exist in Sudan, including movements deriving from the *Mahdi* movement in the late 19th century (see Chapter 18), groups influenced by Sufi revivalist movements (see Chapter 13), and modern Islamist movements. Although periods of temporary truce have occurred, southern rebels resist the efforts of the north to strengthen its control of the country, especially when this involves the likely imposition of Islamic law as state law. Some people accuse the north of enslaving non-Muslim southern captives, although Muslims and the Sudanese government (not surprisingly) deny such charges.

The key Islamist reform movement in Sudan is the NIF (National Islamic Front), headed by Hassan al-Turabi. Al-Turabi held various positions in the government headed by al-Bashir and was thought by some to actually be the power behind the scenes. However, possibly because military figures in the government believed al-Turabi was too powerful, he has been under house arrest since 2000. Al-Turabi proclaims himself to be a humble man without political ambitions. Because of the role of Sufism in Sudanese culture, al-Turabi doesn't follow the hard anti-Sufi rhetoric of the Wahhabis (see Chapter 18) and also takes a more egalitarian view on women in Islam. Al-Turabi is one of the foremost Islamist intellectuals.

Tunisia

A socialist party has ruled Tunisia since it gained independence from France in 1956. The status of women is probably better in Tunisia than in any other Muslim country except, perhaps, Turkey. The Islamist An-Nahda party (also called MTI) did well in the 1989 elections. The government, aware of the civil conflict in Algeria, wanted to avoid a similar civil war (and of course to hold onto power) and outlawed the al-Nahda party. Its leader, Rachid al-Ghannoushi, was imprisoned in 1981 and again in 1987 and sent into exile to London in the early 1990s. The crackdown on al-Ghannoushi and his party is somewhat ironic, because he represents a type of Islamist reform that is much less radical and more open to democracy than is true of many more radical movements in other countries.

South Asia

In Chapter 18, I discussed developments in Islam in South Asia prior to independence and in independent Pakistan. In this section, I look briefly at the remainder of South Asia, including Bangladesh, present-day India, and Kashmir.

Bangladesh

Bangladesh was part of Pakistan from 1947 to 1971 and constituted 55 percent of the population, but West Pakistan dominated the country militarily, economically, politically, and linguistically. One thousand miles of Indian territory separated Bangladesh and West Pakistan.

Civil war led to the independence for Bangladesh in 1971, with a mildly socialist orientation. From 1975 to 1991, the nation was ruled by several military leaders, who introduced a moderate Islamic tone into the government. Eighty-eight percent of the population is Sunni Muslim. About 10 percent is Hindu.

Since 1991, two major political parties have alternated in power, the more secular Awami League, and the BNP (Bangladesh Nationalistic Party) that won the last election in 2001 in coalition with two small Islamic parties. One of these smaller parties is the Bangladesh branch of the *Jama`at-i-Islami*, whose aim is to establish an Islamic state under Islamic law (*shari`a* — see Chapter 8). Militant Islamic groups haven't been very active in Bangladesh, but the small HUJI *(Harkat-ul-Jihad-al-Islami)* has carried out terrorist attacks in Afghanistan, India, and Kashmir. One of its leaders signed the 1998 bin Laden *fatwa* of *jihad* against the United States. Although occasional clashes break out between Hindus and Muslims in Bangladesh, the two communities generally get along better there than elsewhere in south Aisa.

India

India is a secular state whose population is overwhelmingly Hindu but whose 12 to 15 percent Muslim population is one of the world's largest. Islamic law applies to Muslims in areas such as family law. Growing Hindu nationalist sentiment over the past two decades has increased tensions between Muslims and Hindus with a number of incidents of mob violence. The most incendiary incident was the destruction of a 16th-century mosque in Ayodhya by Hindu militants, claiming that it was a pre-Islamic Hindu holy site.

Kashmir

Kashmir is a predominantly Muslim state in northwest India. When the British relinquished colonial control of South Asia in 1947, the local ruler chose to be part of India. Disputes over Kashmir caused war between India and Pakistan in 1947 and again in 1965. Since 1987, militant Muslim groups, operating at times with the apparent support of Pakistan, have waged a war of liberation, leading to repressive countermeasures by Indian troops, and about 60,000 people have died. However, Islamist terrorist groups likely represent the agenda of outside Islamist radicals more than that of Kashmiri Muslims. Eighty-two percent of the people polled in a recent election preferred to become an independent state rather than be part of India or Pakistan. Because both India and Pakistan own and test nuclear weapons, all out war between the two nations could have major international consequences.

Southeast Asia and the Pacific

Indonesia has more Muslims than any other country in the world, although it still has significant Christian and Hindu minorities in some regions. Malaysia also has a Muslim majority, but with an even larger non-Muslim (mainly Buddhist) minority than Indonesia. Both countries experienced significant economic development until the Asian economic collapse of the 1990s.

The cultural context of both countries, as well as the Philippines, is significantly different from Islam in South Asia or other countries, despite the fact that Islam came to Malaysia, Indonesia, and the Philippians along the trade routes, with merchants and Sufis being the main means of spreading Islam rather than conquest or immigration of significant numbers of Muslims from other countries. The Pacific region as a whole is also significantly influenced by Japan and China, and therefore a Confucian ethos (but not specific Confucian religious practices) provides a setting for the adaptation of Islam to local culture different than that found in other parts of the world.

Indonesia

Islam spread gradually in Indonesia from the costal trading cities beginning in the 13th century. Although the majority of the population became Muslim, Indonesian Islam incorporated significant elements from local tradition and was a rather easygoing form of Islam. Eventually, some Muslims going on pilgrimage to Mecca came back determined to purge Indonesian Islam of what they regarded as non-Islamic elements. These efforts weren't well received by the local Islamic establishment. Dutch colonialism and Japanese occupation in World War II introduced additional complicating factors.

A strong secularist nationalist movement arose, as did an even more secular communist movement. A unified Indonesia arose after World War II, based not on Islam but on President Sukarno's proclamation of the "five principles" *(pancasila),* including nationalism and monotheism. Efforts of Muslim parties to create a Muslim state fell short of a majority despite the substantial Muslim majority among the population. Islam was accepted by the increasingly authoritarian government, headed by Sukarno, as a religious and cultural force, as long as it didn't challenge the political establishment. Threat of a local communist takeover in the mid-1960s led to the ouster of Sukarno and an increased role for the military in a regime headed by General (President) Suharto. Although Wahhabis are active in Indonesia in support of Islamic reformist movements and in providing funding for Islamic schools (as they do also in Malaysia and Pakistan), traditionalist native Islam remains a strong counter-force. Islamic parties didn't pose a major threat to the Suharto regime.

The largest Islamic party is the NUD *(Nahdatul Ulama)*, whose leader, Abdurrahman Walid, was chosen as president after Suharto's fall. He advocated democracy, pluralism, tolerance, and the recognition of universal human rights, but he wasn't particularly successful as president and was replaced by his vice president, Megawati Sukarnoputri, adding another to the list of modern Muslim countries to have had a female head of state. After an October 2002 nightclub bombing in Bali, the government cracked down on Islamist radical groups, such as the Jemaah Islamiyah, and arrested its spiritual head, Abu Bakar Bashir, who denies any link to the group and attributes the Bali bombing to the American CIA. Such groups have grown during the past several decades, turning to radical action as they failed to gain a sufficient popular following to gain political control of the state.

Jemaah Islamiya is a radical Islamist group whose goal is to establish a pan-Islamic state that would include Indonesia, Malaysia, and the southern Philippines. It supposedly has connections to al-Qaeda.

Malaysia

Malaysia presents a unique situation among Muslim countries and is sometimes touted as a model for a progressive, modern form of Islam. Islam was brought to present Malaysia by merchants in the 14th and 15th centuries, and today, Malaysia is about 60 percent Muslim. The nationalist, mostly secularist government has had to create a national Malaysian identity, balancing the ethnic and religious divergences of three major communities — Malay, Chinese, and Indian.

Throughout most of the modern period Malaysia has been dominated by the coalition led by the UMNO (United Malay National Organization), headed since 1981 by Mahathir Muhammad, who has announced he'll resign in 2003. The main Islamic party, the PAS *(Parti Islam SeMalaysia)*, advocates an Islamic state. UMNO has successfully promoted its own version of moderate Islamization, while advocating pluralism, capitalism, and modernization. Mahathir has aspired to play a leadership role among Muslim states, offering an alternative vision of Islam in the modern world.

Mahathir has been an autocratic ruler and his engineering of the imprisonment of his respected deputy Prime Minister, Anwar Ibrahim, at the end of the 1990s, gathered unfavorable international attention.

Philippines

The same merchants and Sufis that spread Islam to Malaysia and Indonesia carried Islam to the southern Philippines, where Muslims constitute between 5 to 9 percent of the population of the Philippines. Independent sultanates were established, but Muslim control didn't spread north. When the Spanish came in the 16th century, they tried to extend control over all of the present Philippines. Upon independence in 1947, the new government claimed the entire present Philippines.

The MNLF (Moro National Liberation Front) led the struggle for independence or autonomy of the Muslim regions of the south. After some fighting, the government undertook to implement on its own terms an agreement reached at Tripoli in 1976 but never fully ratified. In 1991, a small, radical, militant group, Abu Sayyaf Group (Bearer of the Sword), broke off from MNLF and engaged in terrorist activities, including kidnapping, bombings, and bank robberies. The ASG is generally believed to have links to al-Qaeda and is opposed by the larger MNLF. Since September 11, 2001, U.S. military advisers have aided the Philippine government in combating the ASG.

The Balkan States

Bosnia-Herzegovina, Kosovo, and Albania gained significant Muslim populations when they were part of the Ottoman Empire. After World War II, Bosnia-Herzegovina and Kosovo were part of Yugoslavia, while Albania became a separate communist state. About 20 percent of the population of Yugoslavia was Muslim prior to the breakup of Yugoslavia into its constituent parts in 1992, including 40 percent of the population of Bosnia-Herzegovina. Seventy percent of Albania is Muslim, but religious identity and freedom were restricted in both Yugoslavia and Albania during the communist period. Yugoslavia today consists only of Serbia and Montenegro. Serbia is overwhelmingly Serbian Orthodox (Christian) in religion. Montenegro, whose future link to Serbia is in doubt, has about a 15 percent Muslim minority population.

Bosnia-Herzegovina

With the breakup of Yugoslavia in 1992, Bosnia-Herzegovina declared its independence. Bosnia-Herzegovina is a multi-religious, multi-ethnic nation with Bosnian Muslims, plus Christian Croats and Serbs. By 1992, Bosnian Muslims were highly secularized.

Serbia, the dominant power in what remained of Yugoslavia, invaded Bosnia at about the same time the communists were defeated in Afghanistan. Many *mujahiddin* were looking for the next arena in which to continue their *jihad,* and an estimated 4,000 ended up in Bosnia fighting the Serbs. Although the Serbs committed hideous war crimes, some Muslims were guilty of atrocities as bad as those committed by the Serbs.

Due to a Western arms embargo, weapons were supplied to Muslim forces from Iran via Istanbul, while a number of Muslim countries provided humanitarian aid. Some tension surfaced among Wahhabi-oriented aid workers, who considered it their task to teach pure Islam to Bosnian Muslims. When fighting ceased upon the conclusion of the Dayton Peace Accords in 1995, the *mujahiddin* fighters were asked to leave.

The most prominent Muslim figure in this period, and the Bosnia Muslim member of the three-member presidency until 2000, was Alija Izetbegovic.

Kosovo and Albania

Kosovo is part of Serbia. Despite its Albanian Muslim majority population, Kosovo contains sites of importance in Serbian history. Troubles began between Serbian nationalists and Kosovo rebels in the second half of the 1990s. This led to a NATO air campaign and to stationing NATO peacekeeping forces in the country. Ethnic peace is still elusive, with former Kosovo-Albania rebels attempting to expel native Serbs from Kosovo. Much of the population of Kosovo would like to see some type of union with Albania, with whom they share religious and ethnic affinities. Typical figures cited for Albania are about 70 percent Muslim, 20 percent Eastern Orthodox Christian, and 10 percent Roman Catholic Christian.

Iraq

In 1958, a nationalist, military revolt overthrew the Hashemite monarchy that had been installed by Britain after World War I. Subsequently, in 1963, the secularist-socialist Ba`th party seized control in a military coup and has retained control since that time.

General Saddam Hussein, a member of the Ba`th party, became president in 1979 and has ruled as a virtual dictator ever since. While Saddam is a Sunni Muslim, Shi`ites constitute the majority of the population. A small Iraqi-Shi`ite radical group, *al Daawa al Islamiyah,* has operated inside and outside the country since 1957. During the decade of war with Iran in the 1980s, the Shi`ites, in general, chose country over religion, supporting Iraq over their fellow Shi`ites in Iran.

Iraq's invasion of Kuwait, which it claimed as part of Iraq's territory, led to the Gulf War in 1991. A Shi`ite uprising in the south was ruthlessly suppressed by Hussein's Sunni-based Republican Guard troops. Some leading Shi`ite Ayatollas (Ayatolla Baqir al-Sadr and Ayatolla Khoi) have been executed by the government or have died suspiciously under house arrest.

Hussein has savagely repressed the Sunni-Kurdish population in the north, but the American no-fly zone in the north has resulted in de facto autonomy for three Kurdish provinces. Since the Gulf War, Hussein has tried to wrap himself in the mantle of Islam, adding *Allahu Akbar* (God is great) to the flag and constructing showplace mosques in Baghdad. An anti-Saddam Shi`ite movement, the SCIRI (Supreme Council of the Islamic Revolution in Iraq, also known as SAIRI, for Supreme Assembly) operates from Iran. Although the American government suspects Hussein of cooperating with international Islamic terrorists, these accusations haven't been proved. It's hard to believe, given his past, that Hussein has become a radical Islamist, although he would undoubtedly cooperate with any group if it were to his own advantage.

Lebanon

Lebanon came into being at the end of World War II. A power-sharing arrangement assured stability for a number of years. Marionite Christians, the largest community, got the presidency, Sunni Muslims received the position of prime minister, and Shi`ite Muslims took the less powerful position of speaker of the parliament. The Druze (a religious ethnic movement that arose out of Isma`ili Shi`ism in the 11th century — see Chapter 14) were also a significant power block in the new state.

Another part of the mix was the 120,000 refugees who fled newly independent Israel in 1948. Then, Syria regarded Lebanon as part of greater Syria and in 1976, sent in troops when civil war broke out. The Shi`ite population increased to become the largest group in Lebanon. Amal, a Shi`ite movement under the leadership of Imam Musa Sadr (who disappeared in 1978), revitalized the Shi`ite community.

Inspired by the Iranian revolution and supported by Iran, a more radical Shi`ite group emerged in 1982 called *Hezbollah* ("Party of God"). This group provided educational and social services and became a mainstream participant in Lebanese politics. Hezbollah engaged in terrorist activities, such as the attack on the American Marine base and kidnappings of the 1980s. Hezbollah's main Islamist ideologue was Sheikh Muhammad Fadlallah.

The PLO's (Palestinian Liberation Organization, created in 1964) main base was in Lebanon, from which it raided Israel. In 1982, the Israeli army invaded, forcing the PLO to relocate to Tunisia. Shi`ites of South Lebanon, who felt threatened by the PLO presence, initially welcomed the Israeli troops. That feeling faded as the Israeli army stayed and established a client South Lebanon Army that controlled the south and allowed the massacre of refugees south of Beirut. Political stability was restored with a new power-sharing arrangement in 1993.

In 2000, the Israeli army withdrew, and Hezbollah forces moved in to fill the power vacuum. Hezbollah is committed both to the establishment of an Islamic state in Lebanon and to the elimination of the state of Israel.

Palestine and Israel

Palestine has always been a contested area. For more than 400 years, Palestine was part of the Ottoman Empire. In the late 19th century, the Zionist movement began to promote Jewish immigration to Palestine with the goal of reestablishing a Jewish homeland there. Unable to broker an agreement between Jews and Arabs, the British, who ruled Palestine after World War I, turned the problem over to the United Nations in 1947. A United Nations plan to partition the land was accepted by the Jews but rejected by the Arabs. After British withdrawal in 1948, the Jews declared the state of Israel, and surrounding Arab nations invaded. Many Palestinians fled Jewish-controlled areas and when armistices were signed in 1949, Israel was in control of 75 percent of Palestine. At that point, 30 percent of the population was Jewish (11 percent in 1922). In the 1967 war between Israel and its Arab neighbors, Israel gained control of the remaining territory west of the Jordan.

In the aftermath, the PLO, headquartered in Tunisia, became the major voice of the Palestinians. The PLO, which included Christian and Muslim Arabs, was committed to the creation of a single, secular state in Israel encompassing Jews, Christians, and Muslims. Its head, Yasir Arafat, has shown an amazing ability to survive each new crisis. In the 1973 war, Israel gained control of the Sinai and the Golan Heights area of Syria. In 1979, President Carter successfully brokered the Camp David agreement leading to a treaty between Egypt and Israel.

About this time, a small radical Islamist group, Islamic Jihad, began to engage in strikes against Israel. The first *Infitada* (the name given to the spontaneous, popular Palestinian uprising) began at the end of 1987 and gave rise to the radical Islamist *Hamas* movement, an offshoot of the Muslim Brotherhood in Palestine headed by Ahmad Yassin. *Hamas* had a three-point program:

- Individual spiritual renewal
- Extensive educational and social services
- Military action against Israel.

Its ultimate goal is to drive out the Jews and create an Islamic state encompassing all of Palestine. In 1988, the PLO accepted the existence of the state of Israel, and that paved the way for the Oslo Peace Accords of 1993. By this agreement, in a series of steps, the Israelis would withdraw from 88 percent of the West Bank, leading to an independent Palestinian state. As a result, in 1994, Aragat and the PLO established the Palestinian National Authority (PNA), with Arafat as chairman, to exercised limited government and police authority within some areas of Gaza and the West Bank. Israel called the agreement "generous;" opponents called it "unworkable." Israel would retain security control of significant portions of the Palestinian state, which itself would be divided into four different areas separated by areas retained by Israel.

Israel delayed turning over some areas to the PNA until all attacks against Israel ceased. This wasn't about to happen because Hamas and Islamic Jihad weren't parties to the agreement, and the PNA didn't have the power to control them. Israel, contrary to United Nations resolutions and American pressure, continued to expand Jewish settlements on land that was to be part of the Palestinian state. In September 2000, Israeli defense minister Ariel Sharon, possibly in a bid for Israeli votes in the election for prime minister, made a visit to the area of the al-Aqsa mosque in Jerusalem. Because Jews weren't normally allowed even by the Israeli government in this portion of the former site of the Jewish temple, Muslims naturally regarded this visit, made with great publicity and full police accompaniment, as a provocation. Muslim protests and Israeli countermeasures against the protestors led to the second *Infitada* that continues to the present. Military actions, previously confined to the West Bank, were undertaken by Islamic Jihad and Hamas within Israel — malls, buses, and social events were all targeted, as well as military targets. This triggered Israeli invasions of PNA territory and destruction of Palestinian civil infrastructure. The Palestinian issue remains the strongest political issue uniting Muslims and the main impediment to better Muslim-American relations, due to consistent American support for Israel. With the reelection in early 2003 of Sharon as prime minister by an overwhelming majority (the first prime minister to be reelected in a long time), prospects for an improvement in relations between Palestinians and Israelis are dim at present.

The Former Soviet Union

Muslims were the second largest religious group in the Soviet Union before its collapse. Some Muslim areas, such as Tataristan, were originally part of a Mongol Empire in the 13th century (see Chapter 2), later incorporated into Russia. Other Muslims were incorporated into Russia when it expanded into the Caucasus and Central Asian regions in the 19th century.

Under Soviet rule, religious freedom was restricted, so some religious practices went underground, but in the final years before the breakup of the Soviet Union in 1991, increased religious freedom led to the reemergence of Islam. Former local communist bosses — turned-nationalists — ruled most of the newly independent central Asian republics: Uzbekistan, Turkmenistan, Kazakhstan, Tajikistan, and Kyrgyzstan. Inspired by events in Afghanistan, Islamic radical movements emerged in those countries. Russia cooperated in suppressing those movements, some of which had links with al-Qaeda and the Taliban. So far, none of them have posed a serious challenge.

In the Caucasus mountain region between the Black and Caspian Seas, Azerbaijan became an independent state with a moderate Muslim orientation. Dagestan and Chechnya, further to the north in the Caucasus Mountains, however, remained part of Russia. In 1991, President Dudayev declared Chechnyan independence. Chechnyans have a history of repeated resistance to Russian control going back to the late 18th century. Russian troops re-entered the area in 1994, and are still attempting to pacify the region, resulting in much destruction and loss of life. Just as some Arab-Afghan *mujahiddin* went to Bosnia after the fall of the communists in Afghanistan, others made their way to Chechnya and other places to pursue their vision of a radical Islamic state. Chechnyan terrorists have struck in Chechnya and in Moscow. The Russians say that the rebels are a criminal minority, stirred up by Wahhabis and other Islamic radicals. Muslims regard the conflict as one more episode in efforts of Muslims to resist Russian imperialism.

Syria

Syria is a one-party state whose socialist party, the Ba`th, has been in control since 1963 when a five-year union with Egypt broke up. An Islamist (Muslim Brotherhood) uprising centered in the town of Hama in 1982 was ruthlessly crushed, and an estimated 10,000 to 25,000 people were killed by the government. Since that time, no effective Islamist opposition has operated legally or underground in Syria.

Hafiz al-Asad was president from 1967 until his death in 1994 when his son Bashir succeeded him. The Asad family comes from an Islamic sect, the `Alawis (see Chapter 14), that has rather unorthodox beliefs.

Turkey

Turkey, the only explicitly secularist, Western-style state in the Muslim world was in the news in November, 2002 when a moderate religious party — the Justice and Development party — won a majority in the parliamentary election and formed a new government. The party pledged to continue

Turkey's pro-Western policy, including seeking membership in the European Union, held up due to shortcomings in Turkey's human rights record and a history of military intervention in political affairs. The leader of the party, Tayyip Erdogan, is presently forbidden from serving as prime minister because of a jail sentence he served in 1999 for public reading of an "anti-secular" poem. However, observers expect that the law prohibiting Erdogan from holding political office will be revoked, possibly before this book is published.

Turkey came into being in the aftermath of World War I and the end of the Ottoman caliphate. The "father" of modern Turkey, Kemal Ataturk, saw the future of Turkey in modernization along Western lines and in developing a strong sense of nationalist identity. Nationalism involved eliminating competing ethnic identies ("We are all Turks" is the policy), leading to armed conflict off and on since 1984 with Kurdish rebels (led by the Kurdistan Workers' Party, the PKK) in the southeast. Religion was relegated to the private sphere and any political expression of Islam was repressed. Education was largely secularized and wearing the veil was prohibited for women. Sufi orders were also abolished. Over the last two decades, the government has relaxed its restrictions on religious expression without any fundamental change of national policy and goals.

Turkey has been a strong ally of the United States and has been strongly criticized by other Muslim countries for contacts it has had with Israel.

Part VII
Appendixes

The 5th Wave   By Rich Tennant

"The five core beliefs of Islam really changed my life. Prior to that, my core beliefs had more to do with not buying retail, avoiding day—old fish, and wearing my lucky necktie to the racetrack."

In this part . . .

When will the Islamic New Year or the beginning of the fast during Ramadan occur this year in the calendar most Westerners use? The Muslim calendar is a lunar (moon) calendar, in contrast to the solar (sun) calendar used in the West. So, this part provides the dates in the Western calendar for the major annual Islamic religious observances over the next five years. I also provide a list of the Muslim month names and tell you how to convert any Western date to the corresponding Muslim date, or Muslim date to the corresponding Western date.

This part also includes a selective glossary of the most important technical terms, including many Arabic words and some Persian terms. Turn to the glossary if you encounter a term or word you don't understand, although space precludes listing every possible term.

Finally, I hope your interest in Islam is sufficiently aroused by your reading of this book that you want to dig deeper. The final appendix provides some suggestions as to where to go for additional resources, both print and media.

Appendix A

Counting the Years: The Muslim Calendar

• •

*J*ust as Christians date their calendar from the birth of Jesus and Jews date their religious calendar from the traditional date of the creation of the world, so Muslims date their calendar from the emigration *(hijra)* of Muhammad and his followers from Mecca to Medina in 622 C.E. (also known as A.D.). So, 622 C.E. equals 1 A.H. In addition, Muslims date it from the beginning of the year in which the *hijra* occurred. Thus July 16, 622 C.E. equals 1 *Muharram* (first month of Muslim year) of 1 A.H. (*anno hijrae*, the year of the *hijra*).

Most books published by non-Muslim publishers include only Western dates. This isn't surprising because most of the world now uses the Western calendar, although they may use non-Western calendars for some specific purposes. Until about five years ago, for example, the *Jerusalem Post* (a Jewish newspaper) printed the current date at the top of the paper in the Christian, Muslim, and Jewish dating systems. I didn't immediately notice when they started using only the Jewish and Christian dates, but I assume (perhaps wrongly) that the omission of the Muslim date reflects the increased tensions between Muslims and Jews in Palestine and Israel and, perhaps, a generally more conservative stance by the newspaper.

The Muslim religious calendar is a lunar calendar. As a result, in comparison to a solar calendar, which most of the West uses, each year the same event occurs 11 days earlier, the lunar year being 354 days long (and the solar being about 365 days long). Note that, for civil matters, Muslims often used a solar calendar, in fact sometimes referred to as the *Christian* or *Messianic* calendar — that is, the calendar used by Westerners. After all, farmers need to know when to plant their crops, and this information is linked to the solar, and not the lunar, calendar.

But for religious purposes, the Islamic religious calendar is used. You may encounter the names of the 12 months of the Muslim year, so here they are in sequence, followed by the literal meanings of the month names. Just remember they don't correlate to specific Western months:

- *Muharram:* The sacred month
- *Safar:* The void month
- *Rabi` al-awwal:* The first spring, also called Rabi 1
- *Rabi` al-thani:* The second spring, also called Rabi 2
- *Jumada al-ula:* The first month of dryness, also called Jumada 1
- *Jumada al-akhira:* The second month of dryness, also called Jumada 2
- *Rajab:* The honored month
- *Sha`ban:* The month of division
- *Ramadan:* The scorcher month
- *Shawwal:* The month of hunting
- *Dhul-qa`da:* The month of rest
- *Dhul-hijja:* The month of pilgrimage

Note that the spelling of the names in English will vary slightly from source to source.

At some time, you may want to convert from a Western date to a Muslim date or vice versa. Or you may be curious to find out your birth date in the Muslim calendar. How do you do this? Here's the conversion formula:

- To convert from a Christian (Western) date to a Muslim date, use this formula, where G is the Christian (Gregorian) date and H is the Muslim *(hijra)* date: $H = G - 622 + [(G - 622) \div 32]$. Use this, and you find 1990 A.D., began in the Muslim year A.H. 1410.

- To convert from a Muslim date to a Christian date, here's the formula: $G = H + 622 - (H \div 33)$. This means that the Muslim year 1421 A.H. began in 1999 A.D. $(1421 + 622) - (1421 \div 33) = 1999$.

At times like this, give thanks for the Internet, where you can go to a site such as www.cs.pitt.edu/~tawfig/convert, type in a date, and instantly find the corresponding Christian or Muslim date. With this site, I find that my birth date of November 17, 1936, corresponds to Tuesday, the 2nd of *Ramadan,* 1355 A.H. in the Muslim calendar. Also on the Internet, go to www.moonsighting.com/calendar.html and print out 12-month Islamic and Western calendars for the current year.

Table A-1 shows you the Western dates on which major Muslim religious days will occur for the next five years.

Table A-1

Calendar of Upcoming Muslim Religious Dates

Year	Stand	Adha	1 Muh	Ashur	Maulid	Mi'raj	15 Sha	1 Ram	26 Ram	'Id-Fitr	Stand	Adha
2003	2/10	2/12	3/4	3/13	5/14	9/23	10/11	10/27	11/21	11/25		
2004	1/31	2/01	2/22	3/02	5/2	9/11	9/30	10/16	11/10	11/14		
2005	1/20	1/21	2/10	2/19	4/21	9/1	9/20	10/5	10/30	11/4	12/19	
2006	1/9	1/11	1/31	2/9	4/11	8/21	9/9	9/24	10/19	10/24	12/30	12/31
2007	12/19	12/20	1/21	1/30	3/31	8/10	8/29	9/13	10/8	10/13		

To fit the religious days into the table, I've had to abbreviate. Here are the explanations of the table headings:

- ✔ Stand: Standing at Arafat *(waqfatul-Arafat),* on the 9th day of *Dhul-hijja* (month of *hajj)*

- ✔ Adha: `id al-adha: The feast of sacrifice at the conclusion of the *hajj*

- ✔ 1 Muh: First *Muharram,* the first day of the new year

- ✔ Ashur: `ashura', the 10th of Muharram; commemorates the death of Husayn in 680

- ✔ Maulid: *maulid al-Nabi* on the 12th of Rabi 1, the birth date of Muhammad; also commemorates the birth date of the sixth Shi`ite *imam,* Ja`far

- ✔ Mi`raj: The 27th of Rabi, the night journey and heavenly journey of Muhammad

- ✔ 15 Sha: *Nisf-Sha`ban,* 15th of *Sha`ban* is the Night of Repentance for the coming year

- ✔ 1 Ram: Beginning of month of *Ramadan* in which the required fast *(saum)* occurs

- ✔ 26 Ram: 26th of Ramadan; traditional date on which the Qur'an came down from heaven: night of power (not on the table is another significant date, the death of `Ali, the son-in-law of Muhammad on the 21st of *Ramadan)*

- ✔ `Id al-fitr: Festival of breaking of fast of *Ramadan* on 1st of month of *Shawwal*

Shi`ites celebrate on the 18th of *Dhul-hijja* (the month of *hajj)* the Ghadir al-Khum when, according to their beliefs, Muhammad (after his farewell pilgrimage) stopped at the oasis of Khum and there designated `Ali as his successor. See Chapter 12 for details.

Appendix B

Glossary

• •

*I*n this appendix, you find words and phrases, mainly Arabic, that occur in discussions of Islam. When you've heard too many Islamic terms and just can't keep them straight anymore, this glossary comes to the rescue. I usually don't include terms that occur in only one chapter, because those terms are defined in that chapter. Also, this glossary generally doesn't include people, names of sects or groups, or geographical terms (cities, countries, and regions).

adab: Manners, morals, etiquette (also a type of literature treating these subjects).

adhan: Call for prayer *(salat)*.

ansar: Citizens of Medina who supported Muhammad.

`aqida: Muslim creed of basic beliefs and practices.

`aqiqa: Cutting of hair of newborn child.

arkan al-imam: Five Pillars of Faith — belief in God, His angels, His prophets, and His books; the Day of Judgment; and God's determining all that happens.

`ashura': Tenth of the first Muslim month *(Muharram)* that commemorates the death of Husayn.

aya (plural ayat): Sign or proof of God, also a verse of the Qur'an.

baraka: Blessing associated with Muhammad and some saints.

barzakh: The barrier between life and death that lasts until the resurrection.

basmala: "In the name of God the compassionate, the caring;" this phrase opens every sura but one.

batin: The hidden, esoteric meaning of the Qur'an; see **ta'wil**.

bid`a: Innovation; any deviation from the practices and beliefs of early Islam, regarded by many as a sin.

caliph (khalifa): Title of a Sunni, Islamic ruler; literally means "successor."

dar al-harb: Territory not yet ruled by Muslims (abode of war).

dar al-Islam: Territory ruled by Muslims in contrast to.

da`wa: "Calling" people to Islam; evangelism.

dervish (darwish): The term used to designate Sufis; literally means a "poor person" (Persian).

dhikr: Remembrance; Sufi ceremonies that involve ritual invocation of the names of God.

dhimmi: "Protected people;" initially Christians and Jews — later also Zoroastrians and some other faiths — living in an Islamic state.

din: Religion.

du`a': Voluntary, individual prayer; in contrast to **salat.**

falsafa: Arabic term for philosophy.

faqih: Expert in jurisprudence (law).

faqir: Sufi; dervish.

fard: Indicates an obligatory duty.

fatwa: A decision by an Islamic scholar on a point of Islamic law.

al-Fatiha: The "opening," which is the first sura of the Qur'an.

fiqh: Jurisprudence (law).

fitna: Strife; designates several rebellions that threatened the unity of early Islam.

Five Pillars of Worship or **Five Pillars of Islam** *(arkan al-`ibada, arkan islam):* Confession, daily prayer, saum fast, obligatory almsgiving, pilgrimage to Mecca; not same as the Five Pillars of Faith.

ghayba: Occultation; the concealment of the 12th imam.

ghusl: The major purification before rituals.

hadith: Early tradition about what Muhammad said or did; also one of the roots of the law.

hadith qudsi (sacred hadith): Words of God not in the Qur'an.

hafiz: Person who has memorized the Qur'an.

hajj: Pilgrimage to Mecca — one of the Five Pillars of Worship.

halal: Permitted food and actions.

al-hamdu li-Llah (hamdulah): "Praise to God," a conversational phrase.

hanif: Islam to a monotheist before the time of Muhammad.

haram: Prohibited food and actions.

hijab: One term for a veil.

hilal: New crescent moon marking the beginning of a new month.

hijra : Emigration in 622 C.E. from Mecca to Medina.

hudud: Offenses and penalties defined in Qur'an for some serious crimes; singlular is **hadd.**

`ibada: Service of God, especially worship.

**`id (eid):** `id al-adha (feast of the sacrifice) occurs near the end of the pilgrimage, `id al-fitr (feast of breaking fast) at the end of Ramadan.

ihram: State of ritual purity; especially important on the hajj (pilgrimage).

ihsan: Virtue, ethics.

I'jaz: Inimitability of the Qur'an; that is, nothing is comparable to it.

ijma`: Consensus (agreement either among the entire community of Muslims or among the scholars), one of the four roots of law.

ijtihad: Effort (applied to the work of scholars to interpret the law).

`ilam: Science, knowledge.

imam: Leader of daily prayer; successor to Muhammad among Shi`ites.

iman: Faith, beliefs.

in sha'a-llah: "God willing;" frequently used in conversation.

`isma: Doctrine of the sinlessness of Muhammad and earlier biblical prophets according to the Sunnis; specific to Muhammad and the *imams* among the Shi`ites.

isnad: Chain of transmission that's included as part of a *hadith*.

isra': Muhammad's night journey from Mecca to Jerusalem.

jahiliyya: Time of pagan "ignorance" in Arabia before Muhammad's call.

al-janna: The garden; most common term for paradise.

jihad: "Striving" or "holy war".

jinn ("genie"): Various beings made of fire.

kafir: Unbeliever, atheist.

kalam: Islamic theology as a scholarly discipline.

khanqa: Meeting or dwelling place of a Sufi order.

khitan: Circumcision.

khutba: Sermon at Friday communal noon prayer.

kitab: Arabic word for book, and thus also "the book" (the Qur'an).

kufr: Unbelief or idolatry.

madhhab : Designates one of the recognized Schools of law.

madrasa: Islamic school.

Mahdi: Islamic messianic figures who will appear at end of time.

mahr: Bridal gift, dowry.

masjid: Arabic form of mosque; literally, "place of prostration."

matn: The body or content of a *hadith*.

maulid al-nabi: Birthday of Muhammad; festival celebrating his birthday.

mawla: Used in early period to designate non-Muslim convert who was linked to an Arab tribe by adoption.

mihrab: Niche in mosque wall that marks the **qibla.**

minbar: Pulpit in a mosque.

**mi`raj:** Muhammad's ascent through the heavens during the `isra.

muezzin (mu'adhdhin): The person who gives the call to prayer.

mufti: Person qualified to give a legal opinion; see **fatwa.**

muhajirun: Muslims who emigrated with Muhammad from Mecca to Medina in 622 C.E.

mujaddid: A restorer or reformer who comes to restore Islam at the end of each century.

mulla: Religious scholar (medieval Sunni `ulama`), having leadership roles in Shi`ite Islam.

mushaf: Physical exemplar of the heavenly word (book) of God.

nabi: Prophet (applies to Muhammad, Biblical prophets, and some others).

naskh: A Qur'anic verse that God later annulled, usually referred to as abrogation in English.

nika: Marriage contract.

niyya: The "intention" that must be pronounced before all ritual acts.

pir: One term for a Sufi leader, same as **sheikh.**

qadi: An Islamic judge appointed by a ruler.

qibla: Direction toward Mecca.

qiyas: Analogy, one of the four roots of law.

Qur'an: Basic scripture of Islam, word of God, and one of the four roots of Islamic law.

qutb: The "pole" or axis of the world; the perfect human.

rak'a: Cycle of postures in *salat* (prayer).

Ramadan: The month of fasting *(saum)* from dawn to dust.

rasul: Messenger; apostle as in "Muhammad is the messenger of God."

ra'y: Personal opinion of a scholar on a matter of Islamic law.

riba: Usury; interest from loaning money that is prohibited in Islam.

sadaqa: Charity beyond the required annual **zakat**.

salam alaikum: "Peace be upon you;" a common Muslim greeting.

salat: The five-times-a-day formal prayer ritual.

sama` (listening): Sufi ceremony using music.

saum: Required fast; one of the Five Pillars of Worship.

sa'y: The running between two hills as part of the *hajj* ritual.

sayyid: Title of respect for Muhammad's descendants through Fatima, Muhammad's daughter.

shahada: "There is no God but God and Muhammad is God's messenger."

shari`a: Islamic law.

shaytan: Same as Satan in English; in singular is the same as angel Iblis.

sheikh: Tribal or clan leader (literally "elder"); also used for Sufi leaders.

**Shi`ites:** Smaller branch of Islam that focuses on `Ali and his descendants.

shirk: Associating anything else with God, the worst sin in Islam.

shura: Consultation; bodies that chose or advised the caliph; sometimes used for modern legislative bodies.

silsila (chain): The spiritual family tree of a Sufi.

subha: Prayer beads or rosary used for reciting names of God.

sufi: Islamic mystic (*tasawwuf* is Arabic term for Sufism).

sunna: Customary practice of the prophet and his community.

sunni: Common name for the majority Muslim group.

sura: Common term for the basic 114 units (chapters) of the Qur'an.

tafsir: Commentary on the Qur'an.

tahara: Purification, required before ritual performances.

takbir: The formula "God is Great" *(Allahu Akbar)*.

talaq: Divorce.

talbiyah: The phrase "Here I am . . . " uttered during the *hajj*.

taqiyya: Dissimulation, previously engaged in by some Isma`ili Shiites.

tariqa: "Path," used also of the various Sufi orders.

tasliya: The formula of invocation of blessing upon Muhamamd (peace and blessings be upon him, abbreviated in English PBUH).

tawaf: Counterclockwise circling of the *Ka`ba* as part of pilgrimage ritual.

tawhid: Unity, the most important attribute of God.

ta'wil: Allegorical or esoteric interpretation of the meaning of the Qur'an.

`ulama': Traditional religious scholars of Islam; see also **mulla**.

umma: The universal Muslim community.

`umra: The lesser pilgrimage to Mecca that can be made at any time.

urs: Marriage ceremony.

usul al-fiqh: Roots of Muslim jurisprudence — Qur'an, *hadith, qiyas, ijma`*.

wali: Friend (of God); designation of Sufi saints.

waqf: An Islamic charitable foundation.

wudu': The lesser purification before ritual activities.

wuquf: The ceremony of standing on the plain of `Arafat during the *hajj*.

zahir: The external meaning of a text (opposite of **batin**).

zakat: Specified annual, obligatory almsgiving; one of the Five Pillars of Worship.

ziyara: Visitation; pilgrimage to sites of holy people.

Appendix C

Resources: Digging Deeper

English-language resources for Islam have increased considerably over the past decade and especially since September 11, 2001. In this appendix, I give you a sampling of available resources.

Academic Resources

Most of the books I list in this section are available at a good library, which is good news to your pocketbook, because the large reference works are too expensive for most individuals to purchase. Refer to online booksellers (in the "Islam on the Web" section later in this appendix) for selling prices and publication information.

- ✔ *American Muslims: Bridging Faith and Freedom,* by M.A. Muqtedar Kahn: In this collection of essays, Khan addresses issues facing American Muslims from the standpoint of a person committed both to Islam and to American values of freedom and democracy (Amana Publications, 2002, $14.95).

- ✔ *Approaching the Qur'an: The Early Revelations,* by Michael Sells: This is probably the best current introduction to the Qur'an for non-Muslims. Sells provides his own excellent modern translations of the early suras, and the included CD contains recitations of the early suras by several different reciters (White Cloud Press, 1999, $21.95).

- ✔ *A History of Islamic Societies,* 2nd Edition, by Ira Lapidus: This 2nd Edition is the most comprehensive one-volume history of Islam and contains an extensive bibliography (Cambridge University Press, 2002, $40).

- ✔ *An Introduction to Islam,* 2nd Edition, by Frederick Denny: This is a standard college textbook, with extensive bibliography (Macmillan Publishing Company, 1993, $66). It also has a very useful bibliography.

- ✔ *An Introduction to Shi`i Islam,* by Moojan Momen: The most comprehensive survey of Shi`ite Islam (Yale University Press, 1987, $22).

✔ *Islam in America,* **by Jane Smith:** This is a comprehensive history of Islam in America (Columbia University Press, 2000, $33.99).

✔ *Islam, The Straight Path,* **3rd Edition, by John Esposito:** This widely used textbook is somewhat less detailed than Denny's (Oxford University Press, 1998, $26.95).

✔ *The Isma`ilis: Their History and Doctrines,* **by Farhad Daftary:** The massive but definitive guide to this important group (Cambridge University Press, 1990, $50).

✔ *The Life of Muhammad: A Translation of Ibn Ishaq's Sirat Rasul Allah,* **translated and edited by Alfred Guillaume:** Read this English translation (Oxford University Press, 2002, $25) of the eighth-century biography to see Muhammad as Muslims see him.

✔ *Muhammad: A Biography of the Prophet,* **by Karen Armstrong:** This 1993 book is intended for the general reader (Harper San Francisco, 1993, $15).

✔ *Mystical Dimensions of Islam,* **by Annemarie Schimmel:** Schimmel's in-depth study remains an excellent introduction to Sufism (The University of North Carolina Press, 1975, $21.50).

✔ *The New Encyclopedia of Islam,* **Revised, by Cyril Glasse and Huston Smith:** I frequently use this 600-page, one-volume encyclopedia with 1,300 entries that is aimed at the general reader (AltaMira Press, 2003, $45).

✔ *The Oxford Encyclopedia of the Modern Islamic World,* **edited by John Esposito:** This is the essential reference work for anything pertaining to Islam in the last 100 years (Oxford University Press, 2001, $150).

✔ *The Oxford History of Islam,* **edited by John Esposito:** This large book, with many color illustrations, has 16 topically organized chapters by different experts (Oxford University Press, 2000, $49.95).

The Qur'an

If you want to study Islam seriously, you want to have a copy of the Qur'an. You can buy one or you can consult several translations on the Internet. See Chapter 7 for more information on Qur'an translations.

✔ *The Koran Interpreted: A Translation,* **translated by A. J. Arberry:** Many think this 40-year-old translation is the most faithful in English to the style of the Qur'an (Simon & Schuster Adult Publishing Group, 1996, $20 in paperback).

✔ *The Meaning of the Holy Qur'an,* **translated by Yusuf Ali:** This is the most widely used translation by English-speaking Muslims. Even in its revised version, it has a King James Bible–like style of English. (Amana Publications, 2001, $22).

✔ **Qur'an and Hadith on the Internet:** The Shakir, Pickthall, and Yusuf Ali versions are at `www.usc.edu/dept/MSA/reference/reference.html` along with the major *hadith* collections. Many other sites, such as `www.hti.umich.edu/k/Koran`, have similar resources.

Video Resources

To purchase one of the following videos, try the sources listed under "Islamic publishers and retailers," later in this appendix, or do a search on the Web to find the cheapest price.

PBS in the listings refers to Public Broadcasting System (`www.pbs.org`, if you wish to go directly to the source).

✔ *The Hajj:* Convert and reporter Michael Wolff documents his *hajj* experience on ABC's *Nightline* in 1997 ($20, 25 minutes).

✔ *Islam, Empire of Faith:* This 2001, 150-minute PBS documentary covers the first 1,000 years of Islam ($30).

✔ *Living Islam:* This is a somewhat older, BBC series ($150, five hours).

✔ *The Message:* This 1977 movie about the life of Muhammad stars Anthony Quinn. Its three hours include a documentary about the making of the movie (about $30).

✔ *Muhammad: the Legacy of a Prophet:* PBS premiered this new, two-hour documentary in December 2002 ($30).

✔ *Muslims — A Journey through the Diverse World of Islam:* This is a two-hour PBS *Frontline* report on contemporary Islam ($30, 2002).

Computer Software

Muslims have been quick to take advantage of computers and the Internet. I find the three items listed below reasonably priced and quite useful. Much more is available, and the sources given in the "Islamic publishers and retailers" section of this appendix lists both computer software and other audio-visual resources for sale.

✔ **Alim:** This CD is packed with Qur'ans (English and Arabic, including recitation), *hadith* collections, and much more (ISL Software, $99).

✔ **Al-Qari Plus:** This CD teaches you how to recite the Qur'an in Arabic, even if you don't know Arabic ($59 from Sound Vision).

✔ **SalatBase:** This CD teaches you how to perform *salat* ($49 from Sound Vision).

Islam on the Web

Web sites come and go, so I can't guarantee that all of these sites will still be online when you read this. Each item in the list is representative of a different type of site or resource. Any of the first four lead you to many other useful resources on the Web. Keep in mind, however, that anyone can create a Web site, and, while some sites are useful sources of information, others are useless and misleading.

✔ **Alt.Muslim:** www.altmuslim.com is a good site for Islamic news.

✔ **The Islamic Studies Site of Prof. A. Godlas:** www.uga.edu/islam is perhaps the best academic site about Islam on the Web.

✔ **IslamiCity:** www.islamicity.org is a major Muslim portal site.

✔ **Mamalist of Islamic Links:** www.jannah.org/mamalist has an extensive, categorized list of links to Islamic sites (1,924 links).

✔ **MSAnews:** This e-mail list redistributes current news and reports. To subscribe, send an e-mail to msanews-list-subscribe@topica.com.

Islamic organizations

Chapter 15 provides additional information about Islamic organizations.

✔ **AMC (American Muslim Council):** www.amconline.org

✔ **CAIR (Council on American-Islamic Relations):** www.cair-net.org

✔ **ICNA (Islamic Circle of North America):** www.icna.org

✔ **ISNA (Islamic Society of North America):** www.isna.net

✔ **MAS (Muslim American Society):** http://masba.com

✔ **MPAC (Muslim Public Affairs Council):** www.mpac.org

Islamic publishers and retailers

Some handle a wide range of print and media publications and others distribute mainly their own materials.

- ✔ *Astrolabe:* Books, video, and more at www.islamicmedia.com
- ✔ *Halalco Books:* print catalog available or go to www.halalco.com
- ✔ *IPI (Islamic Publications International):* Print catalog available or go to www.Islampub.com
- ✔ *Kazi Publications:* Print catalog available or go to www.kazi.org.
- ✔ *Sound Vision:* Specializes in audio-visual resources, including the *Adam's World* children's videos at www.soundvision.com

Halalco, IPI, and Kazi all have an extensive line of books, software, videos, and other Islamic items (calendars, prayer rugs, veils, posters, greeting cards, and more). These sources cater to Muslims, and their selection of academic books on Islam by non-Muslim publishers is often limited and selective. For books from non-Muslim publishing houses, check your local library or bookstore.

And Finally . . .

Seek resources in your own community, including local mosques, libraries, and colleges. Inquire about visiting a local mosque or participating in an interfaith discussion group.

Index

• *B* •